Dedicated

to my supportive parents,

and my steadfast friend—

the abyss.

Published by Feral House, Inc.
All Rights Reserved

ISBN: 978-1-936239-43-6
ebook: 978-1-936239-46-7
feralhouse.com

Feral House
1240 W. Sims Way Suite 124
Port Townsend, WA 98368

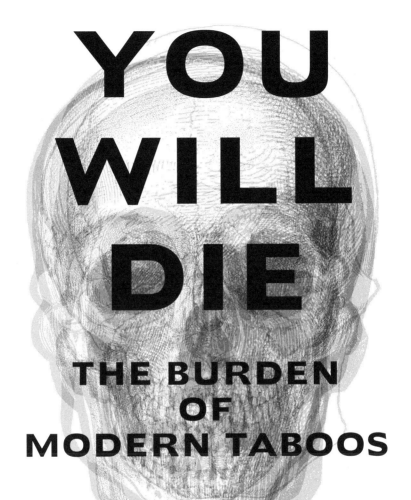

YOU WILL DIE

THE BURDEN
OF
MODERN TABOOS

ROBERT ARTHUR

FERAL HOUSE

CONTENTS

Preface XV

Chapter 1
Introduction: The Burden

I. First Person: Give Me Some Skin 1

II. Aztec Sacrifice: Food for Thought 2

III. Definition of Taboo: Shut Up 5

IV. Spitting: Days of Phlegm 6

V. The Point: Taboos = Bad 8

Chapter 2
Nasal Mucus: Still Picking

I. First Person: The Mucus in Me 11

II. What It Is: Booger, M.D. 12

III. The Taboo: Grow Up 13

IV. Its Origin: Hanky Panky 14

V. Repercussions: Where Did My Septum Go? 16

Chapter 3
Excrement: America Doesn't Know Shit

I. First Person: Doing It Wrong 19

II. What It Is: Good Shit 21

III. The Taboo: Potty Humor 23

IV. Its Origin: Filthy Forefathers 26

    A. Ancient Times: Gods of Poo 26

    B. The Middle Ages: Mountains of Poo 27

    C. 1700–1900: Don't Look at My Poo 31

    D. Twentieth Century: Don't Even Say Poo 33

V. Repercussions: Anal Retentive 35

    A. Facilities: Lazy Shits 35

    B. Technique: Spread and Lift 37

    C. Cleansing: Poo Butt 38

    D. Holding It: Learn to Love Again 39

    E. The Environment: Crapping on the Fish 41

    F. Abroad: Crapping on Third-World Children 43

    G. History: Hidden Turds 44

Chapter 4
Sex I: What It Is: Sex Is Good

I. First Person: A Sex Drive to Nowhere 51

II. Definition: Vagina Meet Penis 54

III. A Basic Human Need: Purity Is Misery 54

IV. Women and Men Have Different Sex Drives:

    Fucking to Love and Loving to Fuck 55

    A. The Differences: Fake Boobs and Fake Rolexes 55

    B. The Evidence: Slutty Men Are Everywhere 60

V. Homosexuality is Biological: Going Gay in the Uterus 63

    A. The Evidence: Manatee Man Love 64

    B. The Religious Argument: Stop Being Gay 67

VI. Children are Sexual:

    Hello, Puberty Starts Before Age Eighteen 69

Chapter 5
Sex II: The Taboo: Sex Is Bad

I. Educational System:

    Premarital Sex Makes You Crazy 79

        A. Arguments for Ignorance: Keep 'Em Dumb *80*

        B. The Curriculum: Be Prepared to Die *81*

II. Censorship: Be Quiet So They Don't Figure It Out 82

III. Criminalization of Sex: Happy Hookers,

    Happy Johns, and Mad Moralists 84

Chapter 6
Sex III: Its Origin: Distorting Jesus

I. American Prude 97

II. Our Genetic Relatives: Sex Was Fun 98

III. Evolution: Help Me Raise This Thing 99

IV. Agriculture: Wives for Sale 101

V. Ancient Rome: Here a Penis, There a Penis 104

VI. Christianity: Turning Jesus into a Prude 106

VII. The Middle Ages: Sex Is a Sin? Who Cares? 111

    A. Penitentials: Did You Come My Son? *111*

    B. Medieval Names: Starring John Fillecunt *112*

    C. The Priests: Stupid and Horny *113*

VIII. The Inquisition: Sex Is a Sin. Meet the Rack. 115

    A. The Process: Torture Is Not Litigious *115*

    B. The Punishment: Burn or Go to Hell *116*

    C. The Effect: Wretched Slavery *118*

IX. The Protestant Reformation: A Monk Wants Sex 119

    A. Catholic Hypocrisy: Hot Papal Orgies *119*

    B. Martin Luther: A Piece of Shit Says Jesus Screwed *121*

    C. John Calvin: Sourpuss *123*

X. Puritan America: God Hates You. Don't Have Sex. 124

CHAPTER 7
SEX IV: ITS ORIGIN: DISTORTING SCIENCE

I. HUMANISM: HAPPINESS (SEX) ON EARTH 133
  A. The Philosophy: Mind Your Business 134
  B. Science: How Come This Wasn't in the Bible? 135

II. VICTORIANISM: SEX IS LOW-CLASS 136
  A. The New Middle Class: Rich and Lame 136
  B. Women as Asexual Victims: Dumb but Not Slutty 136
  C. Children as Asexual Victims: Little Johnny Would Never Want Vagina 138

III. THE MORAL CRUSADERS:
THE SKY IS FALLING! LOCK UP THE SINNERS! 140
  A. What It Is: A Freak-Out! 140
  B. Victorian Prostitution: My Wife Doesn't Suck 142
  C. White Slavery: It's 1910. Do You Know Where Your Daughter Is? 144
  D. The Birth of the FBI: Fighting Interstate Adultery 145
  E. The Saved Victims: Leave Us the Hell Alone 146

CHAPTER 8
SEX V: ITS END?: THE REVOLUTIONS

I. THE 1920S SEXUAL REVOLUTION: WOMEN GET THEIR SEXY BACK 153
II. 1930S–1950S: TOOTHBRUSHES AND COMMIES 155
III. THE 1960S SEXUAL REVOLUTION: SEXUAL HEALING 157
  A. The Courts: Oh Yeah, That Constitution 157
  B. Beats and Hippies: Getting a Peace 159
  C. Helen Gurley Brown:
  Look Ma, I Had Sex and Didn't Die 162
  D. Masturbation: Manual Transmission 164
    1. Philip Roth: The Firing Wad 164
    2. Betty Dodson: All Hell Broke Loose in Her Pants 166
  E. The Media: Spreading the Word for Gay Titty Bars 167
  F. Openness: One Shining Moment 168

IV. THE BACKLASH: AIDS HYSTERIA IS A GREAT RALLYING CRY 171
  A. The Empire Tries to Strike Back Against Facts 171
  B. The Collapse of the Left: Killer Hippies 173
  C. Skewed Stats: When I Was a Boy All We Did Was Chew Gum. Stop Lying. 174
  D. AIDS: I Don't Have It. Do You? [Laughter] 176
  E. God Tells Bush to Stop Fishing and Run for President 179

CHAPTER 9
SEX VI: REPERCUSSIONS:
THE GOVERNMENT WANTS YOUR SEX

187

I. GOVERNMENT: PRUDES GONE WILD
- A. Hypocrisy: I Can Have Sexual Fun,
  But You Can't So I Can Get Your Grandma's Vote 188
- B. Lies: Breaking a Commandment for Something Jesus Didn't Care About 189
- C. Distraction: Stopping Perverts Is the Most Important Issue in the Universe 191
- D. Kill All Child Molesters: Why Civil Liberties Are Important 193
- E. Monetary Cost: Jail 'Em All: Why Are My Taxes So High? 194

II. IGNORANCE: IS DUMB 195
- A. Distortion of Sex Ed: No Birds and the Bees, More Abortions and STDs 195
- B. Distortion of Scholarship: Men Really Are Assholes 197
- C. Distortion of Art: Jesus' Penis 199
- D. Distortion of Teaching: G-Rated Learning Is Boring 200
- E. Distortion of Reality: Maybe Our Culture Is the One That Sucks 201

III. UNHEALTHY SEXUAL ATTITUDES (USA) 203
- A. Shame: My Tinky Is Dinky 203
- B. Overemphasis: Relax, It's Just Sex 204

IV. SEXUAL DEPRIVATION: THE RIGHT TO HAVE SEX WITH A HOT PERSON 207
- A. High-T Males: Blue Balls and Violence 207
- B. High-T Females: The Government Won't Let You Make Money Lying Down 209
- C. Bad Sex: You're Missing Out 211
- D. Bad Marriages: The Rules Committee 212

CHAPTER 10
DRUGS I: WHAT THEY ARE: UNDERRATED

I. FIRST PERSON: I WAS A SCHMUCK 217
II. WHAT THEY ARE: THEY ARE WHAT THE GOVERNMENT SAYS THEY ARE 221
III. YOU CAN'T HANDLE THEM: DRUGS ARE ADDICTIVE 223
- A. Freebasing Caffeine: Administration vs. Substance 223
- B. Avoiding Physical Addiction: Simple 227
- C. Psychological Addiction: Outlaw the Big Mac 229
- D. Instant Inslavement? Please 232
- E. How Addiction Occurs: Not Randomly 233
  1. The Drug: Stop Blaming It 233

  2. Look Deeper: Underlying Issues 235

  3. The Addict: Young and Impulsive 236

IV. You Will Die: Drugs Kill 237

V. You Will Die Slowly: Drugs Are Unhealthy 241

 A. Government Interference Is Dangerous:

  Criminalized Water Would Be Unhealthy 241

 B. It's Not What You Do, It's How You Do It: Duh 242

 C. Functional Alcoholic vs. Junkie: A Matter of Price 242

 D. Drugs Cause Insanity: A Forest Fire of B.S. 243

 E. Shiny Happy Drug Users: The Invisible Majority 244

VI. You Will Kill Me: Drugs Make You Do Bad Things 245

 A. The Drug Made Me Do It: Stop Lying 245

 B. Avoiding Withdrawal Hell: Avoiding the Flu 246

 C. Bananas Cause Crime: The Banana Effect 247

VII. You Only Think You Are Having Fun:

 Illegal Drugs Serve No Purpose 250

 A. Meeting God: Mind Expansion/Religious Reasons 250

 B. I Like You: Social Reasons 254

 C. Ow!: Pain Tolerance 255

 D. Third Wind: Energy 256

 E. Don't Worry, Be Happy: Relaxation 258

 F. A Whole New World: Creativity 258

 G. F The Man: Rebel Cool 261

 H. Custom: Culture 262

 I. It Does the Body Good: Health Reasons 263

 J. Drugs Make Life Fun: Pleasure 264

Chapter 11
Drugs II: The Taboo: You Just Don't Know, You Asshole!

I. The Unsettling Nature:

 No, You Don't Know, You Government Tool! 273

II. The Ignorance: No, Honestly, You Don't Know 274

 A. They Just Wouldn't Do Such a Thing: The Historians 274

 B. Give Me More Tax Money: The Government 276

 C. Brain Shrinkage: The Scientists 277

 D. "Flowers of Destruction": The Objective Media 278

 E. They Must Suffer: The Subjective Media 285

Chapter 12
Drugs III: Its Origin: Racism, Lies, and Cruel Selfish Bureaucrats

I. From the Beginning: Getting High in the Cave 291

II. Lying About the Bible Again: The War on John Barleycorn 293

III. The First Drug War: Prohibition 295

IV. Wright Was Wrong: A Drunk Plays the U.S. and the World 298

V. The Hoover of Drugs:
   A Bald Snake Disregards The Constitution for Thirty Years 301
   A. *Criminalizing Stuff is Fun: Marijuana* 302
   B. *Anslinger Has No Clothes but He Is Still Emperor* 304

VI. Lock Up the Disrespectful Brats: Nixon Was a Tough Guy 307

VII. Carter Tries 309

VIII. Reagan and Crack Incite Panic 309
   A. *You Look Suspicious, Give Me All Your Money: Forfeiture* 310
   B. *Prohibition Creates Crack: The Media Creates a Monster* 310

IX. Reagan and Bush Get Their War On And Lose 314
   A. *Declaring a War on the Coca Plant* 316
   B. *Daily 9/11s: Colombia* 317
   C. *A Boxed Head and a Cardinal Dead: Mexico* 318

X. The Land of the Free Pisses on Other Countries 321

XI. The War Continues: Stay the Stupid Course 323

Chapter 13
Drugs IV: Repercussions: Maybe When It's Your Daughter You'll Give a Shit

I. Do the Crime, Do the Time ... Bitch!: The Land of Liberty? 333

II. What Constitution?: Civil Rights 336
   A. *Chip, Chip, Chip, Gone: Judicial Interpretation* 336
   B. *Snitch Justice* 337
   C. *But the Good Guys Play by the Rules: Please* 339

III. It's Not My Rich White Ass: Classism and Racism 340

IV. Fat White Senators Do Not Scare Them:
   Generation G (For Gangster) 341

V. The Drug Didn't Do This to Little Suzie: The Government Did 343
   A. *Don't Put Me in Jail Because Prohibition Killed Suzie* 343
   B. *Don't Put Me in Jail Because Prohibition Ruined Suzie's Life* 345

VI. My Government Has Fallen and Can't Get Up 346
    A. Bush Got High. Why Can't I?: Hypocrisy 346
    B. Why They Hate Us: The DEA Pisses on the Whole World 347
    C. Tax Addiction Is a Moral Issue: Bloated Bureaucracy 348
    D. Corruption Is a Third-World Thing: Wrong 49
VII. Slandering the Real Lands of the Free 351
VIII. Organized Crime's Lifeline 355
IX. Mission Impossible: Fine, Don't Cut and Run, You Idiot 357
    A. If They Say We Are Winning, They Are Talking Out of Their Asses 357
    B. Economics 101 358
    C. Common Sense 359
    D. What If We Stop Being Pussies? 362
X. Drugs Are Fun: Why Must Everyone Be Square? 363

Chapter 14
The End: Death

I. Death in America: Sanitized and Distorted 369
II. You Will Die: Think About It 372
III. Superficial Seizure: The Ego 373
IV. Seize the Day: Authenticity 376
V. Ecstasy Denied 377

Appendices

Appendix One
Great Philanderers: Twentieth-Century World Leaders 381

Appendix Two
Great Philanderers: American Presidents 385

PREFACE

You Will Die was born out of my misery stemming from youthful ignorance of taboo topics, and was inspired by *Ain't Nobody's Business If You Do* (1996) by Peter McWilliams. That book pointed out the absurdity of victimless crimes. This book explains how taboos have caused McWilliams' arguments for freedom to falter in our supposedly "free" country.

Although victimless crimes were its impetus, *You Will Die* is not limited to taboos with criminal ramifications. While researching, I was amazed to discover the extent to which even minor taboos cause grief and distort our society's views about our past, about what is natural, about what is "right," and about the truth.

The intent of this book is not to advocate all tabooed activities and beliefs, but to present them honestly so that its readers can make their own well-informed decisions. A value judgment that this book does make is that it is wrong to persecute people who come to different conclusions. To criminalize acts that do not harm others is to deny them the pursuit of happiness that inspired the American Revolution.

You Will Die covers scads of history. This is important for four reasons:

(1) By learning how taboos developed, one can appreciate just how frail and dishonest their bases are.

(2) Only by seeing their defenders' policies historically can one appreciate how consistently and thoroughly they have failed; in some cases, for millennia.

(3) By seeing their defenders' propaganda historically one can recognize how deceptive techniques are recycled and easily spot their present forms.

(4) While researching, I was enchanted by the courageous people who have battled irrational persecution from taboos, such as the magnificent Victoria Woodhull, and was appalled by the deceit and hypocrisy used by those who create

and maintain them, such as the despicable Harry Anslinger. Their stories have been glossed over in textbooks, leaving most Americans ignorant about the true heroes and villains of our past. Their stories deserve to be told so that the populace can better discern the true heroes and villains of today.

Their stories also merit coverage so that current leaders realize history will hold them accountable. As soon as memories fade, textbook historians and the popular media will swathe our figureheads in a patriotic sheen so as to reflect America's greatness. For example, the sexploits demonstrated in the appendix, "Great Philanderers: American Presidents," may remain unknown to most Americans, but at least the readers of this book will know just how egregiously hypocritical the American government's billion-dollar sexual morality campaign is.

This book does not have to be read from cover to cover. Feel free to choose sections that interest you from the contents. Outside of the introduction and the end, the chapters are autonomous and are broken into distinct units: (1) a first-person passage that intimately relates how the taboo has affected one person, (2) a section entitled "What It Is," describing the tabooed subject, (3) a section, "The Taboo," describing how the taboo is currently enforced, and self-explanatory sections entitled (4) "Its Origin," and (5) "Repercussions."

Thank you for taking the time to read *You Will Die*. Constructive criticism and insights are welcome and can be made at Suburra.com. The first-person narratives that begin each chapter are a mixture of fact and fiction.

①

INTRODUCTION
THE BURDEN

I
GIVE ME SOME SKIN

Mexico City, fifteenth century A.D.... Nervous anticipation prickles as you watch the ceremony with the other successful Aztec warriors. Poyec, your first captive, is next in the procession. Ignoring the blood seeping past his feet, he steadily climbs the steep stone steps of the temple to Huitzilopochtli singing loudly the songs of his city, "Already here I go: you will speak of me there in my home land . . ."

After the lengthy ascent under the blazing Mexican sun, Poyec's body shines as the priests stretch it over the altar. His placid visage warps momentarily as the flint knife swiftly saws beneath his sternum. But not a sound departs from his mouth, even as the head priest rips his heart from its soupy moorings and holds the trembling, gurgling muscle up for the Fifth Sun to consume.

As the "most precious water" floods the chasm in Poyec's yawning chest his eyes watch the sky. Through this Flowery Death he is now an Eagle Man and his spirit's eight-day journey to the warriors' paradise in the Sun has begun. As your captive, your "beloved son," Poyec has honored you with his stoic exit. His heartless cadaver, left earthbound, is tossed down the temple steps and will be honored further . . .

1

Later that day a solemn dinner at your home ends. Your extended family had a simple meal featuring Poyec's flesh. It was a tearful affair. Although you have brought status to your family, they, like all Aztecs, openly recognize that it is only a period of time before *their* warriors will die the glorious Flowery Death on the battlefield or the killing stone.

You depart when Poyec's skin is delivered. As you pull on his husk, "the container of all that is human," its moist interior sticks to your surface. You work it until it stretches and slides into place. As your father ties Poyec's face around your own, you feel almost as alive as when you grappled with its owner.

In your new suit you will go door to door throughout the neighborhood begging. This ritual allows the citizenry to give you gifts. At homes with infants, you will take them in your arms and perform a brief ceremony to bless them. The night's celebrations will also involve you and other successful warriors dancing with your captives' skinned heads.

Although most of the rituals surrounding your taking of a prisoner of war have been completed, for the next twenty days you will continue to wear Poyec's skin as it rots, hardens, and cracks. Only after twenty days will you remove the putrid and foul casing, or what remains, and be born anew. Through this you will learn the process of death.[1]

II
Aztec Sacrifice
Food For Thought

An expert on Aztec demography estimated that the Aztecs sacrificed 250,000 people a year, or roughly one percent of the population.[2,3] In one famous 1487 sacrifice, the dedication of the Templo Mayor in Tenochtitlán (now Mexico City), possibly 20,000 people were sacrificed.[4] Only the observances of three of the eighteen holidays/months in the Aztec calendar did not involve human sacrifices.

The opening passage describes the "Feast of the Flaying of Men" ceremony that occurred in the Aztecs' second month. The most common type of Aztec sacrifice was portrayed, that is, a captured enemy warrior having his heart removed. However, the

Aztecs not only sacrificed enemy warriors. They also sacrificed slaves, criminals, and innocent Aztec women, children, and infants.

The Aztecs used an array of sacrificial methods that included beheading, slitting the neck, drowning, death by arrows, entombment, starvation, hurling from heights, strangulation, burning, and combinations thereof. For example, one ceremony required that a newlywed couple be thrown into a fire and burned alive, but before they died they were pulled out and had their hearts removed. As shown in the opening narrative, the Aztecs were also creative in their use of the carcasses.

Today these gory practices appear cruel and irrational. Sacrificing innocent people to satisfy bloodthirsty gods? Waging wars on neighboring nations solely for the purpose of capturing prisoners to sacrifice? Cannibalism? However, every cultural practice must be examined in context. Fortunately for its later inhabitants, Eurasia's early societies did not hunt their large herbivores, such as cattle, sheep, and pigs, into extinction before domesticating them. This was not the case in the Mexican region settled by the Aztecs.

Lower-class Aztecs had to survive as almost strict vegetarians. Modern-day vegetarians can get all their nutritional requirements from the vast selection of produce available to them, but the Aztecs were in a more precarious situation. They were frequently short of essential nutrients, particularly during famines.[5]

According to the Aztec religion, catastrophes like famine were a sign of the gods' disapproval and therefore more sacrifices than normal were necessary to bring back the gods' favor. Appeased gods would then provide for them through the sun, earth, and rain. Ironically, the sacrifices themselves were a "godsend," cutting down on the mouths to feed while simultaneously providing needed proteins and fats to the remaining population. In this context, human sacrifice, cannibalism, and the religious system supporting them assisted the Aztecs' survival.[6]

The Aztecs Hernando Cortés ruthlessly conquered for Spain in the sixteenth century were probably ignorant about the economic function of their religious rites. Despite this, the Aztecs did not question the bloodshed—being sacrificed in a Flowery Death was a high honor. To them it was rational. The Aztecs provided for the gods so that the gods provided for the Aztecs.

As the narrator, Mixtli, explains to the appalled Spanish friars in the historical novel *Aztec*:

So, yes, we slew countless [people] . . . But try to look at it as we
did . . . Not one man gave up more than his own one life. Each man
of those thousands died only the once, which he would have done
anyway, in time. And dying thus, he died in the noblest way and for
the noblest reason we knew . . . it seems there is a similar belief
among Christians. That no man can manifest greater love than to
surrender his life for his friends.[7]

III
Definition of Taboo
Shut Up

If an Aztec questioned her religion's rites she would probably have been
severely punished. Religion was, and continues to be, taboo. A taboo is a topic that
a culture prevents its people from discussing freely. The population has been subtly
taught from birth that the prevailing view on the subject is natural, unquestionable,
and correct.[8] *Taboo* can also refer to the thing or action suppressed.[9]

Widespread ignorance is characteristic of taboos. Often the rules of the taboo
have been ingrained at such a young age, sometimes before the baby learns how to
talk, that its reasoning is never explained. When the child grows up the taboo seems
natural and is never critically examined.

People are not exposed to arguments challenging a taboo, and if they are,
they are presented unfairly so they can easily be lampooned. Accurate information
supporting opposing views is difficult to find, so that even those with the moxie to do
independent research cannot get the whole picture. For example, it is unlikely the
Aztecs ever tested whether droughts ended more quickly with or without sacrifices.

A second characteristic of taboos is that broaching them unsettles people. The
mere mention of a taboo can make people nervous. Violating weak taboos elicits
nervous laughter, light ridicule, and comments like "inappropriate," "disgusting,"
"infantile," "gross," and "immature." Violating stronger taboos elicits anger, violence,
and comments like "sick," "offensive," "vulgar," and "immoral."

CANNIBALISM

My Nipples Look Forward to Your Stomach

Not all views protected by taboos are irrational. For example, cannibalism is a modern taboo that is arguably rational, because unlike the Aztecs we easily have enough food to avoid a practice that could encourage murder. However, even if all taboos were logical, we would still be better off without them because free and open debate can improve rational policies as well as irrational ones.

For example, human meat is said to taste delicious—similar, but superior, to pork. Should it be unlawful to eat the meat of people who died naturally or accidentally? If Ms. X offered money to Mr. Y for the right to eat him upon his natural death and he agreed, would both parties not be happier?

If this sounds fantastic, consider the case of Armin Meiwes. In 2004, the German Meiwes ate and killed Bernd-Jürgen Brandes at Brandes' request. Brandes was a successful forty-three-year-old corporate manager and this fulfilled his sexual fantasy. A Brandes e-mail read, "My nipples look forward to your stomach," and prior to Brandes' death both men ate Brandes' sautéed penis.

The German courts grappled with treating this as euthanasia, manslaughter, or murder. Meiwes' initial conviction of manslaughter with an eight-and-a half-year prison sentence was overturned as too lenient, and in 2006 he was convicted of murder and given life in prison.

If the fear of encouraging murder appears overriding in criminalizing Ms. X's behavior, consider the lawful practice of organ donation and its effects in impoverished parts of the world. For another culture's view of cannibalism, consider the Wari', a people who ate their dead. They viewed letting their departed rot in the cold dark dirt just as repulsive as we find eating ours. (Missionaries forced an end to this practice in the 1960s.)

—William Miles, "Pigs, Politics and Social Change in Vanuatu," *Soc. Anim.*, 5(2), 1998.

Strong taboos protect the assumptions around which people have built their lives. People do not like these assumptions challenged. The more vested an interest they have in their views, the angrier they will react. It is particularly unsettling when lifestyle issues are involved. People do not like to even consider that how their parents lived, how they have lived, and how they are raising their kids to live might not make sense.

If a free-thinking Aztec told other Aztecs that their sacrifices had no bearing on nature's behavior, she would likely provoke anger. The suggestion that they were killing people simply for protein and to rid the population of some hungry mouths, rather than to nobly honor the gods, would probably not lead to friendly debate. Unless the listener was a particularly open-minded and courageous Aztec, she would probably not give the radical's theory the slightest consideration for fear of punishment from the gods, and perhaps more importantly, other Aztecs.

These two characteristics of taboos—the ignorance that surrounds them and their unsettling nature—feed off one another. Unsettling people serves as an enforcement mechanism. When irritated people get angry at or mock the taboo transgressor, the transgressor is less likely to address the taboo. When no one addresses the taboo, people remain ignorant. The more ignorant people are about a taboo, the more likely they are to be disturbed by those trying to bring it into the open. It is a self-perpetuating cycle.

IV

SPITTING
DAYS OF PHLEGM

Taboos start as a point of view. In the beginning, supporters make arguments and defend their positions against opposing arguments. Of course, if the people who want to institute their view are more powerful than their opponents, no persuasion is necessary—the view is instilled by force.[10]

Slowly, over generations, as the view on the issue becomes more and more accepted, rational arguments cease to be made. Opposing views are easily shot down with vague words such as "improper," "offensive," and "immoral." Eventually the issue does not have to be defended at all. Opponents are so rare and public opinion is so ingrained that the fairness expected in other debates is disregarded. Anyone who examines the issue at this point is open to character assassination and harassment. The issue is now highly taboo.

The evolution of a taboo can be observed in the Western view of spitting.[11] As recently as the Middle Ages it was a generally felt *need* to spit frequently. It was polite to spit at the dinner table and at any other time. The only prohibitions were that among the genteel one should spit under the dining table instead of on it, and not spit in the washbasin.

In 1530 Erasmus of Rotterdam introduced the social grace of stepping on your spit if it contained phlegm, and also of turning away from people while spitting, so as not to accidentally spit on them. Erasmus also criticized those who spat at every third word in conversation. (This signals how frequently polite people spat, if it only became disagreeable at every third word.)

In 1558 Della Casta of Geneva recommended that spitting be refrained from altogether at meals. By 1672 it was indecent to spit in front of people of rank, such as the nobility. The late 1600s was also the time when handkerchiefs were coming into general use among the upper class. By the early 1700s, the only proper way to spit among the well-bred was directly into one's handkerchief.

We approach the modern view by 1859, when *The Habits of Good Society* admonished that "Spitting is at all times a disgusting habit. I need say nothing more than—never indulge in it. Besides being coarse and atrocious, it is very bad for the health."[12,13]

Currently the prohibition on spitting is so accepted that it is not even mentioned in books of etiquette. *The Habits of Good Society* was a handbook for adults, but in our culture spitting admonitions would only be found in books for young children. Even that might be considered odd, because most children have the spitting ban internalized well before learning how to read.

Our views toward spitting have completed a remarkable evolution. Spitting went from being considered a biological necessity to being a criminal activity, the mere sight of which can cause some to become physically sick.[14,15] During this process, commentators went from giving reasons for progressively tighter and tighter restraint ("spit under the table so it doesn't get in others' food"), to simply bashing it (spitting is a "disgusting habit"), to not needing to mention it at all. It was at these final stages, when opposing views were not even considered, that spitting became a taboo.

V

The Point
Taboos = Bad

In *A Clockwork Orange*, a man named Alex is convicted of murdering an elderly woman.[16] Instead of serving a long prison term, he is subject to draconian aversion therapy. For two weeks his eyelids are pried open and he is forced to watch violent film scenes while being administered drugs that induce severe nausea. After the treatment Alex is released, but now cannot even think of violence without paralyzing and unbearable anguish. The government has brainwashed Alex to censor his own thoughts. This is the power of taboo.

Because of self-censorship, tabooed topics lack open discussion and accurate information.[17] Without these two tools, irrational views cannot be changed. By protecting irrational views, taboos hinder progress toward greater happiness.

This book will demonstrate the burden of modern taboos by covering the irrational taboos currently in American society. The intent of this book is *not* to advocate all tabooed activities and beliefs, but to present them truthfully, so that readers can make their own well-informed decisions. Each chapter will define the taboo, explain its origins, and describe its repercussions for our society. The chapters will progress from less burdensome to more burdensome taboos.

People enjoy belittling the irrational taboos of "primitive" cultures that have come before us. This book intends to show that we have our own follies. Future societies will almost certainly consider some of our unquestioned beliefs silly, irrational, and despicable. Who are our Aztec sacrifices?

NOTES

1. Quotations from David Carrasco, *City of Sacrifice* (1999), pp. 142, 145, 155.
2. Michael Harner, "Enigma of Aztec Sacrifice," *Nat. Hist.*, Apr. 1977, pp. 46–51.
3. Figures are debated. Michael Smith, *Aztecs* (2002), pp. 58, 312.
4. Inga Clendinnen, *Aztecs* (1991), pp. 91, 322.
5. Harner, "Enigma of Aztec Sacrifice."

6. Ibid. and Michael Winkelman, "Aztec Human Sacrifice," *Ethnology*, Summer. 1998, pp. 285–298.

7. Gary Jennings, *Aztec* (1980), p. 213.

8. *Taboo* comes from the Polynesian word *tabu*. Most Polynesian dialects define *tabu* as sacred, but use it informally to describe anything forbidden. Hutton Webster, *Taboo* (1973), pp. 2–7.

9. For example, nasal mucus (NM) is taboo. (1) NM, as a topic, is taboo in that it cannot be freely discussed; (2) NM, as a thing, is taboo in that people find it inherently disgusting; and (3) NM, as an action, is taboo in that one should not touch it.

10. A historic example of this was the Roman Catholic Church during the Middle Ages. Currently, American majorities can also force their views on the rest of country. The only protection minorities have are the courts' enforcement of constitutional protections. The concept of unchecked majorities in democracies is known as "tyranny of the majority." It was a concern of Thomas Jefferson and other American Founding Fathers.

11. The following spitting chronology is from Norbert Elias, *History of Manners* (1982), pp. 153–160.

12. Ibid., p. 156.

13. The writer meant unhealthy for the spitter, not for the other people coming in contact with the saliva. In 1859, Louis Pasteur was still formulating the connection between germs and disease.

14. The District of Columbia, New York City, Philadelphia, and the state of Virginia have all criminalized public spitting.

15. Jeff Ventura, "Spitting Image of America," *Columbia News Service*, 8 May 2002, ret. Columbia.edu, 8 Aug. 2006.

16. The novel by Anthony Burgess was published in 1962.

17. Bad ideas are defeated by argument and persuasion, not by censorship. See John Stuart Mill, *On Liberty* (1859); Thomas Paine's introduction to *The Age of Reason* (1794); and Oliver Wendell Holmes' dissent in *Abrams v. United States*, 250 US 616 (1919).

2

Nasal Mucus
Still Picking

I
The Mucus in Me

Right now I have the repugnant concoction in my stomach of cheap salty crabmeat that I think was probably spoiled, chocolate Tastykake donuts, blueberry bagel, peanuts, and boogers, the latter two being the most plentiful. Do I disgust myself? Naaah.

At this stage of my life I only feel guilty about my nasal habits when my picking causes bleeding. When I am alone in bed at night and blood starts dripping on my pillow is when I think, you know what, maybe I really am a disgusting pig.

These feelings of self-loathing used to be more prominent. As a self-conscious pubescent I thought the immense size of my nose might be my fault, its full figure caused by the constant finger-probing received during its formation. I also felt horrible when I spied my little sister consume something plucked from her nose. I figured that my indiscretions around her before she learned to talk were the cause.

There was also the fear before each childhood doctor's visit that this would be the time the doctor exclaimed, "My God son, half the inside of your nose is torn away. What the hell have you been doing up there?" And then I would have to tell him because if I did not, he would not be able to prevent something serious from happening—like my nose falling off.

Surprisingly, despite doing it everywhere I have avoided the public humiliation that followed a high school peer of mine caught eating a booger. However, I have not gone unscathed. In my mid-twenties I was napping with a woman I was dating when I sensed a breathing impediment.

A quick poke revealed it to be the type of booger that has mucus stretching somewhere deep into your skull. If you can successfully pull the whole apparatus out you are rewarded with the eerily pleasing sensation that a part of your brain is being dislodged. Unfortunately, despite having my back turned to my partner, she saw it all. A high-pitched scream split my head.

I feigned like I was asleep, that I had no idea what I had been doing, and that I was just as repulsed as she was. "I'm afraid to go back to sleep in front of you. What else might I be doing when I'm out?!" I don't know if she bought this sleep-booger-eating defense, but it made an extremely awkward conversation merely highly awkward. How does one explain why they eat their boogers?

To her credit, she did not end the relationship right there. It must have been a shocking sight to the uninitiated. I hoped she would forget, but it's over five years later and she hasn't.

II
What It Is
Booger M.D.

Nasal mucus is more commonly known as snot. Snot is a clear mucus produced in the lining of the nose and in hollow sections of the skull called sinuses. Snot's biological function is to catch dirt and other contaminants in the air to prevent them from entering the lungs.

Millions of tiny hairs in the nasal passages called cilia wave ten times per second, sweeping the snot back toward your throat at the rate of a quarter-inch per minute. Each day a quart of dirty snot ends up sliding into your stomach via the esophagus, where the germs are destroyed by potent digestive juices.[1]

In cold weather the cilia slow down and can even freeze. Without the cilia sweeping, the snot being produced slides right out the nostrils. This is commonly referred to as a "runny nose" or "nasal drip."

The cilia are not to be confused with the bigger hairs that can grow into monstrosities in older men. Those long hairs are called vibrissae. They do not wave like cilia. The vibrissae serve as filters for larger airborne particles. The whole operation works so well that the nose is one of the cleanest parts of your body.[2]

Sometimes snot dries and the resulting product is too large for the cilia to transport. This dried snot is popularly referred to as boogers. Boogers are similar to pearls. Just as an oyster irritant is at the heart of a pearl, a nose irritant, such as a dust particle, is at the heart of a booger. In an oyster, the irritant is coated with nacre to form a pearl. In a nose, the irritant is coated with snot and dries to form a booger. Large boogers can block free air flow.

Abundant snot can also clog the nasal passages. This excess can be caused by an allergy, a virus, or an infection. If the snot is its natural clear color, or white, it is probably an allergy or a virus (a cold), and if it is yellow or green it is probably a bacterial infection. Boogers and excessive snot can be removed by one of three ways: inhalation, exhalation, or manual removal.

III

The Taboo
Grow Up

Nasal mucus is a mild taboo. The social enforcement of not touching or discussing it is not strict. Discussing snot and one's experiences with it, or picking one's nose in public, are likely to be seen merely as immature and rude. Being laughed at is the common reaction. Even the eating of nasal refuse would only get the transgressor labeled as disgusting. Anger would only be aroused in someone socially responsible for the taboo violator, such as an employer or mother.[3] Public handling of nasal mucus has not been criminalized. In line with this mild reaction, not many people have a vested interest in the conventional disdain of nasal mucus.

The taboo has still caused ignorance by keeping nasal mucus out of school curriculum. Most Americans in a high school biology class will learn about the alveoli, the pancreas, and the gall bladder. Odds are they will not find those things interesting to study, nor will they remember anything about them a year later.

In contrast, most kids never learn about nasal mucus. Something people have contact with every day is skipped over. Surveys have found seventy to ninety-five percent of people pick boogers out of their nose and eight percent of people eat them,[4] yet our educational system does not tell us what they are.[5] An entertaining, interesting, and memorable topic is avoided so that teachers can comfortably conform to cultural norms.

IV

Its Origin
Hanky Panky

Nasal mucus did not always have a stigma.[6] In medieval society it was acceptable to clear your airways in a variety of ways. A person could blow her nose in her hands and wipe it on her clothing, or blow it directly into her clothing. One could cover a nostril when blowing, thus magnifying the blast through the open nostril enough to send the mucus flying to the ground. Picking boogers, even eating them, was more common. As with spitting, medieval restrictions were limited to the dinner table: for example, do not get snot on the tablecloth.

The handkerchief changed all of this. Handkerchiefs for cleaning the nose were first used by the "young snobs" of the Italian Renaissance.[7] In the beginning they were expensive luxury items and were seen as a status symbol. "He does not blow his nose on his sleeve" was a way of saying a man was wealthy.[8] As hankies became affordable, more people were able to acquire this prestigious item and distinguish themselves from the riffraff.

By the late 1600s the use of the hanky was common among the upper class. By the 1700s, books of etiquette were adding the restrictions of not using your hanky loudly, and not peering into it after blowing your nose, "as if pearls and rubies might have fallen out of your head."[9] As the handkerchief became more and more

GANG BANG BOOGIE

An example of the repugnance of nasal mucus-eating was when Jasmin St. Claire set an apparent world record by having sex with three hundred men consecutively for the 1996 pornographic film *The World's Biggest Gang Bang Part 2*. St. Claire refused to have sex with one of the participants for eating his boogers while waiting for his turn. (The other two she refused were physically and verbally abusive.) She called his behavior "inappropriate" and "disgusting."

—"Jasmin St. Claire, Episode 3," *Howard Stern Show*, WXRK, 30 July 1996.

accessible (culminating in disposable paper ones in 1930),[10] not using a handkerchief went from being merely impolite—similar to the current view of nail-biting—to being disgusting.

The steep fall of nasal mucus' status is chronicled in the etiquette literature. In the fifteenth century Erasmus used the word "snot" and described its coarseness while advising how to handle it in front of people of honor. In 1729 LaSalle foreshadowed our current avoidance of the word when he referred obliquely to snot as "the filth," and boogers as "what you have pulled from your nose."[11] Currently even oblique references to snot in serious writing risk being labeled juvenile and unnecessary.

Contrary to intuition, the snot taboo did not develop for hygienic reasons. Health is a popular defense for taboos concerning the body, but it usually has nothing to do with their development. As with taboos on spitting, excrement, and sex, the nasal mucus taboo began before the public understood germs and disease. The snot taboo was instead driven by cleanliness as a prestigious sign of wealth and by a growing shame about the body and its functions. This shame will be explored further in the next two chapters.

V

Repercussions
Where Did My Septum Go?

The taboo on nasal mucus is a mild taboo with few societal repercussions. Nose picking and the eating of boogers is not difficult to keep behind closed doors. Being caught in public can be highly embarrassing but it has not been made a criminal act, nor is the shame accompanying picking one's nose or eating its contents enough to weigh heavily on a conscience.[12]

Because of this, even in a book on taboos, some will question the necessity of a chapter on nasal mucus and consider it a joke. However, the inclusion of nasal mucus is important to show the hypocrisy behind taboos. Most Americans would categorize nose picking as gross,[13] yet the most scientific study ever conducted on the topic found the practice to be "almost universal," with over ninety percent of people partaking.[14]

Booger eaters are even more stigmatized. Consumption is so shameful that it is typically not revealed by patients until the third year of psychoanalysis.[15] Despite this, there are 25 million booger eaters in the United States.[16] This compares with 22 million golfers in the United States.[17] There is a significant closeted sub-population that does what America considers repulsive.

This denial extends to the presentation of history. Numerous movies set in the Middle Ages and earlier pride themselves on their accuracy. Yet rarely do these movies portray people blowing their noses in their hands, blowing snot on the ground, picking their noses, and eating their boogers, as kings, queens, and others of those eras did. Artists of those ages had no qualms about representing them in these acts,[18] but this artwork is rarely seen because curators, editors, and collectors have operated under modern taboos in selecting the art worthy of preservation and presentation.[19]

One of the effects of this denial is to prevent a rational approach to nasal mucus. Our nasal mucus taboo is viewed as irrational by most of the world's population. In cultures where blowing in the hand is still common practice, our Western handkerchief usage is seen as a disgusting habit.[20] Other cultures don't understand why anyone would want to package her nasal mucus in a piece of cloth and carry it around when it can simply be left behind.[21]

Our Western revulsion toward touching nasal mucus has a weak basis. Arguments are made that picking is unhygienic and can cause damage to nasal tissue.[22] However, when the fingers are clean and the picking is reserved to boogers (and not the nasal tissue) the practice is harmless. Even when the fingers are not clean the practice is the hygienic equivalent of eating finger food without first washing one's hands. That pervasive American phenomenon can be observed at any fast-food restaurant and those practitioners are not regarded with disgust.

Like any activity, nose picking can be taken to extremes. One psychotic woman picked away her entire nose, and it is estimated that over a million Americans have picked through their nasal septum (the cartilage separating the two nasal passages).[23] Unfortunately the stigma prevents people from getting medical treatment. One afflicted person described her nose picking as follows:

> For the last nine years, every waking moment of every day, whenever possible! I felt so badly about myself at times I [didn't] want to be around people . . . I had surgery to remove scar tissue. I was so desperate . . . believe me we all try to conceal this nasty habit and in most cases I assume people would never see a physician about it, in case they got laughed out of the office."[24]

For the vast majority of nose pickers medical problems do not arise. Instead, unclogged nasal passages are attained through a pleasurable activity,[25] and booger eaters have even reported that boogers are, "quite tasty, salty, to be exact."[26]

NOTES

1.   Stomach acid (hydrochloric acid) is extremely strong and can dissolve stainless steel. The stomach keeps from digesting itself by producing a new mucus lining every two weeks.
2.   Sylvia Branzei, *Grossology* (1995), p. 33.
3.   Men are more comfortable with nose picking than women. James Jefferson and Trent Thompson, "Rhinotillexomania", *J. Clin. Psychiatry*, Feb. 1995, p. 58.
4.   Ibid., pp. 56–59.

5. There are undoubtedly teachers who teach about nasal mucus, however, from my informal research they appear to be rare.
6. The following chronology of nasal mucus handling is taken from Norbert Elias, *History of Manners* (1982), pp. 143–152.
7. Ibid., p. 149.
8. Ibid., p. 145.
9. Ibid.
10. Kleenex facial tissues were developed in 1924 as a makeup remover. In 1930 advertising began emphasizing usage as a disposable handkerchief and sales exploded.
11. Elias, *History of Manners*, p. 147.
12. Jefferson, "Rhinotillexomania," p. 57.
13. In one survey, over two thirds were upset by public nose picking, and a third considered it unacceptable even in private. Ibid., p. 58.
14. Ibid.
15. Ibid., p. 57.
16. Ibid., p. 58, extrapolated to population of 310 million (2010 U.S. Census).
17. National Sporting Goods Association survey, 2010, ret. NSGA.org, 28 Mar. 2012.
18. Elias, *History of Manners*, p. 144.
19. This practice has been more thoroughly documented with excrement and sex and it will be presented in more detail in those chapters.
20. Paul Spinrad, *RE/Search Guide to Bodily Fluids* (1994), p. 94.
21. Ibid., pp. 93–94.
22. Branzei, *Grossology*, p. 13; and Georgie Binks, "Gross Habits That Harm," MochaSofa.com, July 2002, ret. 11 Feb. 2003.
23. Jefferson, "Rhinotillexomania," p. 59.
24. Ibid.
25. An unscientific survey found that almost forty percent of nose pickers find it enjoyable. Spinrad, *RE/Search Guide*, p. 60.
26. Jefferson, "Rhinotillexomania," p. 57

3

EXCREMENT
AMERICA DOESN'T KNOW SHIT

I
DOING IT WRONG

One of my earliest memories is from the bathroom. It is of my father showing me how to wipe: four squares, wipe, fold, repeat. With this orderly and efficient method you could get two or even three wipes out of four squares. My sister's voracious crumpling technique leads me to believe she had a different teacher. Growing up sharing a toilet, it seemed that she used half a roll to clean her ass. This was supported by the speed we went through toilet paper, and by the soggy mounds I witnessed after her forgot-to-flushes.

My first experience away from our toilet for any length of time was at sleep-away camp. I held it for four straight days. I've never had problems holding it. Of course, I've had lots of practice. In middle school I never took bowel movements at school. The bathrooms would usually stink abominably because guys would pee on the radiators. To prevent smoking the stalls had no doors, and the stalls were right by the entrance so that anybody who walked in would see you wiping your butt.

In high school my boycott came to an end. The bathrooms were cleaner and had doors, but perhaps more importantly, I was now an athlete. Like most teenagers, I greatly overestimated the importance of my athletic performance, and one cannot physically excel with weighted bowels.

So greatly did I value my performance that at an away basketball game, I used a solo stall in a cramped locker room while mere feet away the coach was talking to the team. In addition, the stall's frame was severely dented and offered little privacy. When I came out the snickering began.

Apparently, I had focused too much attention on the folding technique from my father's instructional lesson and missed the part about wiping stance. The fear of every kid was manifest that day—people watched me take a shit *and* I did it wrong. If any other teammates stood erect while wiping they made not a peep as the crouchers derisively cooed.

My participation in athletics didn't teach me teamwork, leadership, or discipline, but it did rid me of my guilt. I am no longer a shameful shitter. I am so free that I don't even feel inadequate when I crap my pants every year or so. I don't always make it. It happens. I clean my undergarment the best I can so it doesn't stain the suit and soldier on.

But unfortunately I have not lost all my scruples, and it may be my demise. My body is blessed with a lot of moles, like fifty or so. Besides my mother, no one really appreciated the cancerous threat they posed until I got to graduate school. On the student health care plan, Dr. Kim, my physician, was a young dermatologist-in-training. He too recognized the danger they posed and he knew what had to be done—a mole map.

Dr. Kim searched all over me with his latexed hands to make that map complete—in between my toes, under the hair on my head, even under my scrotum and penis—but there was one place he didn't look. He never looked in my butt crack.

Several months later I was doing a deep wipe of my bum and I felt a bump. After some clever use of mirrors it was confirmed. I had a mole on my asshole. The mole chart was incomplete.

I figured the asshole mole was a good candidate for cancer since it has shit on it every day. Despite this, I could not imagine myself bent over with my anus hanging out while Dr. Kim measured my mole with his little ruler. I never told him. I guess I would still rather risk cancer than make somebody examine my dirty place.

II
What It Is
Good Shit

Excrement includes any waste matter expelled from the body, but this chapter will center on feces, urine, and flatus.[1] Unlike nasal mucus, excrement is too important to the human body to be ignored by biology teachers, so most people have a rudimentary understanding of it. However, because of its taboo nature, teachers still do not give it the coverage that it deserves. For example, most people were taught fecal matter is mainly undigested food. This is false. This section will correct errors like these and delve into the more interesting aspects of excrement.

Feces—Contrary to popular belief, only a third of dry feces is undigested food. Another third of it is dead bacteria from the digestive system and the rest is a potpourri of live bacteria, dead body cells, mucus, etc.[2] The average adult produces seven pounds of feces a day, and a ton of feces a year.[3] All of this detritus must be handled carefully because the ingestion of feces, even indirectly through unwashed hands or tainted water, is a major source of disease.

Feces-contaminated water turned the dreaded cholera into the first global epidemic in the early 1800s. Lightning-quick, cholera can transform a strong, healthy person into a shriveled, blue, dehydrated carcass in mere hours. It is likely that Edgar Allan Poe's story "The Masque of the Red Death" was based on reports of cholera turning joyful parties into a mixture of silent corpses and hysterical people before the evening was through.

Humans are unique in their biological aversion to fecal matter. Most one-stomached animals, such as gorillas and dogs, regularly eat their bowel movements. The vitamins and nutrients that they don't digest the first time around make it worth their while to eat again. Rats are prolific feces-eaters. They eat roughly half of their once-passed-through feces. When rats have been fitted with "tail cups" to prevent them from coprophagy (feces-eating) they suffer from severe malnutrition. As with our one-stomached brethren, many nutrients escape in our stool as well. For example, humans defecate a quarter of the protein in digested potatoes and rice. Since we cannot eat our stool, this protein is wasted.

Urine[4]—Urine, unlike our bowel movements, is sterile and can be consumed by animals and humans without problems.[5] A person's urine is actually cleaner than the saliva or the skin on her face.[6] In other words, drinking the pee of a stranger is more sanitary than kissing a stranger.

Some South American native tribes drink urine as a refreshment, and urine therapy—ingesting or applying urine for its health benefits—is an ancient Eastern tradition practiced all over the world. The former prime minister of India, Morarji Desai (1896–1995), lived to be ninety-nine years old and credited his longevity to his practice of drinking a liter of his own urine a day.

Urine therapy has a surprisingly solid foundation. Urine is ninety-five percent water, two-and-a-half percent urea, and the remaining two-and-a-half percent is a mixture of minerals, salt, hormones, and enzymes. Urine is derived from blood that is taken out of circulation by the kidney. The kidney balances blood content. Just because something must be removed from the blood does not mean that it is unhealthy, it simply means that the blood had too much of it at that moment. This is how so many nutrients end up in urine.

Urine therapy advocates point to several facts when asserting that urine is our body's self-produced health drink. First, we all started out as urine drinkers. Fetuses develop in urine. Amniotic fluid is largely the fetus' urine and the developing fetus drinks and inhales it.[7] Second, many animals drink urine, for example, goats sometimes pee into their own mouths. Third, several cosmetic products and medicines, such as Murine eye drops, uric acid, and Urokinase, are already taken from urine.

Urine therapy is not urine's only use. Fresh urine is also a mild disinfectant that was used on the front during World War II to clean surgical instruments. As urine ages, the urea decomposes into ammonia, giving it a pungent odor and making it a powerful cleaner. Ancient Romans collected urine for use as a detergent or dye, with buyers walking the streets hollering, "Urine. Sell your urine."[8] As such a valued commodity, it was even taxed. Urine traders thought the tax was unfair because they had to work with the powerful stench of stale urine, but the emperor Vespasian rebuffed them by reportedly coining the phrase "money does not stink."[9]

Flatus—In contrast to feces and urine, flatus is not covered in most biology classes. As with nasal mucus, if a teacher were to cover farts she would risk being seen as infantile by her peers. The taboo nature of farts would bring her chagrin and embarrassment, so children are forced to learn about farts from second-rate comedy bits and their own experimentation.

Farts are a gaseous discharge from one's anus. This gaseous discharge comes primarily from the micro-farts of *E. coli* bacteria that live in our guts. The pungent fart smell actually comes from only one percent of the chemical makeup of a fart. Part of this one percent is sulfur and another part is skatole. A fart's flammability comes from hydrogen and methane. Although the volume, frequency, and smell of them vary greatly according to one's diet, everyone farts. An average person expels roughly a pint of gas through a dozen daily farts.[10] Women fart less frequently than men.[11]

Gaseous discharges have large environmental ramifications. The billions of massive dinosaur herbivores who existed during the hundred-million-year-long Jurassic period were prodigious farters. It is believed that this made our climate warmer and helped usher in mammals like ourselves.[12] But the same global warming that made it possible for us to exist may eventually drive us out. As during the Jurassic period, methane is still a significant contributor to global warming. Fifteen percent of annual methane emissions comes from ruminant animals, mainly cows, through their belching and farting. Another five percent comes from animal feces, and another four percent of annual methane emissions comes from termite farts.[13]

III

The Taboo
Potty Humor

The most taboo excreta is feces. The taboos of urine and flatus likely derived from their close relationships to it. From a young age people are taught to be ashamed of their detritus. At an early point they are toilet-trained and then put in solitary confinement when defecating. Parents who once wanted to constantly watch their children suddenly not only want to be away from them, but want the door closed so the child cannot be seen or heard during this act.

Shortly after potty training, it becomes improper to talk about bowel movements. It is only acceptable to mention them in a serious and urgent manner, for example, saying in a hushed voice "Excuse me, mother, I just had a bloody stool and I am concerned." If a child does have the gall to talk casually about excrement, her behavior is "inappropriate" for talking about "disgusting" things. If the child uses it in humor she is "immature" and into "potty humor."

This fecal shame follows people throughout life in a variety of ways. There can be awkwardness when one first uses a bathroom with strangers nearby, or first uses a restroom when a person of authority is using it, for example, a teacher. The fear of defecating around a new target of romantic affection is alluded to in the Ladino (Judeo-Spanish) adage, "If you come for the kisses, you must stay for the farts."[14] For some people these initial feelings of discomfort do not go away and remain as minor neuroses.

In his humorous essay "The Doubler," Raymond Abruzzi discusses the problems created by a person at work who is oblivious to the excrement taboo and transgresses its unspoken rules, for example, using the stall adjacent to the one Abruzzi is using, talking with Abruzzi during the act, making loud defecation noises, etc. In the following excerpt Abruzzi describes his own behavior when he is on the commode and someone enters the restroom:

> I bide my time, sitting patiently until they leave, before I exit the stall. I will often refrain from wiping or squeezing, as I realize these sounds are unappealing, until after the coast is clear. I also do not like to exit the stall in someone else's company, because I cannot escape the feeling of "I did a BAD thing," and don't want to meet their eyes and exchange bathroom pleasantries with anyone when I am feeling so dirty and disgusting about what I have done.[15]

This shame and the widespread availability of bathrooms in America is enough to keep defecation and its kin out of the public eye.[16] Passing wind is more difficult to restrain to private situations for some, but like nasal mucus, mild social enforcement is enough to keep farts out of most social situations.

Unlike nasal mucus, however, the excrement taboo has extended to our legal system. Public defecation is illegal in most municipalities. For example, in Miami, it is punishable by up to a $500 fine and sixty days in jail. This creates a problem for homeless people, many of whom have no choice but to go in public, and are thus legally barred from performing a necessary life function.

Excrement also must be sensitively discussed over the airwaves from six a.m. to ten p.m. Indecent discussion of excretory organs or activities during these hours on broadcast radio or television can result in the federal government imposing a fine or even revoking a station's license.[17]

The federal government tried to restrict indecent discussion of excretion from the Internet as well with the Communications Decency Act of 1996, which was passed overwhelmingly by Congress. This law criminalized any transmission of indecent communications about excrement that could be seen by minors. In other words, anybody who posted on Internet message boards or made a web site would be susceptible to punishment. However, the Supreme Court unanimously declared the Communications Decency Act an unconstitutional violation of the First Amendment's guarantee of freedom of speech, rendering it void.[18]

Excrement censorship by the federal government is done with the stated purpose of protecting children from hearing or viewing "harmful" material. How excretory references are harmful has not been explained. Despite the fact that excrement is included in the government's definition of indecent material, it is overlooked in most government censorship debates, which instead revolve around sex.

If evidence of the harmfulness of excretory references to minors was ever requested, it is likely the government would respond much like a federal court did when the harmfulness of sexual references was challenged in 1995: "Congress does not need the testimony of psychiatrists and social scientists in order to take note of the coarsening of impressionable minds..."[19]

IV

Its Origin
Filthy Forefathers

A. Ancient Times: Gods of Poo

Excrement was not always shameful in Western culture. Ancient religions that predated the Abrahamic faiths (Judaism, Christianity, and Islam) had a close affinity with nature. They believed in animism—the idea that animals, natural objects, and natural phenomena have their own guardian spirits. Unlike the Christian worldview, in which the physical world is separate from the spiritual world, they saw the physical world as being deeply spiritual, and excrement linked humans to this world through the natural cycle.

Humans defecate and the feces return to nature, fertilizing the crops. Humans harvest the crops and eat them, continuing the cycle. (This cycle was easier to observe for peoples whose excrement was not immediately whisked away down pipes, never to be seen again.) In this way excrement symbolizes decay and rebirth, and ancient creation myths all over the world have explained land, oceans, and people as coming from the urine and feces of gods.

Like the animist religions, the ancient Roman religion recognized excrement. They had a god for feces, Stercutius, who was revered by farmers who fertilized their fields with manure, and an alleged god for flatulence, Crepitus, who was invoked by those suffering from diarrhea or constipation. In addition, rain was thought to be the gods urinating.

This benign attitude was extended to the act of excreting as well. Wealthy Romans used to have their chamber pots brought to them at their feasts and would defecate in front of everybody without pausing their frolic.[20] In public, the commoners would go anywhere.[21] While feces were not shameful, it was still not appreciated in roads and stairwells. To keep these areas clean, the Roman government built public latrines. In these classical restrooms dozens of people would sit next to each other, male and female, defecating into troughs with no dividers. Each public latrine had community sponge sticks soaking in buckets of salt water, which the Romans would use to clean their hindquarters.

The respectful view of excrement in the West changed with the adoption of Christianity by the Roman Emperor Constantine in 312 A.D. Christianity and the other Abrahamic religions have demonized excrement.[22] This disdain dates to the creation of the Jewish religion, when rival tribes of the Jews worshipped an array of nature-related gods, among them the dung god, Baal-Peor. Worshippers of Baal-Peor reportedly defecated before the idol's mouth, which resembled an anus. To clearly distinguish itself from the nature religions it abhorred, Judaism established itself as strongly anti-scatological.[23]

Disdain of excrement pervades the Judeo-Christian tradition. According to most interpretations of the Bible, Adam and Eve did not defecate until their exile from the Garden of Eden, angels and other residents of heaven do not defecate, and the Israelites did not defecate during their forty years of wandering in the desert, because the manna provided from heaven was a perfect food.

In current practice, it is against Jewish law to think of holy matters when having an urge to defecate or during defecation. One can also not face toward or away from Jerusalem while defecating. Islam has a similar law regarding Mecca. A tragic example of excrement's offensiveness in these traditions occurred in 44 A.D., when a Roman soldier exposed his rump and farted toward Jews celebrating the Passover in Jerusalem. This insult provoked a riot that reportedly caused ten thousand Jews to be trampled to death.[24]

There are exceptions in the Judeo-Christian heritage, such as the European friars who explained the Americas by claiming they were formed from the animal feces dumped from Noah's ark.[25] However, the overall treatment of excrement is damning compared to Eastern and pagan religions.

B. The Middle Ages: Mountains of Poo

The Roman Empire's coercive installation of Christianity in Europe at the end of the fourth century planted the seeds of the excrement taboo,[26] but the idea of excrement being "bad" and "shameful" would not catch on for another 1,500 years. This delay was largely due to two reasons. First, the European masses held on to their pagan belief that nature was spiritual, although they did so under a Christian veneer. It took the brutality of the Inquisition and the witch hunts at the end of the

Middle Ages to forcefully extinguish this belief.[27] Second, it is difficult for one to be ashamed of something that is everywhere, and in medieval cities excrement and its stench were everywhere.

Europe took a technological step backward during the Middle Ages and sanitation suffered greatly. Lacking the public facilities and underground sewers enjoyed by the Romans, townsfolk had to rely on tossing their excreta into the streets from their windows. "Loo," slang for toilet, likely comes from the French term for "Beware the water." It was yelled out to warn people below the window of an outgoing delivery. People below would shout, "Hold your hand," and scurry off.[28]

When people were outdoors without the aid of a chamber pot, defecating in plain view of everyone was acceptable as late as the 1700s.[29] With human and animal excrement and its accompanying stench all over the streets, contact with it was not the abomination it currently is. Della Casa wrote in his 1609 book of manners for noblemen:

> It is far less proper to hold out the stinking [turd] for the other to smell, as some are wont, who even urge the other to do so, lifting the foul-smelling thing to his nostrils and saying, "I should like to know how much that stinks," when it would be better to say, "Because it stinks do not smell it."[30]

The wealthiest class could afford more privacy. When pressed to defecate in public they could rent a shielding cloak and a bucket from a street vendor who would wander the streets shouting out his service.[31] When nobility retired to their castles, there were small "bathrooms" protruding over the moats. They allowed detritus to fall into the water below and added to the castles' defenses by turning the moats into reeking cesspits. Dark stains running from these windows can still be seen on castles today.

There were a variety of methods by which the cities attempted to dispose of the waste filling their streets. In Nuremberg, Germany, open sewers went from each house to the river. At times the river was completely overburdened and at low tides the detritus would sit and fester. London used its rivers as well. London's Fleet River was so overburdened that it stopped flowing and is now Fleet Street. Before it clogged completely, the smell was so pungent that the monks of the White Friars complained to Parliament that the river's toxic atmosphere had killed several monks.[32] In Paris, feces were dumped outside the city walls. So much accumulated that the walls had to be extended so enemies could not use the mountains of feces as cannon positions.

Despite the dumping, Paris still had a problem, as the Duchess of Orleans commented around 1700:

> Paris is a dreadful place. The streets smell so badly you cannot go out. The extreme heat is causing large quantities of meat and fish to rot in them, and this, coupled to the multitude of people who . . . in the street, produces a smell so detestable that it cannot be endured.[33]

Country folk fared no better. Between eighty to ninety percent of Europe's population were rural peasants who lived in small villages isolated by miles of forest.[34] Prosperous peasants lived in sprawling huts of wood, mud, and thatch. These structures served as barns as well as living quarters, so that pigs, hens, cattle, and humans lived under the same roof. All the people would sleep in one immense bed made of vermin-infested straw pallets. Peasant homes were dark, dank, and filthy, and each had a dung heap in the front yard that rivaled it in size. Less prosperous peasants lived in smaller windowless straw shacks with less livestock and less ordure.

In these surroundings, it was difficult to be ashamed of feces and candor extended to other excreta as well. In the 1500s the English and Dutch would toast someone's health by drinking draughts of urine. Far from being coarse behavior, "drinking flapdragons" was an act of chivalry.[35] Another old English tradition was for wedding guests to drink the bride's urine. At a banquet celebrating the coronation of Anne Boleyn as the new English Queen in 1533, two handmaidens crouched beneath the table to handle her excretions, one with a chamber pot and another with a napkin.[36]

Flatus was also treated casually. Although it has been regarded as low comedy since at least the ancient Greeks,[37] Western culture has not suppressed gaseous discharges in public until relatively recently. In fact, for thousands of years it was

A DIRTY TRICK
The European Advantage

Spending centuries in medieval squalor gave Europeans a tolerance for diseases, such as smallpox, which the relatively clean American Indians lacked. European diseases destroyed Indian populations. When the Pilgrims landed in 1617, an unknown disease introduced to coastal New England by European fishermen only three years earlier had already killed over ninety percent of its Indian population.

—James Loewen, *Lies My Teacher Told Me* (1995), p. 70.

considered unhealthy to hold it back, even deadly. Uninhibited expulsion has been encouraged by such intellectual giants as Hippocrates ("the father of medicine"), Cicero, and Montaigne.

In the early Middle Ages diners belched and farted as loudly as they could to demonstrate their good health and to show gratitude toward their host.[38,39] In the 1600s a European explorer of Africa's Gambia River alluded to uninhibited European flatulence when writing about the Ashanti tribe:

> [The Ashanti] are very careful not to let a fart, if anybody be by
> them. They wonder at our Netherlanders that use it so commonly,
> for they cannot abide that a man should fart before them, esteeming
> it to be a great shame and contempt done unto them.[40,41]

This casual approach to farting was not limited to rugged explorers. In the 1700s the French royal court would have farting contests, engaged in by both men and women, with extra merit awarded to those who could light their gas aflame.[42] But toward the end of this century Western attitudes toward excrement began to change.[43]

C. 1700–1900: Don't Look at My Poo

At the end of the 1700s the taboo on excrement began to tighten its grip for numerous reasons. First, by then Christianity had ruthlessly separated people from their affinity toward nature through the Inquisition and the witch trials.[44]

Second, around 1760 researchers began to associate certain smells with infections and contaminations. They would not understand germs' relationship to disease for another hundred years, so their theories centered on types of vapors, with putrid ones being thought unhealthy.[45]

Third, as with the hanky, being odor-free became a status symbol. Poor people stank; people of means did not.[46] With the rise of the middle class during the Industrial Revolution, more and more people had the means to be clean. This trend extended itself to one's home and streets. The development of the modern toilet in the late 1700s made it technologically possible to reduce exposure to excrement and its funk.

Fourth, controlling the bodily functions was seen as an act of respect in the hierarchical society of the Middle Ages.[47] What was fine to do in front of others was not fine to do in front of kings and dukes. A noted example of this was the case of Edward de Vere, the seventeenth Earl of Oxford. In the late 1500s the Earl broke wind as he bent to kiss the hand of Queen Elizabeth I at court. He was so embarrassed that he left England and traveled for seven years. When he returned the Queen welcomed him home and said, "My Lord, I had forgot the fart."[48]

Yet as businessmen began to gain more power and the aristocracy fell, the clear-cut hierarchy began to melt. There was much greater social interdependence. Whereas before you only had to ingratiate yourself to a handful of people rarely, such as royalty, now you had to ingratiate yourself to a wide variety of people with whom you did business regularly—and it was wise to treat them all like royalty.[49]

Even with all this impetus for change, positive attitudes toward excrement did not exit quietly. Some intellectuals resisted what they saw as unnecessary elitist mannerisms. Gustave Flaubert, the author of the classic *Madame Bovary*, wrote in the mid-1800s, "Let diarrhea 'drip into your boots, piss from the window, shout out shit,' defecate in full view, fart hard, blow your cigar smoke in people's faces . . . belch in people's faces."[50]

A number of the poor found the stale air comforting, which is understandable considering they spent their entire lives in it. Rumors claimed the use of chlorine to eliminate odors was a mass homicide plot against the underclass and in 1832 ragpickers in Paris protested against municipal sanitary measures by rioting and burning dung carts.

Despite the mounting evidence of excrement's dangers, some doctors still insisted it was not harmful. The medical field had a long-established practice of using excrement as medicine, called "Filth Pharmacy." One prominent adherent was Martin Luther, who reportedly ate a spoonful of his own feces daily for its remedial effect.[51] Excreta from a variety of animals and humans (such as the dung of milk-feeding lambs, or urine of an undefiled boy) were prescribed for ingestion, injection, and inhalation. It also had long been customary for doctors to diagnose their patients by tasting small amounts of their stool.

All these doubters were silenced in 1857 when Louis Pasteur established the germ theory of disease. By this time the Victorian Age was underway and modesty regarding sex and excretion was already being taken to extremes. Although the Victorian Era is most noted for its repression of sex, excretion was repressed as well. Chamber pots were hidden in other furniture by the use of secret doors. Some of these devices played music when in use to draw attention away from the deed.

The Victorian obsession with regulating excrement also influenced its toilet training:

> [Mothers in the early 1900s] were taught to commence toilet training as early as possible, to cut down on the drudgery of hand-washing diapers, and, more significantly, to instill early on a sense of order, cleanliness, and respect for authority. Starting as early as one month, they would set aside frequent blocks of time to hold the child over a pot or even strap them down and probe their rectum with soap sticks or glass or porcelain rods until they passed a stool. A rigid toilet regimen was seen as necessary to physical and mental health, and mothers who couldn't toilet train their small infants, which was all of them, were told they were failures.[52]

They were all failures because it is now known that most children are physically incapable of toilet training until their eighteenth month. Before then the nerves used in controlling their excretory functions are not developed enough to resist bowel movements. Toilet training in this era was thus a disciplinary struggle between mothers and children that could last years. Sigmund Freud and other early psychoanalysts believed this strife had long-lasting psychological ramifications—one of them being the internalization that excrement is very bad.

Despite this Victorian shame, excretion would still not become a private activity until the twentieth century. Although the concept of the modern toilet dates to 1596, when Sir John Harrington made one for his godmother, the aforementioned Queen Elizabeth,[53] they did not come into general use among the wealthy until the late 1800s.

In America, indoor flush toilets would not become popular outside of wealthy urban neighborhoods until after World War I, when soldiers returned from Europe raving about them.[54] Until then America's largely rural population depended on outhouses and the age-old chamber pot. Although outhouses could offer privacy, they often did not. They came with as many as six seats, complete with different sized holes for different sized posteriors, and it was common for family members to use the unpartitioned seats simultaneously. Not until the 1920s' housing boom did bathrooms become common, cementing excretion as a private affair.[55]

D. Twentieth Century: Don't Even Say Poo

Another twentieth-century development that allowed the taboo to reach its zenith was mass communication. The early 1900s saw the development of the record player, the radio, movies, and television. Mass communication could be censored much more easily than locally-performed live entertainment, and it was.

The fledgling movie industry was regulated by the Hays Office.[56] The Hays Office expunged any intimations of excretion in movies. In 1936 it sent a letter to United Artists about Charlie Chaplin's *Modern Times*, urging it to eliminate "the business of the stomach rumbling on the part of the minister's wife and Charlie."[57] In 1941 the Hays Office warned Universal Pictures about using the words "stinker" and "stinkeroo" in a W.C. Fields movie.

In 1968 the Hays Office was disbanded by the motion picture industry after several state courts declared its censorship unconstitutional. The Hays Office was then replaced by the current rating system (for example G, PG-13, R). Despite this change, it was not until 1974 that flatus first appeared on screen, in *Blazing Saddles*.

Blazing Saddles had a scene that lampooned cowboy westerns for always showing cowboys eating beans without showing the results. The scene showed the results and was widely criticized. One *New York Times* editorial that lambasted the movie began, "Every society has its unspoken taboos. They linger in the twilight of public consciousness until something called bad taste brings them into the open."[58]

Television was slower to accept flatus freedom. In fact, the television version of *Blazing Saddles* to this day has the cowboys' farting overdubbed with horses whinnying. The word "fart" was first said on the little screen during a critique of the word's use on radio. On an NBC news program in 1982, a segment on X-rated radio went like this:

> Host: "What you are about to hear is going to shock and disgust you, because it's vulgar, even obscene … It's X-rated radio, barnyard radio …"
>
> Clip of Disc Jockey Howard Stern: "Hey, man, I hear your pappy is so disgusting that he takes a bubble bath by farting in a mud puddle."
>
> Host: "Can't something be done to get this filth off the air?"[59]

This treatment is a strong contrast to the relative freedom that flatulence currently receives in the media. Even the family entertainment bastion Walt Disney embraced its comedic value in its G-rated hit movie *The Lion King* (1994), with its farting warthog character, Pumbaa. This media exposure is loosening the excrement taboo's hold on society and returning it to the more natural attitude that has prevailed throughout human history.

V

Repercussions
Anal Retentive

The excrement taboo has stifled talk about excrement, its handling, and the body parts from which it is expelled. The resulting ignorance has had multiple ramifications.

A. Facilities: Lazy Shits

First, the taboo about excrement has influenced the quality of our bathrooms. Technology has transformed all aspects of our lives. Ovens, refrigerators, and blow dryers have all undergone amazing changes in the last fifty years. Toilets have hardly changed since the late 1800s.[60]

The advantages of not having as strong an excrement taboo can be seen in Japan. Many modern Japanese homes have electronic toilets that can heat the seat at preprogrammed times, such as when you wake up in the morning. These toilet marvels also have hydraulic jets for anal or genital cleansing, hot air dryers, and can make sounds to hide any embarrassing ones created by your body. Some of these toilets can even check a person's temperature, blood pressure, and blood sugar and transmit the data to a medical professional.

Yet the most consequential problem with Western toilets is not that they lack these frills but that they are horribly designed.[61] Western toilets make one sit. Sitting is an unnatural position.[62] Evolution has designed human beings to squat when defecating. Most of the world's population squats. Squatting straightens the rectoanal junction allowing an unimpeded path to the anus,[63] and spreads the buttocks allowing for a cleaner and quieter release. In addition, when squatting the thighs exert pressure on the stomach aiding in expulsion. Squatting has a hygienic advantage as well because the rear does not come in contact with anything.

A drawback to squatting is that it takes more energy and older Americans who are new to it may have difficulty. This is not a problem for older people who have been squatting all their lives because their squatting muscles, the upper leg muscles and abdominals, have been developed. These muscles are the same muscles used in expelling excrement and one of the reasons American elderly have constipation is because these muscles have atrophied.[64]

The seated defecation posture's effect on regularity has been known for a long time. One author wrote in 1924 "the adoption of the squatting attitude would . . . help in no small measure to remedy the greatest physical vice of the white race, the constipation that has become a contentment."[65]

The unnatural defecation position that Western toilets require may have graver ramifications than merely constipation. There are reasons to believe that the seated posture contributes to a range of bowel problems—appendicitis, Crohn's disease, colitis, irritable bowel syndrome, colon cancer, incontinence, hemorrhoids,[66] diverticulosis,[67] and heart attacks on the toilet.[68],[69] These afflictions are significantly rarer in Asia and Africa, where the squatting method of defecation is predominant. For the past century doctors have tried to attribute this to diet—particularly lack of fiber. However, diet has not fully explained the difference.[70]

The rationale behind these theories, briefly, is that (1) the sitting method does not promote full evacuation. The leftover fecal material stagnates and can lodge in the appendix, where it causes appendicitis, and to the walls of the lower digestive tract, where it can contribute to Crohn's disease, colitis, irritable bowel syndrome, and colon cancer.

(2) When in the seated position, people perform the Valsalva maneuver to evacuate. The Valsalva maneuver requires a pushing down with the diaphragm while holding one's breath. This unnatural straining can cause heart attacks in the weak and the repeated stress on the lower digestive system over a lifetime leads to incontinence, hemorrhoids, and diverticulosis.

While hundreds of studies have been done trying to connect varying diets to the above problems, the sitting-squatting hypothesis has been practically unexplored.[71]

B. Technique: Spread and Lift

The taboo interferes with Americans' use of facilities as well. Men urinate standing up. This would be acceptable if men aimed at the water in the bowl. However, because they are embarrassed by the sound that is produced from peeing into the water, many men instead aim for the bowl's side walls. This is a smaller target and porcelain is harder than water, ergo, larger backsplashes are created. Just how far urine aimed in this manner can backsplash is known to those who clean bathrooms.

Backsplash is less of a problem with urinals because the urine is usually falling a shorter distance, but even America's urinals are poorly designed to minimize backsplash. When urine leaves the penis, it moves in a tight rotating sheet for the first several inches, after which it breaks into a continually widening spray.[72] A well-shaped urinal would be more like a funnel, trapping this widening spray and directing the backsplash inward.[73]

American women, on the other hand, are not even aware they have the ability to stand and urinate accurately just like men. A woman simply has to make a "v" with her first and second finger, spreading the inside of her labia minora, and lift to the desired angle.[74] The standing method is still popular in rural areas of India and the Philippines, and up until a hundred years ago it was common practice for Western females as well.

For a while, the standing method was making an underground comeback, with the technique spread on a website.[75] One woman was quoted on the website as writing,

> I've used urinals many times when working late at my office (at first, because the men's room is much closer, and now, because I find a urinal to be more convenient). I do it facing, and it works fine now that I know the posture (nothing extreme). I don't make any kind of mess, and don't even have to undress as much as to sit down. I'm starting to think women have been kept in the dark about this for a reason.[76]

Another woman wrote that she improved her technique until she could pee her name in the snow, and complained "My, what our mothers never taught us!!"[77]

One ramification of this technique being buried is that women must stand in arduously long lines at public events waiting to use the restrooms as men fly in and out of their facilities.[78] Ironically most of these women are waiting to use toilets they won't touch anyway. Instead they will acrobatically hover over them.

The topic of hovering leads to a modern marvel of futility—the public restroom. One American survey found that nearly thirty percent of Americans avoid public restrooms altogether and that sixty percent of the people who do use public toilets hover.[79] Women appear to be more apt to hover than men, with one British study showing that eighty-five percent of women hover.[80]

Hovering stems from a fear of coming in contact with toilet seats soiled by other peoples' rear ends. This may appear rational until you consider that a 2002 study found that the average office toilet seat contained forty-nine germs per square inch, while office desktops had roughly 21,000 germs per square inch and office phones had 25,000.[81] In addition, at home many of these hoverers do not shut the toilet lid after flushing, meaning that fecal matter is regularly sprayed on their toothbrush.[82]

The problem with hoverers is that they often miss the hole and leave a pile of their feces sitting on the seat, effectively putting the toilet out of commission for everyone else. Westerners find the Asian squat toilet inappropriate, and yet on any toilet but their own many of them squat and hover, leaving behind foul messes.[83]

C. Cleansing: Poo Butt

Another area in which the excrement taboo hampers progress is cleaning. Here in America toilet paper is used to clean after defecation. But polls show that even among Americans, there is no consensus on how to use the toilet paper. Since it is never talked about most people do not realize they are all using different methods. Most people wipe from front to back from the back. The second most popular method is from back to front from the front.[84] Roughly half the population folds their toilet paper and the other half crumple.[85] The average total of squares of toilet paper used is eighteen.[86]

The first problem with this is that females who wipe from back to front are risking vaginal infections. The second problem is that there are people who are inefficient wipers. Folding is the most efficient method. Crumplers are wasting considerable amounts of toilet paper. If one surmises that half of the population is using twice as much toilet paper as necessary, it is evident that vast forests are needlessly being flushed down America's commodes.

Toilet paper is not used in many parts of the world. One alternative is using the left hand to wash with water, as in Arab countries and India. While many Americans may find this repulsive, the feeling is mutual. Hand wipers do not understand how Americans can expect to get clean with a dry paper wipe.

Their criticism is valid because dry paper leaves residue, particularly on those with an abundance of hair surrounding the anus.[87,88] In 1964 Dr. J.A. Cameron surveyed the underwear of 940 men in Oxfordshire, England, and found contamination in almost half of them, ranging from "wasp-colored stains" to "frank massive feces."[89] Incomplete cleaning can lead to odors, chafing, and infections.[90] Some Americans may dislike the need to wash one's hands after a wet hand wipe, but for proper hygiene one should be cleaning one's hands after the paper method as well. This rule even applies to crumplers who use half a roll of toilet paper.

The main barrier to wet wiping for Americans is the psychological one of touching feces with the hands. Fortunately there is a wet wiping alternative that came on the market in 2001—Kimberly-Clark's flushable pre-moistened Rollwipes. The same company that introduced the tissue is attempting another hygienic transformation, but has already had difficulty advertising a taboo topic. The initial campaign flopped.[91] Ads showed people from behind splashing in water with the slogan "sometimes wetter is better." It was so vague that consumers did not understand what it was.

D. Holding It: Learn to Love Again

The excrement taboo has also forced people to hold in their excrement. Everyone has felt the discomfort from holding in gas around other people, and from holding in bowel movements for lack of an available restroom. However, there are also those who hold in feces because they do not like others to even be aware that they are defecating. For most people this embarrassment is avoided by simply avoiding specifics, for example by saying, "I must use the restroom," and by using euphemisms such as "Excuse me, I must go powder my nose." For the more self-conscious these semantics are not enough cover.

This fear of public excretion has ramifications. School children may be the most at-risk group. Due to their immaturity, the general treatment of their facilities is often cruder, leading to uncleanliness, and the social ramifications of having a loud or malodorous evacuation are worse. Because students are not allowed to leave school premises, they have no alternative. A Swedish study found that thirty-five percent of older students never used the school bathrooms and eighty percent never used them for defecation.[92] In addition to the torment of holding it, this repeated behavior can lead to urinary tract infections, bladder inflammation, constipation, and incontinence. In poorer regions education suffers because some kids solve the problem by not attending at all. In Tanzania, India, and Bangladesh, when schools installed "decent latrines" school enrollment rose by as much as fifteen percent.[93]

Urination is a more frequent necessity than defecation, and for some the anxiety created by the taboo is substantial. The technical term for the affliction is *avoidant paruresis* or "bashful bladder." *Avoidant paruresis* is a psychological disorder in which people fear urinating with other people around. Their fear is so strong that they are physically incapable of peeing. Studies have shown that roughly seven percent of the population, or seventeen million Americans, suffer from paruresis.[94] Most paruretics only have the problem when they are in view of others, such as in crowded urinals, but more severe cases fear any bathroom where there is a possibility of others seeing, hearing, or merely knowing they are urinating.

The intuitive solution of just holding it can be extremely painful. One sufferer explained it thus, "I felt like I was either going to die or I would pass out because the pain was so intense that even if you put a gun to my head, I would not be able to go."[95] Severe paruresis can be life-altering, binding people to their homes. One man dropped out of high school in ninth grade, went to a local college so he could live at home, and stayed in a lousy job for years, all to accommodate his disorder.[96]

Therapy programs, complete with a "pee buddy," pee practice, and relaxation training, have been successful as a cure. The elation of conquering this phobia is clear in Don from California's posting at ShyBladder.org:

> I [now] LOVE to pee—as much as I possibly can. I MADE MYSELF love to pee by loving myself, forgiving the past, living in NOW, and NEVER giving up until I felt in my heart and soul that I was CURED—PERMANENTLY! AND I AM.[97]

At the individual level, the health problems caused by holding one's bladder and bowels are not severe. Perhaps the gravest repercussion of the excrement taboo is that people avoid seeing a doctor for symptoms that involve excrement and the orifices involved. This hesitance costs lives. Britain's stricter excrement taboo is thought to be a reason for the slower diagnosis of gastrointestinal disease and colorectal cancer than mainland Europe, and the correspondingly higher death rate.[98] One British doctor wrote in London's *The Times*:

> I cannot bear to think of the patients I have seen who have kept some intimate symptom secret until they had the opportunity of telling me in the course of their annual medical check of some seemingly embarrassing problem, too distressing to discuss elsewhere. Too often it was rectal bleeding, change in bowel habits, mucus discharge from some orifice or another, blood in the urine, lump in the breast, vaginal discharge and sometimes . . . the shame of no longer being able to control their belching or farting.[99]

E. The Environment: Crapping on the Fish[100]

In addition to damaging our health, the excrement taboo has also damaged the health of the environment. Excrement is an important part of the life cycle. For the latter history of life on this planet, water and land have had separate cycles. Land ecosystems are nutrient-rich and land animals' excrement played a major part in keeping it this way. Animals dropped their nutrient-rich detritus on the ground, where it was assimilated back into the soil to fertilize the plants, thus renewing the process. In contrast, water ecosystems are pure, that is, they are relatively free of nutrients. Aquatic life has evolved in a nutrient-poor environment.

The Western taboo on excrement has destroyed this balance. Whereas East Asian cultures valued their feces and were diligent about returning it to their farmland, Western cultures preferred to dump it in waterways to get rid of it. While Asian farming's productiveness per acre became a wonder and was credited with supporting their immense populations, Western farmland was quickly depleted and needed artificial fertilizers to maintain meager crops.[101]

41

In the late 1800s sanitary engineers in Europe and America were split between adopting the Asian practice of using human excreta as fertilizer and those who believed it should be dumped into waterways. Western politicians, like the members of New York City Council,[102] could not overcome their disdain for turning human waste into plant fertilizer, and the recyclers lost.

Instead of recycling excreta, expensive sewer systems were developed. Water was piped in and out of houses. Whereas before people used five gallons of water per day, water use shot up and now an individual uses roughly ninety gallons of water a day.[103] All of this excreta-laced water was sent back into the water streams. River ecosystems were destroyed as nutrient-rich water created algae infestations that choked out all other life.

The tragedy does not end there. Factories dumping chemicals into sewers lobbied for more. Sewers allowed them to push the cost of their toxic waste onto the public. Industry demand for sewers produced massive public sewer construction projects. Massive public sewer systems were attractive to engineering and construction firms, who supported even more projects. The valuable nutrients of excreta were now hopelessly mixed in sewage with the thousands of man-made chemicals dumped from factories and other household products.

Currently sewage is treated to keep harmful elements out of the waterways. This is expensive, but has been done successfully where local communities are environmentally alert and politically organized. The problem is now what to do with the filtered pollution called sludge. Sludge has been put in landfills, causing ground pollution, incinerated, causing air pollution, and dumped in the ocean. No one knew exactly what its effects were at the bottom of the ocean, but ocean dumping became unacceptable in the 1980s when hypodermic needles and other unsavory items began washing up on recreational beaches.

At present the sludge problem is handled by giving it away as free fertilizer to farmers. While appearing to be a wonderful solution that saves both municipalities and farmers money, it could have grave consequences. It is indeed recycling, but the valued nutrients from human excreta are now being put back into the food chain along with an unknown potpourri of chemicals that includes industrial waste.

The Environmental Protection Agency has deemed treated sludge fertilizer safe, even though its own scientists have testified before Congress that the supporting science is lacking, even "fraudulent."[104] Despite anecdotal evidence that exposure to sludge fertilizer has caused health problems and even death, the dangers of sludge fertilizer remain under-researched.[105] As a result, scientists are still uncertain what effects these chemicals have in the chain of life, which goes from plants to animals to us.[106]

F. Abroad: Crapping on Third-World Children[107]

While developed nations grapple with sludge, impoverished nations still grapple with unprocessed excrement. Just like in medieval European cities, in slums and villages around the globe crap is everywhere. Of the world's seven billion people, 2.6 still have no sanitation whatsoever and defecate on the ground. Ubiquitous feces contaminate drinking water, causing diarrhea—a deadly affliction for children in the absence of health care.

Feces-contaminated water kills a staggering 1.8 million children annually. This number dwarfs the number of people killed by violent conflict, and one dollar invested in sanitation returns seven in saved health care costs and productivity gains. Yet, sanitation "barely registers on the international agenda."[108] As Rose George explains in *The Big Necessity: The Unmentionable World of Human Waste and Why It Matters*, politicians and celebrities do not want to talk about sanitation, much less champion it.

G. History: Hidden Turds

As with nasal mucus, one of the most fascinating effects of the excrement taboo is how history is presented. Artists of past ages had no qualms about representing excretion, but this artwork is rarely seen because curators, editors, and collectors have operated under modern taboos in selecting the art worthy of preservation and presentation.[109] Sometimes art has been modified, as in the case of the Rembrandt painting now entitled "A Woman Bathing in a Stream." The original allegedly portrayed a woman urinating but in a later time period someone painted out the falling stream.[110]

When excretion is presented historically, it's often not treated in the manner befitting its time. An example is the 1984 Oscar-award-winning film *Amadeus*, about

YE GODS!
Mozart's Muck

Examples of the scatology in Mozart's letters can be found in these passages from a missive he wrote to his cousin, Maria Mozart, while in his early twenties (November 5, 1777):

I shit on your nose and it will run down your chin. À propos.

Oh, my arse is burning like fire! What on earth does it mean!—Perhaps some muck wants to come out? Why yes, muck, I know, see and smell you … and … what is that? —Is it possible … Ye gods!—can I believe those ears of mine? Yes indeed, it is so—what a long melancholy note!

He concluded his letter with this story:

I must tell you of a sad thing which has happened just this very moment. As I was doing my best to write this letter, I heard something on the street. I stopped

Wolfgang Amadeus Mozart. In it Mozart is portrayed as an abnormal adult with a strange obsession with flatus. This treatment is echoed in a critic's article:

> There is also something disturbing about Mozart. Even into his twenties he was still very adolescent. Some of the letters he wrote, including those to his sister, are vulgar and immature. Lavatory humor for eight-year-olds may be understood but not for someone who is 21-plus. He wrote about intimate bodily functions and both his parents talked openly about defecation.[111]

During Mozart's life (1756–1791), the excrement taboo was in its infancy. As has been mentioned, during this time period the French royal court was having fart contests. Coupled with the fact that Mozart came from a poor background, a social class in which excremental activity was even less concealed, his bluntness in regard to things scatological is not disturbing.

writing—I got up—went to the window … and … the sound ceased, I sat down again, started off again to write—but I had hardly written ten words when again I heard something. I got up again—As I did, I again heard a sound, this time quite faint—but I seemed to smell something slightly burnt—and wherever I went, it smelt. When I looked out of the window, the smell disappeared. When I looked back into the room, I again noticed it.

In the end Mamma said to me: "I bet you have let off one." "I don't think so, Mamma," I replied. "Well, I am certain that you have," she insisted. Well, I thought "Let's see," put my finger to my arse and then to my nose and—Ecce, provatum est. Mamma was right after all.

—Jim Dawson, *Who Cut the Cheese* (1999), p. 112; Wolfgang Mieder, "Now I Sit Like a Rabbit in the Pepper," *J. Folklore Res.*, Jan.–Apr. 2003, pp. 51–52; and William Stafford, *Mozart Myths* (1993), p. 92.

The excrement taboo has also affected more serious examinations of history. Napoleon's final defeat, the Battle of Waterloo in 1815, is studied by most students at some point, as it prevented Napoleon from making all of Europe France. Why did Napoleon lose? In a four-hundred-word analysis by the BBC, the failure is blamed on mistakes in communication, leadership, and judgment.[112] Curiously, the BBC fails to mention that Napoleon had to leave the battle at its height for several hours because he was stricken with severe diarrhea.[113]

Perhaps Napoleon's untimely bowel movements are irrelevant to understanding Napoleon's defeat at Waterloo, but the following omission is more difficult to comprehend. The atrocities committed by Adolf Hitler have been a popular academic topic over the past fifty years. Studying Hitler is an integral part of American history classes, and the question "What drove Hitler to commit these acts?" is often asked. Theories range from repressed homosexuality to bitterness over being a failed artist.[114] Almost no one mentions that his atrocities could have stemmed from his severe gas problems.

When Hitler was first coming into power in the early 1930s he was already suffering from gastrointestinal pains. At that time he was taking a gun-cleaning oil called Balestol to alleviate the problem. During World War I soldiers sometimes would ingest Balestol in the trenches for upset stomachs, and under the name Neo-

Balestol, the oil was later sold specifically for that purpose. Balestol turned out to be poisonous, and after suffering a particularly bad reaction to it Hitler had it removed from the market.

Hitler's uncontrollable farting continued to be problematic. After other doctors' remedies failed, Hitler began treatment in 1936 with a quack physician, Dr. Theodor Morell. Morell initially had success and became Hitler's primary physician, but over time Hitler's problems grew even worse. One of Morell's later notebook entries regarding Hitler read, "After eating a vegetable platter, constipation and colossal flatulence occurred on a scale I have seldom encountered before."[115]

For the rest of Hitler's life, Morrell injected him with dubious concoctions so frequently that Morrell sometimes had trouble finding an unscarred vein to pierce. Between 1941 and 1945, Morell's journals show that he treated Hitler with seventy-seven different medicines and preparations.[116] One particularly damaging treatment was Dr. Koester's anti-gas pills. These pills contained strychnine and atropine, two deadly poisons. Hitler ingested high amounts of the pills for eight years, and they likely caused his irritability and dementia.

Is it rational that one of the great themes debated by students and scholars in the last half-century is devoid of the information that he was being continuously pumped full of poisonous concoctions, some of which are known to cause insanity?

NOTES

1. Flatus (FLAY-tus) is the scientific word for fart.
2. Our digestive system is loaded with healthy bacteria. One drop of saliva can contain two million bacteria. One drop of colon content contains fifty million bacteria. These bacteria help digest our food, produce vitamins, and occupy niches that would otherwise be available for unhealthy bacteria. Without them we could not survive. Trudy Wassenaar, "Bacteria: More Than Pathogens," Actionbioscience.org, July 2002, ret. 9 Aug. 2006.
3. Roger Luckenbach, "Fecal Matters," *Coast Weekly*, July 1995.
4. Section largely from Coen van der Kroon, *Golden Fountain* (1996).
5. This should be qualified as fresh urine from a healthy animal.
6. Sylvia Branzei, *Grossology* (1995), p. 24.
7. A fetus' urine is very similar to its mother's urine.
8. "Classicist Digs Deep for Truth About Hygiene Habits of Ancient Romans," *Brandeis University News*, 12 June 2000.
9. van der Kroon, *Golden Fountain*, p. 13.

10. Branzei, *Grossology*, pp. 62–63, and Jim Dawson, *Who Cut the Cheese* (1999), p. 10.
11. Dawson, *Who Cut the Cheese*, p. 11.
12. "How Dinosaurs May Have Helped Make Earth Warmer," *San Francisco Chronicle*, 23 Oct. 1991.
13. H. Augenbraun, E. Matthews, and D. Sarma, "Global Methane Cycle," Institute on Climate and Planets, Aug. 1997.
14. Dawson, *Who Cut the Cheese*, p. 65.
15. Abruzzi, "The Doubler," 1998. Available free on the web.
16. Feces and defecation cannot be avoided by some groups, such as pet owners and farmers, making it less taboo with them.
17. The FCC has defined broadcast indecency as "language or material that, in context, depicts or describes, in terms patently offensive as measured by contemporary community standards for the broadcast medium, sexual or excretory organs or activities." "FCC Consumer Facts: Obscene and Indecent Broadcasts," FCC.Gov, 24 Sep. 2007, ret. 1 Sep. 2008.
18. *Reno v. American Civil Liberties Union*, 521 US 844 (1997).
19. *Action for Children's Television v. FCC* (ACT III), 11 F.3d 170 (DC Cir. 1993).
20. A chamber pot is a portable container used as a toilet.
21. Roughly ninety percent of the ancient Romans were commoners, that is, not of the wealthy patrician class.
22. Paul Spinrad, *RE/Search Guide to Bodily Fluids* (1994), p. 90.
23. Ibid., p. 89.
24. Jim Dawson, *Who Cut the Cheese* (1999), p. 8.
25. Spinrad, *RE/Search Guide*, p. 120.
26. Roman Emperor Theodosius criminalized all other religions and any disagreement with the Christian Church in 380 A.D..
27. Helen Ellerbe, *Dark Side of Christian History* (1995), p. 143.
28. Spinrad, *RE/Search Guides*, p. 111.
29. Norbert Elias, *History of Manners* (1982), p. 133.
30. Ibid., p. 131.
31. In the nineteenth century, women's long voluminous hooped dresses allowed them to urinate discreetly in front of others. (Women did not wear underwear until bloomers were popularized at the start of the twentieth century.) Havelock Ellis, *My Life* (1939), pp. 84–87.
32. Julie Horan, *Porcelain God* (1996), pp. 31–32.
33. Elias, *History of Manners*, p. 132.
34. Paragraph from William Manchester, *World Lit Only by Fire* (1993), pp. 50, 52–53.
35. Spinrad, *RE/Search Guide*, p. 94.
36. Richard Zacks, *Underground Education* (1997), p. 136.
37. Jim Dawson, *Who Cut the Cheese* (1999), p. 1.
38. Philippe Aries and Georges Duby, *History of Private Life: From Pagan Rome to Byzantium* (1987), pp. 446–447.
39. Boisterous and malodorous flatus was abundant due to diets comprised almost solely of meat and bread.
40. Dawson, *Who Cut the Cheese*, p. 4.
41. Another explorer wrote of an Ashanti man who farted when bowing before his chief and was so ashamed that he hung himself within an hour. Cultures vary widely on flatus acceptance. The Yanomami of Venezuela use farts as a greeting.
42. Carol Midgley, "Our Gross Domestic Products," *Times*, 28 Aug. 2002.
43. Horan, *Porcelain God*, p. 68.
44. Helen Ellerbe, *Dark Side of Christian History* (1995), p. 143.
45. Spinrad, *RE/Search Guide*, p. 112.
46. Ibid., pp. 112–113.
47. Norbert Elias, *History of Manners* (1982), p. 152.
48. Dawson, *Who Cut the Cheese*, p. 86.
49. An example of this social leveling can be seen in a table mannerism. Whereas eating used to commence when the person of highest rank, for instance the king, was ready, eating now commences when everyone is ready. Elias, *History of Manners*, pp. 137–139.

50. Spinrad, *RE/Search Guide*, p.113.
51. Rose George, *Big Necessity* (2008), p. 8.
52. Spinrad, *RE/Search Guide*, p. 85.
53. She refused to try it and banished him from court for his poor taste. Horan, *Porcelain God*, pp. 48–49.
54. Maureen Francis, "The 'Flush Toilet' a Tribute to Ingenuity," MasterPlumbers.com, 19 Oct. 1999, ret. 12 Oct. 2010.
55. Alexander Kira, *Bathroom* (1966), pp. 10–11.
56. The office was an unsuccessful attempt by movie studios to prevent government censorship. Marjorie Heins, *Not in Front of the Children* (2001), p. 54.
57. Jim Dawson, *Who Cut the Cheese* (1999), p. 116.
58. Urjo Kareda, "Is There Any Future for Bad Taste?" *New York Times*, 18 Aug. 1974.
59. Dawson, *Who Cut the Cheese*, pp. 125–126.
60. Kira, *Bathroom*, pp. v–vi.
61. Ibid., pp. 119–138.
62. Dov Sikirov, "Comparison of Straining During Defecation," *Dig. Dis. Sci.*, July 2003, pp. 1201–1205.
63. Ibid.
64. Kira, *Bathroom*, pp. 120–121; and Berko Sikirov, "Primary Constipation," *Med. Hypotheses*, Feb. 1989.
65. Frederick Hornibrook, *Culture of the Abdomen* (1933, orig. pub. 1924), pp. 77–78.
66. Berko Sikirov, "Management of Hemorrhoids," *Isr. J. Med. Sci.*, Apr. 1987.
67. Berko Sikirov, "Etiology and Pathogenesis of Diverticulosis Coli," *Med. Hypotheses*, May 1988.
68. Berko Sikirov, "Cardio-Vascular Events at Defecation" *Med. Hypotheses*, July 1990.
69. For an overview see "Health Benefits" at NaturesPlatform.com, a site selling platforms that allow squatting on toilet bowls.
70. For example, high fiber intake was not found to reduce the risk of colorectal cancer. Yikyung Park, et al., "Dietary Fiber Intake and Risk of Colorectal Cancer," *JAMA*, 14 Dec. 2005.
71. Sikirov, "Comparison of Straining," p. 1205.
72. Kira, *Bathroom*, p. 141.
73. Ibid., p. 149.
74. The standing technique is not as natural for women as it is for men and their external hose. A web poll done by Denise Decker (see infra) found a success rate of seventy percent for women who tried to learn it.
75. Denise Decker (pseudonym) of Caring Hands, Inc. in Hayden, Idaho, hosted "A Woman's Guide on How to Pee Standing Up" webpage and an active message board from 1997–2002 on Restrooms.org.
76. Ret. Restrooms.org, 3 Feb. 2006.
77. Ibid.
78. Women wait twice as long as men for public restrooms. Allison Janse and Charles Gerba, *Germ Freak's Guide to Outwitting Colds and Flu* (2005), p. 97.
79. 2001 survey by the toilet paper company Quilted Northern.
80. K.H. Moore, et al., "Crouching Over the Toilet Seat," *BJOG*, June 1991.
81. David Williams, "Is Your Desk Making You Sick?" CNN.com, 13 Dec. 2004.
82. Toilets can send fecal matter soaring twenty feet in the air when flushed. This blast occurs not immediately upon flush, but right before all the water has left the bowl. Janse, *Germ Freak's Guide*, p. 96.
83. Almost forty percent of women crouch even when using a friend's toilet. Moore, "Crouching Over the Toilet Seat."
84. Paul Spinrad, *RE/Search Guide to Bodily Fluids* (1994), p. 12.
85. 2004 survey by the toilet paper company Quilted Northern.
86. Spinrad, *RE/Search Guide*, pp. 11–12.
87. Alexander Kira, *Bathroom* (1966), p. 95.
88. The remnants left on hair patches around the anus that dry and harden have been called "butt nuggets" and "dingle berries."
89. Rose George, *Big Necessity* (2008), pp. 46, 247.
90. Kira, *Bathroom*, p. 95.
91. Emily Nelson, "Is Wet TP All Dried Up?" *Wall Street Journal*, 15 Apr. 2002.

92. Grade school bathroom avoidance has also been found in Brazil, Belgium, and Taiwan. Barbro Lundblad and Anna-Lena Hellström, "Perceptions of School Toilets," *J. Sch. Health*, Apr. 2005, pp. 125–128.
93. George, *Big Necessity*, p. 84.
94. Steven Soifer, et al., *Shy Bladder Syndrome* (2001), p. 38.
95. Laura LaRose, "Agony but No Sympathy for Bashful Bladder," *Calgary Sun*, 22 Nov. 2001.
96. Soifer, *Shy Bladder Syndrome*, p. 86.
97. Posting from e-mail sent to Steven Soifer on June 27, 2002. Ret. ShyBladder.org, 9 Aug. 2006.
98. Carol Midgley, "Our Gross Domestic Products," 28 Aug. 2002.
99. Ibid.
100. Largely from Abby Rockefeller, "Civilization and Sludge," *Current World Leaders*, Dec. 1996.
101. F.H. King, "Chapter IX: The Utilization of Waste," *Farmers of 40 Centuries* (1927).
102. Julie Horan, *Porcelain God* (1996), pp. 99–100.
103. "Water on Tap: What You Need to Know," EPA.gov, Oct. 2003, ret. 9 Aug. 2006.
104. Rose George, *Big Necessity* (2008), p. 168.
105. Ibid., p. 165.
106. For more information on sludge go to the website of the United Sludge-Free Alliance.
107. Section from George, *Big Necessity*, pp. 2, 68, 71–72.
108. Ibid., p. 68.
109. For example, "scatological proverb lore has often been suppressed in collections by prudish collectors and publishers." Wolfgang Mieder, "Now I Sit Like a Rabbit in the Pepper," *J. Folklore Res.*, Jan.–Apr. 2003, p. 45.
110. Havelock Ellis, *My Life* (1939), p. 85.
111. David C.F. Wright, "What Makes A Great Composer? Mozart," 2002, ret. MusicWeb-International.com, 2 Oct. 2008.
112. "The Battle of Waterloo," BBC.co.uk, ret. 7 Aug. 2003.
113. David Irving, *Secret Diaries of Hitler's Doctor* (1983), p. 9.
114. Charlie McCollum, "Miniseries Compelling but Not Insightful," *Mercury News*, 18 May 2003.
115. Irving, *Secret Diaries*, p. 119.
116. Ibid., p. 60.

SEX I

WHAT IT IS

SEX IS GOOD

I

A SEX DRIVE TO NOWHERE

Sixth grade was the best year of my life. Sports, hobbies, toys, and friends provided all the enjoyment I needed. I was handsome and liked by the girls. Then puberty struck.

At some point during sixth grade I stayed home sick. Bored, I went through my parents' clothing drawers and found a massage vibrator. I applied it to different parts of my body and when I applied it to my penis, it curiously stiffened and swelled. Manipulation gradually increased the pleasing sensation into my first orgasm. Although the orgasm was a wonderful surprise at the time, I was unaware of its severe consequences.

By seventh grade I was consumed with seeing and touching females. Of course, at exactly that same time, braces were put on my teeth and glasses over my eyes. Moles that were previously barely perceptible were starting to darken and protrude from my face. Guys around me started developing facial hair, body hair, and muscles, while I only grew taller and skinnier. (One particularly precocious classmate would get up on a bench in the locker room after gym class and display the advanced state of his genitalia while berating our inferior models.) Now that I was ready to reciprocate females' affection, it disappeared. And as if to mock my reversed fortunes, females began growing breasts.

Things that had given me joy were now irrelevant. Toys have never been the same. My imagination soon sought assistance for masturbation. Some early aids were photographs of naked African women in *National Geographic* magazines and the lingerie sections of the seasonal Sears' catalogs. I would scour every brassiere photo for the dark suggestion of the model's underlying nipples.

In the mid-'80s, people were just beginning to use personal computers. I had a pirated strip blackjack game that every fifty games or so would allow me to win enough to see the rough portrayal of a completely naked woman. Amazingly, the green squares that represented her nipples and the green triangle that represented her pubis sufficed to make it worthwhile. More creatively, I had a Mad-Libs game in which I would insert sexual words and names of female classmates. The randomly concocted stories that resulted would arouse me incredibly.

Over time the neighborhood boys realized this new interest was a shared one and by pooling our efforts our visual aids improved. We obtained pornography from trash cans, mail boxes, recycling bins and hand-me-downs from older siblings. One friend hit the mother lode when he discovered thirty years' worth of *Playboys* in his grandmother's basement, immaculately left behind by his deceased grandfather. Videos were more difficult to find, but the one or two dubbed VHS cassettes we managed to obtain continuously passed through each of our hands for years. Curiously, despite this pornocopia, no one ever brought up masturbation. That was disgusting. Back then I actually thought I was the only one doing it.

Unfortunately, my experiences with females in the flesh were not as rewarding. The one time I managed a girlfriend was in eighth grade. She never even granted me a kiss. One errant attempt in a back alley nicked her chin, and not much later her friend unceremoniously told me I was dumped. I tried. I dated a lot but the women always ended up with hot jerks. In fact, I still have never kissed a girl from my hometown.

The summer before my senior year in high school I was at a month-long academic program at the University of Pittsburgh. A well-muscled girl from a coal county took a liking to me and my first-ever make-out was her shoving her blueberry Blow-Pop-flavored tongue down my mouth in a dorm stairwell. On the program's last night I broke the rules and snuck up to her room. Unfortunately, I ejaculated during the bumbling but ravenous foreplay, and when she manually went to enter my pants I abruptly left to avoid embarrassment.

Looking back on high school, I should have lowered my aesthetic standards, since the only girls interested in reciprocating physical affections were like me—unattractive. Unfortunately, I continuously overestimated my own appearance. This is partially due to my mother and many of my friends' mothers who said I was tall, dark, and handsome; but a bigger cause was that the mirrors in my house were relatively small with poor (complimentary) lighting.

I did much better with the opposite sex in college, but still could not lose my virginity. It was not from lack of effort. My junior year in college I sat down and tried to list all the women in my life who had explicitly rejected me. I remember that I was relieved to find the list was only about forty names long. I like to tell myself I could have lost my virginity in college if I wanted, and in fact, I was close several times but felt that the first time should be in the bounds of an established and exclusive loving relationship. I guess I believed it should be a well-planned event with flowers on the bed and candles in the windows instead of an ordinary drunken college evening. In retrospect, I greatly regret this conceit.

My junior year in college, I found my "first love." Unfortunately, she was Palestinian. Although the relationship was satisfying, intercourse was not on the menu. The intense Arab familial shame caused by non-virgins (and the occasional stoning of them) intimidated me. In law school, at the ripe age of twenty-four with thousands of self-administered orgasms behind me, I finally lost my virginity. It was a disappointment. Undoubtedly, sex is great, but I believe if I had just gotten it over with in high school a lot of unnecessary pining, moping, and misery would have been avoided.

Since my late start in the world of sexual intercourse, I have not made up for lost time. Although I have been advised by well-meaning friends that women want sex just as much as men do, my experiences have taught me that this is false. Attractive women are willing to have sex with me only after I have wooed them *and* made a commitment, so until I become handsome, rich, famous, or start lying about my devotion, nothing will change. I have accepted this fate, and masturbation and long jogs have kept my libido bearable. It is only when I see an extremely voluptuous woman in something partially revealing or form-fitting that my loin tightens, my craving explodes, and I want to carve my eyeballs out. At those times I hate my life.

II
Definition: Vagina Meet Penis

In its most narrow definition, sex is the penetration of a female's vagina by a male's penis. A wider definition of sex is any activity done with the aim of achieving orgasm. Although the situation is improving, Americans are still largely ignorant about sex beyond the basic mechanics. Because of this, there are the following widespread misconceptions:

III
A Basic Human Need: Purity is Misery

The largest misconception about sex is that it is not necessary to a person's well-being. This is false. Sex is a basic human need for men and women.[1] It is a biological requirement as strong as that of eating and drinking. People will not die if they do not have sex, but the human race will, and that is more important to our genetic programming than the insignificant lives of individuals.

The existence of a sex drive is most evident in sexual desire, that is, the libido, but research is starting to show other ways in which our genetic wiring prods us to procreate. People who do not have sex (1) endure more tension and stress,[2] (2) are unhappier,[3] (3) suffer more from pain,[4] (4) look older,[5] (5) die younger,[6] and (6) have a poorer quality of life.[7] Masturbation satiates the sex drive, but evolution has countered this non-procreative release by making it chemically less satisfying.[8]

Benefits are just beginning to be researched. Government and private foundations have not paid for sex research in the past. Sex is seen as wrong and sinful outside of marriage, and there has been "a palpable fear of what sex researchers might discover and how it might affect moral and religious standards."[9] The American government's refusal to fund sex research stood firm even in the face of the late twentieth-century AIDS crisis.[10] Despite this lack of scientific investigation, the stress of not having sexual release is obvious to (1) the average man, (2) the woman of above-average testosterone levels, and (3) painfully obvious to young men of above-average testosterone levels. These testosterone levels lead to another fundamental misconception.

IV
WOMEN AND MEN HAVE DIFFERENT SEX DRIVES
FUCKING TO LOVE AND LOVING TO FUCK

Partially as a backlash to the eons of repression of women, the feminist movement has promoted the idea that men and women are behaviorally the same and it is only social programming, that is, a sexist culture, that makes them different.[11] In the past thirty years one could be labeled sexist and naive for saying males have a higher sex drive than females.[12] However, as is often the case with taboo topics, what is offensive is true.

Men do have a higher sex drive than women.[13] This should not be interpreted to mean that females do not have a sex drive, but females, *on average,* are much more interested in the social aspects that can surround sex, such as affection, intimacy, and companionship, while men are much more interested in the physical act of copulation itself.[14]

A. The Differences: Fake Boobs and Fake Rolexes

Other sex differences between the sexes include:

Frequency—Men desire more sex than women, are much more sexually active than women (this includes masturbation), and pursue sex with a greater appetite.[15]

55

HIGH-TESTOSTERONE WOMEN EXIST
Thank God

When groups of people are compared it is the averages that are usually analyzed. Critics errantly and annoyingly contest group findings by pointing out the exceptions, that is, the non-average examples.

For example, the fact that men are taller than women is obvious, and it does not lessen the validity of this statement to point out an extraordinarily tall female who is much taller than most men. The same applies when discussing sex drives. The fact that there are women out there much more driven to have sex than most men does *not* contradict the fact that, on average, men are more driven.

For ease of reading, "on average" will not always be used when comparing men and women in this book, but it should always be assumed.

Relationship Arousal[16]—Women are more aroused by the imagination of a sexual relationship. Romance novels have an overwhelmingly female readership. Women who do enjoy pornography tend to like watching a couple having sex, as it is a relationship in action.

Visual Arousal—Men are more visually aroused. The pornography industry has an overwhelmingly male audience. Images of a nude person arouse men but are often too impersonal for women. When women are aroused by pictures of nudes the sex of the nude tends to be irrelevant for they are more interested in its beauty or identification with the featured model.[17]

Even the only pornography magazine directed at women, *Playgirl*, has a large male audience (homosexuals).[18] Males can be aroused simply by a close-up picture of a female vagina. A close-up shot of a penis does not have the equivalent effect with women, because it is far too impersonal.[19]

Status Arousal—If one considers signs of social status, women are more visually aroused than men. One study showed pictures of various men to women and found that the least physically attractive man was more acceptable to sleep with than the most physically attractive man as long as he was depicted wearing a Rolex watch and a designer blazer. Conversely, social status signals had no influence on men, who still focused on physical attractiveness.[20]

Orgasm's Importance—Orgasm matters less to women than it does to men, as affection and intimacy are the primary reasons women like sex.[21] In addition, women are chemically rewarded for foreplay, whereas men require orgasm for their chemical lift.[22]

In line with this, three-fourths of men can always orgasm from vaginal intercourse whereas fewer than a third of women can claim an automatic climax.[23] Some women can orgasm more effectively from stimulation of the clitoris than from vaginal intercourse,[24] in fact, many women cannot achieve the latter at all.[25] Understandably, women are more interested in intimate foreplay than in vaginal intercourse.

Sex Outside of Relationships—Men enjoy sex with acquaintances much more than females.[26] Even women who have positive feelings toward casual sex often report feeling "used" even though they cannot defend the feeling, that is, they cannot say they have been mistreated or deceived.[27] The more partners a women has, the more this anxiety increases, whereas the opposite correlation has been found with men. Men are substantially more likely to desire sex with strangers.[28]

Prostitution has an almost all-male clientele,[29] and even the exceptions to this rule reinforce the differences in libido. For example, the "sex tourism" phenomenon of women from wealthy countries going to underdeveloped vacation destinations for male companionship is often more about romance than sex. These pairings frequently involve courtship and a relationship that lasts for the length of the visit, if not longer.[30]

Partnership Variety—Men enjoy variety in their sexual partners much more than women.[31] Men, whether married, single, or gay, want twice as many partners as their female counterparts, on average, in the next month, and in the next ten years.[32]

This preference is dramatically demonstrated when the opposite sex is removed from the equation—in one study forty-three percent of gay white men had

MEN ON PORN FOR WOMEN
Weary Whacker Needs Nudie Time

One example of pornography that targeted women was the 1990s cable show *Red Shoe Diaries*. It garnered a large female audience by using plot and dialogue to develop sexual relationships.

Male critiques of *Red Shoe Diaries* posted on the web demonstrated the typical male response to this type of porn, "Never—NEVER—bog down a porn show with a plot. No one wants to hear about 'lover's lament' or whatever. All that just takes away from nudie time. *Red Shoe Diaries* SUCKS."

Another male wrote:

> As a late night, sofa-spanker, I demand very little from such soft core smut: one or two happy lesbians lightly licking one another, a round, juicy bottom, glistening beneath incandescent set lights, and perhaps a greedy mouth closing fast over a pointy nipple. I certainly don't expect to get all of these things, but with them, I am at least able to produce a modest amount of friction—enough to induce a mild orgasm. The *Red Shoe Diaries* is the worst kind of torture for a weary whacker like myself; it drones on and on like an episode of *Matlock*, forcing you to lie on the couch, waiting, holding your naked phalus [sic] with the promise of an eventual pleasure burst. But nothing ever occurs. It both saddens and depresses me.

—Ret. JumpTheShark.Com, 5 Sep. 2003; and Ginia Bellafante, "Now, the Sex Files," Time, 10 June 1996.

over five hundred sex partners, whereas zero percent of their lesbian counterparts had reached that number.[33] In committed relationships gay men are much more likely to have sex with someone other than their partner compared to similarly-situated lesbians,[34] even though lesbians in long-term relationships suffer from a phenomenon known as "lesbian bed death."[35]

These contrary sexual attitudes were recognized when the homosexual movement of the late 1960s split between lesbians and gay men. Prominent lesbian author Rita Mae Brown said of her disillusionment with the gay movement and its lack of focus, "Gay guys thought life was a fuckathon... [that] you could just have sex

THE COOLIDGE EFFECT
A Cock Story

The male preference for variety has been called the Coolidge Effect, after President Calvin Coolidge. Reportedly, Coolidge and his wife once toured a farm separately. At the chicken-yard the guide told Coolidge that Mrs. Coolidge, who had come through earlier, wanted it pointed out that the rooster copulates dozens of times a day. Coolidge asked, "Same hen every time?" "Oh no, Mr. President, a different one each time," the guide answered. Coolidge slowly nodded, then said, "Tell that to Mrs. Coolidge."

—David Barash & Judith Lipton, *Myth of Monogamy* (2001), pp. 20–21; and Irving Wallace, et al., *Intimate Sex Lives of Famous People* (1982), pp. 389–390.

with as many people as you wanted with no emotional or physical consequences . . . Which was fine, but it wasn't for me."[36]

Single-Mindedness—Men have a one-track mind,[37] particularly when high testosterone levels are propelling them toward sex.[38] After the goal of orgasm is accomplished and the testosterone level subsides, the man is sometimes left with post-coital remorse.[39] That is, the man can now receive a wider input of information that often includes reasons not to have had sex. Some of the reasons not properly considered can include ramifications of having sex, such as committing adultery, or in the case of masturbation, societal views of masturbation come rushing back, causing feelings of guilt.

Age of Partner[40]—Women of all ages sexually prefer older men. Adolescent boys prefer women several years older than themselves. Young men prefer women roughly their own age. After their mid-twenties, men of all ages sexually prefer women between eighteen to twenty-four years of age, that is, women of optimal fertility.

Desire Peaks[41]—Women hit their highest testosterone levels and highest sex drive right when the egg is produced during the middle of their menstrual cycle.

Male testosterone levels are highest in the morning and lowest in the evening.[42] Men also peak in autumn.[43]

Sexual Aging—Men tend to reach their overall sexual peak, and testosterone peak, around the age of twenty, and then testosterone levels decrease at roughly two percent per year so that by the age of seventy, they are at approximately a third of their peak.[44] Women's sexual drive drops off much more gradually from puberty so male and female sex drives converge over time.[45]

Paraphilias—Unusual sexual preferences are almost an exclusively male phenomenon.[46] Some sources of arousal include exhibitionism (exposing one's genitals to strangers), frotteurism (rubbing oneself against strangers, such as in a crowd), necrophilia, bestiality, and pedophilia.

Lighting—Women prefer having sex in the dark more than men do. Women are not as visually aroused as men and darkness heightens women's superior senses.[47]

B. The Evidence: Slutty Men are Everywhere

Most evolutionists agree that there are "deep and substantial" libido differences between men and women.[48] Despite this, the media,[49] sexuality textbooks,[50] and some academics still assert that these differences stem primarily from socialization or are merely unsupported stereotypes. While it is likely that notions about how men and women should behave accentuate the biological differences by pressuring atypical people to conform, it is highly doubtful that these differences are culturally rooted.

First, there is the vast and overwhelming scientific support of biological sexual differences. Men have been shown to have a stronger sexual desire in studies testing spontaneous thoughts about sex, frequency, and variety of sexual fantasies, desired frequency of intercourse, desired number of sexual partners, masturbation, affinity for various sexual practices, willingness to forego sex, irritability when deprived of sex,[51] initiating versus refusing sex, making sacrifices for sex, and other measures.[52] A comprehensive survey of thousands of articles related to gender differences in sex drive found a "unanimous convergence" supporting males having a higher drive. Not a single study showing female desire to be stronger was found.[53] If the differences were based in socialization, it is unlikely the evidence would be so diverse and consistent.[54]

Second, there is the extreme nature of the differences. In two studies conducted four years apart at Florida State University, eighty-eight men and eighty-eight women were asked by average-looking members of the opposite sex one of three questions, with the following results:

I HAVE BEEN NOTICING YOU AROUND CAMPUS. I FIND YOU VERY ATTRACTIVE. WOULD YOU . . .	WOMEN AGREEING	MEN AGREEING
Go out with me tonight?	50%	50%
Come over to my apartment tonight?	6%	69%
Go to bed with me tonight?	0%	75%

The huge difference in responses to the last question posed is actually moderated. The responses of the men who turned sex down generally belied lack of interest, for example apologizing that they would but they were in a monogamous relationship or offering to do it tomorrow instead. None of the women were apologetic in their refusals of sex.[55,56] If this were merely cultural, it is likely at least one female would have been willing to act on her desire in what could have been a secret occurrence on an immense campus.

These large disparities are not limited to heterosexual college students. Homosexuals portray the behavior of men and women freed from negotiating with the opposite sex's libido. They are also a population willing to defy sexual cultural norms.

In one study, gay men had higher frequencies of sex than lesbians at all stages of relationships. In the first two years of a relationship, two-thirds of gay men but only one-third of lesbians were having sex three or more times a week. After ten years, eleven percent of gay men but only one percent of lesbians were still having that much sex.

Outside of relationships, the difference becomes even more extreme. As already noted, another study found that forty-three percent of gay white men had over five hundred sex partners, whereas zero percent of their lesbian counterparts had reached that number.[57]

Third, some of these differences emerge at a very young age. Prior to puberty, young boys tend to have their first sexual fantasies in response to a visual stimulus. Girls, in contrast, report that their first sexual fantasies occurred in the context of a real or imagined romantic relationship.[58] Boys' fantasies begin several years earlier than girls', despite starting puberty later, and they are more frequent, intense, distracting, sexually explicit, and positive in associated feelings.[59]

Fourth, many of these differences can be tied to testosterone.[60] Testosterone is the hormone that promotes sexual desire in both sexes. Although it appears to have more potency in women,[61] men still have seven to eight times more testosterone than women on average.[62]

Testosterone levels have been associated with sexual arousal in males,[63] and high-testosterone women have sex more often than do low-testosterone women, and with more people.[64] These results have been validated by testosterone therapy in women, in which treated women had higher frequency of sexual activity, sexual arousal, sexual desires, and sexual thoughts.[65]

If testosterone has a marked effect within the sexes, where people are getting the same cultural messages, it is reasonable to assume that the enormous difference in testosterone is a reason for the differences between the sexes as well.

Fifth, our physical features are in line with other species in the animal kingdom where the male pursues sex with greater aggression and frequency. A study in contrast is the katydid (bush cricket).[66] When the male katydid ejaculates he loses about a quarter of his body weight. The human equivalent would be fifty pounds of semen. This load of ejaculate is filled with nutrients, and amounts to about a tenth of the food supply that a female bush cricket will have in her lifetime. As could be expected, men are the choosier katydid sex. Females have the higher sex drive and primarily pursue the males.

Male humans, on the other hand, have an inexhaustible supply of semen, making sex virtually costless. Men would probably not be so biologically eager to have random sex if it cost them fifty pounds in body weight, or if they were at risk of becoming pregnant.

Due to pregnancy, the genetic reward for indiscriminate sex is smaller for women. A prehistoric man who copulated with a dozen women in a week could be rewarded with a dozen descendents, while a prehistoric woman who copulated with a dozen men in a week would still only have one. She would only be genetically rewarded for more intercourse if her partner was a better candidate than the one that preceded him (and his semen was able to win the sperm competition).[67]

Sixth, these differences are cross-cultural. The previously mentioned study that found men want twice as many sexual partners as females polled over 16,000 people scattered over fifty countries on every continent.[68] The fact that these differences occur in widely varying societies proves they are not socially based.

Seventh, it is common sense. Many men and women of above-average testosterone levels do not need science to tell them their urges are not cultural, but chemical. (It is noteworthy that academics, some of whom theorize about sex drives, have below-average testosterone levels as a group.[69])

I am familiar with high-testosterone men who welcomed the lowered libido caused by antidepressants. For the sake of productivity (not constantly thinking about sex) and their relationships (not cheating) they had fought these urges for years. If their urges were cultural, not chemical, antidepressants would not have succeeded where will power had failed.

V

Homosexuality Is Biological
Going Gay In The Uterus

A third popular American misconception regarding sex is that homosexuality is a choice. While undoubtedly some people engage in homosexual behavior by choice, particularly women,[70] the sexual preference for most people is based in their biology.[71] The research supporting this has finally begun to receive American media coverage, but the issue is still presented as if it is debatable due to evangelical Christian opposition. In 2007, fifty-six percent of the population no longer thought homosexuality was a choice,[72] and the choice argument is becoming difficult to sustain as the scientific evidence piles on.

For people familiar with the gay community, scientific evidence was never needed to tell them what they already knew. If homosexuality was a choice, few would choose to endure it. America has treated homosexuals with open scorn. Up until 1973 the American Psychiatric Association referred to homosexuality as a mental disorder. As late as 1990 the United States government, through its Immigration and Naturalization Service, considered homosexuals undesirable. In 2003, the President of the United States implied homosexuals were sinners.[73] Homosexuals were, and still are, disowned by friends, family, and religious communities.[74] It is difficult to believe that this is a chosen path.

Additionally, until recently America's gay culture was underground except for being lampooned and characterized as sinful. It is unclear why adolescents only exposed to homosexuals through hearing supposed "dykes" and "faggots" disparaged would throw away their lives to copulate with people to whom they were not naturally attracted.

Many rural Americans do not have exposure to gays in their communities and think that homosexuality primarily occurs in more liberal cultures. This is a faulty premise, because there probably are gays in their community, but they are closeted. And there would be many more if their gay children had not committed suicide,[75,76] or fled to the bigger cities where they have support in numbers and relative anonymity.[77]

A. The Evidence: Manatee Man Love

The biologic basis for homosexuality is only beginning to be understood. The gist of current theory is that people's brains are formed in the womb. We all start out with a female brain. What makes a male brain begin to take shape is a massive dose of testosterone and other male hormones that occurs six weeks after conception. During this extremely delicate process things can go amiss.[78] The fact that the female brain is the original brain can explain why homosexuality occurs at a much higher rate in males than in females—estimated at two to one.[79] There is simply more opportunity for irregularities to occur in the formation of the male brain.

This sexualizing of the brain can manifest in three areas—(1) physique, for example hermaphrodites; (2) mating preference, (3) and gender, for example, exhibiting masculine or feminine behaviors.[80] Because of these different areas, feminine behavior is not a litmus test for a man being homosexual, although femininity and male homosexuality are closely bound. Feminine boys who prefer passive social activities like playing with dolls and playing house to more competitive and physical exercises like sports do tend to be homosexuals when they sexually mature.[81]

Adult gay men are less feminine. This can be explained in two ways. First, gay men have endured years of socialization from family and peers that is often cruel. Secondly, gay men are attracted to masculinity and must masculinize themselves to attract other gay men.[82]

This predicament was revealed in a review of thousands of gay personal ads, in which the requested traits were masculine ninety-six percent of the time. When advertisers described themselves as either masculine or feminine, ninety-eight percent of the time it was as masculine. In all the ads where someone was specific about a trait he explicitly did not want, the trait was a feminine one.[83]

One gay man's story, which echoes a common theme in the gay community, was, "I met this cute guy at the bar. He seemed so butch and like such a stud, but when I got him home, the first thing he did was throw his legs in the air."[84] This occurrence is also represented in the gay saying "butch in the streets, femme in the sheets."[85]

Although feminine traits can be hidden, it is difficult to erase them completely. Studies have shown that gay men move and speak more effeminately than straight men, giving credibility to those claiming to have "gaydar."[86]

Studies have also found that parts of the gay male brain are more similar to the female brain than to the straight male brain. For example, one cell grouping in the hypothalamus, the area that controls sexual preference, has been found in two studies to be larger in straight men than in females and homosexual men.[87]

Another study showed that fifty-two percent of the identical twins of homosexual men shared their brothers' sexual preference, while with fraternal twins the number was twenty-two percent.[88] This demonstrates that, as with height, homosexuality is influenced by genes but not determined by it. That is, one's genes may make it more likely that when one's brain is formed the abnormalities occur that make one a homosexual.

Other findings point to biology as well. Homosexual behavior has been found in over 450 animal species.[89] The behavior is amazingly diverse from species to species. Male West Indian manatees perform simultaneous oral-genital stimulation (the "69"

65

"REPARATIVE THERAPY"
You Can't Hustle a Hustler

The American Psychiatric Association, the American Psychological Association, and the National Association of Social Workers have all stated that there is no evidence that reparative therapy is possible, and studies have found the success rates to be abysmal.

Despite heavy financial backing by Christian fundamentalists, the largest reparative organization—Exodus International—has been plagued by its high-profile "success stories" returning to gay activities. For example, one of its founders, Michael Bussee, has since married another early Exodus member, Gary Cooper. (They exposed Exodus' questionable methods in the 1993 documentary *One Nation Under God.*) Also, in 2000 the chairman of its board, John Paulk, was caught flirting at a gay bar using his old gay hustler pseudonym, "John Clint."

position) on each other, while male Amazon River dolphins (Botos) will copulate with other male's blowholes. Male Brown-headed Cowbirds will not only solicit mounting from other male brown-headed Cowbirds, but will solicit males of other species, such as house sparrows, and are occasionally successful.

Not only does homosexuality occur in nature, but scientists have been able to manipulate hormones in laboratory rats to produce homosexual behavior. In one study, male rats were castrated at birth and then given estrogen, while female rats had their ovaries removed and were given testosterone. The modified male rats would assume the female mating position with their hinds raised, while the modified females would feverishly mount them and thrust away.[90] And although scientists have not yet isolated genetic markers for homosexuality in humans, they have done so in several species of insects.[91]

Other support for biological causes includes the following: homosexuals are found in widely varying cultural groups throughout history[92]; most homosexuals realize they are attracted to the same sex before the age of ten even though at that age they often do not have the vocabulary to describe this attraction[93]; children raised by homosexual parents are not more likely to identify themselves as gay as adults[94]; and all attempts to turn homosexuals straight through reparative therapy have failed.

Perhaps most damaging to the socialization theorists are the real-life examples. One study followed children reassigned as females because of poorly formed penises at birth. Due to the social construction concept that gender is a product of socialization, it was thought this would be the best route for these children. They were surgically modified as newborns and brought up as females while not being told about their operations.

A study of fourteen of these reassigned children found that by their teenage years half of them had declared that they were males.[95] Remarkably, five of these did so spontaneously. Two made their declarations after the parents came clean about their true past. Of the remaining seven, one wished to become a boy, but accepted her status only to become irate when finally told the truth. Parents of the remaining six were determined never to tell their children the truth of their birth status. Three of these children were withdrawn, and a fourth had no friends. Most of the children in the study have discussed their sexual and romantic feelings, and all of those that have are attracted to females. In addition, all the children have exhibited masculine interests and behavior.

B. The Religious Argument: Stop Being Gay

Despite all the evidence, religious forces still claim that homosexuality stems primarily from two sources. The first is improper parenting. Particularly with males, the culprit is a distant and cold father. As one proponent of this view put it, "Although he has 'defensively detached' from his father, the young boy still carries silently within him a terrible longing for the warmth, love, and encircling arms of the father he never did nor could have."[96]

The second source is childhood sexual abuse that is so psychologically damaging to the child that their natural sexual attraction is distorted.

Both of these characteristics are more prevalent among homosexuals than their straight counterparts, but this does not mean there is causation. It has never been shown that fatherly detachment causes homosexuality as opposed to the opposite—the son's homosexuality causes detachment in the father. It is a difficult adjustment for a homophobic father who is looking forward to playing sports with his son when his son prefers talking on the phone with female classmates.

Gay men have a higher rate of child sexual abuse than their straight counterparts,[97] but this does not mean abuse causes homosexuality. An obvious explanation is that homosexual youth are targeted more frequently *because* of their homosexuality. A gay man is more likely to foster a sexual relationship with a homosexual adolescent than a straight adolescent. Due to the child's sexual orientation, the child may be more likely to submit, and less likely to recognize and report the abuse. (Straight boys are relatively untargeted because women rarely sexually abuse children.)[98]

Another plausible explanation for the higher rate of child sexual abuse among gay men is that homosexual boys are more likely to seek out age-discrepant sexual relationships. (Age-discrepant relationships are when one partner is significantly older than the other.) In America any relationship straddling a state's age of consent, which can range from sixteen to eighteen, can be labeled sexual molestation or abuse.

Considering that homosexual males account for only 2.8 percent of the population,[99] it is understandable that they are more likely to reach across age groups to find partners. For example, if a fifteen-year-old homosexual male is in a high school class of five hundred, chances are there are only seven other homosexual males in his class. Considering some of the others are still closeted or questioning their sexual orientation, the boy is likely to willingly engage someone older and more comfortable with his homosexuality.[100]

Studies bear this out. Unlike straight pubescent girls, straight pubescent boys who have sexual experiences with adults of the opposite sex predominantly view the experiences positively.[101] This may extend to gay boys' experiences with adult men as well. Studies of age-discrepant homosexual relationships have found that often the boys consent to the sexual conduct with the men and in many cases initiate it. These consensual interactions are viewed neutrally or positively by the boy later in life.

If this sounds alarming, look at it as if they were straight. If straight people only made up 2.8 percent of the population and straight girls were closeted, would it be that disturbing if straight teenage boys would try to seduce straight women? And would it be child molestation if they succeeded?

Unfortunately, this nuanced reality is overshadowed by the nightmare repeatedly etched in the public's consciousness of an old man forcing his will through trickery on an innocent prepubescent boy. In the midst of a sensationalized scandal in London, Ontario, sixty men were arrested and police and social workers pressured teenage boys into saying they were victimized, despite the fact they were over the age of consent and willing. One of the boys told the Canadian Broadcasting Company:

> I knew what I was doing... I wanted it. ... [I]t's not a recruitment thing, it's not that you're forced into it. ... [W]hen you're fourteen and gay it's as natural to want to be with a man as it is when you're fourteen and straight and want to be with a girl . . . I was doing it when I was fourteen. I was picking up the guys. It wasn't them picking me up. And you can't be a victim unless you're forced into something.[102]

Sexual predators of gay boys do exist, but categorizing all age-discrepant relationships as traumatic abuse is overly simplistic. The fact that these are often positive experiences instigated by the minors suggests that age-discrepant relationships are not a significant cause of male homosexuality. One study of these age-discrepant relationships found that all but one of the twenty-six boys were aware of their homosexual attractions before the incident occurred—three-and-a-half years before on average.[103]

VI

Children Are Sexual
Hello, Puberty Starts Before 18

With current American attitudes, it is almost criminal to even suggest that children are sexual. In 1997, Surgeon General Joycelyn Elders was fired by President Bill Clinton after answering in the affirmative when a sex educator asked if masturbation could appropriately be discussed in schools to combat sexually transmitted diseases and teenage pregnancy.[104] In 2004, for three-quarters of a second a distant shot of a woman's nipple was televised. Despite it being imperceptible to viewers without replay, a Congressional investigation was launched, censorship penalties were tightened, and a congresswoman cried over the nipple's effects on her fourth-grade son.[105]

Sexual desire in humans begins with the onset of puberty. Commencement of puberty varies widely by individual in both sexes, but the average girl begins having her period when she is twelve and a quarter years old and the average boy is capable of ejaculation at the age of thirteen and a half.[106]

Even before puberty, children are not completely sexless.[107] The genitalia are pleasurable to the touch from birth, with males being capable of erection and females being capable of vaginal lubrication. In addition, sexual behavior is natural in infants and children. Masturbation has been observed in infants as young as seven months, and evidence suggests that children as young as two years old may even experience orgasm. In studies, parents have reported observing two six-year-olds masturbate with objects, imitate intercourse, put their mouths on sex parts, and rub their bodies against other people.

Parents and other caretakers also skew observed sexual behavior by quickly discouraging its existence and thus causing it to be hidden. One study placed children aged three to seven in an environment where only coercive sexual activity or insertion of any object was forbidden. Sexual play was very common, and included genital manipulation and attempts at sexual intercourse. In another study of college-age women, eighty-five percent reported engaging in sexual games with others during childhood, at an average age of seven-and-a-half years. Only fifty-six percent of these experiences were discovered by an adult. Excluding the sex play that was deemed coercive, participants largely reported the experiences as positive.

These positive descriptions reflect sexual mores found in other cultures. For example, Marquesan youth (inhabitants of the Marquesas Islands in French Polynesia) have already had a wide range of sexual experiences by the time they reach puberty, experiences that can include homosexual acts.[108] A boy has intercourse for the first time with a married woman in her thirties or forties, and a girl has her first time with an older man. The young enjoy the benefits of learning sex from those with experience. A daughter with a great number of lovers is a source

DISCLAIMER

This chapter is not recommending sexual activity with minors nor its legalization. It only questions the alarmism, extremism, and hysteria that surround the issue. (The ramifications of which will be discussed in Chapter Nine.) Most of the information presented has been compiled by medical experts seeking to learn how to better *prevent* child sexual abuse, *catch* the perpetrators, and *rehabilitate* the victims.

One of these is William Friedrich, of the Mayo Clinic, who wrote:

> Sexual behavior in children represents to far too many people further proof of the moral decay of our society. Any issue that provokes as strong an emotional reaction as childhood sexuality is obviously in need of a rational discussion . . . Our culture needs information on [childhood sexuality]. Knowledge about sexuality reduces hysteria.

—Betty Gordon & Carolyn Schroeder, *Sexuality* (1995), pp. vii–viii.

of pride to the Marquesans. While societies as sexually liberal with their children as the Marquesans are rare, cultures more liberal than ours are plentiful.

For example, touching of a child's genitalia by adults is accepted in at least seventy societies. Some of the reasons behind cultural acceptance include pacification, gratification, teasing, greeting, and demonstration of gender-specific parental pride. Some European societies that have accepted this behavior in their recent past include Southern Italian and Danish groups. This behavior still accepted in Puerto Rican culture. The following collection of quotes describes behavior in Puerto Rico:

> "[. . .] adults and older brothers and sisters are likely to tease and play with his [infant boy's] genitals, kissing them and remarking on their size, commenting that he is a machito (real little male) or a machote (real he-man)"; "[. . .] parents and friends may play with the boy's genitals until he is around seven years old"; "parents would pull a two-year-old's penis, and inquire for its function. The answer

EXAGGERATED FEARS #1
Internet Predators

The popularity of the *Dateline* NBC television series *To Catch a Predator* (*TCAP*) from 2004–2007 gave the Internet the appearance of a playground run by pedophiles. On *TCAP*, decoys posed in Internet chat rooms as underage kids receptive to sexual overtures. The decoys lured men into homes rigged with cameras (sometimes getting them to strip naked) and then *TCAP's* host, Chris Hansen, came out and chided them on national TV before they were arrested.

Although the unwitting stars of *TCAP* cannot be defended, this anecdotal approach produced a skewed and fearful image of reality, as do the news and crime shows that highlight the most heinous crimes in the nation daily. One CEO of a website that introduces people with shared interests estimated from focus groups that fears inspired by *TCAP* cost him thousands of customers a day.

TCAP's selective presentation was not dishonest, but some of its assertions were. *TCAP* originally stated that at any given moment, fifty thousand child molesters were prowling the Internet. When questioned about this figure, *TCAP* stopped using it (but not before the Attorney General cited it in one of his speeches).

During its May 24, 2006 show, Hansen said:

> *Dateline* touched a major nerve—exposing an epidemic of sexual predators in our country. When we first started our investigation we were told by the National Center for Missing and Exploited Children that one in five children online has been approached by adults looking for sex.

would be, 'For the women!'"; "A two-year-old boy will be asked, 'What is it for?' while an adult pulls at his penis; and sometimes the child will answer, 'For women.' Such a child is called malo (bad) or even malcria'o (badly brought up), but actually the terms are used with some measure of approval"; "As soon as they started talking, they asked them questions about their penis, for whom it was and for what it was needed. They answered it was for the chacha or the girl friend, or to play a trick on the girl friend. [. . .] If they had an

This was false. The survey to which Hansen was referring found nineteen percent of kids aged ten to seventeen had received a sexual solicitation. First, the study's definition of solicitation included any unwanted talk of a sexual nature. When solicitation was defined as attempting offline contact the number dropped to three percent. Second, only twenty-five percent of the "solicitations" were made by people over the age of eighteen. In addition, seventy-seven percent of the solicited "children" were in the fourteen to seventeen age bracket, and of the 1,501 kids surveyed, none had solicitations that led to actual sexual contact.

Another study has shown that many Internet-predator myths are false. For example, instead of being deceptive, fast-moving baby snatchers, most men seeking underage sex online are up-front about their age and their sexual intentions, target teenagers, and foster the relationship for over a month.

As someone who was once a youth and has since spent years teaching, I can vouch that unwelcome sexual solicitations of middle-school girls by their male peers are common outside of cyberspace as well. Similar to the cyber-findings, the actual fruition of these solicitations is extremely rare. They often go something like this: "Baby, will you suck my dick?" and the girl responds, "Fuck off." The much rarer adult solicitation garners the same result. No law enforcement or national news network gets involved. No one goes to jail. Although the young "girls" of TCAP are always eager and willing, real girls are not so vulnerable or naive.

—Steven Levy, "All Predators, All the Time?" *Newsweek*, 3 July 2006, p. 20; "To Catch a Predator," transcript, NBC.com, 24 May 2006, ret. 13 Sep. 2006; K. Mitchell, D. Finkelhor, & J. Wolak, "Risk Factors for and Impact of Online Sexual Solicitation of Youth," *JAMA*, 20 June 2001, pp. 3,011–3,014; and Marilyn Elias, "Survey Paints Different Portrait of Online Abuser," USAToday.com, 1 Aug. 2004.

erection, they were praised and the parents would celebrate it by telling them they had joined the masculine race."[109]

In many parts of the United States these Puerto Rican children could be removed from the home by the government for fear of the children becoming "over-sexually stimulated and [preferring] sexual behavior to sports, dance, or other more appropriate activities," and becoming "promiscuous as adults."[110] The perpetrators could be incarcerated and then registered as sex offenders for decades under Megan's Law.[111]

Due to America's sexually repressive climate, scientific study in the area of children's sexuality is lacking,[112] and there is much that is not yet understood. It is not clear at what point mere pleasure-seeking and curiosity is replaced with the cognitive desire for the opposite sex. However, two things stand out in contrast to popular perception. One, the line between enjoyable sexual play and sexual abuse is not always clear, and two, childhood sexual encounters that are motivated by curiosity are positively perceived by the participants later in life and are associated with better self-esteem and later sexual functioning.[113]

NOTES

1.   This is a prevalent view in the scientific community. Some prominent advocates include William James, Sigmund Freud, and Abraham Maslow. For an overview of the literature see Pamela Regan and Ellen Berscheid, *Lust* (1999), pp. 22–31.
2.   David Weeks, "Sex for the Mature Adult," *Sex. Relation. Ther.*, 17(3), 2002, p. 235.
3.   Andrew Walters and Gail Williamson, "Sexual Satisfaction Predicts Quality of Life," *Sex. Disabil.*, 16(2), pp. 103–115; Ibid., pp. 235–236; and Edward Laumann, et al., *Social Organization of Sexuality* (1994), pp. 351–368.
4.   Barry Komisaruk and Beverly Whipple, "Suppression of Pain," *Annu. Rev. Sex Res.* (1995), pp. 151–186.
5.   David Weeks and Jamie James, *Secrets of the Superyoung* (1998), pp. 21, 82–83, 144.
6.   G. Davey-Smith, et al., "Sex and Death" *BMJ*, 20 Dec. 1997, pp. 1641–1644; and S. Ebrahim, et al., "Sexual Intercourse and Risk . . . ," *J. Epidemiol. Community Health*, Feb. 2002, pp. 99–102.
7.   Laumann, *Social Organization of Sexuality*, pp. 351–368.
8.   S. Brody and T.H. Kruger, "Post-Orgasmic Prolactin Increase Following Intercourse is Greater than Following Masturbation," *Biol. Psychol.*, Mar. 2006, pp. 312–315.
9.   Robert Michael, et al., *Sex in America* (1994), pp. 10–12.
10. A narrow survey of AIDS-related questions was nixed by Sen. Jesse Helms in 1991. (Ibid., p. 28.). Note that in 1992 the federal government spent almost $40 billion on non-defense research, and while studying human sexual behavior was unacceptable, only four years earlier it spent over $107,000 to study the sexual behavior of Japanese quail. ("Golden Fleece Award," Taxpayers for Common Sense, ret. Taxpayer.net, 14 Aug. 2006.)
11. Mary Jane Sherfey, *Nature and Evolution of Female Sexuality* (1966), p. 11, announced this belief. For the ensuing political climate see Anne Moir and David Jessel, *Brain Sex* (1991), p. 12.
12. Moir, *Brain Sex*, pp. 9–10.
13. Sex drive is defined as the desire to have sex.
14. In a study of adulterers, unfaithful men far outnumbered women in the category of one-night stands (twenty-nine percent vs. five percent), whereas unfaithful women outnumbered men in the category of long-term love relationships (forty-one percent vs. eleven percent). Graham Spanier and Randie Margolis, "Marital Separation and Extramarital Sexual Behavior," *J. Sex Res.*, Feb. 1983, pp. 23–48. For more support see the literature overview in Paul Okami and Todd Shackelford, "Human Sex Differences in Sexual Psychology and Behavior," *Annu. Rev. Sex Res.*, 12, 2001, pp. 201–205.
15. Roy Baumeister, Kathleen Catanese, and Kathleen Vohs, "Is There a Gender Difference in Strength of Sex Drive?" *Pers. Soc. Psychol. Rev.*, 5(3), 2001, pp. 242–273.
16. Sect. from Moir, *Brain Sex*, pp. 106, 107.
17. J.M. Bailey, *Man Who Would Be Queen* (2003), p. 94.

18. A former *Playgirl* editor estimated its readership is forty percent men. Judy Cole, "Playgirl's Gay Canard," Nerve.com, 27 Nov. 1997, ret. 16 Sep. 2010.

19. Moir, *Brain Sex*, pp. 106–107.

20. Okami, "Human Sex Differences," p. 197.

21. Moir, *Brain Sex*, p. 109; and Robert Michael, et al., *Sex in America* (1994), pp. 123–124.

22. Any sexual arousal releases oxytocin in females, though higher levels are released at orgasm. Only orgasm and ejaculation release oxytocin in males. Oxytocin reduces and prevents stress. David Weeks, "Sex for the Mature Adult," *Sex. Relat. Ther.*, 17(3), 2002, p. 235.

23. Michael, *Sex in America*, p. 123.

24. The clitoris has the body's highest concentration of nerve fibers—twice as many as the much larger penis. Tina Miracle, Andrew Miracle, and Roy Baumeister, *Human Sexuality* (2002), p. 33.

25. In 1992 four percent of American women over the age of eighteen had never had an orgasm. Michael, *Sex in America*, p. 128.

26. A study asked how willing people would be to have sex with someone they knew for an hour, a day, a week, six months, a year, two years, or five years. Men were more willing at every stage but the last, where it was equal. Okami, "Human Sex Differences," pp. 202–203.

27. Ibid., p. 203.

28. In the 18–44 age group ten percent of women found sex with a stranger somewhat or very appealing, and thirty-four percent of males concurred. Michael, *Sex in America*, pp. 146–147.

29. In Australia, where there is legalized prostitution, 15.6 percent of men had ever paid for sex compared to .1 percent of women. C.E. Rissel, et al., "Sex in Australia," *Aust. N.Z. J. Public Health*, 27(2), 2003.

30. Edward Herold, Rafael Garcia, and Tony DeMoya, "Female Tourists and Beach Boys," *Ann. Tourism Res.*, 28(4), 2001.

31. David Barash and Judith Lipton, *Myth of Monogamy* (2001), pp. 20–21.

32. David Schmitt, "Universal Sex Differences in the Desire for Sexual Variety," *J. Pers. Soc. Psychol.*, July 2003, 85(1), p. 90.

33. Roy Baumeister, Kathleen Catanese, and Kathleen Vohs, "Is There a Gender Difference in Strength of Sex Drive?" *Pers. Soc. Psychol. Rev.*, 5(3), 2001, p. 251.

34. The respective numbers are eighty-two percent to twenty-eight percent. Ibid.

35. After ten years in committed relationships almost half of lesbians, but only a third of gay men, were having sex less than once a month. Ibid., p. 247.

36. Brown was not alone. Robin Morgan announced to 1,500 at a lesbian conference in 1973, "Every woman here knows in her gut the vast difference between her sexuality and that of any [male's] . . . That the emphasis on genital sexuality, objectification, promiscuity, non-emotional involvement, and tough invulnerability, [was] the male style, and that we, as women, placed greater trust in love, sensuality, humor, tenderness, strength, and commitment." David Allyn, *Make Love, Not War* (2000), pp. 251, 253.

37. James Dabbs and Mary Dabbs, *Heroes, Rogues, and Lovers* (2000), pp. 45–46.

38. "Sex Cues Ruin Men's Decisiveness," BBC.co.uk, 19 Apr. 2006.

39. Anne Moir and David Jessel, *Brain Sex* (1991), p. 108.

40. Sect. from Okami, "Human Sex Differences," pp. 219–220.

41. Sect. from Anne Moir and Bill Moir, *Why Men Don't Iron* (1999), pp. 221, 222.

42. An erection, "morning wood," often greets waking men. Lou Schuler, et al., *Testosterone Advantage Plan* (2002), pp. 45, 53.

43. Correspondingly, autumn has more sexual assaults.

44. Dabbs, *Heroes*, p. 16.

45. Men still want sex more frequently in all age groups and at all stages of marriage. Baumeister, "Gender Difference," p. 246.

46. J.M. Bailey, *Man Who Would Be Queen* (2003), pp. 171–172.

47. Women have better hearing and night vision. They are also more sensitive to taste, smell, and physical contact. Moir, *Brain Sex*, pp. 17–19.

48. Steven Rhoads, *Taking Sex Differences Seriously* (2004), p. 48.

49. The LiveScience.com Sex Quiz by Heather Whipps that has been linked from science articles on sites like Yahoo! News and MSNBC since at least 2006 calls this a "cultural misconception."

50. Richard McAnulty and M. Michele Burnette, *Sex and Sexuality*, Vol. 1 (2006), pp. 185–198; Janell Carroll, *Sexuality Now* (2009), pp. 94–96; and Baumeister, "Gender Difference," p. 243.

51. Moir, *Brain Sex*, p. 105.

52. Baumeister, "Gender Difference," pp. 242–273.

53. Ibid., pp. 245, 269.

54. A common critique is that men, as a whole, consistently report more sex partners than women, as a whole. This disparity has been used to argue that men exaggerate their sexuality while women downplay theirs thus creating an illusion of innate difference. However, when sex surveys' under-sampling of prostitutes was considered this disparity disappeared. D.D. Brewer, et al., "Prostitution and the Sex Discrepancy in Reported Number of Sex Partners," *Proceedings of the National Academy of Sciences*, 24 Oct. 2000.

55. Russell Clark and Elaine Hatfield, "Gender Differences in Receptivity to Sexual Offers," *J. Psychol. Hum. Sex.*, 1989, 2, pp. 39–55.

56. No females reported fear as a refusal reason, and studies have repeated the results when safety was assured. David Schmitt, et al., "Are Men Really More 'Oriented' Toward Short-Term Mating?" *Psychol. Evol. Gend.*, Dec. 2001, p. 226.

57. Baumeister, "Gender Difference," pp. 247, 251.

58. Russell Knoth, Kelly Boyd, and Barry Singer, "Empirical Tests of Sexual Selection Theory," *J. Sex. Res.*, 1988, 24, pp. 73–89.

59. Steven Gold and Ruth Gold, "Gender Differences in First Sexual Fantasies," *J. Sex Educ. Ther.*, 1991, 17, pp. 207–216.

60. Men with ring fingers longer than their index fingers have high testosterone levels. "Sex Cues Ruin Men's Decisiveness" BBC.co.uk, 19 Apr. 2006.

61. Steven Rhoads, *Taking Sex Differences Seriously* (2004), p. 50.

62. Baumeister, "Gender Difference," pp. 265–266.

63. Ibid.

64. James Dabbs and Mary Dabbs, *Heroes, Rogues, and Lovers* (2000), p. 101.

65. Baumeister, "Gender Difference," p. 266.

66. Katydid example from Terry Burnham and Jay Phelan, *Mean Genes* (2000), pp. 131–132.

67. Penises and semen are designed to compete with other men's semen inside the reproductive tract. When a woman has sex with two different men within a five day period, the sperm battle it out to fertilize the egg. David Barash and Judith Lipton, *Myth of Monogamy* (2001), pp. 161–172.

68. David Schmitt, "Universal Sex Differences in the Desire for Sexual Variety," *J. Pers. Soc. Psychol.*, July 2003, 85(1), p. 85.

69. Dabbs, *Heroes*, pp. 134–135, 149–150.

70. Women's arousal patterns are significantly more bisexual in nature, that is, less bifurcated between male body and female body stimuli, and lesbians self-report that their sexual orientation is a choice more than gay males. Marco Costa, et al., "Gender Differences in Response to Pictures of Nudes," *Biol. Psychol.*, May 2003. pp. 129–147.

71. This is often presented as there being a "gay gene." This is an inaccurate oversimplification of the issue.

72. This was up from thirteen percent in 1977. "Poll Majority: Gays' Orientation Can't Change," CNN.com, 27 June 2007.

73. When asked his view on homosexuality President George W. Bush said, "I am mindful that we're all sinners, and I caution those who may try to take the speck out of the neighbor's eye when they got a log in their own." Naftali Bendavid, "Bush Calls for Law Defining Marriage," *Chicago Tribune*, 31 July 2003.

74. For a tragic story of one religious man's struggle to deal with his homosexuality that ended in suicide, see Mark Miller, "To Be Gay—And Mormon," *Newsweek*, 8 May 2000.

75. Studies have shown between twenty and forty percent of gay adolescents have attempted suicide. R. Kitts, "Gay Adolescents and Suicide," *Adolescence*, Fall 2005, pp. 623–624.

76. A suicide note left by a gay man read, "I know God will forgive me for doing this thing but that God could never forgive me for having another homosexual thought." Taken from the documentary, *One Nation Under God* (1993).

77. In America's dozen largest cities, the men identifying themselves as gay jumps to 9.2 percent, compared with only 1.3 percent in rural areas. Edward Laumann, et al., *Social Organization of Sexuality in the United States*

(1994), p. 305.

78. The use of the word "amiss" is not meant to imply a value judgment. Amiss is used to mean dissimilar compared to what normally occurs.

79. 2.8 percent of men and 1.4 percent of women self-identify as gay. Laumann, *Social Organization of Sexuality*, p. 293.

80. Moir, *Brain Sex*, pp. 114–116.

81. About seventy-five percent of boys exhibiting "extremely feminine" behavior are gay as adults. About ten percent of girls exhibiting "extremely masculine" behavior are lesbians as adults. J.M. Bailey and Kenneth Zucker, "Childhood Sex-Typed Behavior," *Dev. Psychol.*, 1995, 31(1), pp. 43–55.

82. J.M. Bailey, *Man Who Would Be Queen* (2003), pp. 80–81.

83. Ibid., pp. 77–78.

84. Ibid., p. 84.

85. It is also found in the gay slur "girl top," meaning a feminine gay man who pretends to enjoy being the penetrator.

86. Bailey, *Man Who Would*, pp. 69–76.

87. Ibid., pp. 120–121.

88. J.M. Bailey and Richard Pillard, "Genetic Study of Male Sexual Orientation," *Arch. Gen. Psychiatry*, Dec. 1991, pp. 1089–96.

89. Paragraph from Bruce Bagemihl, *Biological Exuberance* (1999), pp. 31, 58, 126, 340, 603.

90. Terry Burnham and Jay Phelan, *Mean Genes* (2000), pp. 149–150.

91. Bagemihl, *Biological Exuberance*, p. 182.

92. Homosexuality is not a modern concept. In cultures where there is not a stigma on homosexuality people are more willing to cross, and hence blur, the lines, however there have always been a small minority of effeminate men who strongly prefer male sexual relations: for example, the ancient Greek *kinaidoi* and the ancient Roman *cinaedi*. Bailey, *Man Who Would*, pp. 124–138. Lesbians also have been present throughout history (for example, Sappho) but they went relatively unrecorded because of the undervaluation of the female experience and the male view that sex had to involve penetration.

93. Daniela Altimari, "Refusing to Hide in the Closet," *Hartford Courant*, 20 Feb. 2000.

94. C.J. Patterson, "Children of Lesbian and Gay Parents," *Child Dev.*, Oct. 1992, pp. 1025–1042.

95. Study from Bailey, *Man Who Would*, pp. 48–49.

96. Jeffrey Satinover, "How Might Homosexuality Develop?" National Association for Research and Therapy of Homosexuals (NARTH) Collected Papers, 1995, ret. NARTH.com, 15 July 2006.

97. M.E. Tomeo, et al., "Comparative Data of Childhood and Adolescence Molestation," *Arch. Sex. Behav.*, Oct. 2001, p. 535.

98. One study found only seventeen percent of sexually abused boys were victimized by women: a remarkably low number considering how many more straight women there are than gay men. David Finkelhor, et al., "Sexual Abuse in a National Survey of Adult Men and Women," *Child Abuse Negl.*, 1990, 14, p. 22.

99. Edward Laumann, et al., *Social Organization of Sexuality in the United States* (1994), p. 293.

100. This is changing rapidly. In the 1980s the mean age at which homosexuals identified themselves as gay was twenty. By the middle of the 1990s this age had dropped to fifteen. Daniela Altimari, "Refusing to Hide in the Closet," *Hartford Courant*, 20 Feb. 2000.

101. Paragraph from Bruce Rind, "Gay and Bisexual Adolescent Boys' Sexual Experiences," *Arch. Sex. Behav.*, 2001, 30(4).

102. Ibid.

103. Ibid.

104. Judith Levine, *Harmful to Minors* (2003), pp. ix, 185.

105. Betsy Rothstein, "Rep. Heather Wilson," *Hill*, 30 Mar. 2004.

106. Janet Hyde and John DeLamater, *Understanding Human Sexuality* (2008), pp. 106–107.

107. Next two paragraphs from Betty Gordon and Carolyn Schroeder, *Sexuality* (1995), pp. iii, 2–6.

108. Suzanne Frayser, *Varieties of Sexual Experience* (1985), pp. 202–203.

109. Diederik Janssen, *Growing Up Sexually, Volume II: The Sexual Curriculum* (2002), ret. www2.hu-berlin.de, 7 Oct. 2010, p. 233.

110. Judith Levine, *Harmful to Minors* (2003), p. 57.

111. In a Virginia survey, the majority of mental health and legal professionals believed that parents who hug a ten-year-old too frequently, kiss a child on the lips, or appear naked before a five-year-old were "professional intervention" candidates. Ibid., p. 56.

112. Gordon, *Sexuality*, p. xi; and G. Hornor, "Sexual Behavior in Children" *J. Pediatr. Health Care*, Mar.–Apr. 2004, pp. 57–64.

113. Gordon, *Sexuality*, p. 7.

5

SEX II

THE TABOO
SEX IS BAD

The sexual taboo still exists in America due to fundamentalist Christian clout. Although Jesus Christ condemned only one sexual practice—adultery— fundamentalist Christians still strongly believe all extramarital sex is a sin. Not only is it a sin, but it is a sin responsible for most of society's problems.[1] For these people the taboo's maintenance is imperative.

The "sexual revolution" of the 1960s and 1970s did weaken the taboo on sex, and because of this there is currently a generational divide regarding the appropriateness of its discussion. Generally, detailed sex talk is still considered an inappropriate topic for conversation outside of close friends. In addition, there are still legal ramifications for those who transgress America's sexual mores.

I

EDUCATIONAL SYSTEM
PREMARITAL SEX MAKES YOU CRAZY

The ignorance of sexual mechanics stems largely from the censorship in our school systems. Whereas mild social enforcement has been enough to keep the subjects of nasal mucus and excrement out of our schools, sex education is fiercely contested by religious conservatives, whose three main arguments are discussed below.

A. Arguments for Ignorance: Keep 'Em Dumb

(1) *They wouldn't know*—The first argument is that sex education shows kids how to have sex.[2] This is laughable because sex is an instinctual human drive. When they hit puberty, kids will naturally want to have sex *and be able to figure out how to have sex*, whether they are taught how to do it safely or not.

This argument not only counters common sense but scientific studies as well. It has been found that explaining the sex act does not incite sexual fantasizing in children,[3] and over half of kids who masturbate learned how to do it on their own.[4]

(2) *It's the Hippies' Fault*—The second argument is that sex education and the "sexual revolution" have created an adolescent pregnancy crisis that requires a radical return to the good old days of the 1950s when sex was not in our schools or media.[5] This is flawed reasoning because the 1950s had the highest rate of teenage childbearing in twentieth-century America.[6]

Additionally, if sex ed and our "sex-saturated" society have created this "disaster," the Netherlands should be falling off a cliff. The Dutch start comprehensive sex education in preschool and have legalized prostitution. However, Dutch teens begin having sex almost two years later than their American counterparts,[7] and boast a birthrate seven times lower.[8]

(3) *Family Values*—A third argument, which gets less promotion, is that practical consequences do not matter. It is the teaching of "family values" that is the overarching concern. Of course, these are Christian fundamentalist family values. The dark side of this argument is that those that do not follow these values should get the consequences they "deserve."[9]

As will be seen in the next section, this argument is part of a thinly disguised use of the government to establish religion. However, the government's role is not to teach the populace values—in this case, values that counter the practice and beliefs of the majority of Americans,[10] and which are not even practiced by the fundamentalist Christians themselves.[11]

B. The Curriculum: Be Prepared to Die

Despite the flawed arguments of religious conservatives and their lack of public support, they lobby vigorously, and politicians have responded by censoring sex education. The Constitution bars the federal government from regulating for the public good—this is supposed to be the states' domain. However, even in an area traditionally left to the states—education—the federal government flexes its influence through monetary grants.

In 1996 the federal government allocated $250 million to the states for five years for the exclusive purpose of teaching the social, psychological, and health gains to be realized by completely abstaining from sexual activity. Not surprisingly, all the states but California accepted the money and the accompanying restrictions. There were a few local holdouts, like Charleston County, South Carolina, who rejected the money, its school board chairman saying, "Let's not live in a fantasy land . . . [or] play Russian Roulette with the lives of our students."[12]

The fantasy land to which the chairman was referring was the Congressionally-mandated sex education curriculum. Sex education now could *only* teach that sexual activity outside the context of marriage was likely to have harmful psychological and physical effects. Even worse, contraceptive and safer-sex techniques could not be discussed, except to emphasize their failures, and discourage their use.

One of the sex education curricula that meets this conservative standard is "Sex Respect," created in the 1980s with federal money. Its founder, Phyllis Schlafly, protested in 1981 that, "nearly all existing sex education curricula . . . taught teenagers (and sometimes children) how to enjoy fornication without having a baby and without feeling guilty."[13]

"Sex Respect" pushes abstinence based on grossly exaggerated fears of emotional devastation, sexually transmitted diseases (STDs), and death. Its religious basis is barely hidden, as it has advised kids to attend worship services regularly, and has said, "nature seems to be making a statement about the wisdom of keeping sex within marriage through the current epidemic of STDs and teen pregnancy."[14]

Other questionable assertions have included, "there's no way to have premarital sex without hurting someone," the chances of getting pregnant while using a condom are one in six,[15] and a film in which a student asks an instructor, "What if I want to have sex before I get married?" The instructor's response (which has surely garnered cackles in classrooms across the country) is "Well, I guess you'll just have to be prepared to die."[16]

The federal government has instituted a fundamentalist Christian view of sex into our nation's educational system. Educators are not allowed to even answer questions about safe-sex aids, unless to criticize their effectiveness.[17] They are required by law to teach children that "sexual activity outside of the context of marriage is likely to have harmful psychological and physical effects."[18] In other words, American children are being schooled not to orgasm until they are twenty-six.[19]

This program is surreal. In 2003 over sixty percent of American high school seniors had already had sexual intercourse.[20] By the age of eleven, twenty percent of boys are masturbating, and by the age of sixteen, ninety percent are doing so. By the age of sixteen, sixty percent of girls are masturbating.[21] Ninety percent of Americans have sex before marriage.[22] In addition, it is estimated 2.8 percent of males and 1.4 percent of females are homosexual.[23] In a society that does not allow homosexuals to marry, it is cruel to teach that they are never supposed to enjoy an orgasm. Sexual education in America is a very expensive hypocritical joke that spreads shame and misery among its young.

With a multitude of studies unable to demonstrate abstinence-only education's effectiveness, President Barack Obama cut its funding from the 2010 federal budget, but Senator Orrin Hatch added a last-minute provision before the budget's approval to provide $250 million in funding for another five years.[24]

II

Censorship
Be Quiet So They Don't Figure It Out

Thankfully, the truth about sex can now seep out through different channels in spite of politicians' best attempts. As with excrement, communication involving the topic of sex is restricted by our government. Sex must be sensitively discussed over the airwaves from six a.m. to ten p.m. Indecent discussion of sexual organs or activities during these hours on broadcast radio or television can result in the federal government imposing a fine or even revoking a station's license.[25]

Sex censorship by the federal government is done with the stated purpose of protecting children from hearing or viewing "harmful" material. How sexual references are harmful has never been scientifically explained by politicians. These "harms" are only alluded to in vague terms, as Senator Jesse Helms did when he introduced, and passed, a 1998 ban on broadcasting all indecent speech at all hours:[26]

> [W]hat happens when a child unintentionally tunes in and hears or sees material describing, by innuendo, how to have sex? Or when an eight-year-old girl turns on her radio to hear the deejay describe sex acts by the use of metaphors? . . . How much damage will be done? I hope that we will not have to find out.[27]

Scientists have attempted to find out and they have found no damage. In the 1995 federal court case known as *ACT III*, Judge Harry Edwards wrote in his opinion that " . . . the simple truth is that '[t]here is not one iota of evidence in the record . . . to support the claim that exposure to indecency is harmful—indeed, the nature of the alleged 'harm' is never explained.'"[28]

In addition to the government, social enforcement hampers candid discussion about sex. Prior to the "sexual revolution" of the 1960s and 1970s, any talk about sex was discouraged. It was a conversation reserved for a husband and wife to discuss in private, if it was discussed at all. Currently sex is commonly discussed among friends, and the closer the relationship, the more detailed the conversations can be. But discussing sex, particularly in detail, can be offensive to new acquaintances.

III

Criminalization of Sex
Happy Hookers, Happy Johns, and Mad Moralists

As for the act of sex itself, the social punishment is largely reserved to women. In the past fifty years this stigma has been moderated. Previously all women who had sex with someone besides their husband were condemned, but now "slut shaming" is largely reserved for women who frequently have casual sex, that is, sex outside of an exclusive relationship. Despite an erosion in the double standard thanks to some prominent sexually liberated women,[29] females who have sex with too many partners are still called sluts and whores, whereas their male counterparts are called studs. Sluts and whores are thought of as dirty and dumb, whereas studs are thought of as attractive and powerful.

There still remains a large social stigma around homosexuality as well, but homosexuals are not the only unconventional performers who garner derision. Anyone who strays too far from the conventional missionary sexual position risks being branded a pervert. Social enforcement can range from being called kinky behind one's back and avoided (for someone into S&M) to being murdered (pedophiles).[30]

The taboo on sex is still enforced in law. Two adults cannot have consensual sex if there is an exchange of money involved. The sale of sexual services is illegal everywhere except for a few counties in Nevada's desert.

Laws against prostitution are justified on fallacies. These include:

(1) Prostitution degrades women—Prostitution is considered degrading because of our culture's Victorian attitudes toward sex. But large portions of our population no longer share this attitude, including many of the adult women who consensually partake in prostitution. Some sex workers feel more degraded by the slimy men they regrettably had sex with in relationships, and by the legal system that punishes them, than by the men who pay them for sex (johns).[31] A number of them feel sex work is empowering and find it *raises* their self-esteem.[32] One 1986 American study found that ninety-seven percent of call girls liked themselves "more than before" they began prostitution.[33]

84

"Whose theory is it that prostitution is victimless? It's the men who buy prostitutes who spew the myths that women choose prostitution…"—Melissa Farley and Victor Malarek, *New York Times*, March 12, 2008

"There is no victim here…"—Ms. O'Donnell, a sex worker who relishes the time spent with her clients, *New York Times*, March 16, 2008

Those who argue that women should only be financially rewarded for their "minds" disregard models, whose looks are their source of payment. They also disregard female blue-collar workers who are being paid for physical tasks. Critics also imply the poor quality of their own sex lives when they deny that providing orgasms is an improvable skill.

(2) Prostitution endangers women physically[34]—Prostitution is by far the most dangerous occupation in the United States *primarily because* it is illegal.[35] Prostitutes cannot enjoy the safety of brothels, and johns and pimps can get away with treatment unacceptable in other service industries because a prostitute is not likely to go to the police for fear of being arrested herself.

(3) Prostitution spreads disease—Once again, this is primarily the product of its criminalization. In the many parts of the world where prostitution is legal, prostitutes are regulated and required to be regularly tested. In a study of sexual health clinics in the Netherlands, where prostitution is legal, female prostitutes' chlamydia/gonorrhea rates were half those of straight people at large.[36]

In addition, professional sex workers are highly aware of sexually transmitted diseases and know how to spot and avoid them. In a 1988 study of seventy-eight New York City call girls (who had been prostitutes for an average of five years and had an average of 200 sexual partners in the past year), none tested positive for AIDS.[37]

As a former escort wrote, "Until I became a prostitute, I did not even know what the symptoms were. When I started working as a professional, I learned about safe sex practices and how to take care of myself."[38]

A PROUD PROSTITUTE
I Was in Heaven

Norma Jean Almodovar was a Los Angeles police officer before becoming a sex worker. She described one of her years as a call girl as "one of the happiest of my life ... I felt I was in heaven." She wrote:

> Prostitution offered all the things I wanted in a career: I could choose my own hours, see only men I liked, and go to the finest restaurants with clients. And I loved sex. What more could I ask for?

—Norma Jean Almodovar, *Cop to Call Girl* (1993), pp. 62, 139.

(4) Prostitutes do not want to be prostitutes—Prostitution opponents make the incredible argument that no woman would become a sex worker of her own volition. To victimize the entire sex worker population, they must make the absurd claim that all sex workers are either slaves or so drug-addicted/psychologically damaged that they cannot think for themselves.

Sex slaves do exist, but in the United States they constitute a microscopic percentage of sex workers. From 2000–2007 only 1,362 victims of human trafficking were identified by the federal government in the entire U.S..[39] (This number includes those trafficked for non-sexual labor as well.) In that same time period, there were over half a million prostitution arrests.[40] In 2008 there were over five thousand prostitution arrests just on the Strip in Las Vegas.

The argument that all prostitutes are drug addicts or psychologically damaged from abuse is supported by junk science conducted by anti-prostitution activists. Ronald Weitzer, a sociologist at George Washington University, explains that in these anti-prostitution studies "counterevidence is routinely ignored, anecdotes masquerade as evidence, non sequiturs abound, and sampling is biased toward the most disadvantaged segment of the sex industry."[41]

One of the most notable of these "researchers" is Melissa Farley, who publicly asserts that *no* woman would ever choose prostitution and that *all* prostitution is violence against women.[42] Despite the fact her bias is so blatant that it caused

86

A PROUD PORN STAR
Fat, Old, and Ugly

The well known 1970s porn star Seka (Dorothiea Patton), a former high school home-coming queen, said:

> This is something that I want to do—that I've always wanted to do. And I love it. I love getting up in front of a camera and fucking someone until they come all over my face. I don't think I'm being exploited. A lot of those women are probably fat, old, and ugly and probably couldn't do it. That's why they don't like it. If they tried it once they might like it. It's something they've probably never tried so they don't know whether they like it or not.

—*Midnight Blue Vol. 2: Porn Stars of the '70s*, DVD, (2006).

a Canadian judge to deem her testimony "problematic,"[43] media outlets give her voluminous coverage, with a 2011 study of hers released "exclusively" to *Newsweek*.[44] (In contrast, the media routinely ignores sex workers' rights activists, many of whom were once prostitutes themselves.)[45]

Research of Farley's ilk often fails to mention the prevalence of drug and psychological issues in other professions as well. For example, estimates of childhood sexual abuse for *all* women can run as high as sixty-two percent.[46] Anti-prostitution studies also tend to focus on non-random samples of street prostitutes.[47] The ensuing studies, statistics, and media presentations are dishonest because street-based prostitution only accounts for an estimated fifteen to twenty percent of the prostitution in America.[48]

Many street prostitutes have lost control over their lives due to past abuse, drug addiction, and mental health issues. This is why they are desperate enough to risk arrest and public exposure by plying their trade on the street. However, their situation is more about poverty and the war on drugs than it is about prostitution.

Unlike street prostitutes, many escorts are well-educated and cannot easily be framed as victims. The DC Madam, Deborah Jeane Palfrey, employed over 132 women between 1993 and 2006. She required that they be at least twenty-three

GET OFF
Independent Sex Workers Have More Fun

Prostitutes who work for themselves have better experiences than their peers.

In one study of three hundred prostitutes (seventy-five call girls, seventy-five street prostitutes, and 150 Nevada brothel workers), ninety-seven percent of the call girls reported an increase in self-esteem after they began working in prostitution, compared with fifty percent of brothel workers and only eight percent of street prostitutes.

The same study found that seventy-five percent of call girls frequently had orgasms with customers, whereas only nineteen percent of brothel workers and zero percent of street workers did.

A study of Midwestern indoor prostitutes (most of whom worked in bars) found that three-quarters of them believed their lives improved after entering prostitution. The rest reported no change. None said it became worse.

A study of indoor sex workers and street workers found that the former were doing well emotionally, whereas the latter exhibited significant psychological problems.

A New Zealand study of twenty-nine sex workers (twenty-seven indoor workers, two street) found no differences between them and an age-matched sample of non-prostitutes in physical health, self-esteem, or mental health.

years old and have at least two years of college education. Jeannette Angell became a prostitute after receiving a doctorate in social anthropology.[49] Brooke Magnanti worked as a call girl while finishing her doctoral thesis and found sex work "so much more enjoyable" than her previous job as a computer programmer.[50]

To hear the voices of proud women who choose sex work, go to the blog "Bound Not Gagged." For example, this statement from Ms. Honey Pot:

> I have a PhD, viable skills, and many years of experience as a corporate executive. I do this, because I enjoy it. Hearing or reading that we do this because we do not possess options, makes me cringe. I am sick and tired of the old feminist rhetoric that we escorts are victims. I am not a victim. I make my own circumstances. I am doing this of my own free will and loving every minute of it.[51]

> Research on ninety-five call girls in Sydney, Australia, found they were generally emotionally healthy.
>
> Another Australian study found that half of call girls and brothel workers felt their work was a "major source of satisfaction" in their lives and seven of ten would "definitely choose" sex work if they had to do it over again.
>
> All of the escorts examined in one 1979 study were proud of their profession, and eight other studies have found indoor sex workers feel their work had some positive effect on their lives or believed they were providing a valuable service.
>
> —Ronald Weitzer, "New Directions in Research on Prostitution," *Crime Law Soc. Change*, 2005, 43, pp. 217–218.

Unlike Ms. Honey Pot, there are undoubtedly many sex workers who do it primarily for the money. Call girls are paid $300, tax-free, per hour compared to the $10 per hour in alternate fields. However, the same could be said about many jobs. It would also be a more enjoyable profession if it was legalized and did not carry such a stigma—a stigma perpetrated by slut-shaming anti-prostitution activists who deny any rational woman would ever do it.

(5) **Most prostitutes are brought into the business as children**—The statistic that the average age of entry into sex work is thirteen is widespread on the Internet and has found its way into legitimate media such as *Vanity Fair* magazine and ABC's *Nightline*.[52] It appears to have originated from the aforementioned anti-prostitution activist, Melissa Farley.[53] This shocking statistic is a lie, because Farley cites studies that focused on juvenile prostitutes, in other words, the average entry age for *juvenile* prostitutes was thirteen.[54] A different study—from Farley's own book—found the age of entry to be a more believable twenty-three.[55]

Another anti-prostitution lie that has been echoed everywhere from the *New York Times* to CNN is that 100,000–300,000 children are sold into prostitution in America annually. This twisted number actually came from two professors' estimates as to how many children are "at risk" for sexual exploitation. Their numbers included such vulnerable groups as all juveniles living near the Canadian border who have

MOTHER SUPERIOR
Diane Sawyer Would Never Have Sex for Money, Why Are You?

In ABC's 2008 20/20 series "Prostitution in America: Working Girls Speak," Diane Sawyer went about proving that (in the words of the producer) "behind every prostitute is a story of sex abuse, drug dependency, or mental illness. No one chooses this."

Predictably—despite street prostitutes being a small minority of all sex workers—the show focused almost completely on street prostitutes, passed off street prostitute statistics as applying to all sex workers, and only interviewed anti-prostitution experts who believed no woman could possibly choose sex work.

Sawyer doggedly got every prostitute to admit to past sexual abuse, drug use, or mental illness. Any other reason was unacceptable. When one young woman said she did it for the cash, Sawyer grimaced and raised her voice, "Why? You could have gotten some other job … and kept yourself. Why?" After some introspection the woman owned up to being raped when younger and having low self-esteem.

Sawyer ran into difficulty at the legalized Nevada brothel out in the middle of the desert. The women, including a licensed R.N., said they did it for the money. However, one of them privately told Sawyer that "a lot" of the women use illegal or prescription drugs to get through the day. Case closed.

A clip of a casual interchange between a sex worker and an aspiring one showed what might have been said more frequently if Sawyer wasn't shaming her interviewees: "To be honest, it's not much different than going home drunk from your college frat party with a different guy except you're getting paid."

The show was apparently not going to bother to interview any call girls/escorts at all, but in the wake of the New York governor's prostitution scandal they scrambled to get one. Sawyer appeared to finally have met her match with the escort. When asked how she felt about being offered money for sex for the first time, the escort answered "liberated" and added that she was "a very sexual person." Sawyer did not like that answer at all, saying: "It can be a sexual person and at the same time really value the sanctity of your own body."

After challenging the woman about "moral choice" and giving away something that "should not be sold," Sawyer laid it out:

Sawyer: I'm having a really hard time believing that there isn't suffering in you. I don't believe it …. Were you abused as a child?

Woman: No.

Sawyer: Teenager?

Woman. No.

Sawyer: Drugs?

Woman: No.

Sawyer: Emotional problems?

Woman: Yeah, I think I do. I'm afraid to be vulnerable.

Later the woman wrote on her blog (*Debauchette*), that she did the interview because she wanted to break "the old Victorian trope of the broken, dysfunctional, fallen prostitute, incapable of forming her own opinions or making her own decisions."

She also wrote that she was disappointed that the documentary didn't interview more women like her and that they didn't interview any "(real) sex worker activists." Case closed.

—David Bauder, "ABC to Air Prostitution News Special," AP, 19 Mar. 2008; and "Boom," *Debauchette* (blog), 20 Apr. 2008, ret. 3 Sep. 2008.

their own mode of transportation. The actual number of children kidnapped and sold as sex slaves is more likely in the few hundreds.[56]

(6) **Trafficked women are sex slaves**—When anti-prostitution advocates are not using junk science to inflate numbers, they are blurring definitions to achieve the same result.[57] Although the terms "trafficked women" and "sex slaves" are often used interchangeably, they are not the same.

A study of Vietnamese migrants in Cambodia found that out of a hundred "trafficked" women, only six had been tricked into sex work. The rest knew they would be working in a brothel before they left Vietnam and they did it for "economic incentives, desire for an independent lifestyle, and dissatisfaction with rural life and agricultural labor." When "rescue" organizations raided the brothels and "saved" them, they "usually returned to their brothel as quickly as possible."[58]

Emigration for sex work is driven by poverty and barriers to female employment in developing countries and Eastern Europe. If anti-prostitution activists cared more about women and less about sexual morality, they would devote themselves to these issues. Better employment options would give these women more of an incentive to *voluntarily* leave the industry.

EXAGGERATED FEARS #2
AIDS

The risk of contracting AIDS from heterosexual sex in the developed world was greatly exaggerated for political reasons. First, it was thought AIDS would not get governmental interest if it was seen as merely a "gay disease." Second, heterosexual AIDS was used by the left to support sex education, and those on the right to trumpet extramarital sex as evil.

In the late 1980s when the New York City health department carefully interviewed men claiming to be infected by women (as opposed to simply taking their word for it like other health departments), they found that almost no one fell into this category. Closeted gay men and intravenous drug users have an incentive to lie, and when New York City stopped their interviewing process, the heterosexual transmission numbers went "through the roof."

Exposure Route	Risk Per Act
Receptive Anal Intercourse	1.70%
Receptive Penile-Vaginal Intercourse	.08%
Insertive Penile-Vaginal Intercourse	.04%
Receptive Fellatio	.00002%
Insertive Fellatio	.00001%

Note: Being uncircumcised raises risk two times. Presence or history of genital ulcers in either partner increases risk five times. Transmission rates are higher in developing countries, where many people suffer from already crippled immune systems.

—Marie-Claude Boily, et al., "Heterosexual Risk of HIV-1 Infection Per Sexual Act," *Lancet Infect. Dis.*, Feb. 2009; Michael Fumento, "Myth of Heterosexual AIDS," 2 Nov. 1998, ret. Fumento.com, 8 Sep. 2006; Brendan O'Neill, "Exploitation of AIDS," Guardian.co.uk, 12 June 2008; and Beena Varghese, et al., "Reducing the Risk of Sexual HIV Transmission," *Sex. Transm. Dis.*, Jan. 2002.

(7) Legalized prostitution increases coercive trafficking—Anti-prostitution activists claim Sweden's 1999 criminalization caused trafficking in Sweden to go down "dramatically."[59] The evidence to support this has been revealed to be bunkum,[60] but the media continues to repeat it.

Outside of unsubstantiated quotes, there is "absolutely no evidence" that legalized prostitution contributes to the trafficking of involuntary victims.[61] In the United Kingdom, where prostitution is legal, sensationalism about the trafficking of sex slaves led to a massive crackdown using every police force in the country. Eight hundred and twenty-two brothels, flats, and massage parlors were raided. They did not find a single person who had forced anybody into prostitution.[62]

(8) Tougher laws would end prostitution—In the mid-1980s police doubted even a tripling of enforcement efforts could "make a dent" in their respective cities' prostitution problems, and individual cities' crusades against prostitution in the 1970s supported this assertion.[63] Before Saddam Hussein's removal from power in 2003, convicted prostitutes could be beheaded in Iraq. Even in this extreme "tough on crime" climate, poor men could still procure affordable prostitutes.64

(9) Prostitution is illegal everywhere but "freaky" places like the Netherlands—Countries where prostitution is legal include Australia, Brazil, Canada, Colombia, Denmark, England, France, Germany, Greece, India, Italy, Mexico, Switzerland, and Turkey. In these countries, prostitutes are able to organize and advocate for their rights. Durbar, a sex worker collective in India, has over 65,000 members.

The United Nations' Convention on the Elimination of All Forms of Discrimination Against Women (CEDAW) is a 1979 treaty that upholds "the right to a free choice of profession and employment."[65] The United Nations' CEDAW committee has determined that this human right includes voluntary prostitution.[66] The United States is the only democracy not to have signed CEDAW.[67]

Prostitution is not the only sexual behavior that is criminalized. All states criminalize sexual intercourse with minors. The oldest age of consent in America is eighteen. In most states the age of consent is age fifteen or sixteen, however, there can still be vague morality statutes that apply until age eighteen.[68]

Public nudity is also illegal in most of the United States. In 2010 Missouri made it a crime for adults to be naked even in strip clubs where only consenting adults are present. The United States Supreme Court has stated that this is not a violation of the First Amendment's guarantee of free expression because "Public nudity is the evil the state seeks to prevent . . ."[69]

NOTES

1. For a fundamentalist Christian diagram showing how sexual immorality leads to "crime, drugs, murder, suicide, riots, truancy, violence, poverty, litigiousness, and economic weakness," then "social collapse," see Daniel Heimbach, *True Sexual Morality* (2004), p. 38.
2. "The comprehensive safe-sex education message ignores basic human nature—that when given the option between two alternatives, some people will choose the worst alternative." Ret. SexRespect.com, 17 Sep. 2010.
3. Steven Gold and Ruth Gold, "Gender Differences in First Sexual Fantasies," *J. Sex Educ. Ther.*, 1991, 17, pp. 207–216.
4. Most of the remaining children learned from peers or siblings. Roy Baumeister, Kathleen Catanese, and Kathleen Vohs, "Is There a Gender Difference in Strength of Sex Drive?" *Pers. Soc. Psychol. Rev.*, 2001, 5(3), p. 255.
5. ". . . the sexual revolution has proved to be a disaster for American society." Ret. SexRespect.com, 17 Sep. 2010.
6. Stephanie Coontz, *The Way We Never Were* (1992), p. 202.
7. The average age of first teen intercourse is 17.7 versus 15.8 in America. Linda Berne and Barbara Huberman, "European Approaches to Adolescent Sexual Behavior," Advocates for Youth, 1999, p. 5.
8. The birthrate was 6.9 per one thousand women aged 15–19 versus 54.4. Planned Parenthood, "White Paper: Adolescent Sexuality," Jan. 2001.
9. An abstinence enthusiast said, "I have personal friends who have preached abstinence to their kids for a lifetime, and several of them now have teenage kids who are pregnant. And every single one of them tells me that if they had to do it again, they would not do it any differently. Because what they were teaching their kids was right. They had taught them the right values." Esther Kaplan, *With God on Their Side* (2005), p. 197.
10. More than ninety percent of Americans lose their virginity prior to marriage, and parents "overwhelmingly favor" the comprehensive sex-education approach. David Crary, "Most Americans Have Had Premarital Sex," AP, 19 Dec. 2006; and Debra Rosenberg, "Battle Over Abstinence," *Newsweek*, 9 Dec. 2002, pp. 67–71.
11. A 1987 survey of 1,438 teenage members of eight "born again" denominations revealed that, by the age of eighteen, forty-three percent had had sexual intercourse and sixty-five percent had participated in some form of sex play with another person. "Kids Will Be Kids," *Fam. Plann. Perspect.*, Sep.–Oct. 1988, p. 204.
12. Marjorie Heins, *Not in Front of the Children* (2001), p. 147.
13. Ibid., p. 142.
14. Ibid.
15. Over the course of a year, the chance of a pregnancy occurring with correct condom usage is two percent. Christopher Lee, "Condom Information in Abstinence Programs Called Inaccurate," WashingtonPost.com, 28 Apr. 2007.
16. Heins, *Not in Front*, pp. 145–146.
17. Esther Kaplan, *With God on Their Side* (2005), p. 196.

18. §510(b), Title V, Social Security Act, P.L. 104–193.

19. The average age of marriage is 26. (U.S. Census, 2002).

20. CDC, "Surveillance Summaries," 21 May 2004, p. 18.

21. Martha Cornog, *Big Book of Masturbation* (2003), pp. 68–69.

22. David Crary, "Most Americans Have Had Premarital Sex," AP, 19 Dec. 2006.

23. Edward Laumann, et al., *Social Organization of Sexuality in the United States* (1994), p. 293.

24. "Prevention of HIV/AIDS, Other STIs and Pregnancy: Group-based Abstinence Education Interventions for Adolescents," CDC, TheCommunityGuide.org, June 2009, ret. 22 Sep. 2010.

25. The FCC defines broadcast indecency as "language or material that, in context, depicts or describes, in terms patently offensive as measured by contemporary community standards for the broadcast medium, sexual or excretory organs or activities." "FCC Consumer Facts: Obscene and Indecent Broadcasts," FCC.Gov, 24 Sep. 2007.

26. It was later declared unconstitutional. The Court ruled that some safe harbor was necessary for broadcasting so that adults were not completely constrained to the language of children.

27. 134 Cong. Rec. S9912 (26 July 1988).

28. *Action for Children's Television v. FCC* (ACT III), 11 F.3d 170 (D.C. Cir. 1993).

29. Examples include pop star Madonna in the 1980s and early 1990s, with her sexually-themed songs and music videos that included "Like a Virgin" and "Erotica," and her book, *Sex* (1992), as well as rapper Lil' Kim, who has songs like "How Many Licks" (2000), in which she boasts about men who gave her oral sex.

30. Pedophiles are frequent murder targets. "Experts: Convicted Sex Abusers Face Grave Danger in Prison," FOXNews.com, 23 Aug. 2003.

31. Jeannette Angell, *Callgirl* (2004), pp. 8, 13. Also see Norma Jean Almodovar, *Cop to Call Girl* (1993), p. 325.

32. "Long after I had dealt with my addiction to drugs, I still fantasized about my years as a sex worker. I never had such power before or since as I did in those moments just before a man would come. For those five minutes, watching his knees shake and turn to jelly, I had him. He was mine. I was in total control." Margo Caulfield, "Empowered Sex Workers: Do They Exist?" *Research for Sex Work* 3, June 2000.

33. Ronald Weitzer, "New Directions in Research on Prostitution," *Crime Law Soc. Change*, 2005, 43, p. 218.

34. Just as some feminists, like Andrea Dworkin, argue that heterosexual intercourse is inherently violence against women, prostitution is similarly categorized. "When prostitution is understood as violence, however, unionizing prostituted women makes as little sense as unionizing battered women." Melissa Farley, *Violence Against Women*, Oct. 2004, p. 1089.

35. Ronald Weitzer, "Moral Crusade Against Prostitution," *Society*, Mar./Apr. 2006, p. 35.

36. Kate Kelland, "Disease Risk Higher for Swingers than Prostitutes," Reuters.com, 24 June 2010.

37. M. Seidlin, et al., "Prevalence of HIV Infection in New York Call Girls," *J. Acquir. Immune. Defic. Syndr.*, 1988, 1(2), p. 150.

38. Almodovar, *Cop to Call Girl*, pp. 321–322.

39. Jerry Markon, "Human Trafficking Evokes Outrage, Little Evidence," WashingtonPost.com, 23 Sep. 2007.

40. There were 653,500 prostitution related arrests from 2000–2007. "*Easy Access to FBI Arrest Statistics 1994–2008*," OJJDP.gov, 2011, ret. 7 Apr. 2012.

41. Ronald Weitzer, "Flawed Theory and Method in Studies of Prostitution," *Violence Against Women*, July 2005.

42. Melissa Farley and Victor Malarek, "The Myth of the Victimless Crime," *New York Times*, 12 Mar. 2008; and ibid.

43. "I found the evidence of Dr. Melissa Farley to be problematic . . . her advocacy appears to have permeated her opinions. For example, Dr. Farley's unqualified assertion in her affidavit that prostitution is inherently violent appears to contradict her own findings that prostitutes who work from indoor locations generally experience less violence." *Bedford v. Canada*, 2010 ONSC 4264 (CanLII).

44. Leslie Bennetts, "The John Next Door," TheDailyBeast.com, 18 Jul. 2011.

45. These include Amanda Brooks, Robyn Few, Elena Jeffreys, Carol Leigh, Susan Lopez, Maggie McNeill, and Audacia Ray.

46. Most professionals place it between one and three and one and four. Kathleen Faller, *Child Sexual Abuse* (1993), p. 16.

47. Ronald Weitzer, "Flawed Theory."

48. Alexandra Murphy and Sudhir Venkatesh, "Vice Careers," *Qual. Sociol.*, June 2006, p. 137; and Weitzer, "Flawed Theory," p. 944.

49. Jeannette Angell, *Callgirl* (2004), p. 6.
50. "Belle de Jour Drops Her Anonymity," BBC.co.uk, 15 Nov. 2009.
51. Comment left on March 16, 2008, at blog entry "Prostitution 2.0," Bound Not Gagged, 15 Mar. 2008, ret. 3 Sep. 2008.
52. Amy Fine Collins, "Sex Trafficking of Americans," VanityFair.com, 24 May 2011; and Katie Hinman and Melia Patria, "Girls Sold for Sex Online," ABCNews.go.com, 24 Apr. 2012.
53. Melissa Farley, "Prostitution: Factsheet on Human Rights Violations," 2 Apr. 2000, ret. ProstitutionResearch. com, 5 Sep. 2008.
54. Mimi Silbert and Ayala Pines, "Victimization of Street Prostitutes," *Victimology: An International Journal*, 1982, 7:1–4, pp. 122–133; and D. Kelly Weisberg, *Children of the Night: A Study of Adolescent Prostitution* (1985), p. 94.
55. Melissa Farley, *Prostitution, Trafficking and Traumatic Stress* (2004), p. 191.
56. Martin Cizmar, Ellis Conklin, and Kristen Hinman, "Real Men Get Their Facts Straight," VillageVoice.com, 29 June 2011.
57. Ronald Weitzer, "Moral Crusade Against Prostitution," *Society*, Mar./Apr. 2006, p. 36.
58. Multiple studies have had similar findings. Weitzer, "Moral Crusade," p. 37.
59. Leslie Bennetts, "The John Next Door," TheDailyBeast.com, 18 Jul. 2011.
60. Laura Agustin, "Big Claims, Little Evidence: Sweden's Law Against Buying Sex," TheLocal.se, 23 Jul. 2010, ret. 8 Apr. 2012.
61. Weitzer, "Moral Crusade," p. 37.
62. Nick Davies, "Inquiry Fails to Find Single Trafficker Who Forced Anybody Into Prostitution," *Guardian*, 19 Oct. 2009.
63. Houston in 1975 and New York City in 1979. Julie Pearl, "Highest Paying Customers," *Hastings Law J.*, Apr. 1987, p. 789.
64. Christian Caryl, "Iraqi Vice," *Newsweek*, 22 Dec. 2003, p. 38.
65. CEDAW, (1979), Article 11, §1(c).
66. "Report of the CEDAW," A/54/38/Rev. 1, UN, p. 30.
67. Linda Lowen, "Why Won't the U.S. Ratify CEDAW?" About.com, 1 Mar. 2012.
68. For example, Pennsylvania's reads, "Whoever, being of the age of 18 years and upwards, by any act corrupts or tends to corrupt the morals of any minor less than 18 years of age . . . commits a misdemeanor of the first degree." 18 Pa.C.S.A. §6301.
69. *Barnes v. Glen Theatre*, 501 US 560 (1991

6

SEX III

ITS ORIGIN
DISTORTING JESUS

I
AMERICAN PRUDE

Our current era is presented as an "X-rated age," one in which sex is "everywhere" "like never before."[1] It is claimed that sex inundates our media,[2] teenagers are having way too much sex,[3] and that sexual "perversity" and sexual problems abound.[4]

This outlook is extremely skewed because these commentators are comparing us to an erroneous interpretation of 1950s America. The America of the 1950s was not devoid of sex, but as one of the most censorious eras it is easy to portray it that way.[5] In the public arena sex was invisible. When compared to the full gamut of societies throughout the world and throughout history, America's prudishness is revealed to be not normal, or natural,[6] but radical.

Before the West colonized the world, enforced monogamy was a rarity. In one study of 185 human societies, less than sixteen percent formally restricted their members to monogamy, and fewer than a third of those disapproved of both premarital and extramarital sex. Thirty-nine percent of the societies not only tolerated but actually approved of extramarital sexual relations.[7]

II

OUR GENETIC RELATIVES
SEX WAS FUN

To get to this surreal state was quite a journey for mankind. To understand what our "natural" sexual habits are we must go back millions of years ago. Our evolutionary forebears lived in the African jungles. Although no one knows the sexual habits of these early humans, called *Australopithecus*, it is reasonable to assume they were similar to one of our evolutionary relatives who remained in the jungle—the chimpanzees.[8]

Chimpanzees are promiscuous. A female in estrus will attempt to seduce every male available except for her sons and brothers.[9] Sometimes the males will simply line up as long as eight deep and wait their turn. These females are sexually aggressive and will tweak the flaccid penises of males who are not interested.

In a phenomenon that may foreshadow our pair-bonding, some male chimpanzees try to monopolize a female's affections. They may do this by physically keeping other males away or by winning the female over. The latter is much more effective. Male chimps will try to win females by grooming them and giving them food. If the male is successful he will be able to get the female to "go on safari" with him.

With hair and penis erect he will beckon, rock from side to side, flick his penis, wave branches, and stare intently at the object of his desire. When she comes toward him he walks away and hopes that she will accompany him. If he is judged worthy they will disappear into the woods for several days or even weeks for a private affair.

To witness what sex might have been like for our forebears, or just to see what sex is like free of human cultural trappings, one can go to a zoo and admire the bonobos (pygmy chimpanzees). The bonobo is our closest genetic relative. Sex is casual and relaxed for the bonobo, and serves as a social lubricant.[10] For example, if a female wants some of a male's food supply she will copulate with him and the male will share.[11] Whenever there is a source of conflict bonobos will engage in sexual activity, rather than aggression, to relieve the tension. For example, after a male bonobo chases another male away from a female the two may reconcile by rubbing their genitals together.

For those that think that humans invented sex play, bonobos will surprise. Just like *Homo sapiens* sex, bonobo sex is remarkably varied. Bonobos enjoy oral sex, manual stimulation by others, masturbation, and rubbing genitals with members of the same sex.[12] Other remarkably human-like sexual activity includes intense open-mouth kissing and sex in the missionary position—the position preferred by female bonobos. This is noteworthy because it was once thought the missionary position was uniquely human. Even many preliterate societies did not practice it and were taught the more "holy" position by missionaries, hence its name.

III

Evolution
Help Me Raise This Thing

The first humans were hunter-gatherer bands of roughly twenty-five members who ventured out of the jungles into the African savannas.[13] This was considerably more dangerous terrain. Whereas arms provided a climbing advantage in the forest, where the dense trees provided cover, in the open fields early humans were vulnerable to the quicker four-legged predators.

It was in this new environment that humans became bipedal. Standing upright and moving efficiently on two legs gave early people several advantages. They could use their arms for tools and weapons. They could see over the grasses for approaching predators. They could carry things such as collected fruit and scavenged meat. Perhaps most importantly, now that mouths were no longer needed to carry things, they could be used for communication.

The new environment and stance had important ramifications for human sexuality. For one, raising a child was significantly more dangerous. In the savanna the child had to be watched constantly, and with the new erect posture mothers could not sling their babies on their backs. Babies now had to be held. Unlike chimpanzees, the male was now required to assist in the raising of the offspring.

Because of this, humans began to form pair bonds. These bonds were not for life. Early humans practiced what could be called serial monogamy.[14,15] Serial monogamy is the forming of temporary exclusive pair bonds in succession. These bonds usually lasted four years because that is how long it took to raise a child and how long it took early women to begin ovulating again.[16] Children were not independent at the age of four, however, at that age they were weaned and able to join other children in multi-age play groups where the entire community assumed more responsibility for them.

Serial monogamy was not a firm rule. Men would try to keep as many partners as they could afford. However, in the hunter-gathering state in which humans began, men could readily support and defend only one partner from other males' advances, so few men were capable of polygyny (multiple wives or partners).[17]

In fact, most men could not even defend one partner from other male's advances. Discreet "cheating" was common.[18,19] Men would try to have sex with whomever they could, and females would cheat with a more attractive male than their current partner. Men knew of their female mate's proclivity and would guard their mate from others.[20] Despite this, cheating still occurred frequently because men would have to leave to hunt. It was easy to take advantage of these absences when clothes amounted to an animal hide, if anything, a bush could provide cover, and wooing was fast.

Wooing was fast because there was no taboo on sex. Women were still the instinctually choosier sex because, as noted previously, they have a much larger investment in the outcome of sex—pregnancy. Whereas men would cheat with any woman available, women, like their animal brethren, would cheat only with a male superior to her mate, a tactic called "ratcheting up."[21,22] However, early women could tell if a man was superior (strong, attractive, and healthy) to her mate by a quick look-over. Dating was not necessary.

As in every era, there were men and women who could not find mates willing to copulate with them. This leads to an archeological mystery—the Venus figurines.[23] It is believed that early people developed an appreciation of art and a hint of self-awareness roughly three million years ago,[24] and by the end of the Ice Ages, roughly 26,000 B.C., people were carving figurines of women. The most famous is the Venus of Willendorf, found in what is now Austria. She is five inches high, carved out of limestone, originally colored with red ocher, faceless, naked, and has a bulging stomach and breasts.

Around two hundred similarly carved statues have been found in places as divergent as the Pyrenees in Western Europe and the steppes of Southern Russia.

They come in a range of shapes and states of undress, however, they are mostly faceless. There are several theories about the Venus figurines. One is that these were prehistoric pornography. Due to the climate, naked women were an uncommon sight and these figurines, which accent the naked, fleshy hips and breasts could have been masturbatory aids. No male figurines have been found.

One paleontologist wrote that "sex and hunger were the two motives which influenced the entire mental life of the mammoth hunters and their productive art."[25] This is apparent in early peoples' other art forms as well. Another common artifact of the late Ice Ages is the dildo. Although one cannot be certain that these rounded shafts were dildos, they are frequently in the dimensions of modern dildos and some have explicit penis images carved into them, like the double dildo found in what is now the French Pyrenees.

Prehistoric cave and rock art also have sexual themes, which run from a woman having intercourse with two men simultaneously to bestiality. One drawing is of a man having sex with a donkey from what is now Northern Italy. Another drawing from Siberia appears to portray a man on skis having sex with a moose.

IV

Agriculture
Wives for Sale

These sexually free times would come to an end in the New Stone Age or Neolithic era (7000 B.C.). Before the Neolithic, men were the hunters of larger game and women were the gatherers of plants and small game such as turtles, crabs, and mussels.[26] It was a relatively egalitarian society in which resources could not be easily accumulated and everyone was valued roughly equally for their roles.

In the Neolithic, economic changes led to the sexual and social subjugation of women. First, people learned how to farm. Plants were raised, not just gathered, and animals were domesticated. Agriculture allowed successful men to become significantly more powerful than their peers. The domestication of animals allowed men to accumulate them and one strong and talented man could tend his own flock. The weaker and less intelligent men, previously needed for the constant hunting forays, were less valuable. Wealth, property, and female partners could now be stockpiled. In this new stratified society, polygyny occurred more frequently.

Humans learned to castrate the bull to make it a draft animal. With the ox pulling a plough, the female role of plant expert was supplanted as men operated their first power tool.[27] Even with an ox, a plough required greater strength than a hoe. Most women could not handle a plough and their agricultural role was displaced. It was no longer necessary for women to go out and gather, nor for men to venture out on hunting trips. This made it easier for men to guard their partners from other males' sexual advances. Men could simply keep their women at home.

Other changes did not bode well for women. At some point men realized their own role in reproduction. The giveaway may have come from observing domesticated animals' reproduction patterns. Knowing that a child was "theirs" reinforced their instinctual drive to keep other men away from their partners.

This conscious realization that the male played a crucial role in reproduction probably cemented the family unit. It is from this point that female partners will be referred to as wives and male partners as husbands, even though these early "marriages" were nothing like marriage today. Despite the fact that these pairings were often for life, mutual affection was not much of a factor. A male might not even see his wife-to-be until the marriage ceremony.

Marriage first meant that a female belonged to a male. She was property that passed from her father's possession, to her husband's, to her son's. Wives were head servants who bore sons for the husband to pass his property, and bore daughters for the husband to marry off for payment or to cement political alliances. Men could have more than one wife, but only the most successful could afford them. The early civilizations of Egypt, Mesopotamia, and our religious forebears, the Jews,[28] all practiced polygyny, as have the large majority of societies on our planet.

Another repercussion of men understanding that a woman's child belonged to a specific man was that they took steps to assure it was theirs. Sex, for the first time, became wrong outside of marriage. This started the preoccupation with virginity that continues to this day. However, it was only wrong for the female—not the male—

and it was only wrong because it lowered her value by putting any future husband's paternity in doubt.

Law codes from ancient Mesopotamia dating from 1100 B.C. indicate that men were allowed to have extramarital sex but women could be killed for it. Men ran afoul *only* when they had extramarital sex with another man's property, such as his wife or daughter. The plentiful slaves, prostitutes, and females from lower classes were fair game. This property view is seen in the *only* sexual prohibition in the Hebrew Ten Commandments—a man cannot have sex with another man's wife.

Divorce was rare in the early days of marriage simply because there was no need for it. If a wealthy man did not like his wife he could just get another. There was no reason to get rid of the first wife, who was still a useful servant. Poorer men, who could not afford another wife, could go elsewhere for sexual services. The marriage was not for companionship, so the existence of love was not important anyway. Women did not have much say in the matter. The one situation where divorce did occur was when a woman proved infertile, because then she could not fulfill her primary purpose.

These early civilizations were preoccupied with population growth. Hunter-gatherer communities with limited resources were burdened by too many children and frequently practiced infanticide,[29] but on a farm, children were assets because their labor contributions outweighed their expense. They were also important for another growing feature of life—war. Although humans have always warred (as do their genetic relatives, the chimpanzees), war became more prevalent in early agricultural civilizations. Farming allowed the population to grow exponentially and people to accumulate goods and land. There were more people with whom to fight and more things for which to fight. Wars require warriors and large families provide more of them.

With this emphasis on population growth, early civilizations began to clamp down on non-procreative sex. The early Jews were particularly concerned with propagation.[30] They believed the Hebrew God said to the first two humans, "be fruitful and multiply."[31] In line with this, the Hebrew God outlawed homosexuality and zoophilia.[32] Unlike other cultures at the time, the Hebrew proscription on non-procreative sex extended to prostitution. Female prostitutes tried to inhibit pregnancy,[33] and did not provide legitimate children. Despite this, prostitution was still common in Jewish communities, especially for impoverished women, who had few alternatives.

The restrictive Jewish attitude toward sex was based in economics. The act of sex itself carried no stigma, nor was it bad. For that innovation, one must thank the ancient Roman philosophers.

V

Ancient Rome
Here a Penis, There a Penis

As with other early civilizations, the Romans were open about sex. The penis image was a symbol of fertility and prosperity that protected against evil spirits.[34] Penises appeared everywhere.[35] Jewelry, armor, and homes all had phallic symbols. Breads, cookies, and cakes were often made in the shape of penises and vaginas. Penis sculptures were put in gardens to help them grow.

During rural celebrations of the Liberalia, a mid-May festival in honor of the god of fertility, a gigantic phallus was carted around the countryside to bless the people and the land with fertility. This parade culminated with an honored matron putting a wreath on the phallus. These festivals were famous for their licentiousness, complete with public nudity and orgies. The Liberalia was likely the precursor of May Day, with the May Pole replacing the phallus.[36]

Children were not shielded from this sexuality and wore penis amulets as good-luck charms. Minors grew up around off-color jokes and saucy songs and adults thought it funny when children joined in the merriment. Children also saw their father's concubines (mistresses) and pet young men around the home.[37]

Childhood was over for a female at menses. The line was not so clear for boys. A father or tutor judged when a boy was ready to don the adult garb, usually when they started trimming their mustaches. Once deemed an official adult, Roman male youth immediately used a servant's sexual services or rushed down to Suburra to engage a prostitute.[38]

Roman weddings were raunchy, with guests praising the bride and groom in explicitly sexual terms. On the wedding night it was custom that the man would not deflower his bride out of respect for her timidity; instead he would enter her anally.[39] Wedding guests would stand outside the marriage chamber after the ceremony and await the emergence of the groom to announce he had sealed the deal.

Yet in this sexually free environment, a new attitude budded. The stoic school of philosophy in Rome devised that for physical health purposes,[40] *not* moral, all pleasure should be moderated.[41] As a pleasure, sex was to be limited, and for the sake of Rome's survival the best place to limit it to was the marital bed. For perhaps the first time in Western history, a society valued premarital virginity for males. Even masturbation was thought unhealthy for young men, for it was believed that it made boys mature too quickly, producing an imperfect adult.

This restrictive view of sex was supported by other philosophies of the time. These philosophies were heavily influenced by the Greek philosopher Plato. Plato was a dualist: he believed that there was a physical world and a world of ideas. Our souls were trapped in our bodies and yearned to get back to the world of ideas. The physical body would die and decay but the soul was immortal. This exultation of the mind debased the body and everything associated with it, such as excrement and sex.[42]

Another philosophical innovation of the first century A.D. was companionate marriage. In a companionate marriage the partners are close friends. No longer were women to be head servants with whom the husband occasionally had intercourse for the sole purpose of producing legitimate heirs. This concept of marriage being built on affection is still with us today, and it was arrived at by faulty logic.

The Stoics believed firmly that there was a reason for everything. In evaluating the institution of marriage they tried to discern why marriage was a lifetime commitment when producing children did not require that amount of time. They came to the conclusion that if reasonable beings live together all their lives, it must be a type of lasting friendship.[43]

The Stoics were wrong. Lifelong marriage had not developed based on friendship. They made the common mistake of justifying an institution by finding or creating a current function. Roman wives in the times of the Stoics were denied any meaningful work, but lifelong marriage developed when the distant hunter/gatherer ancestors settled into rural communities, like early Rome. In that context, two people were required to manage all of the necessary duties on a farm.[44] Marriages were originally for life because men were allowed to acquire other wives, so there was no need to end a relationship with a wife who was a useful servant.

This new Stoic concept of companionate marriage took place between the first and second century B.C., and two things should be noted. First, just because affection was not in the old concept of marriage does not mean it never occurred. Since the origin of marriage there were undoubtedly times when the man and woman created a strong emotional bond, however, when this happened it usually came after the wedding, not before.

Second, the new concept made it admirable to like your wife. This was quite different from romantically loving your wife. This was also quite different from what actually occurred. One historian believes that the only practical consequences of this new philosophy were that husbands spoke about their wives differently in front of other men and addressed their wives differently in public.[45] Although in the early second century the Romans began requiring a woman's permission for marriage,[46] money, status, and political maneuvering would still play an important role, as they arguably still do.

VI

CHRISTIANITY
TURNING JESUS INTO A PRUDE

Although it is a popular belief in the West that Christianity changed the Roman Empire's values, the reverse is true. The Roman Empire, specifically Emperor Constantine, *literally* defined Christianity. Constantine gathered and presided over the first ecumenical council (a gathering of bishops to determine Christian doctrine) in 325 A.D.. Constantine assured unanimity by banishing all the bishops who would not accept the finished product—the Roman Catholic Church.[47]

Christianity in the first centuries A.D. was a diverse group of countless sects and cults. The varying interpretations of Jesus' life were even more numerous—as late as 450 A.D. there were at least two hundred different gospel versions circulating in just one jurisdiction.[48] The Christianity that was accepted by Emperor Constantine was a hierarchical and authoritarian version that ruled through fear and force.

Emperor Constantine was not interested in the variants of Christianity that stressed love, pacifism, forgiveness, tolerance, and openness—features that were more in tune with Jesus' message. Constantine, who had his wife boiled alive and his son executed, was looking for a religion to unite his armies and the faltering empire.[49] By conforming their religion to meet his needs, Catholic Church leaders were rewarded greatly.[50] In little more than a hundred years, the Roman Empire went from killing Christians to killing non-Christians.

The Roman Catholic Church proved to be a great authoritarian structure, so great that as the Roman Empire crumbled—because of a shrinking ruling class mentally diminished from lead poisoning, a collapsing economy, overextended resources, invading Germanic tribes from the north, and the bubonic plague in the east[51]—the Church became its European successor.

Whereas the Roman Empire largely left its conquered people free to continue their own cultural traditions and to think independently, the Roman Catholic Church did not. It told people what to think. What it wanted people to think was called morality. Anything it did not want people to think was called heresy and was punishable by death.

In the Greek and Roman Empires, the educated upper classes, who could read and write freely, participated in intellectual life. Under the Catholic Church, education and literacy were restricted to clergy who could read and write only Christian literature. Ancient academies were closed, great libraries were burned, and scientific understanding in some areas was set back millennia.[52] This era has aptly been called the Dark Ages.

This intellectual monopoly had huge ramifications for sexuality in the Western world, and influences us to this day. Powerful men in the church articulated the Western view of sex in the name of Jesus Christ, who despite criticizing adulterers (as then defined),[53] never criticized sex directly.[54] Being a Jew, it was likely that he shared their values of that period.[55] These were that premarital sex was not forbidden, sex was not evil, and celibacy was not favored.[56]

107

However, drawing on sexual theories already popular with the Roman Neo-Platonists and Stoics,[57] the following men falsely encoded in Christ's name the enduring concept that sex is evil:

St. Paul (3 A.D.–67 A.D.) — Paul never met Jesus, but when he was around thirty years old he converted to Christianity from Judaism and became a missionary. Paul's writings have become Christian scripture and are a part of the New Testament. His immense contributions to the spread of Christianity have led some to call him its second founder.[58]

However, when it comes to Christianity's view of sex, Paul could be considered its first founder. Paul, like Jesus, was never married. Perhaps because of this bias, Paul wrote to early Christians that celibacy was better than sex, even marital sex, as it allowed one to focus on holy matters.[59] Paul openly admitted that this was his opinion, and that he did not know if Christ spoke on the matter.[60] He also made it clear that he based this advice on his belief that Jesus' second return would happen shortly.[61]

After two millennia it is apparent that living as if Jesus' return is months away is impractical. Considering how Christians have wielded Paul's passage, it is acutely ironic that he wrote that it was not meant to limit people's freedom.

Tertullian (circa 150 A.D.–240 A.D.) — Tertullian was the son of a Roman military officer in Africa. He converted to Christianity in his late forties and made many contributions to Christian theology. Building on Paul's questionable logic,[62] Tertullian argued that marriage was permissible but that God preferred that men and women practice celibacy.

He blamed women for original sin, calling them the devil's gateway.[63] Attractive women threatened males' salvation. Cosmetics were tools of lust and natural beauty should instead be obliterated by concealment and neglect. He advised his wife that when they would meet in heaven there would be no sex, "There will at that day be no resumption of voluptuous disgrace between us. No such frivolities, no such impurities, does God promise to His servants."[64]

St. Augustine[65] (354 A.D.–430 A.D.) — Augustine grew up in North Africa with a macho, unfaithful, pagan father and a meek, virtuous, Christian mother. His mother, Monica, was determined to make him a Christian. At the age of twenty-nine he was still torn between pursuing the sexual bravado of his father or the piety of his mother. He decided to escape his mother by moving to Rome. She tearfully pleaded for him to stay or to take her with him, so he lied to her about the departure date and left her praying in a dockside chapel as his boat left.

She found him two years later and moved in with him. At her bidding, he finally got rid of the concubine to whom he had been faithful for fifteen years and with whom he had a son. Instead, he became engaged to a twelve-year-old girl. Not able to wait the two years for his fiancé to be of marriageable age, he took up with another concubine. At this point he uttered his famous prayer, "Give me chastity—but not yet."[66]

At the age of thirty-two, to his mother's delight, Augustine converted to Christianity after reading St. Paul's words urging Christians not to party but to focus on Jesus Christ.[67] Augustine abandoned his concubine and his fiancé, and returned to Africa to found a monastery of celibate men. Through the voluminous writings that followed, Augustine had an enormous influence on Christian theology, particularly regarding sexual ethics.

Augustine believed that no one could control an aroused sex drive and that if it was not for the restraint of Christian marriage, "people would have intercourse indiscriminately, like dogs."[68] "This diabolical excitement of the genitals" could paralyze rational thought.[69] Proof of its power was his inability to control his erections and his inability to give up his first concubine.[70]

Augustine theorized that the unruly sex drive, like death, was caused by original sin. If Adam and Eve had not eaten the forbidden fruit, sex would have been as God intended it—mechanical and without passion. He compared the sexual body control of people in paradise to people in this world that can wiggle their ears one at a time or who can continuously fart musical notes at will. Because original sin is transferred with semen during the sex act, all people are born sinners.

Augustine believed that to merit God's salvation and be returned to paradise, one must resist the depraved sexual craving. He wrote that although God prefers virgins, for those not up to the task the only acceptable time to have intercourse is when one is explicitly trying to have a child with one's spouse. The sooner a married couple refrained from having this acceptable type of sex, the more approval they would receive from God. Augustine cemented the theological wall between personal affection and sexual expression.

The rhetoric of the Church Fathers was not limited to faulty reasoning. St. Jerome, the virginophile, was so enamored with sexual purity that he fraudulently spun his Latin translation of the Bible (the one adopted by the Catholic Church) so that it appeared more anti-sexual.[71]

It should also be recognized that St. Augustine had a very active sex life before taking up his love of celibacy, and there is no evidence that Tertullian and Paul were sexually restrained as young men. Testosterone levels drop off considerably as men age. For Tertullian, who converted in his forties, and St. Paul and St. Augustine, who converted in their thirties, this suggests hypocrisy.

Lastly, there was opposition to transforming Jesus' religion into an anti-sexual vehicle. One such challenger was Pelagius. Pelagius was a man who disagreed with Augustine's view that original sin was transferred to everyone through semen. He accused Augustine of being heavily influenced by another religion, Manichaeism. (Augustine was formerly a Manichean.) In 416 A.D. Augustine wrote to the bishop of Rome advising him that Pelagius' ideas would threaten the Church's power. An African bishop who was friends with Augustine sent eighty Numidian stallions to the imperial court as a bribe. In 418 A.D. the Pope sided with Augustine and Pelagius was excommunicated.

The Roman Empire, which so heavily influenced Christianity, eventually waned. The first Christian Roman Emperor, Constantine, moved the capital of the Roman Empire from Rome to Constantinople (now Istanbul, Turkey) in 330 A.D.. This move was the result of a steady decline of the Roman Empire's strength in Europe. Over the previous hundred years the Empire had degenerated into an unstable state with generals becoming emperors and then being assassinated in quick succession.

During this tumultuous time the Germanic tribes from the north picked away at the Western Roman Empire province by province. Rome was sacked, first by the Visigoths in 410 A.D., and again by the Vandals forty-five years later. In 476 A.D. the Western Roman Empire officially ended when the German barbarian Odoacer became King of Italy.

VII

The Middle Ages
Sex is a Sin? Who Cares?

The usurpation of power away from Rome was gradual. As the floundering Roman government lost the allegiance of the people, Rome had to rely more and more on German soldiers. By the time Odoacer officially deposed the last Western Roman Emperor, the child Romulus Augustus, most of the soldiers and officers of the Roman army were Germanic.

Relatively little is known about the culture of the Germanic tribes because, unlike the Romans, they had an oral tradition that left no written records. It is likely the Germanic tribes practiced the resource polygyny of the Neolithic era:[72] that is, it was acceptable to have more than one wife, but few men had the resources to do it.

Although German leaders officially adopted Christianity soon after inheriting Europe, it is unlikely their populaces actually practiced it until much later.[73] The rural Germans' Christianity was probably limited to being baptized and adding Christ to their pantheon of gods. Worshipping their old gods and the new Jesus was a way of hedging their divine bets.[74] This would not change until monks and priests slowly penetrated Europe's vast forests.

A. Penitentials: Did You Come My Son?

Priests in medieval Europe used regional guides called penitentials. To understand penitentials, one must understand the practice of confession. Early Christians confessed their sins publicly before other Christians, but by the sixth century, Christians would confess privately to a priest. The priest would forgive the sinner and set a penance. The penance was a voluntary self-punishment to atone for the sin. (Giving money to the Church could substitute for penance and was called an indulgence.) Penitentials were guidelines for setting penances.

The advantage of sex's omnipresence was that it led to continuous sinning. This in turn led to a reliance on priests to continuously purge one's soul for the afterlife and, conveniently, it also produced regular indulgences to the church. Therefore,

111

penitentials categorized sexual sins in great detail. Nocturnal emissions warranted seven days of fasting (eating only bread and water). Masturbation required twenty days of fasting. Coitus interruptus (the withdrawal of the penis immediately prior to ejaculation to prevent pregnancy) warranted two to ten years of penance. Anal intercourse, oral sex, and potions that created sterility were almost as sinful as homicide.[75]

Homosexual acts were explicitly broken down into type of contact, result, and age of participants. For example, in one seventh-century penitential, offenders younger than twenty who kissed were advised to do six special fasts, however, if the kissing resulted in ejaculation, that was upped to ten.[76]

The sexual scrutiny extended to marital sex as well. Marital sex was only acceptable at night, if the participants were partially clothed, and if they used the missionary position. The woman could not be pregnant, nursing, or menstruating. Major saints' days, Lent, Advent, Fridays, and Sundays were off-limits. This left roughly fifty nights a year available for sex.[77] Thinking about sex was also off-limits, with lustful thoughts requiring penance as well. Even the "sin" of marriage required that a couple not enter the Church for thirty days.[78]

B. Medieval Names: Starring John Fillecunt

Getting the populace to associate sex with shame was a slow process, as evidenced by the court and tax records of England at the start of the second millennium. At this point in history surnames (last names) were still not in use, and people used bynames instead. Bynames were often taken from a person's father, for example "John Son of Samuel"; from the name of a town, such as "John of York"; or from an occupation, such as "John the Smith." There were also bynames that came from notable characteristics, and this latter category shows how comfortable people still were with sex.

John Fillecunt (fill cunt) was recorded in 1246 and Bele Wydecunthe (wide cunt) was recorded in 1328.[79] Other bynames included Balloc (testicle), Coyldeor (golden testicles), Assbollock (donkey's testicles), Levelaunce (raise spear, the French version of Wagstaff or Shakespeare), Wytepintell (white penis), Coltepyntel (colt's penis), Cuntles (without cunt), Clawcunte, Preyketayl (penetrate-vagina), Strekelevedy (stroke lady), and Swetabedde (sweet in bed).[80] Numerous streets contained sexual references as well, like Gropecuntelane in London and a Rue Grattecon (Scratchcunt Street) in Paris.

C. The Priests: Stupid and Horny

The Roman Catholic Church's medieval influence on sexual attitudes was dubious. For example, premarital sex was a sin. However, sexual relations between unmarried men and women seemed natural and inevitable. Over one thousand years after Europe was first Christianized, people still could not understand how such conduct could be sinful,[81] and many priests concurred. Reflecting a frustration expressed in other writings of his time, one twelfth-century cleric wrote bluntly, "there are certain stupid priests, [priests] in name only, who believe that simple fornication is a [minor] sin."[82]

Another example of sex's resilience was clerical celibacy. Since celibacy was the spiritually superior state, as early as 385 A.D. Pope Siricius tried to require it for all clergy. This was strongly opposed and largely ignored. It was so disregarded that villages would sometimes insist a priest take a mistress to ensure the fidelity of the parishioners' wives.[83] This was not done in folly, as one remarkable bishop in the thirteenth century fathered sixty-five illegitimate children before being deposed.[84]

The Church's tolerance would not last. By the twelfth century it had grown extremely rich and there was now an added incentive to enforcing clerical celibacy—preventing this wealth from passing out of the Church via heirs.[85] In 1139 A.D. the Church again ruled that the clergy could no longer be married, but the response was not any warmer in this millennium. The outraged clergy in Paris violently drove their bishop out of his cathedral and the royal family had to protect him from further harm. A century earlier the clergy in what is now Wales had burned alive a supporter of clerical celibacy.

Understandably, some fearful bishops refused to publish the decree. Eventually the Church was able to create an unmarried clergy, but not a chaste one. The clergy resorted to mistresses, prostitutes, or a succession of sexual partners to fulfill their "natural instincts."[86] It is estimated that by the sixteenth century England had a hundred thousand prostitutes whose prime customers were clergy.[87]

This toleration of clerical sexual activity, which extended into the twelfth century, was also applied to prostitution. The general attitude was that of St. Thomas Aquinas (circa 1225–1274), who compared prostitution's value to sewers in a palace. If you take away the sewers the palace becomes polluted. Even the venerable Augustine believed prostitution was a necessary evil. One of the greater evils prostitution was thought to prevent was the rape and seduction of honest women by men who did not have a sexual outlet. Dijon, France, used prostitution as a preventative measure for an epidemic of gang rapes.[88]

For this reason, many towns regulated prostitution through taxes or institutionalized municipal brothels. In towns run by the Church, and in some parts of Europe, monasteries ran brothels. In the city of Avignon, in what is now France, there was a Church brothel in which the women spent part of the day praying and handling religious duties and the rest servicing Christian customers.[89] The capital of the Church itself, Rome, is estimated to have had seven thousand prostitutes in 1490. The women lived in houses owned by the church and it was common to see them walking the streets with priests,[90] unsurprising considering several popes maintained "holy brothels."[91]

The relative tolerance for premarital sex, clerical sexual activity, and prostitution for much of the Middle Ages demonstrated the Church's lack of progress in making sex a shameful act in the minds of the people. However, the difficulty of the task must be recognized.

Fewer than one percent of Europe's population were well-born nobility, that is, the class studied in high school history lessons.[92] Rural peasants were eighty to ninety percent of Europe's population and they had no qualms about going naked in the summertime. Most medieval people did not have the luxury of privacy. Parents would be naked and have sex around children and other relatives—often in the same bed— simply because there was nowhere else to go.[93] Many residences consisted of only one room with one hearth as a heat source. Medieval weddings commonly involved a couple being placed in bed together, naked, in front of witnesses.[94] In addition, most Europeans were accustomed to seeing the sexual behavior of farm animals.

Sex in this environment was like eating, a banal and unremarkable event, noteworthy only when it impinged on the property rights of a male, such as a father or a husband. To give sex the psychological weight that it now has was a gigantic endeavor and it required a stronger tool than the confessional.

VIII

The Inquisition
Sex is a Sin. Meet the Rack.

A. The Process: Torture is Not Litigious

During the Middle Ages, people who sinned fell under the jurisdiction of the church courts. Through fees and fines these courts brought in a significant amount of money. Up until 1200 A.D., these courts operated under an accusatory process, much like other medieval courts. Under an accusatory process, the individual had to accuse someone of a crime openly in court and produce witnesses. Court costs were paid by the accuser until the verdict. This process protected defendants against frivolous and malicious cases.

Church lawyers realized that sexual crimes and heresies were difficult to prosecute in this manner. Finding the common requirement of two witnesses was rare and people did not like making these accusations publicly. Proceedings were developed to make prosecution easier.

Under these proceedings *per inquisitionem* a judge began the investigation, called the witnesses, made judgment, and then passed sentence. The accused was denied a right to counsel, not told where or when the offense occurred, and was not told who the witnesses were.[95] The judge could use torture to generate a confession and to root out other wrongdoers. In 1231 A.D. Pope Gregory IX established a formal tribunal to conduct proceedings *per inquisitonem*. It was called the Inquisition.

Over time the Inquisition became a terrifying machine. Answering only to the pope, its power was virtually unchecked. It began as only one prosecutorial option, but predictably became the only one used. The accusatory process was deemed too "litigious."[96] Inquisitors and their assistants were soon allowed to carry arms and had the right to absolve each other of any acts of violence. When torture victims died it was deemed that the devil broke their necks. Inquisitors grew immensely wealthy. They collected bribes from the rich,[97] and could claim all the money and property of alleged heretics.[98]

The Inquisition was officially limited to heresies—that is, false beliefs of church members. However, any act in violation of the Church's canons could be creatively interpreted as false belief. For example, a priest who had a concubine was not punished for his lechery, but for his belief that putting on the sacred vestments purified him in his daily conduction of mass.

B. The Punishment: Burn or Go to Hell

Those found guilty by the Inquisition were not punished. As mentioned above, the Inquisition only prescribed penance. Penance was a "voluntary" deed to redeem oneself with God. Interestingly, the harshest penance was burning at the stake.[99] This was reserved for those who failed to complete their original penance, relapsed into heresy, or refused to confess. Burnings were not common, although it did not take many public mass burnings (*autos da fé*) to have the desired effect.[100]

Other penances were used more frequently. Flogging was commonplace. Every Sunday the heretic was stripped in front of the congregation and lashed by the priest during mass. This could go on for her entire life, or until the Inquisitor remembered/ decided to liberate her. Another prevalent penance was wearing conspicuous orange or red cloth crosses on the chest and back for the rest of one's life.[101] The stigma of these made ridicule common, and employment difficult if not impossible.

The guilty would also be sent on pilgrimages to holy places or on crusades (soldier missions for the Church). Pilgrimages to holy destinations in distant places were no easy task and could take years. Usually the pilgrim would be flogged by a priest at the holy destination, given documentation of his arrival, and then sent back. Families back home could perish without the protection and support of the penitent. However, the Church forbid mitigating penance for age, sickness, pregnancy, or dependents. For socializing with heretics, one ninety-year-old man was required to travel over one thousand miles round-trip from Southern France to Northwest Spain.

Imprisonment was also a common penance. The horrible conditions of medieval prisons meant that inhabitants frequently died of illness or went insane. Because these penances were "voluntary," the request to other jurisdictions for an escapee's capture and return would describe the fugitive as "one insanely led to reject the salutary medicine offered for his cure, and to spurn the wine and oil which were soothing his wounds."[102]

The torture used to judge one's innocence and to root out fellow heretics was even worse than the penances. The most common method of torture was called the hoist or "the queen of torments."[103] In the hoist, a person's wrists were tied behind his or her back with a rope. The person was then lifted by this rope and held elevated for a period of time. In addition to the excruciating pain, the hoist could dislocate one's shoulders and cut the flesh of their wrists. Weights could be added to the person's feet for added effect. Sometimes the victim would be partially lowered with a sudden jerk halting their descent. This could tear limbs asunder.

The Inquisition's form of water torture was called the "Wooden Horse." The Wooden Horse was developed and favored by the Dutch Inquisition. It involved tying someone horizontally to a wooden bench, known as the "horse." An iron band kept the person's head immobile and an iron prong kept their mouth open. The nostrils were plugged, and a strip of linen was shoved down the throat. Water was then dripped onto the linen. As the linen became totally damp the person would be forced to inhale the linen, choking themselves. The linen, often bloodied, would be pulled out before death would occur, and the process repeated.[104]

Another common method was the rack. The rack was a structure on which the accused was laid and secured. Cords would tie the wrists and ankles to beams. A rod would be placed between the cord and the person's limb and then twisted. This twisting constricted the cord, and as it got progressively tighter caused the tearing away of skin and flesh.

Other torture used in the Inquisition included rubbing body parts with lard or grease and roasting them, or lighting aflame only certain body parts through the use of sulfur. Leg-screws, thumb-screws and toe-screws would crush bone. Slowly dripping water on a forehead would bring about insanity.[105] One creative torture technique involved putting a large dish of mice upside down on a victim's stomach. A fire was then lit on top of the dish and the alarmed mice would then burrow into the stomach. Those tortured were often stripped completely naked,[106] and the tools used would frequently be blessed with holy water and inscribed with "Glory be only to God."[107]

C. The Effect: Wretched Slavery

It is difficult to appreciate the effect the Inquisition had on the psychology of the people. Anyone could accuse anyone of anything. Children were to inform on parents, spouses on each other. This backstabbing was encouraged by the fact that merely interacting with heretics was heresy. In 1322 an Inquisitor sentenced three men to perform seventeen pilgrimages. Their malfeasance was that fifteen to twenty years earlier they had seen heretical teachers in their fathers' homes without knowing what they were.[108]

Informants were also entitled to a portion of the heretic's confiscated property, thus adding incentive to anyone looking to settle a grudge.[109] One historian wrote about the Spanish Inquisition, "Petty denunciations were the rule rather than the exception."[110] He gave as an example a woman who was reported to the Inquisition for smiling when hearing the Virgin Mary mentioned.

A Spaniard wrote in the 1490s that: "[People] were deprived of the liberty to hear and talk freely, since in all the cities, towns, and villages there were persons to give information of what went on. This was considered by some the most wretched slavery and equal to death."[111]

As no one could be certain of the piousness of another, distrust seeped into every daily interaction. In 1538 a writer wrote of the Spanish Inquisition's effects in the city of Toledo:

> [P]reachers do not dare to preach, and those who preach do not dare to touch on contentious matters, for their lives and honor are in the mouths of... ignoramuses, and nobody in this life is without his policeman... Bit by bit many rich people leave the country for foreign realms, in order not to live all their lives in fear and trembling every time an officer of the Inquisition enters their house; for continual fear is a worse death than a sudden demise.[112]

Over time, the ruthless Inquisition helped transform rational and natural sexual attitudes into those filled with anxiety and guilt.[113] The Inquisition did not end until 1816.

IX

THE PROTESTANT REFORMATION
A MONK WANTS SEX

The Church's harsh treatment of the general populace did not extend to the rulers of medieval Europe. Although extremely wealthy and powerful, the Church's papal army was insignificant, and relied on the secular authorities to enforce its edicts.[114] The cooperation varied widely from area to area, and from time period to time period. However, the Church's ability to manipulate this situation was critically hampered in the fifteenth century by deepening corruption.

Foul play and malfeasance had been rife in the Church ever since its bureaucratic inception with Constantine. Less than thirty years after his death in 337 A.D., Damasus became pope only after his supporters trapped 137 supporters of his rival in a church and killed them.[115]

Other examples of papal corruption included the ninth century's Pope Stephen VII, who exhumed his predecessor and put the eleven-month-old rotting corpse on trial after garbing it in full pontifical vestments.[116] The tenth century had John XII, who was charged with accepting payments for ordaining bishops, blinding one member of the clergy, killing another by castration, and bedding numerous women, including his own niece. He later had one of his accusers' tongue pulled out, another lost a hand, and another lost a nose and some fingers.[117]

However, John XII was merely ahead of his time in selling an ordination. By the fourteenth century everything was for sale. This not only included positions in the Church (simony), but also rulings, adjudications, indulgences, absolutions, and relics.[118]

A. Catholic Hypocrisy: Hot Papal Orgies[119]

The papacy's degradation hit its nadir at the end of the fifteenth century with Alexander VI, formerly known as Rodrigo Borgia. As a young Cardinal, Borgia received a sharp rebuke from Pope Pius II for throwing an unruly party/orgy in

Siena, Italy, in which Siena's most beautiful young women had been invited but their male relations had not.[120] Borgia would eventually have ten known children.

Four notable children were fathered by Rosa Vannozza dei Catanei, the young daughter of one of his favorite mistresses. According to Roman legend, when Borgia was copulating with Vannozza dei Catanei's mother, his attention was drawn to Vannozza dei Catanei's naked adolescent body lying beside them. Her spread legs were mimicking her mother's thrusts, but with a rhythmic rotation of the hips that so enticed Borgia he swapped partners mid-stroke.

Borgia enjoyed bedding married women and was particularly aroused if he had been the one to officiate her vows. He married Vannozza dei Catanei off to two of her eventual husbands. Despite keeping a stable of women on hand, he did have favorites. When he was fifty-nine, he replaced Vannozza dei Catanei in this role with the "breathtakingly lovely" Giulia Farnese.[121] Conforming to his *modus operandi*, Borgia married the fifteen-year-old off, and following the ceremony, the new husband was told he was needed elsewhere. Farnese was then led to Borgia's bedchamber and as his favorite mistress she was soon known throughout Italy as the bride of Christ.[122]

When Borgia bought the papacy in 1492 and became Pope Alexander VI, his theme parties became stupendous spectacles. The most notorious was the Ballet of the Chestnuts. Approaching the papal palace for a Borgia party one would see living statues, gilded young men and women striking erotic poses devoid of clothing. After the Ballet of Chestnuts' banquet, the fifty most beautiful prostitutes of Rome danced with the guests and simultaneously disrobed. Candelabras and chestnuts were then scattered on the floor and the prostitutes crawled around the candles picking the chestnuts up. The male guests then stripped and ran out on the floor to congress. Servants kept track of each man's orgasms. After everyone was satiated the Pope and his daughter, Lucrezia, gave out awards for those who were able to orgasm the most.

Borgia's children would further his legacy. His beautiful daughter by Vannozza dei Catanei, Lucrezia Borgia, was bright, learned, and had inherited her father's prodigious sex drive. Her father took advantage of the fact that men found her ravishing to cement his political alliances. He first married her off at thirteen and then used his power of annulment to remarry her when it was advantageous. By the age of twenty-one she was renowned for her "orgasmic exploits," with all the positions, groupings, and situations that could entail.[123]

Her brother, Cesare Borgia, was just as sensational. He was an eloquent and gallant killer, skilled at the Italian politics of the time, which were rife with back-dealings and assassinations. Cesare was made a cardinal by his father, an unprecedented maneuver for an illegitimate child. Cesare also employed Leonardo da Vinci and was the model for *The Prince*, written by his acquaintance Machiavelli.

In 1497, Borgia divorced Lucrezia from her first husband by publicly calling him impotent. This was a grave insult and the husband responded that the real reason was because Borgia wanted Lucrezia for himself. Whether or not this was Borgia's motive, it is now known that Borgia was sleeping with her. As this gossip electrified Italy, it was also reported that Lucrezia was caught in a love triangle between her brothers, Cesare and Juan. That summer Juan was found in the Tiber River stabbed to death. Cesare, as a known murderer, was generally assumed responsible.

Lucrezia became pregnant during the absence of her first husband. The original Borgia plan was to hide Lucrezia in a convent during her pregnancy. Unfortunately, Lucrezia's scandalous behavior continued at the convent, and spread to the nuns, whose convent soon became notorious. The formal annulment ceremony of her first marriage occurred when Lucrezia was six months pregnant. Despite wearing a loose dress, the crowd was aware of her incestuous dalliances and when she was officially declared a virgin it broke into guffaws.

Whether the baby boy, Giovanni, belonged to her father or her brother is uncertain. Borgia made two proclamations. The public one announced the boy, Giovanni, to be the son of Cesare and an unmarried woman. A second secret bull declared Giovanni to be the son of Borgia and the unmarried woman. The next husband that Borgia strategically arranged for Lucrezia was eventually murdered by Cesare. Lucrezia would eventually outlive her father, her son, and her brother, Cesare, who was assassinated in 1507, to become a respectable princess.

B. Martin Luther: A Piece of Shit Says Jesus Screwed[124]

While the corrupt papacy was trashing the Church's reputation, two developments were also weakening the Church's position. First, secular power was consolidating in Europe. Powerful kings were emerging that could stand up to the

Church better than their fragmented forebears. Second, communication improved greatly after the invention of the printing press in 1440.

The printing press broke the Church's stranglehold on the written word. What previously had to be tediously hand-copied by monks could now be quickly copied and disseminated. Heretical ideas, which before had to be spread largely by word of mouth, could now be transferred on paper anonymously. In addition, the printing press made the Bible more accessible to the general populace, so that they could finally judge the Catholic Church's interpretation of it for themselves.[125]

Church corruption, consolidated secular power, and the printing press allowed the heresy of a German monk, Martin Luther (1483–1546), to flourish in the sixteenth century. In 1517, Luther nailed a list of ninety-five theses to the church door in Wittenberg (in what is now Germany), questioning the Church's practice of selling indulgences.[126] As discussed earlier, people of means had been buying indulgences from the Church that released them from penance—even for murder.[127] Luther felt that this was a corrupt practice, and one not authorized by the Bible. Without Luther's knowledge, printers made copies of his theses and distributed them.

These printings allowed Luther's ideas to quickly find a wide and supportive audience. Perhaps more importantly, Luther was protected by a prominent German prince, Frederick III of Saxony. After Luther was condemned as a heretic, Frederick III sheltered Luther in his castle under the alias Junker Georg. Numerous German princes adopted Luther's precepts and became Lutherans.[128]

Although there may have been theological reasons behind their conversions, adopting Lutheranism allowed the princes to take back the substantial amount of Church property in their regions, and to save their subjects from paying the Church taxes, fines, indulgences, etc., which all flowed to Rome.[129] These princes formed an alliance that fought the Catholic military forces that soon gathered to stamp out the heresy.

This reform movement was called the Protestant Reformation, after the formal protest filed by these German princes. As one of its first religious leaders, Luther's interpretation of sex was largely adopted into this new branch of Christianity.

Recognizing the powerful sex drive within people, Luther believed that chastity was an unreasonable expectation. (He assumed that even Jesus Christ partook.)[130] To Luther the best Christian was not one who unsuccessfully tried to purge sex from her life, but one who channeled that sex drive into marriage. Instead of trying to be celibate, everyone should marry as soon as possible after puberty. This extended to the clergy. In this way, Luther elevated the status of marriage. Virgins were no longer morally better and marriage was now seen as "the cornerstone of society."[131]

This glorification of marriage may have caused the greater suspicion of single people that followed. In 1572 Wismar, Germany, kicked out of town all unmarried women who were not domestic servants, because these women pretended to sew when in reality they were engaged in "great lewdness."[132] In many places fashions used to attract the other sex, such as cleavage and codpieces,[133] were outlawed. Pastors and authorities also attacked activities where single people could interact with the opposite sex, such as festivals. Dancing was outlawed in many places as it was "the devil's pimp."[134]

Another notable break with Catholicism by Luther was his vehement stance against prostitution. Whereas Catholicism was relatively tolerant, Luther called prostitutes "stinking … tools of the devil."[135] They were soon considered worse than other criminals for, unlike other criminals, they seduced other citizens into sin. Predictably, in the 1500s there was a wave of brothel closings.[136]

Luther and other Protestant leaders discovered, like the Catholic Church before them, that the reward of heaven in the afterlife was not enough to extinguish extramarital sex. In Protestant areas, sins were increasingly outlawed by the secular authorities, thus beginning the "criminalization of sin."[137] Whereas Roman Catholicism put the Church in the bedroom, the Protestant Reformation put the government in there as well. Catholics and Protestants both regarded sexual purity as a sign of God's favor,[138] and they were now competing to be the purest.

C. John Calvin: Sourpuss

The Frenchman John Calvin (1509–1564) was a leader of the Protestants' moral charge. Unlike the entertaining Luther, who enjoyed drinking beer and playing the flute and the lute, Calvin was petite, ailing, and dour. His righteousness began early in life. As a youth his classmates called him "Accusativus" for criticizing and reporting their behavior.[139]

As an adult, Calvin suffered from migraine headaches, indigestion, ulcers, gout, kidney stones, pulmonary tuberculosis, and temper tantrums. Not surprisingly, Calvin's God was a pitiless tyrant, and almost all humans were doomed to his eternal damnation. God's mercy would be shown to a very predetermined few, and nothing one did could affect the outcome. Pious, charitable, or good people had no advantage over anyone else. Calvin considered life to be valueless. He wrote, "We are all made of mud, and this mud is not just on the hem of our gown, or on the sole of our boots, or in our shoes. We are full of it, we are nothing but mud and filth both inside and outside."[140]

With his long thin face and "domed forehead,"[141] Calvin would emerge as the dictator of morals in the city of Geneva, in what is now Switzerland. Calvin ruthlessly had his critics tortured and killed,[142] and enforced his misery on its citizenry. No tomfoolery to take one's mind off of holy matters was allowed.[143] Singing, acting, dancing, church bells, organs ("the Devil's bagpipe"), altar candles, cursing, gambling, playing cards, serving too many dishes at dinner, revealing dress, pictures, statues, elegant hairstyles,[144] rouge, and jewelry were all declared sinful or criminal.

Improper sexuality was severely punished. Single pregnant women were drowned. Calvin was not nepotistic: when his stepson was found in bed with another woman and his daughter-in-law behind a haystack with another man, all four adulterers were executed.

Calvin's strict form of Christianity took hold in other parts of Northern Europe as well. In England there were numerous Protestant splinter groups who believed the form of Protestantism adopted there was not Calvinist enough. They viewed England as a Sodom, a land that God would destroy for its sexual sins. Called Puritans by their detractors, large numbers of them left England to bring Calvin's piety to America.

X

PURITAN AMERICA
GOD HATES YOU. DON'T HAVE SEX.[145]

In 1620 the first group containing Puritans settled in what is now Plymouth, Massachusetts. Over the next several decades thousands more Puritans would arrive in what is now America. From 1629 to 1691 the Puritans lived in a Calvinist theocracy.

124

Consistent with the Calvinist ideal, they lived in strict and orderly communities that closely monitored personal morality. The Puritans wanted to create a society that would be like a "city upon a hill."[146] By pleasing God, God would make them a glory to be admired and imitated by the rest of the world.

Because God would punish the community for the sins of any one person, snooping was encouraged. In colonial times this was easy to do in the small, isolated communities and relatively porous homes. Court documents refer to neighbors peering through holes and pulling out loose boards to spy. Clement Coldom of Gloucester, Massachusetts, ripped a door from its hinges to learn what his neighbor, John Pearce, was doing with "the widow Stannard" at night.[147]

Based on the Bible's Old Testament, the law codes were harsh. Death was the penalty for adultery,[148] bestiality,[149] and sex between males. Lesser punishments were meted for crimes such as overly flirtatious behavior ("lewd and lascivious carriage"), giving one's attention to several suitors ("wanton dalliance"), and courting a woman without first seeking the permission of her parents.[150]

Puritan ministers fulminated against sexuality from the pulpit. Even marital sex was to be moderated, as sex of any type was unclean, and lust damaged both spiritual and physical health. Grave "fire and brimstone" sermons attempted to scare audiences straight with graphic images of hell. If the following passage bores, it should be considered that these orations would last for two to three hours and those whose attention strayed would be hit with a switch.

> The God that holds you over the pit of hell, much as one holds a spider, or some loathsome insect over the fire, abhors you, and is dreadfully provoked: his wrath towards you burns like fire; he looks upon you as worthy of nothing else, but to be cast into the fire ... you are ten thousand times more abominable in his eyes, than the most hateful venomous serpent is in ours. You have offended him infinitely more than ever a stubborn rebel did his prince; and yet it is nothing but his hand that holds you from falling into the fire every moment. It is to be ascribed to nothing else, that you did not go to hell the last night; that you [were] suffered to awake again in this world, after you closed your eyes to sleep. And there is no other

reason to be given, why you have not dropped into hell since you arose in the morning, but that God's hand has held you up. There is no other reason to be given why you have not gone to hell, since you have sat here in the house of God, provoking his pure eyes by your sinful wicked manner of attending his solemn worship. Yea, there is nothing else that is to be given as a reason why you do not this very moment drop down into hell.[151]

Death was considerably more familiar to Puritans than to modern populations, thus providing these endless orations with more relevancy and power. Child mortality rates are estimated to have been around fifty percent, while in some regions one in five colonial mothers could expect to die from childbirth.[152] Life expectancies were low and killing animals was a part of farm life. The potency of these speeches can be seen in the anecdotes of fearful children crying and remorseful adults attempting suicide.

For example, in the late 1600s Samuel Sewall of Boston wrote in his diary that his young daughter, Elizabeth, was sad all day. After dinner she broke into tears causing everyone in the family to cry. Elizabeth revealed after questioning that she was afraid of going to hell. In another incident, Sewall lectured his ten-year-old son, Sam, about the need to prepare for death, and recorded, "He seemed not much to mind, eating an apple."[153] However, later that night during prayers Sam cried and expressed a fear of death.

Despite this intense enculturation, sex and nudity were still common sights. Simple homes still did not provide privacy and some scenarios have been recorded. One female recalled being in bed with her siblings and her mother when they were joined by a man. Her mother instructed them to "lie further or else shee would kick us out of bed."[154]

The court records of the Puritans betray their reputation for vanquishing sex. In practice, use of the death penalty for sexual offenses was extremely rare. As long as one confessed and paid the penalty, the congregation was likely to quickly reinstate the person without a loss of status.

The language of the offenders is revealing as well. Abigail Bush of Westfield was censured in 1697 for commenting that her father's new wife was "as hot as a bitch."[155] In a 1771 bastardy case John Harrington denied being the father of a child. He stated on the record, "I fucked her once, but I minded my pullbacks. I sware I did not get it."[156] He was convicted.

Lastly, the Puritans reported on each other's sexual indiscretions surprisingly infrequently, considering the encouragement and ability to do so.[157] In 1664 in Concord, Massachusetts, the meddling of Thomas Pinion led to a derisive satiric verse being posted to the church and addressed to "cunstable" Thomas Pinion.[158] This revolt against prudery was not limited to Concordians; a new worldview was growing in Europe that was trying to do the same to the cunstables of Christianity.

NOTES

1. Kathleen Deveny and Raina Kelley, "Girls Gone Bad?" *Newsweek*, 12 Feb. 2007, pp. 3, 41.
2. Marc Peyser, "Family TV Goes Down the Tube," *Newsweek*, 23 Feb. 2004; and Daniel Henninger, "Jacksonian Era," *Wall Street Journal*, 6 Feb. 2004.
3. Nancy White, "Plain-Talk," *Christian Science Monitor*, 6 Aug. 1999.
4. Suzanne Fields, "Janet and a Shameless Culture," *Washington Times*, 5 Feb. 2004.
5. At this time radio was established and television was emerging. Because of the limited number of broadcast channels and the national distribution of programming, the government could censor the information people received like never before. Before this, people received their information from localized and splintered sources, such as books, newspapers, and personal conversations, which were impossible to censor completely.
6. Monogamy used to be reported for ten to fifteen percent of all primate species, and roughly three percent of all mammals. However, DNA tests are revealing that in these supposedly monogamous species "cheating" is rampant. David Barash and Judith Lipton, *Myth of Monogamy* (2001), pp. 10, 146.
7. Clellan Ford and Frank Beach, *Patterns of Sexual Behavior* (1951), pp. 107–108, 113.
8. Helen Fisher, *Anatomy of Love* (1992), p. 131.
9. Estrus is the recurrent state in female mammals in which they are capable of conceiving and most willing to mate.
10. Bonobo information primarily from Frans de Waal, "Bonobo Sex and Society," *Scientific American*, Mar. 1995, pp. 82–88.
11. This tit for tat by the bonobos, chimpanzees, and other primates suggests prostitution is natural to our species.
12. Bonobos have a sexual sign language of at least twenty-five signs. Two are "spread your legs," and "adjust your genitals." Bruce Bagemihl, *Biological Exuberance* (1999), pp. 66–67.
13. The following description of early evolution is from the theorizing of Helen Fisher. Fisher, *Anatomy of Love*, pp. 144–149.
14. Ibid., pp. 152–154.
15. In 2010 Christopher Ryan and Cacilda Jethá argued in *Sex at Dawn* that early humans engaged in group marriage and that multi-partner bonds are our natural state (pp. 44–45). A few of the reasons why I disagree include the phenomenon of sexual jealousy; the fact that most current hunter-gatherer cultures are monogamous albeit with plenty of adultery (Barash, *Myth of Monogamy*, p. 136); and group marriages'/polyamory's failure to gain popularity, for example, the failure of the group marriage movement following the

publication of Robert Rimmer's *The Harrad Experiment* in 1966. For a scholarly critique of *Sex at Dawn* see Ryan Ellsworth's 2011 article in *Evolutionary Psychology*, "The Human That Never Evolved."

16. Four years is the usual birth spacing in primitive societies. Ovulation is suppressed longer from continual nursing, more exercise, and poorer diet. Four years is also the modern worldwide divorce peak, suggesting a "four year itch" that could be biologically based. Fisher, *Anatomy of Love*, 152–154.

17. Barash, *Myth of Monogamy*, p. 136.

18. Ibid.

19. "Cheating" is a debatable label because early humans behaved instinctually. Cheating occurred because they were driven by desire, and any repercussions were based on the emotion of anger. Explicit commitment was beyond their complexity.

20. In some indigenous societies, men time their wives' absences when the wives go into the bushes to defecate or urinate.

21. Barash, *Myth of Monogamy*, pp. 67-70.

22. A similar term, "trading up," is applied to modern men who drop their partner to get "better" ones when they become rich.

23. Information on Venus figurines is taken from Timothy Taylor, *Prehistory of Sex* (1996), pp. 115–123.

24. Scientists base this on the Makapansgat pebble, a pebble that remarkably resembles a human face, and that was apparently brought back to a cave by an early human. Ibid., p. 99.

25. Karel Absolon, quoted in Taylor, *Prehistory of Sex*, p. 120.

26. Males' better spatial ability arguably stems from hunting large game, while women's better night vision and hearing arguably stems from finding small game in dark thickets and water.

27. Information on Neolithic transformation is primarily drawn from Reay Tannahill's chapter, "Man Into Master" in *Sex in History* (1980), pp. 38–55.

28. Western Jews practiced polygyny until 1000 B.C.. Some Eastern Jews practiced polygyny into the twentieth century. Richard Posner, *Sex and Reason* (1992), p. 49.

29. As late as the nineteenth century there was an Australian tribe that ate every tenth baby born to keep the population down to what the territory could support. Tannahill, *Sex in History*, p. 31.

30. Ibid., p. 70.

31. Genesis 1:28 (King James Version).

32. Zoophilia, or bestiality, was relatively common in the pastoral societies of that era. Tannahill, *Sex in History*, p. 71.

33. Early civilizations practiced contraception. The early Egyptians used crocodile dung and acacia tips (which produce lactic acid, the active ingredient in modern spermicides) as forerunners of the diaphragm. It is also likely coitus interruptus (the withdrawal method) has been used since semen was connected with pregnancy. High-class Greek prostitutes used anal intercourse.

34. John Clarke, *Roman Sex: 100 B.C.–AD 250* (2003), p. 97.

35. The ideal penis for the ancient Greeks and Romans was small. Large ones were portrayed for comic effect. In a 423 B.C. play a warning is given, "If you do these things I tell you . . . you will always have a shining breast, a bright skin, big shoulders, a minute tongue, a big rump and a small prick. But if you follow the practices of the youth of today, for a start you'll have a pale skin, small shoulders, a skinny chest, a big tongue, a small rump, a big ham and a long . . . winded decree." Aristophanes, *Clouds*, trans. by Alan Sommerstein (1982), pp. 107–108.

36. Thomas Wright, *Worship of the Generative Powers* (1865), pp. 77–82, 91–94.

37. Like their Greek predecessors, Roman men enjoyed boys sexually. However, the emotional and mentoring aspect of these relationships exalted by the Greeks was reduced to seduction and outright purchase— beautiful boys could cost as much a farm. Morton Hunt, *Natural History of Love* (1959), p. 66.

38. Suburra was Rome's roughest slum, thick with prostitutes, actors, gladiators, gypsies, beggars, hustlers, and thieves.

39. Paul Veyne, *History of Private Life: From Pagan Rome to Byzantium* (1987), pp. 34–35.

40. Throughout history, societies have believed sex saps men's strength. Reasons for this pervasive belief are males' sleepiness following orgasm, inability to ejaculate repeatedly, sexual decline with age, and the belief that semen is a vital substance. Martha Cornog, *Big Book of Masturbation* (2003), p. 33.

41. Veyne, *History of Private Life*, p. 24.

42. Hypatia was the beautiful head of the Platonist School of Alexandria when the Roman Catholic views on sex

were being cemented by St. Augustine and she taught many influential Christians. In line with Platonism, she chose to remain a virgin. When a student communicated his passionate love for her, she lifted her dress above her waist and said with contempt, "This, young man, is what you are in love with, and not anything beautiful." Hunt, *Natural History of Love*, p. 102. She was later hacked to death with oyster shells by Christian monks because against God's commandments she presumed, as a female, to teach men. Riane Eisler, *Chalice and the Blade* (1988), pp. 132–133.

43. Veyne, *History of Private Life*, pp. 36–37.
44. Fisher, *Anatomy of Love*, pp. 106–107.
45. Veyne, *History of Private Life*, pp. 42–43.
46. Hunt, *Natural History of Love*, p. 82.
47. Helen Ellerbe, *Dark Side of Christian History* (1995), p. 20.
48. Morton Smith, *Jesus the Magician* (1978), p. 2.
49. Ellerbe, *Dark Side*, p. 17.
50. Ibid., pp. 14–29.
51. The assertion that the Roman Empire collapsed because of sexual immorality is false. Its sexual conduct was the same during its ascent as it was during its decline. Richard Posner, *Sex and Reason* (1992), pp. 234–235.
52. Ellerbe, *Dark Side of Christian History*, p. 44.
53. Adultery at that time was defined as sex involving a married woman and any man other than her husband. Therefore, a married man having sex with an unmarried woman was not adultery.
54. Jesus spoke approvingly in *Matthew* 19:12 of men who made themselves eunuchs (men without testicles) for heaven. Although it is now accepted that Christ meant this allegorically, thousands mutilated themselves in the centuries following his death. Morton Hunt, *Natural History of Love* (1959), p. 103.
55. Vern Bullough and James Brundage, *Handbook of Medieval Sexuality* (1996), p. 33.
56. Judaism valued the virginity of their unmarried women, not their men. There was not even a Hebrew word for a male virgin. Michael Satlow, *Jewish Marriage in Antiquity* (2001), p. 120.
57. The influential early Christian Clement of Alexandria directly copied the marital principles of the Stoic Musonius without crediting his source. Paul Veyne, *History of Private Life: From Pagan Rome to Byzantium* (1987), p. 47.
58. David Noss and John Noss, *History of the World's Religions*, 9th ed. (1994), p. 509.
59. "An unmarried man worries about how to please the Lord. But a married man has more worries. He must worry about the things of this world, because he wants to please his wife. So he is pulled in two directions. Unmarried women and [virgins] worry only about pleasing the Lord, and they keep their bodies and minds pure . . . What I am saying is for your own good—it isn't to limit your freedom." 1 Corinthians 7:32–35 (CEV).
60. "In my opinion that is what should be done, though I don't know of anything the Lord said about this matter." 1 Corinthians 7:6 (CEV).
61. "My friends, what I mean is that the Lord will soon come, and it won't matter if you are married or not . . . This world as we know it is now passing away." 1 Corinthians 7:29-31 (CEV).
62. Sexually satisfied people may be able to focus on holy matters better than the sexually frustrated. Bernard Murstein, *Love, Sex, and Marriage* (1974), pp. 105–106.
63. Elaine Pagels, *Adam, Eve, and the Serpent* (1988), p. 63.
64. Morton Hunt, *Natural History of Love* (1959), p. 116.
65. Largely from ibid., pp. 117–122.
66. Ibid., p. 119.
67. St. Paul's words were, "So behave properly, as people do in the day. Don't go to wild parties or get drunk or be vulgar or indecent. Don't quarrel or be jealous. Let the Lord Jesus Christ be as near to you as the clothes you wear. Then you won't try to satisfy your selfish desires." Romans 13:13–14 (CEV).
68. Pagels, *Adam, Eve, and the Serpent*, p. 141.
69. Ibid., p. 140.
70. Merry Wiesner-Hanks, *Christianity and Sexuality in the Early Modern World* (2000), p. 31.
71. His fabricated passage is in the Book of Tobit. This is a canonical book in Catholicism, but not in Protestantism. Uta Ranke-Heinemann, *Eunuchs for the Kingdom of Heaven* (1990), pp. 16–17.
72. Wiesner-Hanks, *Christianity and Sexuality*, p. 34.
73. James Russell, *Germanization of Early Medieval Christianity* (1994), pp. 152–153.

74. William Manchester, *World Lit Only by Fire* (1993), p. 12.
75. Reay Tannahill, *Sex in History* (1980), p. 152.
76. Ibid., p. 158.
77. Wiesner-Hanks, *Christianity and Sexuality*, p. 37.
78. Murstein, *Love, Sex, and Marriage*, p. 113.
79. *Cunt* was not obscene until the 1700s. James McDonald, *Wordsworth Dictionary of Obscenity and Taboo* (1988), p. 36.
80. Names arguably sexual were Haldebytheheved (hold by the head) and Overandover. Ruth Karras, *Sexuality in Medieval Europe* (2005), p. 124.
81. Vern Bullough and James Brundage, *Handbook of Medieval Sexuality* (1996), p. 41.
82. Ibid., p. 13.
83. Murstein, *Love, Sex, and Marriage*, p. 92.
84. Tannahill, *Sex in History*, p. 144.
85. Henry Lea, *History of Sacerdotal Celibacy in the Christian Church*, 4th ed. (1932), pp. 264, 279.
86. Henry Lea, *History of the Inquisition of the Middle Ages: Vol. 1* (2005), p. 31.
87. Murstein, *Love, Sex, and Marriage*, p. 116.
88. Bullough, *Handbook of Medieval Sexuality*, pp. 245–246.
89. Tannahill, *Sex in History*, p. 279.
90. Ibid., pp. 279–280.
91. Barbara Walker, *Woman's Encyclopedia of Myths and Secrets* (1983), p. 824.
92. William Manchester, *World Lit Only By Fire* (1992), p. 21.
93. Ibid., p. 53.
94. Ruth Karras, *Sexuality in Medieval Europe* (2005), p. 154.
95. Lea, *History of the Inquisition*, pp. 437, 444.
96. Ibid., p. 401.
97. Ibid., p. 477.
98. G.G. Coulton, *Inquisition and Liberty* (1969), p. 81.
99. Authority for burning was taken from Jesus' words, "If you don't stay joined to me, you will be thrown away. You will be like dry branches that are gathered up and burned in a fire." John 15:6 (CEV).
100. The term *auto-da-fé* is Portuguese for "act of the faith." Victims were gagged or had their tongues cut out so that they could not speak to the crowd to elicit sympathy. *Autos-da-fé* were often performed during holidays to attract larger crowds.
101. Lea, *History of the Inquisition*, pp. 467–469.
102. Lea, *History of the Inquisition*, p. 459.
103. Edward Peters, *Torture* (1996), p. 68.
104. John Swain, *Pleasures of the Torture Chamber* (1995, orig. pub. 1931), p. 177; and Michael Kerrigan, *Instruments of Torture* (2001), pp. 84–86.
105. Jean Kellaway, *History of Torture and Execution* (2003), p. 59.
106. Swain, *Pleasures of the Torture Chamber*, p. 178.
107. Homer Smith, *Man and His Gods* (1952), p. 286.
108. Lea, *History of the Inquisition*, p. 466.
109. Henry Kamen, *Spanish Inquisition* (1997), p. 176.
110. Ibid.
111. Ibid.
112. Ibid., p. 178.
113. Vern Bullough and James Brundage, *Handbook of Medieval Sexuality* (1996), p. 15.
114. For example, the Inquisition did not handle executions because they were unseemly. It had the secular authorities handle them, and if they refused, they were excommunicated.
115. Peter De Rosa, *Vicars of Christ* (1988), p. 38.
116. Stephen VII shouted at the corpse, "Why did you usurp this See of the Apostle?" A teenage deacon crouched nearby replied, "Because I was evil." The accused pope was convicted, had his atrophied blessing fingers (first three of the right hand) cut off and was then thrown in the Tiber River. Richard Zacks, *Underground Education* (1997), p. 217.

117. Ibid., pp. 217–218.
118. Barbara Tuchman, *Distant Mirror* (1978), p. 26.
119. Section largely from William Manchester, *World Lit Only By Fire* (1992).
120. Pope Pius II was no fuddy-duddy himself. As a bishop, he had fathered multiple children by multiple mistresses.
121. Ibid., p. 78.
122. A marble sculpture of Farnese still sits in St. Peter's Cathedral. The nude sculpture was covered with a metal garment by the Victorian-era pope Pius IX.
123. Manchester, *World Lit Only By Fire*, pp. 81–82.
124. Before the Holy Roman Emperor at the Diet of Worms in 1521, Martin Luther asserted, "I am as much a piece of useless, stinking shit as anyone else, if not more." Heiko Oberman, *Luther* (1992), p. 108.
125. Europe was largely illiterate so written communication was still limited to select segments of the population.
126. The nailing of the theses is probably a myth. It is more likely he simply sent them in a humble letter to his superiors.
127. Manchester, *World Lit Only By Fire*, p. 37.
128. Numerous German priests converted as well. Authorities at the time, such as Emperor Ferdinand, believed the Church's unbending approach to clerical celibacy was their sole motive. Uta Ranke-Heinemann, *Eunuchs for the Kingdom of Heaven* (1990), pp. 113–114.
129. In 1522 the Church owned an estimated fifty percent of the wealth in Germany. Manchester, *World Lit Only By Fire*, p. 132.
130. Luther stated that Jesus probably had sex with Mary Magdalene and several other women so as to fully appreciate man's nature. Martin Luther, *Table-Talk*, as described in Morton Hunt, *Natural History of Love* (1959), p. 222.
131. Merry Wiesner-Hanks, *Christianity and Sexuality in the Early Modern World* (2000), p. 64.
132. Ibid., p. 84.
133. Codpieces were a fashionable version of modern jockstraps and were used to accent the bulge of the male genitalia.
134. Wiesner-Hanks, *Christianity and Sexuality*, p. 86.
135. Ibid., p. 65.
136. Ibid., p. 86.
137. Ibid., p. 93.
138. Ibid., p. 259.
139. Bernard Cottret, *Calvin: A Biography* (2000), p. 19.
140. Jean Delumeau, *Sin and Fear* (1990), p. 27.
141. Hunt, *Natural History of Love*, p. 227.
142. When a poster accusing Calvin of gross hypocrisy appeared on his pulpit, a suspect was arrested on no evidence. After the suspect was tortured for a month he "confessed." As punishment he was lashed and nailed to a stake and then decapitated. William Manchester, *World Lit Only By Fire* (1992), p. 190.
143. Calvin insisted he wanted people to be happy and advised they play quoits (ring toss). Hunt, *Natural History of Love*, p. 227.
144. One woman was jailed for four days for having her hair at an "immoral" height. Manchester, *World Lit Only By Fire*, p. 191.
145. The Puritans were not the only European settlers to come to America, but they are the focus because of the "potent American morality" that they spread. By the Revolutionary War, three quarters of America's white population was Puritan. James Morone, *Hellfire Nation* (2003), pp. 10, 31–33.
146. John Winthrop, "A Modell of Christian Charity," 1630.
147. John D'Emilio and Estelle Freedman, *Intimate Matters* (1988), p. 29.
148. Only after 1660 did the letters A.D. become a common punishment for adultery. They would either be branded into the forehead or they would have to be worn for life.
149. Puritans thought human/animal sex could create "monstrous offspring," therefore animals were also given the death penalty. In 1642, sixteen-year-old Thomas Grazer of Plymouth admitted to having intercourse with "a mare, a cow, two goats, five sheep, two calves, and a turkey." Before his execution he was forced to pick his

partners out of a sheep lineup and they were "killed before his face." D'Emilio, *Intimate Matters*, p. 17.

150. Merry Wiesner-Hanks, *Christianity and Sexuality in the Early Modern World* (2000), p. 228.
151. Jonathan Edwards, "Sinners in the Hands of an Angry God," 8 July 1741.
152. D'Emilio, *Intimate Matters*, pp. 25–26.
153. Hunt, *Natural History of Love*, p. 231.
154. D'Emilio, *Intimate Matters*, p. 17.
155. Morton Hunt, *Natural History of Love* (1959), p. 233.
156. Peter Laslett, et al., eds., *Bastardy and Its Comparative History* (1980), p. 361.
157. Wiesner-Hanks, *Christianity and Sexuality*, p. 238.
158. D'Emilio, *Intimate Matters*, p. 18.

SEX IV

ITS ORIGIN

DISTORTING SCIENCE

I

HUMANISM
HAPPINESS (SEX) ON EARTH

By the 1800s, the fruition of a long process would have consequences for the Puritans' strict sexual ideals. After the turn of the first millennium, the Crusaders (1096–1204) and then merchant traders were exposed to Muslim civilizations in Spain and the Eastern Mediterranean. The Muslims had translated and saved the academic texts of the ancient Greek and Roman scholars that were destroyed by the Roman Catholic Church. In this way, non-Biblical works of literature, philosophy, and science made an unauthorized return to Europe.

These classical texts sparked a renewed interest in learning called the Renaissance (1400–1700). The invention of the printing press (1440), the immigration of Greek scholars from Constantinople prior to the collapse of the Eastern Roman Empire in 1453, and the Protestant Reformation (sixteenth century) further damaged the Church's intellectual lockdown. After one thousand years of static, independent thinking was reborn. This led to innovations in philosophy and science, both of which would remake society, including its handling of sexuality.

A. The Philosophy: Mind Your Business

The broad philosophical outlook that grew through the Renaissance is now called Humanism. Humanism stressed reason and focused attention on the here and now—life on Earth. Christianity as developed through the Roman Catholic Church had stressed faith and focused attention on the afterlife—heaven and hell. Instead of the salvation of the soul, humanism stressed "life, liberty, and the pursuit of happiness."[1]

The United States of America was born out of the humanist ideal in 1776, and the first amendment of its constitution pointedly separated church and state. Although the first amendment was not yet binding on the states, the Puritans' enforcement of morality by the community was replaced with an emphasis on individual choice that was reflected even in religious circles.[2] State regulation of morality diminished, and the United States' first currency was not inscribed with "in God we trust," but "mind your business."[3] The Puritan belief that an individual's private sins could doom the community lost power. Accordingly, in the late eighteenth century and early nineteenth century criminal justice no longer focused on moral crimes.[4]

These attitudes were influenced by an English humanist philosopher named Jeremy Bentham. In the late 1700s, Bentham created a theory of ethics called utilitarianism. Under this theory the goal of laws was to maximize pleasure and minimize pain. This was an alternative to the religious-based codes whose goal was to mold a godly society.

Bentham believed government should not concern itself with moral crimes such as those related to alcohol, suicide, or consensual sex. He believed that these crimes were usually petty, that individuals knew what made them happy more than politicians did, and that in this area politicians were prone to trample on liberty due to a "thousand little prejudices."[5] These crimes would later be called victimless crimes because the only "victims" were the people choosing the actions.

In the early nineteenth century Bentham's godson, John Stuart Mill, would further develop the concept of a government based in humanism. Mill was passionate about liberty and believed that individuality and "experiments in living" needed to be protected from the government's enforcement of conventional morality.[6] His line drawing on criminalization can be abbreviated to "Your rights end where his nose begins."[7]

B. Science: How Come This Wasn't in the Bible?

Whereas Christianity had based its primary source of knowledge in the Bible, humanism based its primary source of knowledge in science, and by the eighteenth-century the reemergence of science had produced profound technological advances.

In 1776 James Watt's refinement of the steam engine sparked the Industrial Revolution that would fundamentally change the way people lived. Other eighteenth century innovations, such as crop rotation and the horse-drawn hoe, replaced inefficient family farms with large commercial ones. The unemployed farmers moved to the cities for work in the new factories.

The growth of factory-based cities changed numerous power relationships. In the growing middle class the dynamic between spouses was altered. Previously farmers and textile workers worked at home where domestic duties and toil for income blurred. Now the husband left home for the factory and the wife stayed behind to handle responsibilities such as raising children. He was now the "breadwinner."

Cities also undermined community control. The great size and diversity of city populations provided anonymity and choices that were unavailable to young adults in smaller rural communities. Men were increasingly free of parental control in the cities, as the dispensation of hereditary land lost its importance.

This freedom would not remain unencumbered. The aspiring elitists of the growing urban middle class wanted to distinguish themselves from those above and below them. True to their Puritan forebears, they did this by clamping down on sexuality. The strict propriety that arose is now known as Victorianism.[8] In addition, the theme of "mind your business" that sparked the birth of our country and the humanist ideals of Bentham and Mill would soon wither under the new strategy of religious moralists—the moral crusade. These political movements would now define the battles over sexual freedom.

II

VICTORIANISM
SEX IS LOW-CLASS

A. The New Middle Class: Rich and Lame

The rich middle-class men of the eighteenth century aspired to be upper-class, but affluence did not suffice. The upper class was still defined by the aristocracy and landed gentry, who both inherited their wealth. Both groups considered commerce dirty, and resented the power accumulating in the social class below them.

Since these new-money men could not marry the actual princesses of the aristocracy, they made princesses of their wives. In an attempt at aristocratic prestige, they used their wealth to treat the middle-class wife as a "lady." The middle-class wife had domestic servants to handle all the chores and to raise the children. Shielded from the "harsh reality" of the outside world, she could not go outside without a chaperone for protection. She was not educated,[9] and was discouraged from taking an interest in anything of substance that might "corrupt" her. Unfortunately, unlike the actual ladies of the royal nobility who had the resources to travel and entertain themselves with or without their equally carefree husbands, the middle-class gentlewomen were caged pets.

B. Women as Sexual Victims: Dumb but Not Slutty

Under the new secular vision of society, it was no longer enough for religious moralists to base criminal sanctions solely upon their interpretations of the Bible. To keep the government in the bedroom, the moralists needed (1) to find victims and (2) find science to "prove" they were harmed.

The coddled Victorian middle-class woman would be the first to fit the bill. In the late eighteenth century and early nineteenth century the concept of the delicate and virtuous female expanded to include sexuality.[10] New scientific understanding of male sperm and the female egg debunked the belief that a woman had to orgasm to conceive.[11] This myth had forced men to concern themselves with the sexual pleasure of women when procreation was intended. Now that female orgasms were no longer necessary or "natural," moralists were able to deny females their sexuality.

The medieval view of women was that they were as lustful as men.[12] The new "scientific" view spread by moralists was that women did not have sexual feelings. The Surgeon General under President Abraham Lincoln, William Hammond, wrote that it was unlikely that women experienced the slightest degree of pleasure even one-tenth of the times they engaged in sex.[13]

Another doctor wrote that excessive sexual engagement and arousal could contribute to cancer.[14] The view that female sexual desire was an illness led in 1868 to doctors prescribing clitoridectomies. They would diagnose a woman by manually stimulating her breasts and clitoris. If they observed a reaction they would excise the latter. The astounding naiveté of the times is demonstrated by the women who thought their clitoridectomy scars "as pretty as the dimple in the cheek of sweet sixteen."[15]

These men of science did not always hide their bias. The widely read nineteenth-century physician William Acton wrote, "the majority of women (happily for society) are not very much troubled with sexual feelings of any kind . . . . Love of home, of children, and of domestic duties are the only passions they feel."[16] The doctor's overarching commitment to the patient's health, which dated back to Hippocrates, was now secondary to sexual morality.[17]

Protestant leaders used these new "scientific" findings to anoint females as the protectors of morality. Eliza Duffey wrote in 1873 that "The purity of women is the everlasting barrier against which the tides of man's sensual nature surge."[18] Men used this ideal to defend the double standard.

Although many sexually active people knew the sexless female to be a myth, the propaganda still had a demonstrable effect on women's attitudes. Previously there were more women trying to divorce because of their partner's impotence than men trying to divorce because of sexual deprivation. In the Victorian era this reversed.[19]

When Dr. Clelia Mosher interviewed some women born in the early 1800s most of them believed sex was a necessity only for men and that a woman could "do without." Only half of the women expressed sexual desire and only half could say they found sex agreeable at least occasionally.[20] Another sex researcher spoke to a seventy-year-old woman who was married in the middle of the Victorian Era and was the mother of several children. She revealed something that would have been shocking even to the colonial Puritans—she had never seen a naked man.[21]

C. Children as Asexual Victims:
Little Johnny Would Never Want Vagina

Women were not the only ones to lose their sexuality in the nineteenth century. Children of both sexes would lose theirs as well. Sexual desire begins in humans with the onset of puberty around the age of thirteen, and youthful sexuality has been openly recognized throughout history.

In ancient Greece the sexual relationship between a man and his adolescent protégé was more hallowed than between a man and his wife. In ancient Rome, a boy's first ejaculation was celebrated at the Liberalia, a festival in honor of the god of fertility. Throughout the Middle Ages children were exposed to sex and nudity simply because privacy and clothing were frequently luxuries.

In addition, medieval children were often married off as soon as possible. With an average life expectancy of only thirty years and high infant mortality rates, it was important to begin childbearing as soon as possible.[22] The common minimum legal age for marriage was twelve for girls and fourteen for boys.[23] Because of this, many boys and girls were undoubtedly married and sexually active *before* beginning puberty. (Before the 1900s female puberty came years later than it does now.)[24]

Surprisingly, America's current obsession with the sexual purity of children is not rooted in a fear of them having sexual intercourse, but with them pleasuring themselves.[25] The concept that would torture children's conscience for over two centuries began in 1710 with the publication of *Onania; Or, the Heinous Sin of Self-Pollution*.[26] As its title suggests, it was primarily a religious attack on masturbation but also contained "scientific" supporting evidence. The immensely popular tome asserted that masturbation caused memory lapses, acne, impotence, and insanity.

In 1758 a well-regarded Swiss physician, Samuel-Auguste Tissot, affirmed *Onania*'s claim that masturbation was unhealthy. He added his own collection of dangers, which included tuberculosis, jaundice, incontinence, and loose teeth. Dangers specific to females included cramps, ulceration of the womb, lengthening

138

and scabbing of the clitoris, and a crazed libido that he called "uterine fury."[27]

Tissot's endorsement of masturbation's peril opened the gates for others. Masturbation was eventually to be blamed for seemingly every affliction. A partial list included constipation, rickets, epilepsy, vision and hearing problems, headaches, abnormally sized penises, nymphomania, irregular heartbeats, sickly offspring, feeble-mindedness, and early death.

Two dietary institutions were created out of this war on childhood masturbation. The graham cracker was invented in 1829 by the religious zealot Sylvester Graham, in part because the bland cracker was thought to cool the body's passions, as opposed to meat and spicy foods, which would incite them. Dr. John Kellogg had a similar intent when he invented corn flakes in 1896, unintentionally launching the breakfast cereal industry.[28] If corn flakes did not serve their purpose, Kellogg recommended an enema.[29]

The actions taken against masturbation were not limited to diet. Things to avoid also included tight lacing, featherbeds, licentious novels, and irregular bowel movements. Devices employed were chastity belts for girls, spiked penile rings for boys, and straitjackets for both. Although not common, extreme surgical methods used on the genitalia were cauterization (burning), infibulation (sewing the vagina shut), clitoridectomy, and castration. These heinous mutilations are no longer practiced, but one body modification that rose to American prominence in an effort to reduce masturbation is still with us—circumcision.[30]

In the late 1800s the ballyhoo over childhood masturbation began to subside. Germs and viruses were discovered and they eventually exculpated masturbation from many of its alleged crimes. Although masturbation continued to be blamed for illnesses that could not be explained, primarily mental health diseases,[31] by the 1920s masturbation was accepted as a safe emergency sexual release when done in moderation. However, as late as 1940 the United States Naval Academy still mandated that admission candidates be rejected if the examining surgeon found evidence of masturbation.[32] It would not be until the mid-twentieth-century sex research of Alfred Kinsey revealed that almost everyone was doing it that experts finally considered it completely harmless.

By that point attitudes about childhood sexuality had been set. Childhood was to be completely devoid of sexuality. This enforced purity had philosophical as well as medical roots. A concept had spread through the eighteenth and nineteenth centuries that children would not become sexually active if they were not exposed to sex. This was based on the concept of the *tabula rasa*, or blank slate, introduced by the humanist John Locke in 1693.[33] The popular view gradually became that parents and educators were responsible for a child's development. The historic image of the wild child who needed taming was now replaced with that of an innocent vessel whose shortcomings were merely reflective of those around it.

By 1875, the Victorian sex expert William Acton would lay out the current fundamentalist Christian view: "With most healthy and well-brought-up children, no sensual idea or feeling has ever entered their heads, even in the way of speculation. I believe that such children's curiosity is seldom excited on these subjects except as the result of suggestion by persons older than themselves."[34]

The transformation of the child was now complete. Children were sexless beings, and any sexual activity on their part was the blame of parents and society. Both their morality and their physical health depended on denying them any exposure to sexuality whatsoever. They were officially victims.

III

The Moral Crusades
The Sky Is Falling! Lock Up the Sinners!

A. What It Is: A Freak-Out!

The rise of secular humanism and the separation of church and state forced moralists to develop a strategy. No longer could behavior be criminalized solely on questionable interpretations of the Bible. Now there had to be a demonstrable victim and a demonstrable harm. The first part was accomplished. Women and children were now the "victims" and there was "science" supporting their "harms." The next stage was to use these ingredients to alter other peoples' behavior.

In *Hellfire Nation*, James Morone describes the moral crusades that continually enlarge our government and whittle away at the liberties provided by our country's humanist founders.[35] Moral crusades begin with an assertion that society is suffering because of its sins and that reform is urgently needed. Religious moralists first try to get miscreants to conform with threats of eternal damnation. With the rise of humanism this threat lost its power, and it now has to be accompanied by warnings of earthly dangers. When citizens still do not conform, moralists then launch a crusade, and turn to the politicians to demand criminal prohibitions that will save the "victims" and society.

Moral crusades have three common features:

(1) Absolutism—Usually such crusades are based on a questionable interpretation of the Bible that does not allow for rational scrutiny. There is only right and wrong, good and evil. The goal is easy to understand and simple. Research and factual analysis are not welcome, and compromise is not an option.

(2) Alarmism—Extremists make the claim of an impending Apocalypse, the second coming of Jesus in which the world will be destroyed and people will be judged to go to either heaven or hell. The less shrill merely assert that the current time is more sinful and troubled than any before it and is therefore ripe for collapse. They refer back to the idealized "good old days" that were supposedly free from sin. Fears are stoked by lies, gross exaggerations, and broadly-applied anecdotal evidence, for example, a condom once broke and therefore condoms are dangerous.

(3) The Other—Perhaps most importantly, all crusades have an enemy, the other. The enemy is pure evil. This is usually a group that cannot defend itself through the democratic process due to its small numbers. It may be a racial/ethnic group or any group that has a shared interest, such as prostitutes or recreational drug users. The group is often one that is stigmatized, so that prevalent prejudices can be used to rally public support. These minorities often must be protected by the courts, which enforce the liberties guaranteed in the Bill of Rights.

Although the Bill of Rights was written by the United States' founders for this exact purpose—protection of minorities from the tyranny of the majority and a power-hungry government—judges who enforce these rights are labeled "activist judges." Judges also have the unpopular role of ensuring due process for the accused.

During moral crusades, as during the Inquisition, the sound policies developed over centuries to prevent the innocent from being wrongly convicted suddenly become too "litigious" and problematic in the face of this great evil.

B. Victorian Prostitution: My Wife Doesn't Suck

One of the first sexual moral crusades to sweep the nation was the war on prostitution. As the middle-class wife was transformed into a sexless angel, many men believed they were doing their wives a favor by taking their sex drive elsewhere.

This perception was supported by the many Victorian physicians who said that only prostitutes enjoyed and desired sex.[36] The "asexual" wife, combined with the complete void of even the most basic sexual education, often made marital sex a dull affair. One Victorian man compared sex with his wife to having a bowel movement.[37]

Not surprisingly, prostitution boomed in the nineteenth century. There was an estimated one prostitute for every twelve males in major Western cities.[38] (In modern America, there is estimated one prostitute for every two thousand males.[39]) The infection of sexually transmitted diseases (STDs) boomed as well, with one expert estimating that at one point sixty percent of American men had either syphilis or gonorrhea.[40]

Until the late nineteenth century, doctors did not even know what gonorrhea and syphilis were, and mistook them for stages of the same illness. These are not minor ailments. Although both exhibit unsavory genital sores and discharge in early stages, late stages of syphilis can be characterized by personality changes, a shuffling gait, a bobbing head, insanity, and death.

Despite its moralistic approach to other sexual matters, such as education and female sexuality, the medical profession did not see prostitution as a moral issue but as a public health issue.[41] It recommended that prostitution be legalized and regulated. This model was already used by some European countries, and the United States Army used it with the prostitutes who followed troops during the Civil War. In Memphis, the Army had set up a system whereby prostitutes were medically inspected weekly and granted licenses. The fees women paid for these licenses were used to support a hospital ward where infected prostitutes were treated.[42]

Several cities debated regulation during the Victorian Era, but St. Louis was the first to enact it in 1870. The forces of morality gathered quickly. Protestant clergy, former abolitionists, and women's rights activists led a crusade consisting largely of middle-class women. The victims who desperately needed to be saved were the prostitutes themselves.

Prostitutes were portrayed as miserable people who, as young virtuous women, had been tricked, seduced, or forced into the sex trade by evil licentious men. Former abolitionists compared legalized prostitution to legalized slavery in the antebellum South, and women's rights groups opposed legalized prostitution on the grounds that it would not control venereal disease. According to them, venereal disease could only be defeated by ending the practice of prostitution.

In an act of beautiful symbolism that combined the two asexual victims of lust, women and children, the anti-prostitution forces had a group of young virginal girls in white dresses present a hundred thousand signatures against legalized prostitution to the Missouri state legislators in 1874. The American experiment with regulated prostitution ended.

The anti-prostitution crusade would lay dormant for several decades. In the cities, nobody seriously thought prostitution could be vanquished, and no one tried to wipe it out completely.[43] Christian morality and humanist liberty coexisted in what one historian has called the "Victorian Compromise."[44] During the 1800s there was an unspoken agreement that moral sins were criminal only if they were done openly where they could offend the general citizenry.

During a time when most young men were initiated into sex by prostitutes and Washington, DC had its "female lobbyists" who stayed in town only as long as Congress was in session, the Victorian Compromise was deeply hypocritical, but it worked. Prostitution was relegated to red-light districts in lower-class sections of cities where the morality of the middle classes would not be offended. Government and police officials were paid by the madams to look the other way, and as long as boundaries were observed, the prostitutes avoided prison and had the safety of brothels.

C. White Slavery: It's 1910.
Do You Know Where Your Daughter Is?

The victimhood of the prostitutes and the evil of their sex-driven male patrons were not powerful enough symbols to overthrow the Victorian Compromise. Because the prostitutes' victimhood was doubtful, and the sex-driven men were actually normal husbands, more potent symbols were needed by the anti-prostitution crusade. These would be provided by a magazine article.

In 1909, *McClure's* reported that white slavery had come to America. Jewish flesh traders were stealing innocent girls from the countryside and forcing them to work in locked brothels. The anonymous john from decades earlier was now a Jew. The victims were no longer stray women in the corrupt cities, but sheltered girls plucked from America's rural heartland. The anti-prostitution crusade was set afire.

Hysteria fanned through the media. One best-seller had on its cover a mother protectively holding her daughter and staring at a wanted ad that read, "Sixty-thousand innocent girls WANTED to take the place of sixty thousand white slaves who will die this year."[45] White slavery films were popular as well, with titles such as *Traffic in Souls, House of Bondage,* and *Is Any Girl Safe?*

Chinese, Mongolian, Italian, and Irish immigrants were also supposed to be complicit in the trade. These "despicable foreigners" were destroying America's virtue.[46] Preachers who walked through cities reported hearing midnight shrieks of "My God, if only I could get out of here!"[47]

Within months of the *McClure's* article, President Taft promised action. Representative James Mann of Illinois drafted legislation to give the federal government the power to stop the crisis that incompetent city governments couldn't. The Mann Act granted the federal government the power to apprehend any criminal who transported a female across state lines for the purpose of "prostitution or debauchery, or for any other immoral purpose."[48]

D. The Birth of the FBI:
Fighting Interstate Adultery

The United States Constitution purposely did not give the federal government a police force or police power. However, the federal government was allowed to regulate interstate commerce, and just as it would do countless times in the future to criminalize almost anything it wanted, it took advantage of this clause to give federal agents jurisdiction in the Mann Act. Opponents of the bill believed that this would unleash a federal police force that would grow unchecked, but they were steamrolled by the hype.

The bill's proponents assured critics that their only goal was to eradicate white slavery which, as one of them described, was "a thousand times worse and more degrading in its consequences on humanity than any species of human slavery that ever existed in this country."[49] The Mann Act became law in 1910.

The two-year-old federal police agency, the Bureau of Investigation, was put in charge of enforcing the Mann Act. At the time of the act's passage, the Bureau had only thirty-five agents. Congress was suspicious of a federal police organization and had given it little funding, but with this weighty white slavery scourge hoisted upon it, the Bureau grew from a small Washington office to a national presence with offices in every state and large city.[50]

The Mann Act's critics were prophetic. The federal police force would change its name to the Federal Bureau of Investigation (FBI), and under the leadership of J. Edgar Hoover from 1924 to 1972, would grow into an extremely powerful organization that would involve itself in almost every aspect of American life,[51] keep secret files with embarrassing information on prominent Americans to blackmail those who opposed it,[52] and regularly use unconstitutional investigation and enforcement techniques.[53]

As will be shown, the Mann Act would not have been the Bureau's meal ticket if it had focused on the white slave trade. However, church groups predictably began lobbying for a literal interpretation of the Mann Act's text, which criminalized transporting women for any "immoral purpose." Because of this, the Bureau became a federal investigator of adultery.[54]

This "crime" was rampant, and fighting it kept tax money flowing into the Bureau. From June 30, 1922 through June 30, 1937, the FBI investigated 50,500

145

alleged violations of the Mann Act. During the 1920s, the large majority of these would be for noncommercial violations.[55] Statistics from specific federal districts showed that seventy-one percent of those convicted of noncommercial Mann Act violations received jail time.[56] Typical complaints to the FBI of noncommercial violations were of the home-wrecking variety, made by crossed husbands, wives, and fathers, but they could come from anybody, as this 1927 complaint from West Palm Beach (which resulted in an investigation) demonstrates:

> There is a J.S. Nouser Liveing at 727 Kanuga drive with a woman that he not married to and they was on a trip this summer to california and new Yory they stoped at the pennsylvania Hotel in new york as man and wife i think this agants [against] the man ack [Mann Act] and should be looked in to.
>
> yours very truly
> from a mother[57]

Prosecutions for noncommercial violations of the Mann Act began to peter out in the late 1920s, as juries began refusing to convict defendants. However, the act continued to be used to jail controversial people who would be less sympathetic to juries, including unpopular political figures and black men who openly cavorted with white women. The first black boxing heavyweight champion, Jack Johnson, was the most famous example of such racial targeting when he was imprisoned in 1920 for sending his white girlfriend money for a train ticket. As late as 1960, the early black rock-and-roller Chuck Berry was imprisoned under the Mann Act in a highly questionable case.

E. The Saved Victims: Leave Us the Hell Alone

As for the white slave trade that relit the crusade and originally armed the federal government, it was a myth. After carefully interviewing 1,106 women, a New York investigation team found no evidence of a slave trade. The results were the same everywhere. One reformer wrote in 1913:

> I have entered at least 2,500 houses of ill-repute and talked
> face to face with possibly 15,000 of these women and I . . . do not
> hesitate to tell you that they are wedded to their ways and that
> they laugh and make fun of those who try to help them.[58]

Psychologists listed a potpourri of reasons women would voluntarily resort to prostitution, which included being weak of will, unhappy, ignorant, impoverished, lonely, and the most common, neglected and abused by family. However, a more conspicuous cause, given scant attention by moralists, was the economics. Former stenographers were paid five times more as prostitutes, domestic servants up to twelve times more, and factory workers up to twenty times more.[59]

Perhaps most shocking was a lesson that moral reformers had first discovered decades earlier in the battle against legalization—women enjoyed it.[60] In the mid-1800s reformers put up halfway houses for released female prisoners, many of whom were prostitutes. The reformers assumed that if given the chance to leave the city and become honest domestic servants they would surely do so. However, as Boston reformers noted it was "extremely difficult to persuade inmates of brothels to forsake their road to ruin."[61] By and large, the prostitutes did not consider themselves fallen women, nor did they want to adopt the middle class' frigid sexual culture.

White slavery investigators quoted one woman who said she was "tired of drudgery as a servant. . . I'd rather do this than be kicked around like a dog in a kitchen by some woman who calls herself a lady." Another said, "there is more money and pleasure in being a sport."[62] Sally Stanford, a madam, wrote that the numerous women begging to work in her house were a "continual nuisance" and most of them were far from destitute.[63]

Debunking the white slavery myth was not as exciting as its creation. Most of the concrete examples of white slavery that led to the moral fury—"For God's sake do something!"—were traced back to District Attorney Edwin Sims and Chicago Prosecutor Clifford Roe, who not surprisingly were friends of Congressman Mann. These few examples were blatantly exaggerated. Despite these revelations, the Bureau of Investigation continued its battle against adultery unabated.

The white slavery panic managed to end the Victorian Compromise. Famous

HOOVER
Repressed G-Man?

One scientific study has shown a correlation between repressed homosexuality and homophobia. This could explain J. Edgar Hoover's sexual conservatism and zealous prosecution of consensual sex crimes despite the fact he was probably gay.

Hoover eagerly gathered evidence of homosexuality, legally and illegally, to use against political opponents. (For example, during Dwight Eisenhower's presidential campaign, Hoover gave Eisenhower's running mate, Richard Nixon, information on alleged homosexual crimes committed by Democratic candidate Adlai Stevenson.) However, he also had FBI agents quash information about his own sexuality. Therefore, unlike the sexual reputations he illegally tarnished (such as Martin Luther King's), his own sexual activities remain open to conjecture.

The evidence is as follows: Hoover never demonstrated any interest in women. He had effeminate characteristics. There were always rumors surrounding his sexuality. He lived with his mom until her death when he was forty-three years old. His associate of over forty years was fellow bachelor Clyde Tolson. Tolson was five years Hoover's junior, was "ruggedly handsome," and had a "remarkably fast ascendancy" within the Bureau to the office adjoining Hoover's.

Hoover and Tolson were inseparable. They ate lunch together every day and dinner together almost every night. They vacationed together, staying in adjoining rooms, and they took adoring photos of each other.

When Hoover died in 1972, Tolson inherited Hoover's estate, and moved into his home. They are now buried beside each other in the Congressional Cemetery.

—H.E. Adams, L.W. Wright, and B.A. Lohr, "Is Homophobia Associated with Homosexual Arousal?" *J. Abnorm. Psychol.*, Aug. 1996, pp. 440–445; and Ronald Kessler, *Bureau* (2003), pp. 13, 30, 43–45, 93.

red-light districts that were shut down included Houston's Happy Hollow, Chicago's Levee, and the infamous Storyville in New Orleans. Despite this, the prostitutes and their clients did not disappear as hoped. They simply moved to the streets.

The wealthier prostitutes became call girls who were put in danger by meeting johns in unfamiliar locations. The poorer prostitutes became streetwalkers who faced even more danger, in addition to higher risks of imprisonment and police harassment.[64] The safe confines of the brothel run by the madam were replaced by the often violent world of the male pimp.

One frustrated ex-mayor wrote:

> Why is it constantly necessary to do something *to* people? If we can't do something *for* them, when are we going to learn to let them alone? Or must this incessant interference, this meddling, this mauling and manhandling, go on in the world forever and ever?[65]

NOTES

1. Thomas Jefferson, "Declaration of Independence," 1776.
2. The 1740s' religious revival, the Great Awakening, stressed personal responsibility. John D'Emilio and Estelle Freedman, *Intimate Matters* (1988), p. 40.
3. "Mind your business" appeared on the continental dollar of the Revolutionary War. It was designed by Benjamin Franklin. "In God we trust" did not appear on American currency until 1865.
4. Lawrence Friedman, *Crime and Punishment in American History* (1993), p. 128.
5. Jeremy Bentham, *Introduction to the Principles of Morals and Legislation* (1996, orig. pub. 1789), p. 290.
6. Ibid., p. 291.
7. Richard Posner, *Sex and Reason* (1992), p. 3.
8. The terms *Victorianism* and *Victorian Era* come from Britain's Queen Victoria (ruled 1837–1901). Her disgust with bodily functions, such as sex and breast-feeding, and her strict decorum characterized the era. For example, queens had always given birth before dozens of government officials. She limited viewing to her doctor, her nurse, and her husband. Carolly Erickson, *Her Little Majesty* (1997), pp. 90, 222, 272.
9. Nineteenth-century intellectuals believed women were incapable of higher education. The philosopher Georg Hegel believed men were to women as animals were to plants.
10. Nancy Cott and Elizabeth Pleck, eds., *Heritage of Her Own* (1979), pp. 165–168.
11. In colonial New England, pregnancy was proof of an accused rapist's innocence because it meant the victim enjoyed it.
12. Ruth Karras, *Sexuality in Medieval Europe* (2005), pp. 39, 80.
13. Bernard Murstein, *Love, Sex, and Marriage* (1974), p. 254.
14. Ronald Pearsall, *Worm in the Bud* (1969), p. 204.
15. G.J. Barker-Benfield, *Horrors of the Half-Known Life* (1976), p. 132.
16. John D'Emilio and Estelle Freedman, *Intimate Matters* (1988), p. 70.
17. The distinguished British physician Sir James Paget advised that a physician should never support immoral behavior even if the patient suffered because of it. Murstein, *Love, Sex, and Marriage*, p. 255.
18. D'Emilio, *Intimate Matters*, p. 70.
19. Ibid., p. 80.
20. Ibid.
21. Morton Hunt, *Natural History of Love* (1959), p. 318.
22. William Manchester, *World Lit Only By Fire* (1992), p. 55.
23. Ibid., p. 67.
24. In 1840, 16.5 was the average age of the first period. M. Rees, "The Age of Menarche," *ORGYN*, Winter 1995, pp. 2–4.
25. Marjorie Heins, *Not in Front of the Children* (2001), p. 8.

26. Onanism refers to masturbation. The term comes from the biblical passages about Onan in *Genesis* 38:8–10. Onan "spills his seed" and then God punishes him with death. Past interpretations of "spills his seed" were that Onan masturbated, however, it is now generally recognized that Onan performed coitus interruptus, *not* masturbation. Uta Ranke-Heinemann, *Eunuchs for the Kingdom of Heaven* (1990), pp. 85–86.

27. Walter Kendrick, *Secret Museum* (1987), p. 89.

28. Kellog was a Seventh Day Adventist. Their founder, Ellen White, learned in an 1863 vision from God that masturbation can turn a boy into a crippled imbecile, and in a female it can cause inward head decay. As for those children that do not curtail the habit, "They must die." Ellen White, "An Appeal to Mothers: The Great Cause of the Physical, Mental, and Moral Ruin of Children of Our Time," 1863.

29. Richard Zacks, *History Laid Bare* (1994), pp. 385–386.

30. Martha Cornog, *Big Book of Masturbation* (2003), pp. 35–36.

31. In a 1959 study fifty percent of medical school seniors in Philadelphia and twenty percent of their faculty believed masturbation led to insanity. David Allyn, *Make Love, Not War* (2000), pp. 128–139, 321.

32. Alfred Kinsey, Wardell Pomeroy, and Clyde Martin, *Sexual Behavior in the Human Male* (1948), p. 513.

33. John Locke, *Thoughts Concerning Children* (1693).

34. Bernard Murstein, *Love, Sex, and Marriage* (1974), p. 251.

35. *Hellfire Nation: The Politics of Sin in American History* (2003).

36. Morton Hunt, *Natural History of Love* (1959), p. 319.

37. Ibid., p. 317.

38. Reay Tannahill, *Sex in History* (1980), p. 356.

39. Derived from J.J. Potterat, et al., "Estimating the Prevalence and Career Longevity of Prostitute Women," *J. Sex Res.*, May 1990, pp. 223–243.

40. D'Emilio, *Intimate Matters*, p. 203.

41. Ibid., p. 147.

42. The Army set up a similar program in Nashville after it first transported all the Nashville prostitutes to Cincinnati. This relocation program was abandoned when they all came back.

43. Lawrence Friedman, *Crime and Punishment in American History* (1993), p. 131.

44. Ibid., p. 127.

45. James Morone, *Hellfire Nation* (2003), p. 262.

46. Ibid., p. 265.

47. Ibid., p. 262.

48. Ibid., p. 266.

49. David Langum, *Crossing Over the Line* (1994), p. 43.

50. Ibid., p. 49.

51. Ronald Kessler, *Bureau* (2003), p. 9.

52. Ibid., pp. 114–118.

53. An early example was the Palmer Raids (1919–1920), where thousands were arrested for their political beliefs. A program marred by illegal tactics was the Counter Intelligence Program (COINTELPRO), which ran from 1956 to 1971. The only reason it was stopped was because a group called the Citizens' Commission to Investigate the FBI broke into an FBI field office in 1971 and mailed out documentation of the program to Congress and the media. They were never caught. Ibid., pp. 96, 156.

54. The presidents of this time, Woodrow Wilson (1913–1921) and Warren Harding (1921–1923), were both adulterers. Future president Franklin Roosevelt was also having his first extramarital affair at this time. See Appendix Two.

55. Langum, *Crossing Over the Line*, p. 148.

56. Ibid., p. 150.

57. Ibid., p. 148.

58. James Morone, *Hellfire Nation* (2003), p. 268.

59. Ibid., p. 270.

60. An example was Jack Johnson's Mann Act "victim" Belle Schreiber. Schreiber, the daughter of a Milwaukee policeman, voluntarily left a Chicago secretarial job to join the "sporting life."

61. D'Emilio, *Intimate Matters*, p. 203.

62. George Kneeland, *Commercialized Prostitution in New York City* (1917), pp. 104–105.

63.   Lawrence Friedman, *Crime and Punishment in American History* (1993), p. 326.
64.   As for police harassment, arrested prostitutes were often paraded through the streets to be jeered by righteous onlookers. Mayor Brand Whitlock of Toledo commented, "We found that the police, if they were brutal enough, could drive the girls off the streets. Of course, after a while the poor things … would come back. Then the police would have to practice their brutalities all over again." Morone, *Hellfire Nation*, p. 272.
65.   Brand Whitlock as quoted in Ruth Rosen, *Lost Sisterhood* (1982), p. 18.

8

Sex V

Its End?

The Revolutions

I

The 1920s Sexual Revolution
Women Get Their Sexy Back

Just as the Industrial Revolution fostered the sexuality of the Victorian Era, another round of societal changes would change sex in the 1920s.

As before, increased independence of young adults played a large part. Family control was lessened by the growing number of kids attending high school.[1] High schools allowed young men and women to socialize outside the family's purview. The car, a "house of prostitution on wheels," would also increase freedom.[2] With cars youth could take advantage of the growing forms of commercial recreation, such as movie theaters, dance halls, and amusement parks. Supervised courtship that occurred in parlor rooms and porches was being replaced by the dating system, with stages such as "going out" and "going steady."[3]

New attitudes were also coming into prominence. Some had been spread by feminist reformers like Victoria Woodhull, who believed in free love.[4] Free love was the idea that love, not marital status, should legitimate sexual relations.[5]

153

Other attitudes came from the new scientific field of psychology. Sigmund Freud's ideas were gradually introduced into American society during the 1910s, and the general concept that reached the masses was that an omnipresent sexual instinct drove society forward, and that its repression could cause psychological suffering.[6]

The youthful independence and new attitudes were flaunted by the fashionable young women of the 1920s, known as flappers. Whereas a newspaper in 1872 could slyly portray Woodhull as disreputable by illustrating her with an exposed ankle (still covered by stocking),[7] the flappers wore skirts just below the knee and bared their arms. They wore makeup, previously the fancy of only prostitutes and actresses. Flappers also smoked and drank like men, used '20s slang like "big cheese," "baloney," and "the cat's meow," and enjoyed the nightlife enlivened by the innovations of electric lighting, air conditioning, and jazz.

The flappers may have been the ones displaying their released sexuality, but covert behavioral changes were widespread. Prostitution declined significantly in the twentieth century. Males who came of age after the first World War (1914–1918) went to prostitutes half as often as the prewar generation.[8] Although the Mann Act's defenders took credit, reports pointed to another cause.

A typical entry was made in Newark where investigators wrote that they found:

> A large number of girls and young women who sin sexually in return only for the pleasures given or the company of the men with whom they consort . . . They have no ethical standards and believe . . . that they have a right to the pleasures they can gain from their bodies.[9]

Perplexed vice crusaders classified this new female breed "clandestine prostitutes" or "charity girls."[10] Prostitution was declining not because of the FBI but because women were now having non-marital sexual intercourse for free. Whereas the typical Victorian man had his first sexual intercourse with a prostitute, the typical twentieth-century man now had his first intercourse with a girlfriend.[11]

The new sexuality was changing not only when it was done but how it was done. Women began disrobing for sex and experiencing orgasm.[12,13] Sexual variation, including oral sex, mutual masturbation, and non-missionary coital positions, increased as well.[14]

Although it appeared to be a historic revolution for those in the midst of it,[15] the 1920s were merely returning to sexual normalcy after the frigid Victorian Era. While women explored their sexuality more than their Victorian mothers, they were not promiscuous. Petting parties were a common phenomenon for teens and young adults. As the name implies, kissing and fondling were enjoyed, but "bamey-mugging" was not.[16] As with the Puritans, premarital sex was usually reserved to one partner with the expectation of marriage.

As always, the youthful independence was contingent upon location and wealth. In the middle of the twentieth century, one young man still groused, "I'll tell you, it's really tough getting it in a small town. Everyone has their eyes on you and especially on the girl. You can hardly get away with anything."[17]

II
1930s–1950s
Toothbrushes & Commies

The Roaring Twenties abruptly ended in 1929, when the stock market crash launched the Great Depression. For the next twenty years America would be preoccupied with crushing poverty and the Second World War.

During this time consumerism became America's driving force. A capitalist economy flourishes when people are kept in a permanent state of discontent and spend their lives seeking satisfaction through buying material goods. This discontent is maintained with advertising, and advertisers learned that in a sexually repressed society sex was (1) a source of discontent and (2) drew attention.

Entire industries, such as cosmetics, sprang up to help people feel sexually attractive. Even in advertisements for products that had nothing to do with sex, attractive models and seductive poses were used to grab attention. The omnipresence of sexual advertising in society gradually accustomed people to seeing sex, even if only through the allusions that slipped past the censors.[18]

In the 1930s, the hungry, unemployed populace had more important things to think about than the vices of others and their views changed accordingly.[19] In religious circles, Jesus' message of sharing and helping others took precedence over prudery,[20] but by the late 1940s postwar prosperity allowed charity to be once again pushed aside.

In addition, the commencement of the Cold War created an "other" to stoke a new round of moral crusades.[21] Communism's atheism made Communists the ideal enemy to rally around. Communism was not simply a different ideology. Communism was evil. *Life* magazine wrote in 1955 "It seems pretty clear that Communism is a form of Satan in action, to be resisted by all means at all times."[22]

In the 1950s, religion and patriotism blurred into one.[23] In a symbolic act of the times, the Pledge of Allegiance was amended in 1954 to include "under God." So popular was the bill that after the Senate unanimously passed it, the House of Representatives' Democratic sponsor and the Senate's Republican sponsor fought over who would get credit. They compromised by standing side by side proudly reciting the new pledge in unison as President Dwight Eisenhower signed the bill into law.

This new religious spirit was harnessed and turned against sex. Congressional committees in the '50s repeatedly made absurd connections between left-wing politics and the exposure of obscenity to minors.[24,25] However, America's gullibility to sexual paranoia was waning due in large part to the work of Alfred Kinsey, a zoology professor at Indiana University. In 1948 and 1953, the world's foremost expert on gall wasps published groundbreaking sex studies. These best-sellers reduced sexual ignorance.

The Kinsey reports revealed that "deviant" sex such as masturbation, homosexual sex, extramarital sex, oral sex, and even bestiality were not as rare as people thought. Kinsey estimated that nineteen out of every twenty American males had broken a law having sex.[26] Either some of these things were not perverted, or the majority of Americans were perverts.[27] No matter how that question was answered, millions of sexually "abnormal" Americans were relieved to learn they were not alone.

Although polls showed that a large majority of the public approved of scientific sexual research,[28] Kinsey was intensely attacked. An Indiana Roman Catholic newspaper wrote that Kinsey's studies "pave the way for people to believe in

156

communism."[29] J. Edgar Hoover, as head of the FBI, wrote in *Reader's Digest* that Kinsey's work threatened "our civilization" and "our way of life," and had the FBI open a file on him.[30]

III

THE 1960s SEXUAL REVOLUTION
SEXUAL HEALING

Although a popular concept, the idea of the 1960s Sexual Revolution is misleading. The "revolution" actually began in the 1950s with the Beat artists and their prosecution, and extended into the late 1970s. The change in sexual activity was predominantly an acceptance among middle- to upper-class white women of premarital sex with a male in a committed relationship (although no longer with the expectation of marriage). This is not the population-wide transformation from purity to promiscuity portrayed by conservatives like former President George W. Bush.

A. The Courts: Oh Yeah, That Constitution

By mid-century the sexual censorship of celebrated literary figures, which began with the crusading zealot Anthony Comstock in the 1880s, was embarrassing not only to literary highbrows but mainstream Americans as well.[31] The religious/patriotic moral zeal of the 1950s brought continuous prosecution, however, the culture had changed. Whereas Victorian censors had operated with the middle class behind them, the new crusaders now found themselves to the right of most Americans.[32]

Courageous publishers openly "broke" the obscenity laws, suffering imprisonment and financial devastation so that the constitutionality of the obscenity laws could be challenged in court.[33] One of these was Barney Rosset, who published Henry Miller's *Tropic of Cancer* in 1961. Now considered one of the greatest novels of the twentieth century,[34] at the time Rosset was required to defend himself in sixty separate obscenity cases, costing him over $1.9 million in legal fees.[35]

Tropic of Cancer passages like the following attracted the government's prosecutorial wrath:

> O Tania, where now is that warm cunt of yours, those fat, heavy garters, those soft, bulging thighs? There is a bone in my prick six inches long. I will ream out every wrinkle in your cunt, Tania, big with seed. I will send you home to your Sylvester with an ache in your belly and your womb turned inside out. Your Sylvester! Yes, he knows how to build a fire, but I know how to inflame a cunt. I shoot hot bolts into you, Tania, I make your ovaries incandescent. Your Sylvester is a little jealous now? He feels something, does he? He feels the remnants of my big prick. I have set the shores a little wider, I have ironed out the wrinkles. After me you can take on stallions, bulls, rams, drakes, St. Bernards. You can stuff toads, bats, lizards up your rectum. You can shit arpeggios if you like, or string a zither across your navel. I am fucking you, Tania, so that you'll stay fucked. And if you are afraid of being fucked publicly I will fuck you privately. I will tear off a few hairs from your cunt and paste them on Boris' chin. I will bite into your clitoris and spit out two franc pieces . . . [36]

Buoyed by the scientific backing of Kinsey's publications and the softening of popular attitudes, and seeking relief from the obscenity cases clogging the courts, judges began critiquing the extremely broad obscenity test—obscenity was anything that could arouse anybody.[37]

In 1949 a spirited Philadelphia judge, Curtis Bok, wrote a scathing critique arguing that this test was ridiculous because some "moron" could be aroused by a "seed catalogue." Regarding inadvertently harming children, he wrote that by the time his own young daughter would be interested in reading adult books she would have learned the "biologic facts of life." As Bok put it, there is:

> . . . something seriously wrong at home if those facts have not been met and faced and sorted by then . . . . I should prefer that my

own three daughters meet the facts of life and the literature of the world in my library than behind a neighbor's barn, for I can face the adversary there directly.[38]

In 1959 the Supreme Court first responded to the lower judges' complaints by refining the test for obscenity. The high court would continue its modifications in later cases and by the mid-1960s it was clear that literature could no longer be censored by local police departments.[39]

Just as the Great Depression put the pettiness of criminalizing personal vices into perspective in the 1930s, the Vietnam War's military draft had the same effect in the 1960s. It was difficult to fathom how the government could force Americans to risk their lives "for freedom" in Vietnam, while simultaneously denying them the freedom to read, view, and have sex however they pleased.

In 1965 the Supreme Court declared Connecticut's ban on contraception unconstitutional,[40] and in so doing announced that implicit in the Bill of Rights was a right to privacy. This reasoning would play a part in blocking government interference in such notable cases as *Roe v. Wade* in 1973, which protected a woman's right to an abortion in the first trimester of pregnancy, and *Lawrence v. Texas* in 2003, which protected consensual adult sexual contact such as male-on-male anal sex.

Although the battle over censorship still continues over pornography and live adult entertainment,[41] the wall had been broken. The words and images released by the courts would continuously chip away at Victorian prudishness and the sexist double standard.

B. Beats and Hippies:
Getting a Peace

This battle over censorship was integral to the "hippie" youth movement of the 1960s and 1970s. The hippies' roots were in 1950s San Francisco, where avant-garde writers collected around the City Lights paperback bookshop in North Beach. They called themselves Beats, and would meet to discuss philosophy and experiment with literary forms and non-conventional sex.[42] They were disillusioned with mainstream values and were inspired by the black hipster of Northern ghettoes who, excluded by white society, listened to jazz and had liberal views on sex and drugs.[43]

In 1957 City Lights owner Lawrence Ferlinghetti published a book titled *Howl and Other Poems*, by the Beat Allen Ginsberg. The local police captain arrested a City Lights clerk for selling it and issued a warrant for Ferlinghetti. *Howl* opened with the famous lines, "I saw the best minds of my generation destroyed by madness, starving hysterical naked/dragging themselves through the negro streets at dawn looking for an angry fix," and went on to celebrate homosexual desire. Among Ginsberg's generation were those:

> who let themselves be fucked in the ass by saintly motor-cyclists and screamed with joy,
>
> who blew and were blown by those human seraphim, the sailors, caresses of Atlantic and Caribbean love,
>
> who balled in the morning in the evenings in rosegardens and the grass of public parks
>
> and cemeteries scattering their semen freely to whomever come who may …[44]

The presiding judge, Clayton Horn, found Ginsberg's book had some redeeming social importance, and therefore was not obscene, adding "life is not encased in one formula where everybody acts the same or conforms to a particular pattern."[45] The failed *Howl* prosecution backfired immensely by drawing national media attention to the Beats. By the early 1960s, San Francisco was teeming with would-be writers sporting the Beat look of black turtleneck, goatee, and berets.

In August 1965, the young Beat Jefferson Poland staged a nude "wade-in" with two women at a San Francisco beach.[46] Poland was a founder of the Sexual Freedom League, and believed that anti-nudity ordinances were a denial of basic civil liberties and contributed to sexual repression. With a cheering crowd and several press cameramen as witnesses, Poland waded into the icy water with only a flower behind his ear. The crowd held a banner that read, "Why be ashamed of your body?" and chanted, "Sex is clean! Law's obscene!" Upon returning to shore Poland and his cohorts were arrested and the story made the national news, as he had hoped.[47]

160

Poland was arguably the first hippie.[48] His natural look with the long hair, flower, and brazen nudity was a contrast to the prevailing sophisticated look of the Beats and the jackets and ties of ordinary college males. Poland's sex movement would never be supported by mainstream youth, however, his style and his method of peaceful demonstration would become characteristic of the hippie movement and its protest of the Vietnam War.[49]

Contrary to popular perception, hippies were not promiscuous. Although the term free love was bastardized to mean having sex with anybody at anytime, most hippies were followers of Victoria Woodhull's free love, that is, sex was legitimated by love, not marital vows.[50] Hippies believed sex was innocent and not to be hidden, but still believed it was best when in a relationship.[51] One woman who identified herself as a hippie at Yale in 1971 explained the unwritten rule of the counterculture: "You were supposed to be in a monogamous relationship—serial monogamy, maybe— but monogamy nonetheless. There's only one woman I ever met who really felt like 'anyone at anytime.' I considered her a rogue."[52]

In fact, the vision of the liberated woman as someone who would have sex with all comers was likely fostered by males desiring easy sex. This male ideal was manifest in the sexually voracious science fiction heroine Barbarella of the 1960s, who would subdue foes by disrobing. Many women found Barbarella insulting, as well as hippie slogans like "Free Land, Free Dope, Free Women," and "Peace, Pussy, Pot."[53] Sexist attitudes were prolific in the counterculture of the late 1960s. Women who proposed to add women's rights to the more popular causes of racial equality and ending the Vietnam War faced catcalls such as "she just needs a good screw," "take it off!" and "take her off the stage and fuck her!"[54]

The cartoonist Robert Crumb said about San Francisco's Haight-Ashbury district, ground zero of the hippie movement, "Guys were running around saying, 'I'm you and you are me and everything is beautiful so get down and suck my dick.'"[55] In 1967 a resident gave an even more sinister view. In addition to claiming that rape was as common as "bullshit" on Haight Street, he wrote:

> Pretty little sixteen-year-old middle-class chick comes to the
> Haight to see what it's all about and gets picked up by a seventeen-
> year-old street dealer who spends all day shooting her full of speed

again and again, then feeds her three thousand [micrograms of acid] and raffles off her temporarily unemployed body for the biggest Haight Street gang bang since the night before last.[56]

C. Helen Gurley Brown:
Look Ma, I Had Sex and Didn't Die

The crux of the sexual "revolution" was that the double standard was greatly weakened and premarital sex (independent of marital expectations) was acceptable behavior for middle-class women,[57] so it's not surprising that one historian credits its launch to the 1962 publishing of *Sex and the Single Girl* by Helen Gurley Brown.[58,59]

In *Sex and the Single Girl*, Brown brazenly admitted to having a long history of casual sex before finally marrying at the age of thirty-seven. Not only did she admit to it, but she proudly reveled in it. She described her first attempt at intercourse with a male relative at age eleven,[60] and the more successful episodes that occurred frequently through her schooling years and eighteen different secretarial jobs. Perhaps the most provocative aspect of her book was not that she had premarital sex, but that she did and there were no negative ramifications.

The previous format for presenting casual sex was demonstrated by the 1956 novel *Peyton Place*, by Grace Metalious. It used sexual intrigue and foul play to become a best-selling sensation.[61] Metalious detailed the physically mature seventh-grade character, Betty Anderson, pleading for rough sex from her wealthy boyfriend, Rodney Harrington:

> "Come on, honey," she whimpered. "Come on, honey," and his mouth and hands covered her. "Hard," she whispered. "Do it hard, honey. Bite me a little. Hurt me a little."
>
> "Please," murmured Rodney against her skin. "Please. Please." His hand found the V of her crotch and pressed against it.
>
> "Please," he said, "please."
>
> It was at this point that Betty usually stopped him. She would put both her hands in his hair and yank him away from her, but she did not stop him now. Her tight shorts slipped off as easily as if they

162

THE FILTHY SPEECH MOVEMENT:
Fuck You

Poland's disrobement was inspired by the publicity garnered by the short-lived filthy-speech movement, which had just occurred on the nearby campus of the University of California at Berkeley.

The filthy-speech movement began when a Beat was arrested for holding up a paper that read "fuck." (The Beats' artistic appreciation of the word "fuck" can be seen in the title of the 1962 Beat journal *Fuck You: A Magazine of the Arts*.)

Four students were then arrested for setting up a "Fuck Fund" table to raise money for the arrested Beat, and reading aloud the final passage from D.H. Lawrence's respected *Lady Chatterley's Lover* (1928), with lines such as:

My soul softly flaps in the little pentecost flame with you, like the peace of fucking. We fucked a flame into being. Even the flowers are fucked into being between the sun and the earth. But it's a delicate thing, and takes patience and the long pause.

A fraternity was also harassed for passing out "I Like Pussy" buttons, as was a campus magazine that wrote an article on the controversy called, "To Kill a Fuckingword."

—David Allyn, *Make Love, Not War* (2000), pp. 48–49.

had been several sizes too large, and her body did not stop its wild twisting while Rodney took off his trousers.

"Hurry," she moaned. "Hurry. Hurry."[62]

This passage proves that 1950s entertainment was not limited to sexless utopias, however, it also reflects the 1950s in that on the very same page Anderson learns that she is pregnant. Lust was appropriately rewarded by fate.

Unlike Anderson, Brown was not fictional, and by happily and proudly announcing that she had an active sex life she lessened the guilt of countless similar women who had negatively viewed themselves as "sluts."[63]

Brown would become editor of *Cosmopolitan*, and during her thirty-two-year

163

helm the magazine was transformed into a successful publication that trumpeted female sexuality in articles like "Career-Proof an On-the-Job Affair" and "Phone Sex and the Single Girl."[64]

D. Masturbation: Manual Transmission

Despite being the most common sexual activity, masturbation's approval in the public sphere has been slow in coming. Even though the myth of its harmfulness has largely withered, it is still a source of guilt and embarrassment for millions.[65] The extent that it has become accepted is due in large part to two pioneering artists who vividly exposed the marvel of masturbation.

1. Philip Roth: The Firing Wad

One of the first public admissions of masturbation was made by the fictional character Alexander Portnoy in Philip Roth's 1969 novel *Portnoy's Complaint*. In describing his life to his psychoanalyst, Portnoy revealed:

> Then came adolescence—half my waking life spent locked behind the bathroom door, firing my wad down the toilet bowl, or into the soiled clothes in the laundry hamper, or splat, up against the medicine-chest mirror, before which I stood in my dropped drawers so I could see how it looked coming out. Or else I was doubled over my flying fist, eyes pressed closed but mouth wide open, to take that sticky sauce of buttermilk and Clorox on my tongue and teeth—though not infrequently, in my blindness and ecstasy, I got it all in the pompadour, like a blast of Wildroot Cream Oil. Through a world of matted handkerchiefs and crumpled Kleenex and stained pajamas, I moved my raw and swollen penis, perpetually in dread that my loathsomeness would be discovered by someone stealing upon me just as I was in the frenzy of dropping my load. Nevertheless, I was wholly incapable of keeping my paws from my dong once it started the climb up my belly. In the middle

of class I would raise a hand to be excused, rush down the corridor to the lavatory, and with ten or fifteen savage strokes, beat off standing up into a urinal. At the Saturday afternoon movie I would leave my friends to go off to the candy machine—and wind up in a distant balcony seat, squirting my seed into the empty wrapper from a Mounds bar. On an outing of our family association, I once cored an apple, saw to my astonishment (and with the aid of my obsession) what it looked like, and ran off into the woods to fall upon the orifice of the fruit, pretending that the cool and mealy hole was actually between the legs of that mythical being who always called me Big Boy when she pleaded for what no girl in all recorded history had ever had. "Oh shove it in me, Big Boy," cried the cored apple that I banged silly on that picnic. "Big Boy, Big Boy, oh give me all you've got," begged the empty milk bottle that I kept hidden in our storage bin in the basement, to drive wild after school with my vaselined upright. "Come, Big Boy, come," screamed the maddened piece of liver that, in my own insanity, I bought one afternoon at a butcher shop and, believe it or not, violated behind a billboard on the way to a bar mitzvah lesson.[66]

In the book, Portnoy goes on to describe how he continues to masturbate obsessively even though a penis freckle leads him to think his masturbation has given him cancer, and how he used his sister's cotton panties and images of a physically developed classmate, Lenore Lapidus, to masturbate. He also relates the masturbatory challenges of lost ejaculate and privacy in a household of meddling parents.[67]

Portnoy's Complaint was an instant best-seller and is now regarded as one of the literary gems of the twentieth century.[68] Adolescent boys across America finally had someone with whom they could relate. Whereas Portnoy was fictional, women had their own real-life counterpart in Betty Dodson.

2. Betty Dodson: All Hell Broke Loose In Her Pants

Dodson was born in 1929 and began masturbating at the age of five. Later as a girl she used a mirror to look at her genitals and was horrified. Her inner lips (labia minora) hung out from her outer lips. Although this was completely normal, she believed that she had stretched them out from masturbating. Later in life she was taught that she should not pleasure herself with her clitoris, only with a man and his penis. Even her sexually liberal friends put down masturbation.

Dodson was sexually frustrated in her first marriage. Her husband orgasmed too quickly and she never orgasmed. Sex was followed by embarrassed silence and became more and more infrequent. After he would fall asleep she would masturbate under the covers, "without moving or breathing, feeling sick with frustration and guilt the whole time."[69]

Dodson eventually divorced and in the 1950s moved to New York City to study illustration. Unlike her fellow artists who drew solitary nudes, Dodson drew nudes having sex. In 1968 her life-size images of figures having intercourse were displayed at the Wickersham Gallery next to the Whitney Museum. Eight thousand people came to see her work, and because they were displayed in the gallery's windows, they were also viewed by the general public.

Although labeled "shocking" by the press, it was not until her second show, when she wanted to include four images of women masturbating, that "all hell broke loose."[70] The director finally allowed two images that included one six-foot drawing of her friend, legs spread and clitoris erect, using a vibrator.

Dodson went on to become an advocate for masturbation and female sexual awareness. As a writer she has stressed that women learn to celebrate the diversity of female body types and be "cunt positive." Women have written to Dodson thanking her for introducing them to self-induced orgasm. Those who were already masturbating have written to express their relief, "Ever since I saw your drawing I've felt better about myself—not so guilty, not so alone, not so weird after all."[71]

166

E. The Media: Spreading the Word for Gay Titty Bars

Although the popular media was simply revealing diverse sexual practices that had been around forever, it still had profound effects. People who were not aware of these activities learned of their existence, and people who were already practicing these activities learned they were not alone. The media attention spread the practice of countless sexual activities and reduced their stigma.

One institution at the forefront of this publicity was *Playboy* magazine, started by Hugh Hefner in 1953. As the first magazine to include photographs of nude women, Hefner took precautionary measures to fend off censors. *Playboy* began by not showing the pubic region, with the first shot of pubic hair not occurring until 1969.[72] Hefner also presented sex and nudity in a sophisticated and mature manner. The magazine's logo was an innocent bow-tied bunny and it ran non-sexual material by respected writers. There were no references to masturbation, despite its obvious masturbatory potential. *Playboy's* cautious entry into pornography cleared the way for later, more brazen magazines, such as Bob Guccione's *Penthouse* in 1965 and Larry Flynt's *Hustler* in 1974.

Playboy also cleared the way for more than magazines. An article on arguably the first American topless bar, San Francisco's Condor Club, made it and its star dancer, Carol Doda, sensations, and launched a topless bar craze in the mid-'60s.[73] Doda was one of the first celebrities to use silicone injections to augment the size of her breasts. Her new breasts "set the city on fire."[74,75]

By repeatedly reminding people that sex could be used solely for pleasure, *Playboy* indirectly legitimized homosexuality in liberal portions of society.[76] *Playboy's* rise coincided with the blossoming of a gay cultural underground.

Although homosexuals had gathered in American cities for at least a hundred years, it was not until after World War II that a gay subculture became identifiable.[77] World War II provided a nationwide "coming out" experience.[78] Psychiatrists seeking to prevent the "mentally unstable" from entering the military would thoroughly question inductees about homosexual behavior.[79] After propagating the concept of homosexuality to every recruit, the war then provided unsupervised sex-segregated isolation to large populations of men and women who otherwise would have been married.

Bob Ruffing, a chief petty officer in the Navy, related how "eye contact" would tip him off to other gay servicemen. "Pretty soon you'd get to know one or two people and kept [sic] branching out. All of a sudden you had a vast network of friends."[80]

Returning soldiers, who had accepted their sexual identities and developed homosexual social networks during the war, chose to congregate in port city neighborhoods like San Francisco's Castro and New York City's Greenwich Village. In 1964 *Life* magazine wrote an article about the gay subculture of San Francisco, saying "this social disorder, which society tries to suppress, has forced itself into the public eye because it does present a problem—and parents especially are concerned."[81]

Life declared San Francisco America's "gay capital."[82] If San Francisco was not yet in that position, the *Life* article helped, as gays all over the country read it and moved there. Following suit, smaller cities ran newspaper articles about their own neighborhoods infested with the "pernicious sickness."[83] These articles unintentionally promoted the growth of the neighborhoods by directing isolated gay youth from surrounding areas.

In these urban neighborhoods, certain bars became associated with gay patrons and the institution of the gay bar developed. Although it did not replace the covert public courtship, or "cruising," that occurred at certain city streets, parks, bus, and train stops, gay bars helped to alleviate the social isolation of homosexuality. In fact, it was a violent revolt by patrons against a police raid on a "seedy" Greenwich Village gay bar, the Stonewall Inn, that grew into a weekend of rioting on the evening of Friday, June 27, 1969.[84] This revolt started the gay liberation movement.[85]

F. Openness: One Shining Moment

The 1920s returned America to the pre-Victorian attitudes in which middle- and upper-class women had sex drives. The 1920s returned American women to the Puritan practice of having premarital sex with men they intended to marry. The 1960s and 1970s rolled back some of the Puritan restraint as well.

From the mid-1960s onward the premarital sex rates of white females surged upwards and closed the gap between them and their male peers.[86] Not only were they having premarital sex but it was increasingly occurring in relationships where there was not a definite expectation of marriage. Cohabitation became a visible trend in the 1970s.

The age of first sexual intercourse for white women decreased from roughly eighteen and three-quarters to just below seventeen and three-quarters.[87] Young women were also increasingly engaging in masturbation, although not at the levels of their male counterparts. Oral sex was also becoming commonplace, and anal sex was more pervasive.[88] Among married couples, a good sex life was being seen as central to a good overall relationship.[89]

These changes were occurring behind closed doors and were largely hidden from public view. More alarming to moralists was the openness with which society was publicly accepting sex. In the conservative American political climate at the start of the third millennium, it is difficult to remember how open the late 1960s and 1970s were.

Starting with the commercial success of *Deep Throat* in 1972,[90] hard-core films (showing sexual penetration) were screened in mainstream movie theaters and a few television broadcasters even began reviewing pornographic films.[91] Surprisingly, juries in conservative towns across America ruled *Deep Throat* deserving of First Amendment protection. In one 1973 survey, a quarter of the respondents said they had watched an X-rated film in the previous twelve months.[92] (This was five years before the VCR would allow private home viewing.) Even the former First Lady Jacqueline Kennedy Onassis went and saw one.[93]

In 1969 the sexual musical romp *Oh! Calcutta!* opened off Broadway.[94] Its opening was attended by celebrities such as Shirley MacLaine, Joe Namath, Julie Newmar, and Hedy Lamarr. A comical series of sexual vignettes intended to provoke and titillate, it included naked actors and actresses simulating acts such as sex and date rape.

The creator, Kenneth Tynan, insisted that the show be choreographed by "a non-queer," and that it include "no crap about art or redeeming literary merit."[95] At the end of the show, the entire naked cast spoke out loud conjectured thoughts of the audience, "I mean what is the point, I mean what does it prove? . . . Nudity is passé . . . . That's my daughter up there . . . If they're having fun, why don't they have erections?" The show was a hit with tourists and moved to Broadway, where it broke the record for the longest-running show in Broadway's history.

Another sample of the times was the Manhattan sex club the Continental Baths, which was a nationally known hotspot in the 1970s. Located in the basement of the exclusive Upper West Side's architectural marvel the Ansonia Hotel, it began as a gay bathhouse that featured cabaret-style entertainment. Singers Bette Midler and Barry Manilow both began their careers there,[96] and Midler made the Continental Baths a sensation when she mentioned it on Johnny Carson's *Tonight Show* in 1970.

Soon the club was catering to heterosexuals as well, and straight sex joined the gay sex in the Continental's back rooms. The club was so accepted that Mayor Abraham Beame and Congresswoman Bella Abzug made campaign speeches there and Bloomingdale's stores sold Continental Baths towels.

A taste of its atmosphere is found in Manilow's description of the public-address system's interruptions of a singer's performance:

> LIZ (singing): The night is bitter, the stars have lost their glitter.
> PA: *Free VD tests on Monday in Room 312!*
> LIZ: And all because the man that got away; No more his eager call, the writing's on the wall; The dreams you've dreamed have all gone astray.
> PA: *The orgy room is off limits for the next hour while it's being cleaned, thank God.*
> LIZ: The road gets rougher, it's lonelier and tougher; With hope you burn up, tomorrow he may turn up.
> PA: *A very strange implement has been left in Room 210. Would the kinky person please claim the thing.*[97]

With the influx of suburban heterosexual patrons, the Baths became unpopular with gays. In 1977 new owners changed the name to Plato's Retreat and began catering exclusively to heterosexuals. Plato's Retreat received a positive review from the mainstream magazine *New York* in 1977,[98] and was reportedly frequented by celebrities such as Sammy Davis, Jr., Richard Dreyfuss, Madonna, Paul Newman, and conservative movie icon John Wayne.[99] *Time* magazine estimated that in 1977 over 6,500 men and women visited each month.[100]

Plato's Retreat did not tame down the sex. One New Yorker recalled:

I was at a party with a great friend and this party turned into an orgy. I distinctly remember being in a bedroom with two women making love when my friend walked in and said "Come on, forget about this, we're going to Plato's Retreat." I said, "What, are you crazy?!" Plato's Retreat had only been open three weeks. I was furious. But let's just say I wasn't sorry we left the party. Plato's Retreat was unbelievable. I had never in my life seen anything like this and probably never will again. I mean, thirty, forty couples all making love at the same time, it was amazing, you cannot believe it. Ahhh, those were the days.[101]

Those were the days that are never brought up by sexual conservatives and the media. Instead they chose to label 2007 as an *unprecedented* time of sexual openness that may be turning America's children into "prosti-tots," largely because one female celebrity was caught sans panties in a paparazzo's photograph of her exiting a car.[102] The days when female celebrities went to swingers' sex clubs sans panties has largely been erased from the collective memory.

IV

The Backlash
AIDS Hysteria is a Great Rallying Cry

A. *The Empire Tries to Strike Back Against Facts*

The religious right did not stand passively by as the courts prevented censorship. Conservative commentators decried the "flood" of pornography "deluging" the nation,[103] and politicians wholeheartedly agreed that pornography was a national concern. However, politicians and prosecutors needed evidence that pornography harmed society. Scientific evidence would show the courts that they were not merely using the police to force Victorian sexual morality on the entire population.

In 1967, Congress authorized the Presidential Commission on Obscenity and Pornography to study the causal relationship of pornography on antisocial behavior for two years and then recommend tactics. The Commission was a remarkably objective attempt to cut through a polarizing issue with factual analysis. The Methodist theologian on the commission said "I consider the birth and ensuing work of this commission to have been a milestone in the history of human communications— the first time in history in which men cared about the problem enough to seek the truth about it through the best methods known to science."[104]

If the commission was a milestone in scientifically seeking the truth regarding sex, it would not be repeated. The majority of commissioners recommended that all laws regulating the sale of erotic material to adults be repealed and that sex education for children be bolstered. Despite funding a number of surveys, retrospective studies, and fourteen controlled experiments, no evidence of pornography causing antisocial behavior was found. In fact, the evidence suggested that those deprived of exposure to sexual material were *more* likely to be antisocial.

Studies showed that compared to sex offenders, the average person had significantly greater exposure to erotic materials during adolescence. In one study, incarcerated rapists were found to have an average age of eighteen for first exposure to images of heterosexual intercourse, while the average age for the general population was fifteen.[105] In Denmark, rapes plunged after censorship ended in 1967, and continued to fall as sexually explicit materials permeated Danish commerce.[106] Even the popular conception that exposure to pornography resulted in "calloused attitudes" toward women was found to be unwarranted, and in fact, no negative impact on character could be found.[107]

Despite the Commission finding that sixty percent of Americans agreed that there should be no restrictions on the sale of erotic materials to adults,[108] the Senate voted sixty to five to completely reject the Commission's report.

To dam the pornographic flood, President Richard Nixon installed the conservative Warren Burger as Chief Justice of the Supreme Court. In a 1973 ruling, Burger allowed obscenity to once again be judged by local community standards. Although the Burger court reestablished that the United States of America could easily ban books, its enforcement has been sporadic.[109]

B. The Collapse of the Left: Killer Hippies

The cultural tide turned in the 1970s. The Weatherman group was bombing government buildings and Charles Manson's cult was on trial for committing gruesome murders. In 1975 only an empty gun chamber prevented Manson adherent Lynette "Squeaky" Fromme from assassinating President Gerald Ford. These fringe groups represented a microscopic percentage of the counterculture, but their violence allowed authorities to brand the entire movement as a threat to America's safety.

Another contributing factor to the left's demise was the withdrawal of American troops from Vietnam in 1974. Opposition to the war had unified and inspired divergent progressive interests, and the end of American bloodshed weakened the movement considerably.

During this fracturing, the feminist movement turned completely against First Amendment sexual protections. Feminists began attacking the recently liberated pornography as a "bastion of misogyny." They were incited by the sexist attitudes prevalent in the industry, its sadomasochistic imagery, and its sometimes demeaning portrayal of women.[110]

Feminists chose not to acknowledge that sexist attitudes were also prevalent in most of the 1970s corporate world. Nor did they recognize that although sadomasochism is the achieving of sexual pleasure through the giving and receiving of pain, it is consensual and women are prominent in both roles.[111] The female sadist, the dominatrix, is the epitome of womanly power.

In focusing on the demeaning portrayals of women in pornography, feminists ignored the fact that men were often portrayed in ways that were just as vile. For example, the inflammatory June 1978 cover of *Hustler* had a woman's legs sticking out of a meat grinder with meat coming out the other end. However, in 1977 *Hustler* had portrayed a man grinding his own penis.[112]

The feminist position against pornography was galvanized in the mid-1970s. It began with a *New York Post* article in October 1975 that reported snuff films were allegedly being made in South America and imported into the United States.[113] Snuff films are extreme erotica featuring real rape and murder. Were South American actresses being killed so that American men could be diabolically titillated?

Four months later a shoddy horror movie featuring a pornographic murder entitled *Snuff* opened in New York. Filmed in Argentina, its tag line read, "Made in South America . . . where Life is CHEAP!" Feminists nationwide went berserk with a wave of protests. In Rochester, New York, women picketed the theater carrying *Snuff* for four days straight and smashed a window to destroy the *Snuff* poster. In California, an anonymous group of women threw bricks through four theaters' box office and lobby windows, and another theater had cement dumped down its toilets. High-profile feminists pressured the Manhattan district attorney into launching a murder investigation.[114]

The reaction to *Snuff* was astounding, because the movie was a hoax. A B-movie distributor named Allan Shackleton capitalized on the buzz around the *New York Post* article and purposely presented his cheap movie as an actual snuff film. It is likely that the film's initial protesters were even paid by Shackleton.[115] The horribly amateurish portrayal of the alleged murder in *Snuff*, for example tomato sauce blood and a detached finger reappearing attached, suggests that its frothing critics never bothered to watch it.

Despite the fact that no snuff films have ever been found, their symbolic appeal was too appealing for feminists to care.[116] Snuff films were the feminist metaphor for pornography incarnate—men's lust literally killing women. Shortly after the *Snuff* hysteria, stopping pornography became feminism's primary focus.[117]

C. Skewed Stats:
When I was a Boy All We Did was Chew Gum. Stop Lying.

While leftist activists floundered and broke ranks, the oil crisis of 1973 hit the economy. In retaliation for supporting Israel in the Yom Kippur War, the Arab members of the Organization of Arab Petroleum Exporting Countries (OPEC) refused to export to the United States. This quadrupled the cost of oil and caused the worst recession since the Great Depression of the 1930s.

The affluence of post–World War II America had allowed young adults to be less concerned with preening themselves for corporate employment and more involved in social causes.[118] In the harsh 1970s job market, youth could no longer afford such independence, further decimating the left.

Facing the collapsing economy, politicians did not take responsibility for the government policies that contributed. Instead, as they have throughout history, they found it easier to distract the populace with imagined sexual crises.[119] Increases in rape, teen pregnancy, and sexually transmitted diseases were held up as the just desserts of the "sexual revolution."

This deceitful rhetoric was distilled in a cute and unsubstantiated critique of society. It is still reformulated every several years to fit the alarming youth behavior *du jour*, and takes advantage of the positive bias of human memory.[120] It is usually presented in a form similar to the following:

Top Disciplinary Problems in School

1940	1990
1. Talking out of turn	1. Drug abuse
2. Chewing gum	2. Alcohol abuse
3. Making noise	3. Pregnancy
4. Running in the halls	4. Suicide
5. Cutting in line	5. Rape

None of this was based on facts.[121] Teen pregnancy rates hit their highest twentieth-century level in 1957. However, most of those girls were married by the time they gave birth, so there were more unwed teenage mothers in the 1970s.[122] Changing marriage patterns—not changing sexual habits—were the cause. "Shotgun weddings" became rarer as women gained financial independence and bastardy's stigma lessened. Moralists still use the unwed mother figure to foster false images of 1950s sexual purity, forgetting the 1950s' loveless forced marriages.[123]

Arrests for forcible rape did quadruple between 1958 and 1975.[124] However, this was because the feminist movement had pressured the criminal justice system into taking rape seriously.[125] Prior to the 1960s it was extremely difficult to convict a rapist.[126]

Some of the hurdles were that women's testimony had to be corroborated and evidence of resistance was required. In addition, there was a strong bias against convicting rapists who knew the victim (now referred to as "date rape"), and promiscuous women or women who dressed provocatively were often deemed to be "asking for it."[127] For example, a gunpoint rapist was acquitted in 1971 because the unmarried victim had a lover.[128]

Due to the low probability of successful prosecution and the stigma applied to the victim it is reasonable to assume victims often chose not to report.[129] Although it is incredibly naive and counterintuitive to believe that rape did not occur prior to the sexual revolution, as an emotionally charged issue this assertion was an effective smear of sexual freedom.

Another argument made in these lists is that students did not suffer from sexually transmitted diseases in the good ol' days. The prevalence of sexually transmitted diseases did rise in the 1970s. However, this was because a medical respite had been provided. Since the 1940s, gonorrhea and syphilis could be easily cured with penicillin. This brought about a remarkably anxiety-free sexual atmosphere that lasted through the 1970s. This respite, combined with the proliferation of the birth-control pill, contributed to a decline in condom usage, but in 1979 the herpes virus was discovered. Genital herpes was not debilitating and its oral equivalent (cold sores) carried little stigma. Despite this, genital herpes was publicized as payback for the sexual good times and the media made it a national crisis.[130] Even the supposedly objective *Time* magazine wrote in its cover story, "Perhaps not so unhappily, [herpes] may be a prime mover in helping to bring to a close an era of mindless promiscuity."[131]

D. AIDS: I Don't Have It. Do You? [Laughter]

The discovery of herpes was followed by the discovery of acquired immune deficiency syndrome (AIDS) in the early 1980s. Unlike herpes, AIDS was deadly; however, its initial appearance in America was confined to the gay community, so whereas herpes had quickly garnered headlines, AIDS was ignored.[132] Publicizing AIDS would mean discussing homosexuals and anal sex.

President Ronald Reagan, keeping his word to the Christian Right who helped elect him,[133] kept sex sacred and did not mention the word AIDS in a speech until five years into the epidemic, when over five thousand Americans had already died and countless more were infected.[134] This White House press briefing, with Reagan's Press Secretary Larry Speakes on October 15, 1982, is demonstrative:

Q: Larry, does the President have any reaction to the announcement—the Centers for Disease Control in Atlanta, that AIDS is now an epidemic and have over 600 cases?

MR. SPEAKES: What's AIDS?

Q: Over a third of them have died. It's known as "gay plague." (Laughter.) No, it is. I mean it's a pretty serious thing that one in every three people that get this have died. And I wondered if the President is aware of it?

MR. SPEAKES: I don't have it. Do you? (Laughter.)

Q: No, I don't.

MR. SPEAKES: You didn't answer my question.

Q: Well, I just wondered, does the President—

MR. SPEAKES: How do you know? (Laughter.)

Q: In other words, the White House looks on this as a great joke?

MR. SPEAKES: No, I don't know anything about it, Lester.

Q: Does the President, does anyone in the White House know about this epidemic, Larry?

MR. SPEAKES: I don't think so. I don't think there's been any—

Q: Nobody knows?

MR. SPEAKES: There has been no personal experience here, Lester.

Q: No, I mean, I thought you were keeping—

MR. SPEAKES: I checked thoroughly with Dr. Ruge this morning and he's had no—(laughter)—no patients suffering from AIDS or whatever it is.

Q: The President doesn't have gay plague, is that what you're saying or what?

MR. SPEAKES: No, I didn't say that.

Q: Didn't say that?

MR. SPEAKES: I thought I heard you on the State Department over there. Why didn't you stay there? (Laughter.)

Q: Because I love you Larry, that's why. (Laughter.)

MR. SPEAKES: Oh I see. Just don't put it in those terms, Lester. (Laughter.)

Q: Oh, I retract that.

MR. SPEAKES: I hope so.[135]

This response can be sharply contrasted with more recent administrations' reactions to epidemics.[136] Patrick Buchanan, who later became Reagan's White House Communications Director, helped explain the White House response when he wrote in a 1983 column, "The poor homosexuals—they have declared war upon nature, and now nature is exacting an awful retribution."[137] Buchanan also later helped illuminate the White House's silence:

> Homosexuality involves sexual acts most men consider not only immoral, but filthy. The reason public men rarely say aloud what most say privately is they are fearful of being branded 'bigots' by an intolerant liberal orthodoxy that holds, against all evidence and experience, that homosexuality is a normal, healthy lifestyle.[138,139]

In 1987 Reagan himself wondered aloud about AIDS, "Maybe the Lord brought down this plague . . . [because] illicit sex is against the Ten Commandments."[140]

While the Reagan administration publicly chose a tactful hush, others did not. In 1977, the singer and actress Anita Bryant successfully had a gay anti-discrimination law repealed in Florida on the theme that homosexuals abused and recruited children. She referred to homosexuals as "human garbage" and, like the Aztecs, traced drought to divine dissatisfaction on the issue.[141] Her "Save Our Children" campaign inspired similarly successful campaigns across the country and sparked the current fundamentalist Christian political movement via televangelist Jerry Falwell.[142] At her request, Falwell would begin his political career with an anti-gay rally in Miami. Two years later he would found the fundamentalist Christian political organization the Moral Majority, which helped elect Ronald Reagan president in 1980.

The 1970s' rational approach to sex was derailed by AIDS. Predictably, as it spread to the general population the political right would blame the sexual "revolution," *not* the painfully slow governmental response.[143] When Surgeon General C. Everett Koop advocated in 1986 that people use condoms and children receive sex education, the religious right was livid.[144]

Fundamentalist Christians believed safe-sex education would be "grammar-school sodomy classes," and instead called for mandatory testing and a quarantine of those afflicted with the disease.[145] Falwell stated that quarantining people with AIDS was not more unreasonable than quarantining cows with brucellosis, but that it would not likely occur because "homosexuals constitute a potent voting bloc and cows do not."[146]

AIDS refueled the Christian fundamentalists' anti-sex crusade. In a 1986 sermon covered by ABC, Falwell dished up standard fare when he preached that AIDS was God's judgment against America for embracing immorality. AIDS illustrated that it was the end of days and that his listeners were possibly the last generation before Jesus Christ's second coming.[147]

Politicians were also well aware of AIDS' potential. At a conference on "How to Win an Election" sponsored by a Christian fundamentalist group in 1985, Newt Gingrich, future Speaker of the United States House of Representatives, said:

> [AIDS] is something you ought to be looking at . . . AIDS will do more to direct America back to the cost of violating traditional values, and to make America aware of the danger of certain behavior than anything we've seen . . . For us it's a great rallying cry.[148]

E. God Tells Bush to Stop Fishing and Run for President

This rallying cry would continue through Ronald Reagan, George H.W. Bush, Bill Clinton,[149] and culminate in the election of a Christian fundamentalist, George W. Bush, to the presidency in 2000—a man who ran for president instead of going fishing because God told him to.[150]

Like his religious predecessors of the past two millennia, W. Bush blamed society's problems on sex:

> The sexual revolution that began in the 1960s has left two major problems in its wake. The first is the historic increase in non-marital births that have contributed so heavily to the nation's domestic problems including poverty, violence, and intergenerational welfare dependency. The second is the explosion

of sexually transmitted diseases that now pose a growing hazard to the nation's public health.[151]

And just like his predecessors, he believed he could stop sex by arming the government with the Bible. Through his abstinence-only funding, W. Bush funneled *billions* of dollars to organizations whose explicit mission was to convert people to Jesus Christ.[152] In addition, W. Bush, like his father and Reagan before him, packed the courts with moral conservatives.[153] Instead of legal scholars, W. Bush appointed "common-sense judges who understand that our rights were derived from God."[154]

Common-sense judges who look to God, rather than the accumulated wisdom of centuries of legal scholarship, tend to hear from God exactly what the judge's personal mores dictate. They tend to defer to Congress on sexual privacy matters with judicial justifications similar to "Congress does not need the testimony of psychiatrists and social scientists in order to take note of the coarsening of impressionable minds . . ."[155] Congress does not need the testimony because Congress' interpretation of the Bible is the same as theirs.

In this judicial environment it was not surprising that in 2005 former Attorney General Alberto Gonzales made a new anti-obscenity squad in the FBI and announced that fighting the producers of pornography (of consenting adults for consenting adults) would be "one of [his] top priorities," causing even law enforcement to snicker.[156,157]

When the courts are filled with judges chosen for their religious zeal, rather than their legal reputations, they cease to be a check or a balance on the legislature. The protection from Bible-touting politicians that the courts have given to our bedrooms, our books, our computers, is currently looking frail.

NOTES

1. From roughly ten percent in 1900 to roughly two-thirds in 1940. U.S. Dept. of Education, *120 Years of American Education: A Statistical Portrait* (1993).
2. Robert Lynd and Helen Lynd, *Middletown in Transition* (1937), pp. 163–164.
3. Going steady allowed teenage girls to obtain some sexual experience while preserving their reputations.
4. A former prostitute, she was the first woman to run for president and she and her sister were the first female Wall Street stock brokers. She said of women who gloried in never experiencing sexual desire, "No

sexual passion, say you. Say, rather, a sexual idiot, and confess that your life is a failure . . ." Barbara Gold-smith, *Other Powers* (1999), p. 149.

5. The Victorian marriage was unjust. A wife had no legal rights, could be beaten as long as death did not result, could not refuse sex, and could be recaptured if she ran away.

6. John D'Emilio and Estelle Freedman, *Intimate Matters* (1988), pp. 223–224.

7. Amanda Frisken, *Victoria Woodhull's Sexual Revolution* (2004), p. 97.

8. Alfred Kinsey, et al., *Sexual Behavior in the Human Female* (1953), p. 300.

9. D'Emilio, *Intimate Matters*, p. 214.

10. Ibid.

11. A 1938 study found that twenty-eight percent of those born between 1890 and 1900 had lost their virginity before marriage, in contrast to over half of those born after 1910. Lewis Terman, *Psychological Factors in Marital Happiness* (1938), p. 331.

12. Fully a third of the women born before 1900 usually remained clothed during sex, in contrast to only eight percent of those born during the 1920s. Kinsey, *Sexual Behavior in the Human Female*, p. 365.

13. Starting with the women born after 1900, each successive generation of women experienced orgasm more frequently from sexual intercourse than those before them. Ibid, p. 380.

14. Ibid., pp. 360–364.

15. Ben Lindsey and Wainwright Evans, *Revolt of Modern Youth* (1925), pp. 18, 32.

16. Barney-mugging was sexual intercourse. Males who frequently attended these parties were known as snug-glepups.

17. Winston Ehrmann, *Premarital Dating Behavior* (1959), p. 87.

18. D'Emilio, *Intimate Matters*, p. 279.

19. James Morone, *Hellfire Nation* (2003), pp. 347–349, 365–366.

20. Ibid., pp. 347–349.

21. Their threat was severely exaggerated. By 1956 the Communist Party USA's membership had dropped to 5,000 with at least 1,500 of these being undercover FBI informants. One FBI counterintelligence head said that by the mid-1950s, "The Communist Party was basically a bunch of discussion groups." Ronald Kessler, *Bureau* (2003), pp. 96–97.

22. John Jessup, "The World, the Flesh, and the Devil," *Life*, 26 Dec. 1955, p. 143.

23. Morone, *Hellfire Nation*, p. 381.

24. Marjorie Heins, *Not in Front of the Children* (2001), p. 51.

25. One example of this was comic books. They were an addictive "marijuana of the nursery" that could turn a child into a "sex maniac." A Senate committee toured the country in the early 1950s and confirmed the threat. Morone, *Hellfire Nation*, p. 397.

26. Alfred Kinsey, Wardell Pomeroy, and Clyde Martin, *Sexual Behavior in the Human Male* (1948), p. 392.

27. Kinsey's surveys were flawed in that he did not use a scientific sampling of the population. (Due to the political climate this was not feasible.) However, Kinsey's theme that sex beyond marital missionary intercourse was significantly more pervasive than Victorian America acknowledged has remained valid.

28. D'Emilio, *Intimate Matters*, p. 287.

29. Stephen Whitfield, *Culture of the Cold War* (1996), p. 186.

30. Heins, *Not in Front of the Children*, p. 53.

31. Ibid., p. 48.

32. D'Emilio, *Intimate Matters*, p. 284.

33. A notable publisher was Samuel Roth (1893–1974) who spent years imprisoned for obscenity convictions. Another was Ralph Ginzburg who was indicted by Robert Kennedy. A comedian who fought censorship despite legal persecution was Lenny Bruce.

34. Ranked the fiftieth best novel of the twentieth century by the Modern Library Board, a division of Random House, July 1998.

35. Adjusted to 2012 dollars. David Allyn, *Make Love, Not War* (2000), p. 65.

36. Henry Miller, *Tropic of Cancer* (1961, orig. pub. 1934), pp. 5–6.

37. Test from the English case of *Regina v. Hicklin* (1868).

38. Heins, *Not in Front of the Children*, pp. 49, 284–285.

39. Allyn, *Make Love*, p. 70.

40. *Griswold v. Connecticut*, 381 US 479 (1965).
41. A more recent example was the prosecutions of Larry Flynt, publisher of *Hustler* magazine, as portrayed in the movie, *The People vs. Larry Flynt* (1996).
42. Beat was black slang for exhausted. Allyn, *Make Love*, p. 26.
43. D'Emilio, *Intimate Matters*, pp. 275–276.
44. Barry Miles, ed., *Howl* (1986), pp. 3–4.
45. Ibid., p. 174.
46. Poland would later legally change his name to Jefferson Fuck and then to Jefferson Clitlick.
47. It was well known that then-president, Lyndon Johnson, swam naked in the White House pool. Allyn, *Make Love*, p. 42.
48. Ibid.
49. The hippie movement was unorganized, ergo there were multiple themes, such as anti-materialism, anti-war, mysticism, back-to-nature, racial equality, socialism, and drug usage.
50. Allyn, *Make Love*, pp. 99–102.
51. Hippie guru Timothy Leary was particularly outspoken in his criticism of promiscuity and his support of monogamy.
52. Allyn, *Make Love*, p. 100.
53. Ibid., p. 103.
54. Judith Hole and Ellen Levine, *Rebirth of Feminism* (1971), pp. 112, 134.
55. Abe Peck, *Uncovering the Sixties* (1991), p. 51.
56. The resident was Chester Anderson. Ibid., p. 47.
57. Allyn, *Make Love*, p. 5.
58. Ibid., p. 10.
59. The launch was aided by the birth control pill's 1960 debut, which freed women to have sex as casually as men. Ibid., p. 40.
60. It was a failure because her vagina was too tight.
61. It also became the first successful TV soap opera in the 1960s.
62. Grace Metalious, *Peyton Place* (1956), p. 203.
63. Allyn, *Make Love*, p. 16.
64. Wendy Martin, April 1998, p. 138; and Lori Campbell, p. 130.
65. In the early 1990s half of all masturbators felt guilty. Robert Michael, et al., *Sex in America* (1994), p. 166.
66. Philip Roth, *Portnoy's Complaint* (1969), pp. 17–19.
67. Several late 1990s movie gags that put national attention back on masturbation were from *Portnoy's Complaint*—including *There's Something About Mary* (1998) where ejaculate goes unnoticed in hair, and *American Pie* (1999), where the liver is replaced with a pie.
68. Ranked the fifty-second best novel of the twentieth century by the Modern Library Board, a division of Random House, July 1998.
69. Allyn, *Make Love*, p. 140.
70. Ibid., p. 141.
71. Ibid., p. 142.
72. In 2001 the first playmate appeared without pubic hair.
73. At the time they were popularly known as go-go clubs.
74. Reportedly from 34B bra size to 44D. Allyn, *Make Love*, p. 25.
75. Elizabeth Haiken, *Venus Envy* (1997), p. 247.
76. Gay playwright Larry Kramer credits Hefner with doing more for gay liberation than anyone else. Allyn, *Make Love*, pp. 161-162.
77. John D'Emilio and Estelle Freedman, *Intimate Matters* (1988), pp. 123, 288.
78. Ibid., p. 289.
79. Ibid., pp. 288–289; and Allyn, *Make Love*, pp. 322–323.
80. John D'Emilio, *Sexual Politics, Sexual Communities* (1983), p. 26.
81. "Homosexuality in America," *Life*, 26 June 1964, p. 66.
82. Paul Welch, "The 'Gay' World Takes to the City Streets," *Life*, 26 June 1964, p. 68.
83. "The Homosexual in America," *Time*, 21 Jan. 1966, p. 42.

84. Allyn, *Make Love*, pp. 145–146.

85. D'Emilio, *Intimate Matters*, p. 318; Allyn, *Make Love*, p. 146; and George Chauncey, *Gay New York* (1994), pp. 2, 373–374.

86. Paragraph from D'Emilio, *Intimate Matters*, pp. 331, 334.

87. As of 1992, the average age of first intercourse for a white woman born between 1942–1951 was roughly eighteen and three-quarters years old, vs. seventeen and three-quarters for a woman born between 1952–1961. Robert Michael, et al., *Sex in America* (1994), p. 90.

88. As of 1992, there was a forty-four percent chance a woman born between 1942–1951 had performed fellatio, vs. seventy percent for a woman born between 1952–1961. Participation in anal sex for these two groups were twelve percent vs. twenty-four percent. Michael, *Sex in America*, pp. 140–141.

89. Philip Blumstein and Pepper Schwartz, *American Couples* (1983), p. 201.

90. *Deep Throat* chronicles Linda Lovelace's search for sexual pleasure, which proves elusive because her clitoris turns out to be located in her throat. In the opening, a man is performing cunnilingus on Lovelace and as she takes out a cigarette she apathetically asks, "Do you mind if I smoke while you eat?"

91. Allyn, *Make Love*, pp. 184, 234.

92. Tom Smith, "The Polls—A Report: The Sexual Revolution?" *Public Opinion Quarterly*, Fall 1990, p. 428.

93. It was *I Am Curious (Yellow)* (1969). "Photographer Says Mrs. Onassis Used Judo on Him," *New York Times*, 6 Oct. 1969, p. 36.

94. The title is a play on the French pun, "Oh! Quel cul t'as!" which means "Oh, what an ass you have!"

95. Allyn, *Make Love*, p. 121.

96. Manilow performed at the Baths for New Year's 1970. Goaded on by the naked crowd and disinhibited by alcohol and marijuana, he disrobed and hit the water too. Barry Manilow, *Sweet Life* (1987), pp. 100–101.

97. Liz Torres sang. Ibid., p. 99.

98. Dan Dorfman, "Franchising Sex," 28 Nov. 1977, pp. 38–40.

99. "Inside Tale of Plato's Flesh Pit," *New York Post*, 23 June 2003.

100. John Leo, "Is There Life in a Swinger's Club?" *Time*, 16 Jan. 1978, p. 53.

101. Allyn, *Make Love*, p. 238.

102. Kathleen Deveny and Raina Kelley, "Girls Gone Bad?" *Newsweek*, 12 Feb. 2007, p. 41.

103. Ibid., p. 184.

104. *Report of the Commission on Obscenity and Pornography* (1970), p. 374.

105. Paragraph from ibid., pp. 236–237.

106. Ibid., pp. 230–232.

107. Ibid., p. 202.

108. Allyn, *Make Love*, p. 188.

109. In the middle of the Civil War (1863), a Union captain wrote to President Abraham Lincoln complaining of the large number of pornographic photos being passed around by soldiers and officers. Lincoln does not appear to have shared the captain's concern, as there's no record of Lincoln doing anything about it. Richard Zacks, *An Underground Education* (1997), pp. 306–307.

110. Allyn, *Make Love*, pp. 280–281.

111. Sadomasochistic imagery was trendy in 1974. Department store catalogs would show scenes suggesting assault and a Rolling Stones' billboard pictured a bruised woman and read, "I'm black and blue from the Rolling Stones." Ibid., p. 280.

112. Ibid., p. 289.

113. Ibid., p. 281.

114. Carolyn Bronstein, *Battling Pornography* (2011), pp. 86–91.

115. Whitney Strub, *Perversion for Profit* (2011), p. 231.

116. Ted McIlvenny, caretaker of over 350,000 sex movies for the Institute for the Advanced Study of Human Sexuality, says that in his twenty-five years of following the porn business, he's only seen three films where someone died. Two of them were accidental, with a man dying of a heart attack during an S&M scene and another man accidentally suffocating during an autoerotic asphyxiation. The third was a Moroccan religious film that showed a hunchbacked child torn apart by wild horses while men stood around and masturbated. Cecil Adams, "Is There Such a Thing as a Snuff Film?" ChiReader.com, 2 July 1993.

117. Allyn, *Make Love*, p. 281.

118. Allyn, *Make Love*, p. 273.
119. Ibid., pp. 273–274.
120. W. Richard Walker, John Skowronski, and Charles Thompson, "Life Is Pleasant," *Rev. Gen. Psychol.*, 2003, 7(2), pp. 203–210.
121. The original lists were created in the early 1980s by a Dallas fundamentalist Christian, T. Cullen Davis, to attack public schools. The lists were later used by California's governor, California's Department of Education, CBS News, and George Will in a *Newsweek* editorial. When a journalist finally tracked it to Davis and asked for evidence, Davis responded, "How did I know what the offenses in the schools were in 1940? I was there. How do I know what they are now? I read the newspapers." Barry O'Neil, "The History of a Hoax," *New York Times Magazine*, 6 Mar. 1994, pp. 46–49.
122. Stephanie Coontz, *Way We Never Were* (1992), pp. 39, 202.
123. Between one-quarter and one-third of the marriages formed in the 1950s eventually ended in divorce, and during that decade two million legally married people lived apart from each other. National polls in the 1950s found that twenty percent of couples considered their marriages unhappy. Ibid., pp. 35–36.
124. From 3,680 to 17,524. U.S. Bureau of the Census, *Statistical Abstract of the United States* (1960), p. 143; (1976), p. 163.
125. This culminated in the late 1970s with husbands no longer being immune to rape charges by their wives, and the institution of rape-shield laws that protected accusers from having to testify as to their sexual histories. Lawrence Friedman, *Crime and Punishment in American History* (1993), pp. 430–434.
126. In 1969, New York City had 2,415 complaints of rape, 1,085 arrests, and only eighteen convictions. Ibid., p. 432.
127. Ibid.
128. Diana Russell, *Politics of Rape* (1984), pp. 11–12.
129. Almost two thirds of rapes still go unreported. Callie Rennison, "Rape and Sexual Assault," Dept. of Justice, Aug. 2002.
130. David Allyn, *Make Love, Not War* (2000), p. 292.
131. John Leo, "New Scarlet Letter," *Time*, 2 Aug. 1982, p. 66.
132. Randy Shilts, *And the Band Played On* (1988), pp. 109–110.
133. "Reverend Reagan," *New Republic*, 4 April 1983, pp. 7–9.
134. Its first speech mention was in "Message to the Congress on America's Agenda for the Future," 6 Feb. 1986.
135. Jon Cohen, *Shots in the Dark* (2001), pp. 1–2.
136. In 2005 President George W. Bush announced the National Strategy for Pandemic Influenza (Bird Flu) and submitted a $7.1 billion emergency budget request to Congress for preparedness funding. This was prior to the global human death toll breaking one hundred, with no deaths yet occurring in North America. In 1983 Reagan only wanted to raise federal spending for AIDS from $14.5 million in 1983 to $17.6 million in 1984. By 1987, the United States was the only major Western industrialized nation still without a coordinated education campaign. Shilts, *And the Band Played On*, pp. 359, 589.
137. Patrick Buchanan, "AIDS Disease," *New York Post*, 24 May 1983.
138. Patrick Buchanan, "New Morality and Barney Frank," *Bangor Daily News*, 4 Sep. 1989.
139. The administration's hostility is verified by Reagan's surgeon general. C. Everett Koop, "AIDS," *Koop* (1991), pp. 194–239.
140. Edmund Morris, *Dutch* (1999), p. 458.
141. She believed California's drought could be God's punishment for the state's liberal antidiscrimination laws. Tom Mathews, "Battle Over Gay Rights," *Newsweek*, 6 June 1977, p. 16.
142. William Martin, *With God on Our Side* (1996), pp. 197–200; and Shilts, *And the Band Played On*, pp. 43–44.
143. Shilts, *And the Band Played On*, p. 474.
144. Koop was a fundamentalist Christian hero for his role in making abortion opposition an issue in the mid-1970s. For the first five years as surgeon general he had been instructed by the administration to stay silent on AIDS. After telling his superiors he could not be quiet any longer, his ensuing AIDS straight talk immediately turned him from a religious-right hero to a pariah. Koop, "AIDS," *Koop*, pp. 194–239.
145. Shilts, *And the Band Played On*, pp. 588–589.
146. Dennis Altman, *AIDS in the Mind of America* (1986), p. 67.
147. Susan Harding, *Book of Jerry Falwell* (2001), pp. 156–161.
148. "Newt Set Strategy for Religious Right—10 Years Ago," *Freedom Writer*, Feb. 1995.

149. Clinton fired his surgeon general for discussing masturbation and signed the bill that officially deemed extramarital sex harmful.

150. W. Bush told a televangelist that he preferred to be a retired governor buying fishing lures at Wal-Mart, but God wanted him to run for president because America would need him. Stephen Mansfield, *Faith of George W. Bush* (2003), p. 109, and Jim Wallis, "Dangerous Religion," *Sojourners*, Sep./Oct. 2003.

151. George W. Bush, "Working Towards Independence—The President's Plan to Strengthen Welfare Reform," Feb. 2002, ret. from WhiteHouse.gov on 14 June 2006.

152. One missionary said, "Our mission was to spread the Gospel of Jesus Christ throughout the world. We put that in our proposals and said, 'If we don't get funded, so be it'. And we got the money." W. Bush pushed funding for domestic abstinence-only teaching to $250 million annually. $1.5 billion of his global AIDS initiative was tagged for abstinence-only teaching. Esther Kaplan, *With God on Their Side* (2005), pp. 42, 217.

153. Reagan was arguably the first modern president to insist on ideological purity in his judicial nominees. More than a third of Reagan's second-term nominees were rated as barely qualified by the American Bar Association (ABA) as compared to six percent for his predecessor, Jimmy Carter. W. Bush cut the ABA out of the process altogether. Ibid., pp. 262–263, 266–267.

154. "Remarks Prior to Discussions with President Vladimir Putin of Russia and an Exchange with Reporters in Kananaskis," *Weekly Compilation of Presidential Remarks*, 1 July 2002, p. 1099.

155. *Action for Children's Television v. FCC* (ACT III), 11 F.3d 170 (D.C. Cir. 1993).

156. This led one exasperated FBI agent to say, "I guess this means we've won the war on terror," and an experienced national security analyst to say, "It's a running joke for us." It has also resulted in quips such as, "Honestly, most of the guys would have to recuse themselves," and "I already gave at home." Barton Gellman "Recruits Sought for Porn Squad," *Washington Post*, 20 Sep. 2005.

157. Some U.S. attorneys did more than snicker, as resistance to these prosecutions was reportedly a factor in at least two of the controversial attorney firings that led to investigations and Gonzales' eventual resignation. Josh Gerstein, "Porn Prosecution Fuels Debate," Politico.com, 31 July 2009.

SEX VI

REPERCUSSIONS
THE GOVERNMENT
WANTS YOUR SEX

America's sex taboo has four general repercussions that contribute to unhappiness—government dysfunction, widespread ignorance, unhealthy attitudes, and sexual deprivation.

In the government, hypocritical politicians censor the schools and our media, and criminalize consensual adult sexual activities. To justify this enforcement of sexual morality, they grossly exaggerate sex-related dangers and lie. Their dishonesty damages the government's credibility, distracts voters from substantive problems, erodes civil liberties, and results in fallacious policies that cost billions.

Government censorship has caused widespread ignorance. Past censorship has left sex scholarship far behind other academic areas. The resulting ignorance regarding homosexuality and the different male and female sex drives causes shame, guilt, and persecution. The transformation of high school sex education into abstinence celebration programs causes more sexually transmitted diseases, abortions, and unwanted pregnancies. G-rated high school textbooks have turned fascinating subjects, like history and world cultures, into bores. The resulting ignorance in these areas allows a majority of Americans to believe their sex laws are normal and that sexual freedom would be disastrous.

Lastly, because of the taboo millions are prevented from having sex by law (since those unable to find a sexual relationship cannot pay for it), and millions more are ashamed to explore the gamut of sexual pleasure.

I

GOVERNMENT:
PRUDES GONE WILD

A. Hypocrisy: I Can Have Sexual Fun,
But You Can't So I Can Get Your Grandma's Vote.

The hypocrisy can be seen clearly in America's last four presidents. Ronald Reagan, George H.W. Bush, Bill Clinton, and George W. Bush have built the billion-dollar federal abstinence-only sex education program that teaches that all sex outside of marriage is damaging.[1]

None of these men restrained their own sexual behavior to the marital bed. (Details in Appendix Two.) Three of the four have not been able to constrain their sexual behavior to the marital bed *even* while married. The man who first fiscally forced the program on the states could not even keep his extramarital sex out of the Oval Office.

Reagan bedded so many young Hollywood beauties between his two marriages that he lost track of their names. He abandoned one after impregnating her and was accused of date rape by another.[2] Despite these sexual shenanigans, as president he formed the Meese Commission. This farcically biased and unscientific investigation sought to prove pornography was harmful to adult viewers so that it could be criminally prosecuted.[3] As a 40-year-old man, Reagan was using models half his age as disposable sex toys, yet he later wanted to make it criminal for men to *view pictures* of models having sex.

The billions of dollars that the last president, W. Bush, extended to combat

AIDS internationally was hamstrung by morality. Roughly $1.5 billion of the aid was tagged specifically for abstinence-only teaching. Missionary groups receiving this money were allowed to use faith-based approaches and reject any HIV-prevention strategy they found morally objectionable.[4]

Money was forbidden for any group that did not pledge opposition to prostitution. Even though sex workers in third-world countries are some of the hardest hit by AIDS, under these constraints humanitarian groups were not even working with them for fear of losing funding.[5]

All this was from a man who was asked by a reporter what he talked about with his presidential father and responded, "pussy,"[6] and whose brother, Neil Bush, testified to having sex with prostitutes in Asia numerous times while married to his first wife.[7]

The hypocrisy extends beyond presidents, however, there is not enough space to cover all the congressmen and women who have fought to straitjacket our populations' sexuality to the marital bed, while their own behavior has been egregiously different.[8] Perhaps their hypocrisy should not be surprising because it merely reflects the hypocrisy of those who elect them.[9]

B. Lies: Breaking A Commandment
for Something Jesus Didn't Care About

Usually the comments about pornography are merely misleading, as when Senator Orrin Hatch said "[Pornography] can be very addictive and harmful."[10] This statement is technically true, however, if you define *addictive* and *harmful* that broadly then the same could be said of pizza.

Other statements are more egregious. Representative Joseph Pitts said on the floor of the House of Representatives in 2005, "[T]he cause and effect between pornography and crime, violence against women and children, rape and child abuse, is clearly defined." That same year Representative Charles Pickering stated in a Congressional hearing, "[A] culture of obscenity leads to a greater culture and exploitation of children. . . . They contribute to each other. And until you address both, you are going to see a dramatic increase."[11] These wild claims have no scientific support.

The lies are not limited to individual politicians. Ann Jordan, the Director of The Initiative Against Trafficking in Persons at Global Rights, had to write an April 2005 letter,[12] co-signed by eight female academics in related fields, to the State Department pointing out the numerous lies in the fact sheet on the department's website titled "The Link Between Prostitution and Sex Trafficking."

One of its most egregious deceits said that "[w]here prostitution is legalized or tolerated, there is a greater demand for human trafficking victims and nearly always an increase in the number of women and children trafficked into commercial sex slavery."[13]

A problem occurs when these lies are vigorously publicized. For example, people of all ages see federally funded television advertisements like this one from 2002:

> **Voiceover:** In ten seconds, you'll hear this father spread a lie. He's a good dad, who's trying to help his son. But if he doesn't know the truth, he can't tell the truth.
> *Screen:* HERE COMES THE LIE.
> **Father:** They'll keep you safe. They'll keep you safe. They'll keep you safe.
> **Voiceover:** Condoms will not protect people from many sexually transmitted diseases and you could be spreading lies to your children.[14]

For informed people this fearmongering may be comical, but the young girls who get pregnant because government ads and sex education teachers say condoms do not work will likely miss the humor.[15] This disinformation destroys the government's credibility. Helpful information that our government and schools give in the future will be disregarded.

In addition, financing and pushing fake science on the populace hampers factual inquiry. Resolving the issues of our day is difficult even when honest information is being presented. When the United States' government is spending billions on spreading fake science, the resulting quagmire of mixed messages can make the search for truth appear overwhelming.

C. Distraction: Stopping Perverts
is the Most Important Issue in the Universe

Obfuscation may be the purpose because sexual alarmism distracts the population from truly debilitating concerns. One hundred years ago "white slavery" hysteria focused the nation's attention on the apparition of white girls being forced into prostitution, and legislative action was promptly taken. At the same time, hundreds of thousands of children were working long hours in factories without inciting similar outrage or action.[16]

Child predators are still media and political darlings. In the early 1980s, an uproar surrounding child kidnapping led to voluminous legislation and missing kids' faces on milk cartons. Representative Paul Simon stated at the time, "The most conservative estimate is that fifty thousand young people disappear each year because of stranger kidnapping." The actual number was closer to two or three hundred a year.[17]

When California Governor Pete Wilson signed into law the chemical castration of child molesters in 1996 he stated that child molesters "have a drive to do what they do . . . three out of four will commit a new offense or parole violation within two years." This was false. The rate was closer to twenty-five percent, with many of those being technical violations.[18] (The recidivism rates for pedophiles are among the lowest of the criminal population.)[19]

Unlike white slavery, missing children and child molestation are not a myth. However, the popular conception that drives the hysteria is that of kids being snatched by a pedophile from the mall and ending up molested and dead. This is extremely rare. The overwhelming majority of missing children are runaways or are kidnapped by a family member, such as a parent in a custody battle.[20] Likewise, the overwhelming majority of child molestations are done by someone the child knows intimately, usually a parent or guardian.[21]

A Department of Justice study determined that roughly forty-six American children are abducted and killed by strangers in a year. Kidnappings by strangers that do not result in death amount to roughly 115.[22] To put that into perspective, sixty-six Americans die a year from being struck by lightning.[23] Meanwhile, these extremely rare cases of child kidnapping and murder continue to drive the belief that kids must be monitored at all times, and that all child molesters must be chemically castrated, jailed for life, tracked for life, or executed.[24]

One California father recently wrote about the predator paranoia at his young son's school.[25] In the article, one mother said she did not think she would *ever* let her son ride his bike around the block alone, saying "The world is a very different place now than it was when we were growing up." (She attributed the increased danger to the Internet.) Parents like her were the reason why the school did not allow elementary-age children to bike to class. When the writer suggested walking or biking as an answer to the school's traffic problems at a PTA meeting, others responded with disbelief. One father referred him to the Megan's Law website and suggested another traffic solution: "Get rid of all the predators. Then you won't have any more traffic."

This fear-driven "house-arrest" of children is occurring nationwide. It has alienated America's youth from nature,[26] made them fearful,[27] and has contributed to a tripling of the childhood obesity rate since 1980.[28]

On a broader level, predator hype distracts the public and its political discourse. Smog in the United States is responsible for thousands of premature deaths a year and billions in health care costs. The most susceptible to its harms are children and the elderly. A unanimous recommendation for more stringent air quality standards by a 2008 Environmental Protection Agency advisory panel has been brushed aside by both President George W. Bush and President Barack Obama.[29] Since deaths due to smog do not inspire the same excitement as deaths due to sexual abuse, the media and the politicians are relatively muted.

D. Kill All Child Molesters:
Why Civil Liberties are Important

Those who commit sexual crimes against children deserve punishment, however, the reaction to the heinous kidnapping/rape/murder of Megan Kanka in 1994, which inspired Megan's Law, is similar to punishing all future murderers for the heinous crimes of serial killer, necrophile, and cannibal Jeffrey Dahmer. This political overreaction to isolated atrocities in the area of child molestation occurs regularly and there are repercussions.

192

When politicians beat their breasts and create barbaric *mandatory* punishments for molesters, they do not point out all the molesters who are not monsters. Although it is a crime worthy of punishment, do taxpayers really want to spend $29,000 annually to imprison a man for years who flashes a girl or grabs a girl's chest?[30,31] Is it wise to give this man a scarlet letter through sex offender registration instead of giving him a chance at treatment with the carrot of redemption?

Another twist is that one third of all sex offenses against minors are committed by other juveniles.[32] This figure does not include the numerous young adults who have sexual relations with teenagers across the age of consent lines.[33] Age of consent laws are frequently used by parents who do not like their daughter's boyfriend. In these cases charges are brought against the will of the "victim."[34] Thirty-two states apply sex offender registry requirements to kids.[35] It is questionable how many of these kids and young adults deserve to be publicly branded forever as baby-rapers.[36]

The repercussions extend to non-molesters as well. The legal rules politicians tear down for sex offender cases protect innocent people from unjust prosecution. For such a loathsome crime it is easy to falsely accuse, as no evidence of injury is necessary. When I was a teacher in 2003 I physically took an eighth-grade girl to the principal's office by her arms. She later accused me of knocking her down during the trip to look up her skirt. The only witnesses were her two good friends. I was fortunate that the two went against their friend and told the truth, but the girl's mother still believed the story because "her daughter would never lie to her." As the mother of a minor it would have been her decision to press charges and if she was wealthier, or I was wealthier, she might have.

One protection of the accused that politicians usually target in molestation cases is the statute of limitations. This rule prevents charges from being made so long after an alleged offense that a defense would be difficult. How would I be able to defend myself against that girl's charges if she did not make them until 2013?

DNA testing has shown that accused does not mean guilty. When it can be used in criminal investigations it clears the named subject *a third of the time*.[37] The heinous nature of child molestation allows politicians to overlook the difference.

E. Monetary Costs: Jail 'Em All.
Why Are My Taxes So High?

In addition to the billions spent on abstinence-only education, billions are also spent on criminalizing consensual adult sex. One of the only studies of the cost of prostitution enforcement was done in the mid-1980s.[38] It found that in Dallas the average arrest, court, and incarceration costs amounted to roughly $2,900 per prostitution arrest, and that large cities spent an average of over $16 million on prostitution control every year.[39] Half of the sixteen cities studied spent more on prostitution control than on either education or public welfare. Although judges are loath to use strapped prison space on prostitutes, police still focus resources on prostitution.

This prioritizing is not without consequences. During Houston's crusade against prostitution in 1975, eleven percent of the police department's criminal investigative force handled prostitution cases exclusively. While Houston waged this failed prostitution battle, reported felonies increased and their rate of arrest decreased. In the mid-1980s, Cleveland spent eighteen officer hours on prostitution duty for every violent offense that failed to yield an arrest.

This was at a time when national polls showed (1) ninety-four percent of people who called the police believed they should have responded faster than they did, (2) less than half the population could say prostitutes did more harm than good, and (3) people ranked prostitution's severity 174th out of 206 offenses. "A store owner knowingly puts 'large' eggs into containers marked 'extra large'" placed 175th.

II
IGNORANCE IS DUMB

A. No Birds and the Bees, More Abortions and STDs

The federal government has been replacing sex education with abstinence-only education for over a quarter of a century. In 2009 a CDC panel reviewed sixteen studies of abstinence-only programs and judged them ineffective at promoting their only goal—abstinence. The same panel analyzed over fifty studies of comprehensive sex-ed programs and found they reduced sexual activity, increased the usage of birth control/protection, and reduced the occurrence of STDs.[40]

Although federally mandated sexual disinformation is counteracted by parents and the Internet,[41] the youthful ignorance is still astounding. This is particularly true among the poor, who are more likely to not have involved parents or Internet access. In a poll of thirteen- to fifteen-year-olds from disadvantaged areas in seven cities, seventy-four percent thought that letting semen drip out of the vagina after sex prevents pregnancy, seventy percent did not know that douching is not a form of birth control, and fifty-six percent did not know that a female cannot get pregnant through oral sex. This may appear to be harmless innocence until it is realized that almost a third of these children had already had sexual intercourse.[42]

This ignorance has resulted in significantly higher teenage rates of pregnancy, abortions, and sexually transmitted diseases than in countries with sex-ed. The following chart shows how America compares to Canada, France, and Sweden on these issues. Canada has more sex-ed than America, although approaches vary by province. France and Sweden have compulsory sex-ed in their schools.

The blatant disregard of scientific evidence while dumping billions into abstinence-only education is bewildering.[43] It suggests that fundamentalists *want* sexually active teens to suffer. By keeping teenagers ignorant their fear tactics become valid, because unprotected sex *is* dangerous.[44]

There are two problems with this "let sinners rot" strategy. First, by hijacking America's public school systems via the federal government, not only are the children of fundamentalist Christians being punished, which is arguably their parents' prerogative, but so are children of impoverished families.

195

BUSTING HOS IS FUN SON
The Law Enforcement Angle

Why do police departments continue to focus on investigating prostitution? Here are two motives:

(1) Prostitution cases dramatically raise "closed by arrest" rates. The mid-1980s prostitution study of sixteen cities found that prostitution was one of the only offenses for which nearly one hundred percent of "reported incidences" resulted in arrest. Eighty-three percent of the violent or property crimes reported in those cities were *not* closed by arrest.

(2) Police enjoy the work. Prostitutes pose less danger to officers than real criminals.

WE'RE #1 IN GONORRHEA
MORALITY OVER REALITY[45]

	USA	CANADA	FRANCE	SWEDEN
Percent Who Had Sex Before Age 18	63	53	50	65
Percent of Women Having a Child Before Age 20	22	11	6	4
Abortions per 1,000 15- to 19-Year-Old Females	29.2	21.2	10.2	17.2
Incidence of Gonorrhea per 100,000 15- to 19-Year-Olds	572	59	8	2

Second, there is the question of the rights of the children of fundamentalist Christians. Do parents have the right to bar factual information from their children, particularly when it involves a public health concern? The European Parliament has recognized that children have a right to sex education irrespective of their parents' wishes.

In addition, the entrapment methods employed are enjoyed. As one officer said when describing the newly-leased cars and clothes used, "we've got to look like guys with money to burn." Their time is often spent around women in massage parlors and modeling studios, and they can have the prostitutes perform sex acts on them without themselves being criminally liable. Even where they are not authorized to partake, one vice division supervisor's comment is telling: "My wife won't let me go undercover. She doesn't trust me. There are some good-looking women out there and a lot of fast talking and a lot of temptation."

—Julie Pearl, "Highest Paying Customers," *Hastings Law J.*, Apr. 1987, pp. 769–800; and Tom Jackman, "Spotsylvania Deputies Receive Sex Services in Prostitution Cases," *Washington Post*, 13 Feb. 2006, p. B01.

B. Distortion of Scholarship: Men Really are Assholes

The taboo has also hindered the academic study of sex. In the past, cultural artifacts were intentionally hidden or destroyed. In the sixteenth century Spaniards systematically demolished sexual objects found during their sacking of the Americas.[46]

Perhaps the most famous archeological purging was of Pompeii in Italy. When excavated in the 1700s, the numerous sexual frescos, statues, and other artifacts were either trashed or removed to a secret chamber in Rome. Although more recent excavations in Pompeii have been opened to the public complete with sexual images, shame still reigns. Tourists are falsely told that these areas were brothels when they were actually places like public baths.[47]

Censorship has not only hampered the study of sex culturally but also biologically. The court systems' protection of First Amendment rights in the 1950s and 1960s first set the groundwork for American scholarship in these areas to begin,[48] however, the taboo still contributes to a lack of funding.

The study of homosexuality's biological causes is one area that is just beginning to blossom. Scientific evidence of its biological nature has only recently received academic acceptance.[49] This belated finding refutes the notions that gay people choose their sexuality and that they can voluntarily change—notions that have often been behind homosexual persecution.

The delay of research into inherent biological differences regarding male and female sex drives has been another cause of grief. Understanding that men are biologically predisposed to view sex more as a physical act, whereas women are predisposed to see it as an emotion-laden bonding activity, illuminates the callousness of some men toward sex transgressions. These transgressions range from cheating to rape.[50]

Understanding different sexualities does not excuse sexual transgressions, but it helps to bridge the chasm between the male and female conceptions of the breach—a chasm that causes considerable pain. Currently people often acknowledge gender differences but not their biological underpinnings. Communication is reduced to clichés with men saying, "It was just sex," and women saying, "All men are assholes."

Understanding different sexualities also allows these differences to be better navigated. The fact that men innately desire sex more frequently than women gives women power in relationships. This can be a source of conflict unless the male rewards the woman for meeting his additional sexual needs with non-sexual inducements.

SEXUAL POLITICS
According to Testosterone (T) Levels[52]

	Pro-Criminalization of Sexuality (low T)	Anti-Criminalization of Sexuality (high T)
Women	Most women	High-T women
Men	Low-T men	Most men
Age	Senior citizens	Teens, young adults
Professions[1]	Academics, farmers, ministers, white-collar workers	Actors, athletes, field soldiers, blue-collar workers

The countless biological differences between male and female sexuality (see Chapter Four) help explain more than relationships. For example, testosterone levels help illuminate sexual politics. People with low testosterone levels are more

198

likely to believe that criminal regulation will put an end to extramarital sex because they have a lower, and more controllable, libido themselves.

This is particularly apparent in regards to age. Older people are led to believe that they control their behavior better because they are wiser,[51] and wisdom can be taught to youth. However, this is a hypocritical stance regarding sex because they now have a lower sex drive, and a lower sex drive cannot be taught to youth.

C. Distortion of Art: Jesus' Penis

Western art has developed within the Christian sexual ethic. Nudity is a rarity in paintings. Sex and its various permutations are even rarer. Sexual artwork is almost never seen because curators, editors, and collectors have operated under modern taboos in selecting the art worthy of preservation and presentation.

Frequently, sexual works of art have been modified. One of the world's greatest paintings, Michelangelo's Sistine Chapel (sixteenth century), is an example. Michelangelo managed to portray nudity over objections,[53] but shortly after Michelangelo's death loincloths were painted over it and some figures were completely redone.

Nudity was a common sight in everyday life up until the Victorian Era, so the abundance of coverage in art is inaccurate. A prominent example of this inaccuracy is the portrayal of Jesus Christ on the cross. He is almost always portrayed with a loincloth. This is a false image as Jesus was almost certainly crucified naked.

Although dishonesty is inherently bad, arguably even in art, Christ's portrayal provides an example of possible consequences. At least one historian believes an honest crucifix might have prevented the repeated Jewish slaughters that dot Europe's history. His reasoning is that a naked Jesus would have forced Christians to recognize their savior's Jewishness every time they saw his circumcised penis.[54]

D. Distortion of Teaching:
G-Rated Learning Is Boring

American high school students hate history, considering it boring and irrelevant.[55] They are by and large correct, as history textbooks distort or leave out anything that might reflect badly—like sex—upon America, Christianity, or past leaders. History is presented as an unstoppable march toward progress, with things getting better all the time. Recent history is largely ignored and glossed over because students' parents lived through it and might recognize the propaganda.[56]

This has left Americans ignorant.[57] Boring history classes do not capture students' attentions and the bland white-washed factoids memorized for tests are soon forgotten. G-rated history is as popular with teenagers (and adults) as G-rated movies. Topics such as the Protestant Reformation would be intriguing and memorable if the Roman Catholic Church's hypocritical view on sex was revealed with examples of the Borgia popes, and the English split was revealed as the soap opera it was. Henry VIII's sexual machinations with the lusty Anne Boleyn, which resulted in Mary I, "Bloody Mary," and Elizabeth I, "Bloody Bess," would rival television's sauciest fare.

Instead the Church's nefarious activities are presented tactfully, as in this example from one texbook: "Devout Germans denounced the practice of letting bishops buy their positions. Many Germans resented the worldliness, lack of piety, and greed of some members of the clergy."[58]

The sexual Olympics being practiced by the papacy has been reduced to "worldliness" and "lack of piety." In regard to the English split from the Roman Catholic Church, the matter is often reduced to King Henry wanting a male heir and splitting when the Church did not grant him an annulment. Henry's bevy of beddings and beheadings are ignored, as are the sexual passions behind them.

History lessons should not be a litany of sexual factoids. Knowing that Napoleon Bonaparte was a butt man,[59] while the French king he was born under, Louis XV, was a breast man,[60] has roughly the same value as memorizing the battle dates of the French Revolution. However, by removing all sexually-related information a better understanding of historical figures' psyches and their accomplishments is lost.[61]

Sexuality, character flaws, and eccentricities are inherent to everyone.

G-SPOTTING
In The Ass

The orgasms stemming from the female G-spot and the male prostate are exalted but little understood. The G-spot, an ultra-sensitive vaginal area, was identified in 1950 by its namesake, Ernst Gräfenberg. Scientific evidence of its existence is lacking, with one expert calling it the "gynecologic UFO." However, the absence of evidence may simply stem from the "ridiculous" absence of laboratory research into this tabooed part of the female anatomy. Similar cursory scientific treatment is given to the male prostate gland's arousal ability. (The semen milking of mammals for research is often done via prostate stimulation.)

This evidentiary void is changing. Recent tests suggest the G-spot is the female prostate (the Skene's glands). This would explain the striking similarities between female descriptions of G-spot sensations and male descriptions of prostate sensations—orgasms that, as opposed to penis or clitoral orgasms, are directed inward and encompass the "full body." It would also explain the G-spot's connection to female ejaculation (prostate controls male ejaculation) and the reason some women do not have a G-spot (ten percent of women have underdeveloped Skene's glands).

—Nicola Jones "Bigger is Better . . .," *New Scientist*, 3 Jul. 2002; Alice Ladas, Beverly Whipple, and John Perry, *G Spot* (2005), p. 134; Fernando Santos & Sebastião Taboga, "Female Prostate," *Anim. Reprod.*, Jan./Mar. 2006, p. 6; Roy Levin, "G-Spot," *Sex. Relation. Ther.*, 2003, 18(1), p. 118; and Jonathan Margolis, *O* (2004), p. 162

Their purging may explain why youth can empathize more with troubled modern celebrities than lionized heroes from the past. Presenting accomplished historical figures truthfully and realistically would allow youth to better relate to them, and in turn be more likely to aspire to their heights.

E. Distortion of Reality:
Maybe Our Culture Is the One That Sucks

The sexless historical and cultural landscapes presented in schools indoctrinates students into thinking that America's sexual scruples were and are universal. This allows people who blame sex for society's problems to be taken

201

seriously. An accurate presentation of history would teach people that moralists and politicians have been using sex as a scapegoat and grossly exaggerating its dangers for two thousand years. It would also show that for two thousand years authoritarian sexual repression has failed.

An example of the effects of this socialization was when President Bill Clinton's sexual indiscretions endangered his presidency in the late 1990s. If the population knew of the numerous infidelities of hallowed presidents and world leaders (see Appendices One and Two), more people would have been disgusted with the circus that was his impeachment.

Accurate presentations of other societies' sexual attitudes cannot be found even in award-winning big-budget R-rated movies.[62] If the effort to recreate other cultures' dress was extended to their sexual mores, fewer citizens would fear sexual freedom.

For example, the original Americans, the Indians, varied widely across tribe and region in their sexual conventions.[63] However, most of them did not associate either nudity or sexuality with sin or shame, and tribes frequently accepted premarital intercourse, polygamy, and homosexuality. There were other common traditions. Children were usually allowed to masturbate and engage in sex-play. Sex with partners outside the marital bounds was more acceptable. Many tribes had men who chose to live like women. These men, whom the Europeans called "berdache," bore no stigma.

In the Indians' looser sexual atmosphere, the sale of sex was unknown and rape was extremely rare. Unlike the Spanish settlers who believed the rape of Indian women was their right of conquest, Indians did not sexually assault white captives.

The Indians' "gross sensuality and unnatural vice" greatly disturbed some Europeans, such as John Smith, who was troubled when young Indian women would welcome him to their tribe by offering to sleep with him.[64] When missionaries tried to instill monogamy, they argued it allowed men to know which children were theirs. An Indian once replied, "You French people love only your own children but we all love all the children of our tribe."[65]

Although Indians did not try to convert Europeans to their lifestyle, a phenomenon occurred that is completely absent from American history textbooks.[66] Europeans converted anyway. This occurred all along the Atlantic coast. Benjamin Franklin observed, "No European who has tasted Savage Life can afterwards bear to live in our societies."[67] Another man wrote: "There must be in the Indians' social bond something singularly captivating, and far superior to be boasted of among us; for thousands of Europeans are Indians, and we have no examples of even one of those Aborigines having from choice become Europeans."[68]

When captives were to be exchanged following battles, Europeans, especially the children, had to be "bound hand and foot" and forcibly returned to white society, while Indian prisoners went back to their own "with great signs of joy."[69] These embarrassing scenes often tarnished European victories. To stop the flow, Europeans used force. Hernando De Soto posted guards to prevent desertion and in many places defectors faced heavy penalties, including death.

Europeans were attracted to the freedom Indians enjoyed as individuals.[70] Teaching modern American students of the Indianization phenomenon would expose them to different sexual worldviews, and show that when people have had a choice, our mores were rejected.

III
Unhealthy Sexual Attitudes (USA)

One historian has written that sexual morality is "a purposeful myth that has been productive of more guilt and misery than any other aspect of human or divine law."[71] A sign of the sex taboo's continuing health is that sexual activities are still shameful for many.[72]

A. Shame: My Tinky Is Dinky

Sexual shame occurs in numerous ways. One example is the penis industry. A large portion of the male population suffers from insecurity and depression over the length of their penises.[73,74] Several misconceptions contribute to this angst. First, large penises have not always been the idealized size, just as enormous female breasts have not always been the idealized size. Second, since most American men only see erect penises in pornography they have a distorted view of the truth.[75] Third, the flaccid penis size does not have a correlation to the erect penis size.[76] This misconception is demonstrated by the fact that almost two-thirds of men seeking penis enhancement are concerned not about their erect penis size, but its size when limp.[77]

This misconception about flaccid penis size has even made its way into presidential politics. When Representative Calvin Dooley was running for Congress in 1992 he frequently told an anecdote about using the House of Representatives gym with President George H.W. Bush. The crowd-pleaser had the following punch line: "It's quite an experience to be a lowly freshman congressman in the shower with the President of the United States (pause) and to look over and see (long pause) that the leader of the free world is (longer pause)…a…well…er…just an average little guy."[78]

Pornography actresses have begun presenting an artificially uniform view of female genitalia as well. Many get excess labia lips and clitoral hoods trimmed and now genitalia modification is surging in popularity. One plastic surgeon said that patients frequently tell him, "I thought I was normal and I watch these movies with my boyfriends and now I feel like I must be a freak."[79]

B. Overemphasis: Relax, It's Just Sex

It's an irony that our culture's sexual taboo has magnified sex's psychological power. By focusing on its repression, society has actually increased its centrality.[80] Victorian prudery led to the flourishing of pornography,[81] and the asexual Victorian wife created the omnipresence of prostitution.[82]

This paradox has been noticed by journalists investigating sexually free environments. One said of the 1970s swingers' club Plato's Retreat, "Oddly enough, there is less sexual electricity in the air than at a Rotary Club party."[83] A Plato's Retreat security guard who manned the orgy room nightly remarked, "You stand here long enough, and you see everything. You lose some of your uptightness about sex, but some of the mystery gets destroyed. Pretty soon it's like watching wrestling on TV. Boring."[84]

A journalist who visited Copenhagen after Denmark became the first Western country to lift all prohibitions on pornography made by and for adults found that:

> With so much of the tension removed from the subject, it
> seems to be discussed less than in similar circumstances in New

GROW UP
Clinton's Impeachment Was About Sex

President Bill Clinton was impeached in 1998 for lying under oath, but those familiar with the law knew he was impeached for what he lied about—having consensual sex with his intern.

The lie was a trivial crime. The testimony was in a civil sexual harassment suit that was (1) filed three days before the statute of limitations expired, (2) backed and goaded by right-wing political activists who have admitted their aim was to take down the president, (3) eventually dismissed as groundless, and (4) the lie was only remotely related to the case. It is highly unlikely that criminal perjury charges would ever be brought in such a minor matter. The lie would merely be punished by the presiding judge, and that is what happened. (The president was fined.)

Even if criminal charges were brought, the writers of the Constitution never intended for mere criminal acts to remove a president. High crimes and misdemeanors were an abuse of the office that endangers the state. To be capable of impeaching him on such a petty offense, especially in light of the deference shown to the two preceding presidents in the Iran-Contra affair, was a farce.

—Cass Sunstein, "Impeachment? The Framers Wouldn't Buy It," *Washington Post*, 4 Oct. 1998.

York ... Time and again I tried to steer the conversation around to good old sex ... only to have it steered right back to such familiar topics as the raising of children, the war in Vietnam, and the impossibility of finding a large enough apartment.[85]

This dissipation of sex's "shocking" nature has been reproduced in laboratory conditions. Three studies have found that people became less fearful of pornography after actually being exposed to it.[86] The repression of sex is what gives this natural function such power.

Conservatives fear that without criminal sanctions sex would be everywhere, whereas the opposite would probably be the case. Prostitution is an example. Poor women work the streets and are a nuisance because brothels are illegal. Prostitution regularly makes headlines whenever a prominent madam or a celebrity is caught.[87]

205

HORNY?

Natural Ways to Lower Male Testosterone (T) Levels

(1) Lose at something or be humiliated. It can be a physical or intellectual defeat.

(2) Allow something with which you are closely attached to lose. For example, testosterone causes aggressiveness and wife abuse increases in Washington, DC, not when its football team loses, but when it wins.

(3) Do not anticipate sex. Anticipation raises testosterone levels. This effect is known colloquially as "blue balls."

(4) Do not compete.

(5) Get married.

(6) Exercise intensely. With both weight resistance and aerobic exercise, testosterone levels initially go up, but during the recovery period they sink below baseline levels.

(7) Do not look at things that arouse you and do not interact with attractive women.

(8) Orgasm. Orgasms lower levels. Testosterone levels are reduced significantly more through orgasm from sexual intercourse than from masturbation.

(9) Sleep less.

(10) Eat soy and licorice root. Avoid meat and zinc. Drink and smoke.

—James Dabbs & Mary Dabbs, *Heroes, Rogues, and Lovers* (2000), pp. 87–93, 102, 120–121; M.S. Tremblay, J.L. Copeland, and W.V. Helder, "Effect of Training Status . . .," *J. Appl. Physiol.*, Feb. 2004, p. 531; S. Stoleru, et al., "Neuroanatomical Correlates of Visually Evoked Sexual Arousal," *Arch. Sex. Behav.*, Feb. 1999, p. 1; T.H. Kruger, et al., "Orgasm-induced Prolactin Secretion" *Neurosci. Biobehav. Rev.*, Jan. 2002, p. 31; and J.R. Roney, Z.L. Simmons, and A.W. Lukaszewski, "Androgen Receptor Gene Sequence . . .," *Proc. Biol. Sci.*, 7 Jan. 2010, p. 57.

American television programs frequently feature it because it is scandalous.[88] If it was legalized, advertising could still be legally limited, and sex workers would be off the streets and out of the media.

IV

SEXUAL DEPRIVATION:
THE RIGHT TO HAVE SEX WITH A HOT PERSON

A. High-T Males: Blue Balls and Violence

America's sex taboo comes down hardest on males who lack the looks, power, or wealth to attract sexual partners.[89] The pain of this group can perhaps best be described by someone who was a woman and then became a man. Here a transsexual describes life after the first testosterone shots began the transition:

> Overnight, my sex drive rocketed through the roof. I think that, by now, it's sailing somewhere over Cleveland. I rapidly developed a new hobby and understood why unenlightened mothers warn their sons to keep their hands outside the covers. I also had a newfound understanding of the eighth-grade boys I used to teach. They were restless and inattentive, and I often wondered if they'd been fathered by space aliens. Now I knew their dilemma, and if I ever return to teaching, I'll be much more sympathetic. In fact, it would probably behoove all middle school teachers, both male and female, to try a few shots of testosterone before their first teaching assignment—the women, so they could understand, and the men, so they could remember. Between the sexual fantasies, the activity that quelled them, and running to the mirror every five minutes to see if hair had sprouted anywhere, there was little time for much else.[90]

If moralists were serious about stopping extramarital sexuality, instead of trying to repress youthful libido through the dangerous tactics of fear and ignorance, they should offer temporary chemical castration. At least with chemical castration, the high-testosterone youth in our population would not have to go through the misery of an unquenched biological drive.[91]

Repressing high testosterone males has broad repercussions. Anti-sex feminists and moralists continue to assert that pornography causes sexual violence, but after forty years of attempting to validate this theory the scholarly evidence remains weak.[92] There is also a phenomenon that heavily supports the opposite view—pornography reduces sexual violence. Pornography has become considerably more accessible due to the rise of VCRs in the 1980s and the Internet in the 1990s. As availability has increased rape figures have plummeted in America.[93]

	1984	1985	1994	1995	2004	2005
Rapes per 1,000 people[2]	2.5	1.9	1.4	1.2	.4	.5

In Japan there was also a dramatic decrease in rape as pornography proliferated between 1972 and 1995.[94] This inverse link between rape and sexual liberation can also be seen with the American Indians.[95]

The link between repressive religious beliefs and sexual crimes, sexual deviancy, and sexual dysfunction has long been recognized.[96] In 2006 the United Kingdom released statistics showing its incarcerated sex criminals were significantly more religious than their imprisoned peers.[97] An expert in sexual abnormalities has stated that the majority of patients with deviant sexual fantasies and behaviors "described a strict anti-sexual upbringing in which sex was either never mentioned or was actively repressed or defiled."[98]

The ramifications of sexual repression may extend far beyond rapists and sexual deviants. A cross-cultural analysis of four hundred pre-industrial societies found that those that had negative attitudes toward extramarital sex were more likely to have a high incidence of theft, have slavery, and be extremely warlike. They were also more likely to kill, torture, and mutilate their enemies.[99]

This correlation between sexual repression and violence was found to exist with nineteen-year-old American college students as well. Students approving of violence were more likely to agree that prostitution should be punished, responsible premarital sex was disagreeable, and that society should interfere with private sexual behavior between adults.[100]

DEATH OF A VIRGIN
The Moral Argument for Prostitution

In the fall of 2001, fifteen-year-old "Jack" was dying of cancer and had a last wish. It was not to meet an oafish sports star or to go to a lame theme park. Jack wanted to have sex. In a poignant situation that occurs regularly in the Western world, where minors are not sexual and sex cannot involve money, a pubescent boy was going to die a virgin. Luckily for Jack he confided his wish to one gutsy person—a nurse, definitely not his religious parents.

Jack had sex with a prostitute. Having sex with a minor for money, this prostitute would be a heinous criminal in America and under Megan's Law could be subject to lifelong tracking. Was Jack psychologically or physically scarred? It will never be known because he died a month later—"very, very happy."

—Lucy Clark, "Moral Minefield of a Boy's Dying Wish," dailytelegraph.com.au, 21 Dec. 2001.

BRAVE WORKERS:
It's Criminalized to Protect Them?[105]

Profession	Annual Murders per 100,000
Prostitutes	204
Soldiers in Iraq War	100
Taxicab Drivers	18
Police and Detectives	4

B. High-T Females: The Government Won't Let You Make Money Lying Down

America's sex taboo comes down hardest on women who have high testosterone levels and those who are willing to have sex for money. High-testosterone females who enjoy casual sex are branded as "sluts" and are more likely to suffer from the ignorance imposed by the religious right and our federal government.

209

EXTREME TABOO
Handballing

Handballing, or fisting, is an extraordinary activity in that it arguably violates three taboos—excrement, sex, and death. Handballing is the act of penetrating another person's rectum, perhaps even the colon (large intestine), with one's hand. Its participants come almost entirely from a subculture of gay men called leatherfolk, who enjoy sadomasochism (S&M) and black leather. Even within the gay community, leatherfolk and fisters are a small and poorly understood fringe group.

Predictably, there are numerous misconceptions about handballing:

(1) It is sexual torture. Handballing does not focus on the infliction of pain—although parts of the process can be painful—and therefore arguably does not even belong in the S&M category. Handballing causes intense pleasure for those who partake in it. It has been described as an "internal massage" of the male's erogenous prostate gland and other internal organs. ("It's like silk sliding through my guts.") The anus itself is capable of sexual stimulation and to have it stretched can be intensely pleasurable. (Non-fisters may be able to compare this to the pleasure sometimes felt when passing a large stool.)

A word often applied to the sensation of having a fist inside one's rectum is *fullness*. Many men ejaculate while being fisted and other men report having full body orgasms that are superior to their penis orgasms. (Some women draw a similar distinction between vaginal and clitoral orgasm.)

(2) It is about feces. Handballing is not about being sexually stimulated by feces (coprophilia). Internal cleansing is a detailed ritual in the fisting community. It involves a preparatory diet and anal douching. Those who do not prepare properly can have trouble finding partners.

(3) It is brutish. To slip a hand in another person's anal canal is not an easy task even with large amounts of lubrication. It takes skill on the part of the insertee ("Top") and the recipient ("Bottom"). Bottoms sometimes require years of training to be able to relax the sphincter muscle enough to take another's fist without pain.

Tops usually do not insert the fist directly as that would be agonizing to most Bottoms. Usually a well-lubricated hand that is opened and curved is guided through the anus. In the rectum there is space for the hand to take the shape of a fist. Some experienced Bottoms, known as "pigs," can take large portions of the arm even above the elbow. For this to be done the Top must be familiar with the internal layout of the colon.

(4) It is casual and anonymous. Handballing is not a sexual activity prone to random encounters. Fisters are a tight community where reputations as safe and skilled fisters are earned. Part of the appeal of handballing is that it requires a level of trust unequaled by other sexual conjoinings. A Top can severely injure a bottom, as he literally has the Bottom's life in his hand, and a Bottom can snap a Top's forearm with his sphincter.

With fisting, a Bottom is literally taking the Top into him. The Bottom is being lifted up from the inside. When a Top goes deep into a Bottom he can feel the Bottom's heart beating. He can feel the aorta. Fisting is perhaps the ultimate in physical intimacy and sessions can last hours. Taking the metaphor of being inside another person to such an extreme makes handballing a spiritual experience for many of its practitioners. One writer calls handballing the gay man's "gift from the gods."

—Mark Thompson, ed., *Leatherfolk* (2001), pp. xv–xvi, 130, 150, 169; and Tim Brough, *First Hand* (2005), pp. i, xv, xxvii, 23, 49.

The sale of sex is illegal purportedly to protect women. This justification is a sadistic joke. Female sex workers face incarceration and, perhaps worse, the permanent branding of a criminal record. Prosecuted women who may have been able to move on to more accepted forms of employment are now constrained to prostitution because of employers' misgivings.[101]

Because of criminalization, prostitutes are afraid to go to the police and therefore are susceptible to horrific violence and murder by their customers.[102] Lastly, the victimless nature of the "crime" of prostitution invites corruption (since there is no one to blow the whistle) and the abuse of prostitutes by police officers themselves.[103,104]

C. Bad Sex: You're Missing Out

The taboo also results in bad sex. For women this primarily occurs in that ignorant men do not realize that what brings a woman pleasure is not the same as what brings them pleasure. Although this situation has improved considerably since the peak of the sexual taboo in the Victorian Era, it is still deficient.[106]

For men this primarily occurs when conventional morality prevents them from taking advantage of their natural disposition for variety and obtaining the pleasures of professional sex workers. Although the federal government and moralists insist that sex is best when in the confines of a loving relationship, not everyone agrees. One patron of call girls compared sex with an experienced call girl to eating at a fine restaurant. He said that sex with a partner and eating a home-cooked meal are delicious, but a trained professional can delight in ways amateurs cannot.[107]

Lastly, the taboo restrains both men and women from exploring the fascinating psychological realms of kinky sex. Even the mere sampling of alternatives to the missionary position is hindered. Perhaps because of the excrement taboo, an erogenous zone that is particularly ignored in Western culture is the anus, and specifically for males, the rectum's prostate gland.

As a gay man speaking to an undergraduate sexuality class said in response to the question, "Do you really enjoy it when a man with a large penis has anal sex with you?"—"Honey, you don't know what you are missing."[108,109]

D. Bad Marriages: The Rules Committee

Finally, the taboo's denial of biological differences between the sexes prevents open dialogue between partners about the rules of their marriage. In their 2010 book *Sex at Dawn*, Christopher Ryan and Cacilda Jethá argue that fulfilling the biological male desire for "sexually novel partners [is] one of the most important social changes required in Western societies to promote marital happiness."[110]

In their view, strict monogamy kills marriages through sexual monotony. The ramifications are high rates of sexless marriages, cheating, divorce, and single motherhood. As alternatives they suggest couples consider open marriages, swinging, polyamory, or taking the French attitude that one-night stands and affairs are not necessarily indictments of a loving marriage.

Ryan and Jethá understand that alternatives to strict monogamy may appear distasteful, particularly to women. Monogamy may be best for any one couple and the above list of alternatives is incomplete, however, the sex taboo should not silence discussion. It is important that partners be honest with each other about what they want, what works for them, and what makes them happy.[111]

In 1988 the governor of Colorado, Roy Romer, faced a media rumpus when his lengthy extramarital affair was publicly revealed. Instead of issuing the stock apologies he told the "tittering reporters" at a press conference that his wife of forty-five years was aware of the relationship, accepted it, and that their marriage was solid. He went on to say:

> What is fidelity? Fidelity is what kind of openness you have, what kind of trust you have, which is based upon truth and openness. And so in my own family, we discussed that at some length. And we have tried to arrive at an understanding of what our feelings are, what our needs are, and work it out with *that* kind of fidelity.[112]

NOTES

1. Marjorie Heins, *Not in Front of the Children* (2001), pp. 142–143.
2. Kitty Kelley, *Nancy Reagan* (1992), pp. 77–82.
3. David Allyn, *Make Love, Not War* (2000), p. 195.
4. Esther Kaplan, *With God on Their Side* (2005), pp. 188–189, 217.
5. Nellie Bristol, "US Anti-Prostitution Pledge Decreed Unconstitutional," *Lancet*, 1 July 2006, pp. 17–18.
6. Kitty Kelley, *Family* (2004), p. 584.
7. N. Bush did not admit they were prostitutes, however, in each encounter strangers would inexplicably knock on his hotel door, enter, have sex with him, and then leave. He did admit their behavior was "very unusual." "Bush Brother's Divorce Reveals Sex Romps," CNN.com, 26 Nov. 2003.
8. The righteous circus surrounding Clinton's 1998 impeachment led to numerous philanderers being exposed. A few congressional hypocrites of the last decade include Rep. Henry Hyde, adulterous affair; Rep. Newt Gingrich, adulterous affairs; Rep. Bob Livingstone, adulterous affairs; Rep. Bob Barr, licked stripper's nipple and left family to marry adulterous lover; Rep. Dan Burton, illegitimate child; Rep. Helen Chenoweth, adulterous affair; Sen. Tim Hutchinson, left family to marry adulterous lover; Rep. Sue Myrick, adulterous affair; and Rep. J.C. Watts, two illegitimate children.
9. Fifty-eight percent of people who said premarital sex is always wrong also admitted that they themselves had sex before they were married. Robert Michael, et al., *Sex in America* (1994), p. 239.
10. Senator Orrin Hatch, "Hatch: Pornography Is Not Free Speech," Press Release, 16 Mar. 2005.
11. Citizens for Responsibility and Ethics in Washington, "Addicted to Porn," 10 Mar. 2001, p. 9.
12. Ret. GlobalRights.org, 23 Apr. 2006.
13. "Link Between Prostitution and Sex Trafficking," Department of State, 24 Nov. 2004, state.gov, ret. 14 Apr. 2006.
14. Kaplan, *With God on Their Side*, p. 204.
15. When this ad was airing, teenage Planned Parenthood clients were showing up saying "condoms aren't as safe as everybody seems to think," and "my boyfriend says they don't work." (That they were still coming in suggests these new beliefs did not halt their sexual activity.) Ibid.
16. Stephanie Coontz, *Way We Never Were* (1992), p. 13.
17. James Kincaid, *Erotic Innocence* (1998), p. 78.
18. Ibid., pp. 94–95.
19. Judith Levine, *Harmful to Minors* (2003), p. 26, and Kincaid, *Erotic Innocence*, p. 95.

20. Levine, *Harmful to Minors*, p. 24, and Kincaid, *Erotic Innocence*, p. 78.

21. Pamela Schultz, *Not Monsters* (2005), p. 201, and Steven Levy, "All Predators, All the Time? Maybe Not," *Newsweek*, 3 July 2006, p. 20.

22. These figures are for "stereotypical kidnappings." When looser definitions are employed, such as including temporary detainments and abductions by a parent, figures are much higher. David Finkelhor, et al., "Nonfamily Abducted Children," NISMART-2, DOJ, Oct. 2002.

23. National Safety Council, "Odds of Death Due to Injury, United States, 2002," NSC.org, ret. 3 July 2006.

24. *This section is not meant to belittle the harm of child molestation or the need for its punishment.* Punishment is needed, but the taboo on child sexuality pushes it beyond rational justification. For a similar argument from a college professor and mother, who was molested as a child and went on to interview molesters in prison, see Pamela Schultz, *Not Monsters* (2005), pp. xvi, 185–186, 200–201.

25. L.J. Williamson, "Let Kids Outdoors," LATimes.com, 29 Mar. 2007.

26. By 1990 the radius around the home where children were allowed to roam alone shrunk to a ninth of what it was in 1970. Richard Louv, *Last Child in the Woods* (2005), p. 124.

27. Forty-one percent of children age eight to eleven worry about being safe in their neighborhoods. Ibid.

28. Current rate is fifteen percent. Williamson, "Let Kids Outdoors."

29. Christopher Doering, "Obama Backtracks on Smog Plan," Reuters.com, 2 Sep. 2011.

30. Lisa Lambert, "Cost of Locking Up Americans Too High," Reuters.com, 2 Mar. 2009.

31. In 2005 I represented a man (no prior record) charged with grabbing a boy's crotch (outside of boy's pants). He would have been publicly registered as a sex offender but a jury found him not guilty.

32. Michele McNeil, "Concerned About Juvenile Sex Offenders . . . .," *Education Week*, 2 Mar. 2007, p. 18.

33. A Florida prosecutor said, "Almost every day we get cases where you're dealing with the kind of person that you want to exclude [from sex offender laws], but our hands are tied by all of these statutes." Stephanie Garry, "Young Love," MiamiHerald.com, 9 Mar. 2007.

34. I represented a defendant in a case of this type.

35. McNeil, "Concerned About Juvenile Sex Offenders."

36. Wisconsin and Ohio considered making sex offenders have flourescent green license plates. Todd Richmond, "Wisconsin Considers Green Sex Offender Plates," AP, 13 Mar. 2007.

37. Victor Weedn and John Hicks, "Unrealized Potential of DNA Testing," *Natl. Inst. Just. J.*, Dec. 1997, p. 23.

38. Prostitution enforcement data from Julie Pearl, "Highest Paying Customers," *Hastings Law J.*, Apr. 1987, pp. 769–800.

39. Figures are adjusted from 1985 dollars to 2012 dollars. Over half of New York City's female prison population were convicted prostitutes at the time of the study. Pearl, "Highest Paying Customers," p. 779.

40. "Prevention of HIV/AIDS, Other STIs and Pregnancy," CDC, TheCommunityGuide.org, June 2009, ret. 22 Sep. 2010.

41. Marilyn Elias, "Teens Turn to Internet for Information on Sex," *USA Today*, 17 Oct. 2005.

42. Poll conducted 1996–1997. Michael Carrera et al., "Knowledge about Reproduction," *Social Policy*, Spr. 2000, pp. 41–49.

43. A consensus statement by the NIH said the abstinence-only "approach places policy in direct conflict with science and ignores overwhelming evidence that other programs would be effective." Judith Levine, *Harmful to Minors* (2003), p. 102.

44. Esther Kaplan, *With God on Their Side* (2005), p. 170.

45. Jacqueline Darroch, et al., "Differences in Teenage Pregnancy Rates," *Fam. Plann. Perspect.*, Nov./Dec. 2001, p. 244.

46. Timothy Taylor, *Prehistory of Sex* (1996), p. 17.

47. John Clarke, *Roman Sex* (2003), pp. 120–121.

48. Clarke, *Roman Sex*, p. 63; and Ruth Karros, *Sexuality in Medieval Europe* (2005), pp. 150–151.

49. J.M. Bailey, *Man Who Would Be Queen* (2003), p. x.

50. For example, coach Bob Knight's quote, "I think that if rape is inevitable, relax and enjoy it." "Bob Knight's Outburst Timeline," 14 Nov. 2006, ret. USAToday.com, 8 May 2007.

51. President George W. Bush avoids discussing his past behavior with, "When I was young and irresponsible, I was young and irresponsible." Kitty Kelley, *Family* (2004), pp. 578–579.

52. This chart predicts the *average* attitudes of these groups.

53. When the pope's Master of Ceremonies, Biagio da Cesena, criticized the nudity, Michelangelo painted da Cesena's likeness in the Sistine Chapel as Minos, judge of the underworld.
54. Peter De Rosa, *Vicars of Christ* (1988), pp. 4–5.
55. Paragraph from James Loewen, *Lies My Teacher Told Me* (1995), pp. 1–3, 9, 24.
56. In the early 1990s, only 2–4 percent of college students said that they had any substantial treatment of the Vietnam War in high school. Ibid., pp. 233–247.
57. Jay Mathews, "'Greatest Generation' Struggled With History, Too," *Washington Post*, 9 Mar. 2004.
58. Marvin Perry, ed., *History of the World* (1985), p. 336.
59. Napoleon had a buttocks fetish. He described his first wife's bottom as "the prettiest little backside imaginable," and when one of his mistresses wore skintight white pantaloons he went into a "near frenzy." Irving Wallace, et al., *Intimate Sex Lives of Famous People* (1982), p. 335.
60. The philandering king asked if a suggested paramour had "a good bust." The recommending attendant replied that he had not looked. The king scolded him saying, "You are a booby! That is the first thing one looks at in a woman." Ibid., p. 333.
61. Ibid., p. 15.
62. Recent exceptions were the movie *Apocalypto* (2006) and the television series, *Rome* (2005). Predictably, a *Rome* review on Amazon.com by "Hispania" read, "[*Rome*] exaggerated the sex and violence to appeal to our baser selves." Ret. 21 June 2006.
63. Following two paragraphs from John D'Emilio and Estelle Freedman, *Intimate Matters* (1988), pp. 7–9.
64. Ibid., p. 7.
65. Ibid., p. 8.
66. James Loewen, *Lies My Teacher Told Me* (1995), p. 101.
67. Ibid.
68. Peter Farb, *Man's Rise to Civilization* (1978), p. 262.
69. Frederick Turner, *Beyond Geography* (1992), p. 245.
70. Loewen, *Lies My Teacher Told Me*, p. 101.
71. Reay Tannahill, *Sex in History* (1980), pp. 425–426.
72. In the early 1990s half of all masturbators felt guilty about it. Robert Michael, et al., *Sex in America* (1994), p. 166.
73. This is exhibited by the copious Internet spam and other advertising for ineffective penis enlargement pills. Internet analysts have estimated one in four unsolicited Internet ads are for penis enlargement. This would not occur if men were not buying. "Life, Liberty and the Pursuit of a Penis of Unlikely Dimensions," *Australian*, 8 July 2003.
74. A Korean study showed that men who believe they have small penises are more depressed. Hwancheol Son, et al., "Studies on Self-Esteem of Penile Size in Young Korean Military Men," *Asian J. Androl.*, Sep. 2003, pp. 185–189.
75. Melissa Healy, "Intimate Makeover," *Los Angeles Times*, 13 Mar. 2006.
76. H. Wessells, T.F. Lue, and J.W. McAninch, "Penile Length," *J. Urol.*, Sep. 1996, pp. 995–997.
77. N. Mondaini, et al., "Penile Length is Normal in Most Men Seeking Penile Lengthening," *Int. J. Impot. Res.*, Aug. 2002, pp. 283–286.
78. Another time Dooley referred to H.W. Bush's penis as a "little stick." Kitty Kelley, *Family* (2004), p. 495.
79. Healy, "Intimate Makeover."
80. Marjorie Heins, *Not in Front of the Children* (2001), p. 26. This is also a theme of Michel Foucault.
81. Ibid.
82. Reay Tannahill, *Sex in History* (1980), pp. 355–356.
83. John Leo, "Is There Life in a Swingers' Club?" *Time*, 16 Jan. 1978, p. 53.
84. Sam Keen, "Voyeur in Plato's Cave," *Psychology Today*, Feb. 1980, p. 88.
85. Tom Buckley, "Oh Copenhagen," *New York Times Magazine*, 8 Feb. 1970, p. 46.
86. *Report of the Commission*, p. 202.
87. For example, Hugh Grant in 1995, Heidi Fleiss in the mid-1990s, and in the late 2000s, Deborah Jeane Palfrey.
88. HBO's *Cathouse* (2005, 2007).

89. Women have a much easier time finding short-term temporary sex partners. See Chapter Four.

90. Matt Kailey, *Just Add Hormones* (2005), pp. 50–51.

91. Depo-Provera is used to chemically castrate sex offenders in some states. In one instance, a gay male couple requested Depo-Provera so that they would be less tempted to have sex with other men. The men are now enjoying its effects in a monogamous gay relationship. James Dabbs and Mary Dabbs, *Heroes, Rogues, and Lovers* (2000), p. 101.

92. Even Neil Malamuth, who has spent his career trying to find a causal relationship since meeting with feminists in 1979, admitted in an exhaustive analysis of numerous studies that "for the majority of American men, pornography exposure (even at the highest levels assessed here) is not associated with high levels of sexual aggression..." Neil Malamuth, Tamara Addison, and Mary Koss, "Pornography and Sexual Aggression," *Annu. Rev. Sex Res.* (2000), p. 85.

93. In addition, the states with the least amount of Internet access had an increase in rapes, while the states with the most access had a decrease. Anthony D'Amato, "Porn Up, Rape Down," Northwestern Public Law Research Paper No. 913013, 21 June 2006.

94. Milton Diamond and Ayako Uchiyama, "Pornography, Rape and Sex Crimes in Japan," *Int. J. Law Psychiatry*, 1999, 22(1), pp. 1–22.

95. John D'Emilio and Estelle Freedman, *Intimate Matters* (1988), pp. 8–9.

96. Gerald Davison and John Neale, *Abnormal Psychology, Rev. 6th Ed.* (1996), pp. 340–342, 372–373.

97. The ratio of those professing a faith in the general prison population to those not was 2:1. For sex criminals it was 3:1. Dominic Kennedy, "Prison Figures Show a Link Between Sex Crime and Religion," TimesOnline.co.uk, 25 Nov. 2006.

98. John Money quoted in Judith Levine, *Harmful to Minors* (2003), p. 12.

99. James Prescott, "Body Pleasure and the Origins of Violence," *Bulletin of the Atomic Scientists*, Nov. 1975, p. 14.

100. Ibid., p. 15.

101. For an example, see Jeannette Angell, *Callgirl* (2004), p. 232.

102. A study found that ninety-four percent of street prostitutes had been raped by a customer. J. Miller, "Gender and Power on the Streets," *J. Contemp. Ethnogr.*, 1995, 23, pp. 427–452.

103. Police easily extort sex from prostitutes. Donna Gentile, a San Diego street prostitute, was an example. She reported extortion in the mid-1980s. The offending officer was fired but was not prosecuted. Gentile went to jail. She left a tape with her lawyer predicting the police were going to kill her and was soon found dead with a broken neck. For more see Norma Jean Almodovar's *Cop to Call Girl* (1993), pp. 223–225, 329.

104. Julie Pearl, "Highest Paying Customers," *Hastings Law J.*, Apr. 1987, p. 785.

105. Prostitute figure from J.J. Potterat, et al., "Mortality in a Long-Term Open Cohort of Prostitute Women," *Am. J. Epidemiol.*, 15 Apr. 2004, pp. 783–84. Soldier figure from 2,426 casualties of combat of the 650,000 serving from March 2003 to the end of 2006, iCasualties.org, ret. 3 Jan. 2006, and Pamela Hess, "Analysis: U.S. Reserves Returning to Iran," UPI, 28 Dec. 2006. Others from Eric Sygnatur and Guy Toscano, "Work-related Homicides: The Facts," *Compensat. Work. Cond.*, Spr. 2000, pp. 4–5.

106. Twenty percent of women orgasm only sometimes during sex with their primary partner. Another four percent orgasm rarely and another four percent never do. Robert Michael, et al., *Sex in America* (1994), p. 128.

107. Personal conversation had on the streets of New York City's Upper West Side circa 2000.

108. J.M. Bailey, *Man Who Would Be Queen* (2003), p. 57.

109. Anal sex is not universally accepted among gay men. Almost twenty percent of men who self-identify as gay or bisexual have never been the receiver in anal intercourse. Gregory Herek, Jared Jobe, and Ralph Carney, *Out In Force* (1996), p. 31.

110. *Sex at Dawn*, p. 295.

111. Dan Savage, "Do Monogamous Gay Couples Exist?" TheStranger.com, 20 June 2012.

112. Christopher Ryan and Cacilda Jethá, *Sex at Dawn* (2010), p. 311.

DRUGS I
WHAT THEY ARE
UNDERRATED

I
I Was a Schmuck

Growing up in a small rural town, I was an All-American boy—class president, three-sport letter winner, top five percent of my class, blah, blah, blah. I didn't do drugs. In high school, I drank an occasional beer just to separate myself from the holier-than-thous and to show that I didn't swallow the anti-drug propaganda hook, line, and sinker. At the time, I did not realize that the sinker was irrelevant because the hook was firmly in my head.

I had too much to risk to join the merrymakers in their drug use. My future was bright. I was young and spry. I was the golden boy who was going places. No one even tried to peer-pressure me into doing anything. In retrospect, I wish someone had.

I felt superior to the kids who drank, did drugs, and had fun. I knew from teachers and the press that they were due for alcoholism, addiction, arrest, or a premature death behind the wheel of a car. One teacher familiar with the large number of students who drank and drove warned that our high school was long overdue for a fatality of that sort. Of the thousands of kids in my area, the only student who died behind the wheel had fallen asleep. All the drinking drivers, the pot smokers, and the acid droppers never suffered. I figured they were just lucky. They were frolicking now, but they would eventually pay for disregarding the wisdom of our elders. They had to . . . because if they didn't, I was a schmuck.

At George Washington University in the mid-'90s, as with almost every college, drinking was so prevalent that any stigma it might have had in high school was lost. It was impossible to maintain, because for every idiot who drank and did idiot stuff there were dozens of responsible students who drank and just had a good time. Most of the non-drinkers abstained only for religious reasons. The other non-drinkers didn't drink because they did not have access to it, which usually meant they did not have many friends. A group of friends of any size often had at least one connection to someone who was twenty-one or somehow had an ID.

In college I soon learned that alcohol played an integral role in the relationships between the sexes. Because of my limited exposure to alcohol, I still believed the demon drug myth. That is, alcohol *causes* women to have unprotected sex. That was one of the tenets of anti-alcohol messages. Women shouldn't drink to excess because they would spread their legs to the whole world and not require it to wear a condom. Movies and television reinforced this with hungover women waking up with naked strangers in their beds, befuddled as to how the stranger got there, regretful.

Perhaps I should have realized that this was all an exaggeration, but instead I learned by embarrassing myself. In the beginning of my freshman year I went to a club with a female friend and a male friend. We all started drinking and when we were ossified the female started making out with the male. I naively thought that since she was in the throes of alcohol she didn't care who she kissed, so I shoved my head in there and tried to get in on the hot action.

I also learned that alcohol's pharmacological effects had little to do with its social value. Alcohol minimized the nervousness and fear of rejection that hitting on another person entails—liquid courage—but more important than lowered inhibitions was the *pretense* of lowered inhibitions. For example, one night I tried to make out with a dorm neighbor while grinding on her on a club dance floor. She politely refused and I moved on to grind on another poor lass. When I ran into her days later, I apologized for my aggressiveness, blaming it on the alcohol and she

218

amicably concurred that it was the alcohol. We both knew I would try to make out with her stone sober right there in the hallway if it was socially acceptable, but alcohol had saved face.

Alcohol would also serve as a scapegoat when people had sexual relations with someone who was not up to their friends' aesthetic standards. Males would also use it to justify brutish behavior. "I'm not a racist sexist asshole. I just had too much to drink." Women would also use it to protect from being labeled easy. "I'm not a slut. I just had too much to drink."

Women also know men are more likely to hit on a drunk woman than a sober one. The joke that a woman's pick-up line is often "I'm really drunk" is funny because it is true. Again I learned this firsthand. At one of my first college house parties there was a pretty woman loudly proclaiming her inebriation and stumbling about rubbing up on random guys. I grabbed her ass. She sobered up immediately, berating me as an asshole pervert and telling everyone in earshot what I had done. Apparently, when the unattractive dude moved in the game was over. I quickly left the party before she could round up a posse of frat boys to beat me for sexual harassment.

Since then, I have suspected that alcohol does not make people lose control of their actions. The dozens of times I've observed women sleep with someone "because they were drunk," the man was always someone in whom they were interested anyway. I've never witnessed a woman sleep with the broke, smelly, fat, ugly fellow or the homeless guy "because she was drunk."

Alcohol played other roles my freshman year. I did not lose my virginity because I had been taught that a woman could not give consent for carnal relations when she was intoxicated with the devil's brew. Looking back, I was a damn fool. No means no, but yes means yes even if alcohol is involved.

My most dramatic experience with alcohol is a void. One night I was ecstatic to have the ID of a friend who shared my big nose, brown hair, and elongated stature. Never having an ID before, this was an opportunity for greatness. I went to a club with my friend, Pookie, met some pretty Georgetown nursing students, tried to buy them as many drinks as I could before the drink special ended at 11 p.m. and then woke up the next morning in the hospital. Apparently I passed out at the club, and since I was underage, the club workers quickly dumped me outside on the sidewalk (after taking my wallet). Some kind freshmen who had seen me around campus got me an ambulance, or so I'm told. When I told my parents my dad laughed, my mom cried.

In college, alcohol wasn't the only drug I used. To stay awake during finals I sucked on tea bags. I also learned to smoke. I liked to smoke cigarettes when I got intoxicated. Everybody told me I would become addicted but I never have. I also learned to smoke marijuana and did so occasionally. I remember potheads telling me about its unjust treatment, their conspiracy theories regarding DuPont, and that George Washington used to smoke it. I laughed them off. Silly potheads. Why would the government lie about marijuana? It had more important things on its agenda.

I did not have much exposure to "hard" drugs in college but I did visit a high school friend attending Gettysburg College. He had always experimented with drugs—all drugs. He told me about his pleasurable experience with heroin, however, cocaine was his drug of choice. I always considered him my proxy. He was an intelligent and responsible individual, and I figured if drugs did not wreck his life, they probably would not have wrecked mine. He is currently getting his doctorate in psychology, still does hard drugs on occasion, and has never had any dependency problems— outside of cigarettes. Still, it was not until law school that the drug charade collapsed.

I was very lucky to get into New York University Law School in Manhattan. It was ranked as one of the top five law schools in the country. My classmates were extremely smart, extremely hardworking, and extremely driven. Unlike me, these people had received straight A's in college, and these were A's at places like Harvard and Yale. Most of them would go on to make $100,000+ starting salaries at big Manhattan law firms where they would work 60+ hour weeks.

To my surprise many of them did drugs. Even more surprising is that it was not the kids at the bottom of the class, it was some of the best of the best. One friend of mine who went to Harvard undergrad and who did well in law school smoked marijuana almost daily. His smoke buddy had gone to Yale undergrad and would eventually graduate in the top ten percent of our class and write for the prestigious *Law Review*—two amazing accomplishments at any law school, much less NYU. Not only did they smoke marijuana regularly, but they had a fondness for whippets. Whippets are nitrous oxide, or laughing gas, and they kept canisters of the stuff in their stash.

Another law school friend of mine was an older man who engaged in futures trading during law school. It was through him that I met some unbelievably wealthy and successful elites. For example, one gentleman was a high-ranking banker who had his own private zoo in Africa. I was shocked to discover that these high achievers casually used cocaine on weekends. They had been using it for years. They weren't addicts. They didn't know of anybody who overdosed. And they had a blast on it. Some of my friends who had never tried it snorted some one night, and besides having fun bragging to people that they were high on coke it wasn't a big deal.

II

What They Are
They are What the Government Says They Are

The dictionary definition of a drug is "a substance that acts on the nervous system . . . especially one causing addiction."[1] The ignorance surrounding the previous taboos was slowly enculturated over millennia. The ignorance surrounding the drug taboo is relatively recent and has been caused by media sensationalism and government propaganda in the twentieth century.

One result of this brainwash has been to change the popular definition of the word *drug* to fit the government's laws. Legal drugs are good; illegal drugs are evil. As President George W. Bush said: "We must reduce drug use for one great moral reason: over time, drugs rob men, women, and children of their dignity and of their character… When we fight against drugs, we fight for the souls of our fellow Americans."[2]

There are two characteristics of a drug: (1) its effect on the nervous system and (2) its addictive qualities. Both of these concepts have been corrupted by the government to justify its criminal laws. The latter has been so corrupted that it is arguably meaningless. Other concepts have been warped as well. Drug abuse has been defined by the scientific community as the continued use of a drug despite negative consequences.[3] The government's definition of drug abuse is any use that it does not approve. The government has unofficially decided using a drug for pleasure equals abuse.[4] This is sanctimonious drivel considering that a great many politicians, prosecutors, and law enforcers enjoy alcohol after a day of work.

To pull every recreational drug from the government's vast lie hole is impossible due to space limitations. However, it should be understood that the law of utility applies to an illegal drug's popularity. Most drug users are *not* stupid. A drug becomes popular because it provides more benefit than harm to its responsible users.[5] Although some users have a "desire to erase" themselves,[6] most do not.

TYPES OF RECREATIONAL DRUGS:
High, Low, or Whoa[7]

Type	Description	Examples
Hallucinogens	Changes sensual perceptions	Marijuana, LSD, mescaline, psilocybin
Hypnotics	Causes sleep and stupor	Barbiturates, Valium, Xanax
Narcotics (opiates)	Relieves pain and induces euphoria	Heroin, morphine, codeine, OxyContin
Sedatives, Depressants	Depresses central nervous system, decreasing mental and physical energy	Tranquilizers, alcohol, Quaaludes, marijuana
Stimulants	Excites and increases mental and physical energy	Caffeine, tobacco, cocaine, amphetamine

This chapter will expose only some of the drug perversions. However, the rule of utility should make one question the assertions of the media and government whenever a drug takes its turn as the most evil drug of the moment. The Internet has given scientists a way to respond to false and misleading propaganda, however, these scientists are not well-funded and their responses are not publicized. One must look for them.[8]

Some major distortions surrounding drugs are:

III

YOU CAN'T HANDLE THEM
DRUGS ARE ADDICTIVE

A. Freebasing Caffeine: Administration vs. Substance

The popular perception is that illegal drugs are outlawed because they are powerfully addictive. This is a myth. The three legal drugs—nicotine, alcohol, and caffeine—are no less addictive than supposedly "hard" drugs and significantly more addictive than others.

It may appear ludicrous that caffeine and cocaine are comparable, but this demonstrates how effective the anti-drug campaign has been since cocaine was outlawed in 1914. Before the drug war, the inherent "evilness" separating these substances did not exist. Here is a German pharmacologist in 1927 decrying America's prohibition of alcohol: "[Alcohol] causes as little harm to others as the voluntary taking of morphine or cocaine, or the intoxication by caffeine by taking too much coffee."[9]

Currently the popular view is that caffeine and cocaine are worlds apart, but they are chemically similar stimulants.[10] The vast difference in their effects stems from how they are consumed. Caffeine is readily available in beverages. Ingestion is the slowest and least efficient method to take a drug because of the lengthy rigors of the digestive process. (The quick "high" from most caffeinated beverages is psychological or from the large sugar content.)

Before criminalization, cocaine was used much like caffeine is used today. South Americans have chewed coca leaves and drunk coca tea for thousands of years. Thomas Edison, Ulysses S. Grant, H.G. Wells, Henrik Ibsen, Jules Verne, and Pope Leo XIII all enjoyed drinking cocaine wine, Vin Mariani.[11] Grant used it to give him the energy to write his memoirs.

Cocaine also came in chewing gum, lozenges, teas, and elixirs. The most famous of the latter is Coca-Cola, which had roughly two lines of cocaine per twelve ounces.[12] (This explains its name; cocaine comes from the coca plant.) Coca-Cola's popularity did not falter when it was legally targeted for containing cocaine because the cocaine was replaced with a comparable stimulant, caffeine.[13]

223

The criminalization of a substance immediately creates incentives for it to take a more potent form.[14] With the danger of arrest, it is important to make something concealable for possession, use, and transportation. In addition, punishments are based on quantities, with larger weights receiving more severe penalties. Potent forms of a drug carry less risk because they weigh less than milder forms. With the arbitrariness of mandatory minimum sentences, mere tenths of an ounce can have severe consequences. For example, in Pennsylvania if a person delivers less than the weight of a dollar bill in heroin she may receive probation. If she delivers more, she is facing a two-year mandatory minimum.[15]

When a drug only comes in powder form the culture of moderate use that surrounds it disappears. Now that cocaine's criminalization is approaching the century mark, its mild forms have long been forgotten, and instead cocaine now comes in the form of crack.

It is questionable whether crack would even exist if cocaine had remained legal.[16] Crack is cocaine chemically modified to allow it to be easily smoked. It is the same substance enjoyed by Edison and Grant, however, the cocaine is hitting the brain faster than if it was snorted or drunk. The effect is significantly more intense, and significantly shorter in duration.

The influence of administration on addictiveness can be seen on the addictiveness chart below with the example of amphetamine. Just as cocaine is the same substance whether snorted or smoked, amphetamine and its related compound, methamphetamine, are the same substance whether snorted, injected, or smoked. Smoked cocaine and methamphetamine are more addictive, not because they affect the brain differently but because the effect is more intense.

Caffeine's crack version has not been created because there is no need for it. Because it has not been criminalized, super-high caffeine doses are readily available in the safer beverage form such as the appropriately-named energy drink, Cocaine. For the more adventurous there are caffeine pills like No-Doz. Although much rarer incidences—because legalization allows caffeine to be drunk—young people are still hospitalized for enormous caffeine intakes, which can lead to hallucinations and death,[17] and just like with other stimulants (cocaine, amphetamines), chronic abuse leads to addiction and correlates with psychosis and a host of other problems.[18]

Most people who think cocaine and caffeine are dissimilar have never tried

COFFEE FREAK
Balzac's Caffeinism

The famous writer Honoré de Balzac (1799–1850) was a caffeine addict for thirty-five years. His coffee binges would stretch for weeks when writing. Toward the end of these binges his tolerance was so high he had to resort to eating finely ground coffee on an empty stomach to maintain the "affair."

He wrote that this dry method caused him to become "brusque, ill-tempered, about nothing," but on the positive side, "ideas quick-march into motion like battalions of a grand army to its legendary fighting ground, and the battle rages."

Balzac learned not to go out in public in this state after once making a fool of himself. His caffeine abuse killed him at the age of fifty-one.

—Bennett Weinberg & Bonnie Bealer, *World of Caffeine* (2001), pp. 120–122.

cocaine. Journalists and screenwriters trying to capture Joe and Mary Schmo's attention portray cocaine as a chemical siren capable of overwhelming bliss. In reality, experienced cocaine users cannot tell the difference between a single dose of cocaine and an equal dose of the local anesthetic lidocaine.[19] Here is a more grounded description that predates 1980s propaganda:

> The effects of [snorting] cocaine upon the average individual are so subtle that many users do not recognize a reaction until one is pointed out to them... Serious dopers hate it. Cocaine has no edge ... It does not alter your perception; it will not even wire you up like the amphetamines. No pictures, no time/space warping, no danger, no fun, no edge. Any individual serious about his chemicals—a heavy hitter—would sooner take thirty No-Doz. Coke is to acid what jazz is to rock. You have to appreciate it. *It* does not come to *you*.[20]

DRUGS' ADDICTIVENESS:
How Bad Do You Want It?[21]

Rank	Drug	Score (0–100)
1	Nicotine	99
2	Ice, Glass (smoked methamphetamine)	98
3	Crack	97
4	Crystal (injected methamphetamine)	92
5	Valium	83
7	Seconal (barbiturate)	82
8	Alcohol	81
9	Heroin	80
10	Crank (snorted amphetamine)	80
11	Cocaine (snorted)	71
12	Caffeine	70
13	PCP	57
14	Marijuana	22
15	Ecstasy (MDMA)	20
16	Psilocybin (mushroom)	19
17	LSD	16
18	Mescaline (peyote)	15

METHODS OF ADMINISTRATION:
How Hard It Hits[22]

Method	Time to Hit Brain
Smoking	7–10 seconds
Injection—vein	15–30 seconds
Injection—muscle or skin	3–5 minutes
Snorting (nasal passages' mucous membranes)	3–5 minutes
Contact with mucous membrane—eye	3–5 minutes
Contact with mucous membrane—skin	15–30 minutes
Ingesting (varies widely by stomach content)	20–30 minutes

B. Avoiding Physical Addiction: Simple

A person is physically addicted to a drug when the body suffers withdrawal symptoms if denied the drug. Physical addiction to a recreational drug is not enjoyable because the body has adjusted to having it constantly and is now tolerant of the drug. That is, the drug is no longer providing the pleasing effect but merely allowing the user to feel normal. Withdrawal symptoms can be barely noticeable with some drugs, such as marijuana, and fatal with others, such as alcohol. Contrary to popular perception, becoming physically addicted to a drug is not easy. One must acclimate the body to *always* having it in one's system. Physical addiction to a drug *cannot* occur if the body is cleansed of it between usages.

Most drugs are processed from the body in half-lives. That means no matter how much of a drug is in one's system at a point in time it will always take the same time period to cut that level in half. That time period is the drug's half-life.

Most illegal drug users are occasional users, for example, they use only on the weekends. It is impossible to become physically addicted to a drug by using it only once a week, and more frequent usage can be done safely in moderation. For example, a person cannot become physically addicted to alcohol by having four twelve-ounce beers a day. Nor would someone become physically addicted to heroin or cocaine if they drank opium or coca tea every night. (Opium is the precursor of heroin.) Of course, the weaker forms of these drugs have long disappeared with criminalization so more caution is now required. However, even with the injection of heroin, physical addiction cannot occur if a day of usage is always followed by two of non-usage.[23]

WHEN CAN I GET HIGH AGAIN?
Half-Lives[24]

Note: Individual rates vary wildly based on factors like age, health, sex, weight, race, and heredity. Other drugs can play a factor as well, for example, caffeine metabolization can be increased by up to fifty percent by cigarette usage and decreased by two thirds by oral contraceptive usage.[25]

Drug	Half-Life (hrs)	Duration of Effects for Common Dosage (hrs) b
Alcohol	†	1 (ingesting) [3]
Caffeine	6 [4]	1.5–5 (ingesting)
Cocaine	.8–1.5 a	3–5 minutes (smoking) .25–.5 (snorting)
Heroin	2–4 a	4–5 (intravenous) 3–5 (smoking)
Marijuana	10–40 a	4–10 (ingesting) 1–4 (smoking)
Methamphetamine	11 [5]	4–8 (intravenous) 1–3 (smoking) 2–4 (snorting)

The reason addicts are a small minority for every recreational drug is that even before addiction is reached, constant use is *not* enjoyable. This is true with all activities. Doing anything nonstop gets boring. For example, there are people who enjoy playing online video games but very few enjoy playing them literally all the time. Video games are not perceived as a dangerously seductive pleasure even though one study found that .7 percent of video gamers played over eighty hours a week, and at least ten "ultra-Web" users have died of blood clots from sitting too long.[26]

Drugs are the same way. Some people will not like a drug, some people will like a drug, and a very small percentage will want to do it whenever possible. This can be seen with the legal drug alcohol. Many people enjoy drinking periodically but the person who enjoys being drunk for weeks on end is rare. This is not because of willpower, but because it ceases to be fun. Drugs provide recreation by causing unique sensations.[27] When used continuously for a lengthy duration the sensation ceases to be unique. (As opposed to when physical addiction is attained and the sensation ceases to be felt.) This sentiment was expressed by the champion boxer Mike Tyson in 1998:

> I did a lot [of drugs] when I was a kid ... I never got hooked. If you get hooked on drugs, you must not have a thing to do in your life. You know how boring drugs are? Being high all the time? You know how fucking boring that is?[28]

That is why drug users who become addicted are usually not using drugs to "party"—the biggest fear of anti-drug zealots—but to escape a real-life problem or to medicate. Ironically, these are the same reasons anti-drug zealots, who can afford health care, are purposely addicted to antidepressants (depression) and amphetamines (attention deficit disorder, weight loss) by their physicians.

C. Psychological Addiction: Outlaw the Big Mac

Another way the government has skewed the definition of addiction is through the hazy concept of psychological addiction. Illegal drugs such as marijuana have virtually no physical withdrawal symptoms.[29] Most hallucinogens, like LSD, not only are not physically addictive but they do not have *any* effect if taken less than several days from the last ingestion.

To defend its criminalization of these substances, the government has argued that these drugs are psychologically addictive. The application of the term *addictive* to drugs considerably less physically addictive than ingested caffeine makes the term applicable to any enjoyable activity. No one would assert we should criminalize the following activities, all of which turn into harmful compulsions for some people: having sex, surfing the Internet, watching television, playing video games, shopping, tanning, texting, and eating junk food.

A popular diet book compared junk food's fix to that of recreational drugs, with good reason. The brain manipulates the same chemicals that recreational drugs manipulate to make us feel hungry and to reward us for eating. Quickly ingesting a large amount of sugar dramatically raises serotonin—the same chemical influenced by cocaine and caffeine.

A large sugar dose creates a quick "chemical high" that "boosts our mood, makes us feel better, or masks the stress, pain, boredom, anger, or frustration that we may be feeling," but this high is then followed by a "big chemical downfall."[30] Studies have shown the obese have brain reward centers similar to those of drug addicts.[31] Comparing crack addiction rates to the adult obesity rate of thirty-four percent led Dr. Nora Volkow, the director of the National Institute on Drug Abuse, to declare in April 2012 that food was more addictive than crack.[32]

HARD DRUGS AREN'T THAT HARD
DRUG USAGE OF POPULATION IN 2010[33]

	CRACK	HEROIN	METH
Lifetime Usage	9,158,000	4,126,000	13,012,000
Past Month Usage	378,000	239,000	353,000
Percentage of lifetime users who used in the past month	4.1%	5.8%	2.7%

IS PHYSICAL ADDICTION THAT BAD?
Ask a Coffee Drinker

The typical American consumes two hundred milligrams of caffeine daily. This makes her an addict. At that intake rate, tolerance can be built in weeks. What this means is that caffeine is no longer giving the typical American a "boost," but instead only getting her back to normal functioning. Her daily cups of joe are merely maintenance doses allowing her to avoid withdrawal.

Caffeine withdrawal usually begins in twelve to twenty-four hours, explaining daily coffee rituals. Some common withdrawal symptoms are headaches, fatigue, and increased irritability. Caffeine withdrawal can last for a week and severe cases can be incapacitating.

Widespread addiction can explain the 1990s' gourmet coffee explosion begun by the Starbucks Corporation. Starbucks' coffees have double the caffeine of grocery-store coffee. The average medium-sized Starbucks' coffee drink (sixteen ounces) contains 320 milligrams of caffeine. For perspective, a can of Coke (twelve ounces) or a cup of brewed tea (eight ounces) has roughly fifty milligrams.

—"Caffeine Corner," *Nutrition Action Health Letter*, Dec. 1996; Roland Griffiths and Geoffrey Mumford, "Caffeine," 2000, ret. acnp.org, 23 Mar. 2007; and Michael McCarthy, "Caffeine Count," *Wall Street Journal*, 13 Apr. 2004.

The evidence that addictions to lawful activities are similar to addictions to unlawful substances is overshadowed by shoddy sensationalized studies that imbue drugs with an unholy power. One experiment loved by anti-drug advocates demonstrated that monkeys "preferred cocaine to life itself" when some monkeys chose cocaine over food and some overdosed.[34] It is usually not explained that these monkeys were tethered to a cocaine-administrating apparatus in an isolated cage with little to stimulate or soothe them but the drug that was administered intravenously when they hit a lever. It was the equivalent of locking a human in a prison's "hole" with nothing but a never-ending intravenous coke supply surgically implanted in her body.

Understandably, scientists have criticized this study as being inapplicable to humans, and other studies have shown that animals kept in more realistic settings have been less drawn to drugs than their shackled kin.[35] If anything, barbaric animal addiction studies like this one support the thesis that drugs are more likely to be used destructively by those suffering—not the thesis that drugs can overpower everyone.

The pleasure received from eating a piece of one's favorite dessert is not the same as snorting a line of cocaine, however, they are a lot more similar than the government and the media suggest. To deny that many people would get more pleasure from the dessert is giving cocaine too much credit. The addictive powers of all recreational drugs have been immensely exaggerated. If you tried crack or heroin you probably would not become addicted—even though you might enjoy the experience.

D. Instant Enslavement?: Please[36]

Hype

Note: Dependence is a technical definition that requires meeting three of seven criteria. Neither physical addiction nor a negative effect on one's life is required.[40]

With heroin, "everyone . . . is a potential addict," "addiction can start with the very first dose," and "with continued use addiction is a certainty."[37]

"Crack is the most addictive drug known to man," causing "almost instantaneous addiction."[38]

"Ninety-five percent of meth users become addicted after just one use."[39]

Reality

Drug	Percent	Support
Tobacco	32	Thirty-two percent of fifteen- to fifty-four year-old tobacco users had experienced dependence.[a]
Heroin	23	One study found that twenty-three percent of fifteen- to fifty-four year-old users had experienced dependence[a] Less than thirteen percent of high school seniors who had tried heroin had used it more than five times in the last month.[c]
Cocaine	17	After first trying cocaine, five to six percent of people become dependent within two years,[6] fifteen to sixteen percent within ten years.[b] Seventeen percent of fifteen to fifty-four year-old users had experienced dependence.[a]

Alcohol	15	After trying alcohol, two percent of people develop a dependence within one year, twelve to thirteen percent within ten years.[b] Fifteen percent of fifteen to fifty-four year-old users had experienced dependence.[a]
Marijuana	9	After trying marijuana, one percent of people develop a dependence within one year, and eight percent within ten years.[b] Nine percent of fifteen- to fifty-four year-old users had experienced dependence.[a]
Crack		Less than eleven percent of high school seniors who had tried crack had used it more than five times in the last month.[7] No abuse was found in hundreds of users of medically-prescribed crack.[8]
Ice (Smoked Meth)		Less than nine percent of high school seniors who had tried ice had used it more than five times in the last month.[c]

E. How Addiction Occurs: Not Randomly

Addiction is an intense involvement people fall into for solace when they cannot find gratification in the rest of their lives.[41] A destructive addiction is a symptom of deeper problems and some people are significantly more susceptible to this symptom than others. The locus of addiction lies in people, not substances. This is why the decriminalization of hard drugs by countries has not been found to affect their addiction rates.[42]

1. THE DRUG: STOP BLAMING IT

Blaming individual substances for an addiction is fallacious because addicts can form unhealthy relationships with whatever is available to them. There will always be something accessible to abuse, whether it is alcohol, sex, lottery tickets, home shopping channels, or glue.

If heroin were to magically disappear, addicts would not be cured unless their underlying issues were resolved. This was demonstrated in the summer of 1972 when a shipping strike temporarily broke the heroin supply to Eastern U.S. cities. Heroin was so scarce that its price ballooned five-fold. In Washington, DC, the methadone-treatment program for opiate addicts had a *decrease* in applicants that summer. The urinalysis of DC arrestees found that all of the heroin addicts simply switched to barbiturates or amphetamines.[43]

If cocaine were to disappear instead, many cocaine addicts might turn to alcohol for respite. As can be seen in the following chart, someone diagnosed with cocaine dependence is 6.6 times more likely than someone without a cocaine dependence to develop a dependence on alcohol. This lack of discipline is not limited to other chemicals, as shown by the substantial overlap between drug and behavioral addictions.

CHEMICAL OPTIONS:
Dependence Predicting Transition from First Use to Dependence on Other Substances[44]

Predictor Diagnosis	Nicotine Dependence	Alcohol Dependence	Cannabis Dependence	Cocaine Dependence
Nicotine		3.52	2.99	2.74
Alcohol	3.05		4.24	3.32
Cannabis	4.31	7.39		3.83
Cocaine	3.08	6.64	6.33	

BEHAVIORAL OPTIONS:
LIFETIME ESTIMATES OF SUBSTANCE USE DISORDERS IN BEHAVIORAL ADDICTIONS[45]

Note: The percentage of the general population that has experienced substance use disorders is 14.6 percent.[46]

BEHAVIORAL ADDICTIONS	LIFETIME ESTIMATES OF SUBSTANCE USE DISORDER
Compulsive Buying	21%–46%
Compulsive Sexual Behavior	64%
Food Addiction	32.6% [9]
Internet Addiction	38%
Kleptomania	23%–50%
Pathological Gambling	35%–63%

2. LOOK DEEPER: UNDERLYING ISSUES

Destructive addictions often artificially compensate for an unbearable psychological weight. Unless the underlying issues are fixed or at least managed, one unhealthy release will only be replaced with another. The following are some of the factors that have been documented to drive addictions:

Mental Health Issues—Those with a mood disorder, anxiety disorder, personality disorder, or ADHD are much more likely to become dependent on nicotine, alcohol, marijuana, and cocaine. For example, those who have been diagnosed with a mood disorder are almost three times as likely to become dependent on cocaine as their peers.[47]

Poverty—Surveys of drinking have long found that despite being more likely to abstain, those from lower socioeconomic groups are still "much more often" problem drinkers.[48] A more recent study has found that income serves as a predictor for more than just alcohol dependence. People in the poorest income bracket (making less than $19,999 per year) were almost three times as likely to become dependent on cocaine or cannabis as those in the wealthiest bracket (making more than $70,000).[49]

War—In the 1970s there was concern over the postwar return of the twenty percent of Vietnam veterans who had been addicted to heroin. However, after being home for three years in a gentler environment only twelve percent of those addicted veterans still had a habit.[50] Roughly half of the returnees did not receive any addiction treatment and their success rate was the same as those who did.

3. The Addict: Young and Impulsive

Not everyone is equally likely to use toxic addictions to escape from distress. The following factors predispose a person to addiction:

Genes—An adoption study has shown that the biological father's drinking patterns predict a son's alcoholism, while the adoptive father's does not. Boys whose biological fathers were severe alcoholics had an alcoholism rate of eighteen percent with an alcoholic adoptive father, and seventeen percent with an adoptive home free of parental alcoholism. Another study, based on twins, found shared genes did not correlate with experimentation with illicit drugs. However, if an identical twin was dependent there was a forty percent chance the other twin was also dependent.[51]

Addictive Personality—People with substance or behavioral addictions score highly for sensation-seeking and impulsivity, and low for harm avoidance.[52] This is not surprising. An addict is arguably someone who chooses the sensation an activity provides at levels that are harmful. Impulsivity is the tendency to act without weighing the future consequences of one's actions. Addictive behavior provides immediate pleasure, whereas the benefits of moderation are often distant and abstract (for example, long-term health, more stable work/family life).

Youth—Not only are older people much less likely to become dependent on something,[53] they are also much more likely to end dependencies. In line with this, addictive personalities weaken over time. Older adults report being less impulsive, sensation-seeking, and risk-tolerant than their younger peers.[54]

The idea that addiction is for life is a myth. The vast majority of addicts "mature out" of their addictions and most of them accomplish this without treatment.[55] Maturing out is so pervasive that a national 2010 survey found that only .1 percent of people sixty-five or older had abused or been dependent on an illegal substance in the past year. The highest level was reached by nineteen-year-olds (9.3 percent), from which the number rapidly decreases.[56]

IV

You Will Die
Drugs Kill

The popular perception is that illegal drugs are highly dangerous. As a public defender I stood by countless people convicted of drug charges and listened to the judge justify the state's harsh sentences ad nauseam with fearsome words such as "This stuff will kill you." The judge was locking the defendant up and ruining the defendant's employment opportunities because if she did not, the defendant would surely die.

This categorization of dangerous and benign chemicals is a myth. The way a chemical affects the nervous system depends on the amount administered. For example, drinking too much water can become deadly by lowering blood sodium levels and engorging brain cells. Fatal water overdoses periodically occur.[57] In contrast, minuscule amounts of the deadly poison arsenic have been used as a recreational drug in the past and have recently been approved for the treatment of leukemia.

The only reason illegal drugs are so deadly is *because* they are illegal.[58] Because the market is underground, drugs come with adulterants and users have difficulty knowing the amount of the drug they are taking. In addition, drugs only come in their most concentrated form. If illegal drugs were decriminalized, deaths from overdose would be as rare as those from legal drugs such as alcohol.

Even on the black market some drugs are virtually impossible to consume to the point of permanent damage. Some of these innocuous drugs are marijuana, LSD, and mushrooms (psilocybin).[59] (When damage does occur from "using" these drugs it is almost always because something else was taken, for example, a toxic mushroom.)

Perhaps nowhere is the gap between a substance's actual deadliness and its perceived deadliness as wide as with the "killer drug"—heroin.[60] Most heroin overdoses are the result of uncertainty about potency, which could be avoided with legalization.[61],[62] Additionally, fatal heroin overdoses usually take over an hour,[63,64] and they can be counteracted by an antidote—Narcan (naloxone). Narcan acts within minutes and is so effective that sometimes people near death will receive it and promptly "get up and walk away."[65] Despite there being no danger of Narcan overdose, Narcan is illegal and so tightly controlled that strict limits on its use by paramedics have cost lives *even when* paramedics were present.[66]

Cocaine's deadliness is also greatly exaggerated. Deaths from recreational use occur but are extremely rare, particularly when the drug is not injected.[67] The safety ratio of snorting cocaine is fifty percent higher than that of drinking alcohol.[68] Cocaine is still used medically as an anesthetic, and a survey of intranasal cocaine administrations during surgery in amounts comparable to recreational use found a .005 percent fatality rate.[69] For comparison, aspirin is deadly to .08 percent of people taking it for more than two months.[70]

Most American fatality figures are based on cocaine-*related* deaths. Whenever someone dies with cocaine in their system the death can be deemed cocaine-related.[71] One review of 935 cocaine-related deaths in New York City found that less than twelve percent were even *possibly* related to the pharmacological effects of cocaine.[72]

State totals of annual cocaine-related deaths can break one thousand, like the total cited in a 2006 Florida article.[73] The European Union, which tightly defines cocaine-related deaths as "acute deaths in which cocaine is present without opiates," estimates its annual total at several hundred.[74] The European Union's population is over fifty percent larger than that of the entire United States.

The media seems completely ignorant of this massive disconnect between using a drug and being killed by a drug. The above-mentioned Florida article—in a section entitled "A Silent Killer in Suburbia"—cites the "cocaine-related" death of one male mortgage broker in his fifties who was hit by a car while jogging at night.

Lastly, cocaine strains the heart and should not be used by those with weak ones.

In 2007 the rocker Ike Turner died. The headlines read "Cocaine Killed Ike Turner," and articles focused on his past drug usage, even though at the time of his death he was so weak from advanced emphysema that he could barely move around.[75] If he died straining to climb stairs would stairs have killed him? If he died after downing several Red Bulls would caffeine have killed him? (Excessive caffeine intake can cause heart palpitations.)

DECLARING A WAR ON STAIRS:
What Kills[76,77]

Cause of Death	Annual Deaths
Tobacco-Related	435,000 a
Obesity-Related	400,000 a
Alcohol-Related	85,000 a
Adverse Reaction to Prescribed Drugs	76,000 [10]
Medical Errors in Hospitals	71,000 [11]
Motor Vehicle Accidents	44,757 b
Suicide	31,484 b
Firearm-Related	29,000 a
Homicide	17,732 b
Illicit Drug User-Related	17,000 a
Aspirin/NSAIDs	16,500 [12]
Prescription Drug Errors	7,000 [13]
Crossing the Street	6,047 d
Workplace Injury	6,000 [14]
Motorcycle Accidents	3,676 c

Drowning Accidents	3,306 [b]
Malnutrition	3,153 [b]
Choking on Small Objects	2,828 [d]
Accidental Falling—Stairs or Steps	1,588 [c]
Electrocution	874 [d]
Accidental Discharge of Firearm	730 [b]
Choking on Food	640 [d]
Accidental Falling—Ladders or Scaffolding	417 [c]
Alcohol Overdose	317 [15]
Tylenol (acetaminophen) Overdose	100 [16]
Peanut Toxicity	75 [17]
Hornets, Wasps, & Bees	66 [c]
Contact with Hot Tap Water	51 [d]
Lightning	47 [c]
Ecstasy (MDMA) Toxicity	3–9 [18]
LSD Overdose	0
Marijuana Overdose	0

FAT AND DEAD:
Fatalities[78]

Demographic	Annual Deaths per 1,000
Tobacco Smokers	15
Obese People	11
Illegal Drug Users	2.6

V

You Will Die Slowly
Drugs are Unhealthy

As with their legal brethren, popular illegal drugs are not unhealthy with occasional and moderate use. One of the most corrosive drugs in the public's opinion is heroin. The heroin junkie sits at the core of the taboo on drugs. Governments are fond of showing a series of mug shots that progress from a person's first arrest until their last. The visual transformation is provocative, disturbing, and extremely misleading.

A. Government Interference Is Dangerous:
Criminalized Water Would Be Unhealthy

First, this degradation is not from heroin. Outside of being chronically impotent and constipated, opiate addiction is "minimally injurious to the body."[79] In fact, with measured administration the typical addict is "able to function quite well and live a long and normal life."[80] This is a sharp contrast to lifelong addicts of the legal drugs alcohol and tobacco, which destroy, respectively, the liver and lungs.

The internal degradation of the body comes from the impurities found in black-market heroin. Common adulterants include sugar, starch, talcum powder, baking powder, or powdered milk.[81],[82] This is problematic when heroin is injected. Injectable legal medications are sterile and dissolve easily in blood. Street drugs are not sterile and are often crushed by the user.

Uncrushed fragments and insoluble contaminants can lodge in tiny blood vessels in the heart, brain, and eyes, and cause hemorrhage, stroke, and blindness. Many intravenous users try to remove these fragments by filtering the drug through a piece of cotton. This results in tiny cotton fragments entering the bloodstream, causing a strong immune reaction called "cotton fever." Cotton fever begins ten to twenty minutes after injection and causes miserable side effects for twelve to twenty-four hours. Repeated injections of contaminants lead to debilitating diseases and infections.

B. It's Not What You Do, It's How You Do It: Duh

Not all illegal drugs are as harmless to the human body as heroin. However, this extends to legal drugs and food as well. One merely needs to listen to American pharmaceutical advertisements to know how many *possible* side effects accompany the ongoing use of any drug.

The health dangers touted with recreational drugs are usually based on extreme use over many years. To see how skewed this portrayal is watch *Super Size Me!* (2004), a documentary that follows a man who eats only at McDonald's for *just* one month.

> . . . I gained twenty-four and a half pounds, my liver turned to fat and my cholesterol shot up sixty-five points. My body fat percentage went from eleven to eighteen percent . . . I nearly doubled my risk of coronary heart disease, making myself twice as likely to have heart failure. I felt depressed and exhausted most of the time, my mood swung on a dime and my sex life was nonexistent. I craved this food more and more when I ate it, and got massive headaches when I didn't.

I would suggest that on average, people who eat at McDonald's every day will be substantially less healthy than a person who uses a drug such as crack, heroin, or methamphetamine once a week. It is unlikely this premise will be touched in the mainstream media or scientific circles any time soon.

C. Functional Alcoholic vs. Junkie: A Matter of Price

People are forced into desperate and unhealthy lifestyles to finance their addictions.[83] When heroin was criminalized in 1915, the cost per ounce shot from $6.50 an ounce to about $100 an ounce.[84] Heroin addicts are forced to deal with criminals regularly and need money to support the artificially sky-high prices of heroin. It is estimated that the prices of marijuana, cocaine, and heroin are a hundred times higher than they would be in a free market.[85]

Heroin addicts are more likely to commit crimes than alcoholics because their substances cost exorbitantly more. A parallel can be seen in post-World War II Europe, where there was a cigarette shortage that drove up their value. Nicotine addicts were reported stealing, trading away prized personal possessions, and engaging in prostitution in order to obtain tobacco.[86]

INFLATED PRICES
Veins of Gold[87]

Street value of one gram of pure:	Dollar Value
Heroin	$375
Methamphetamine	$160
Cocaine	$100
Gold	$12
Marijuana	$12
Alcohol	$.06

D. Drugs Cause Insanity: A Forest Fire of B.S.

Ever since the nineteenth-century yellow journalism of newspaper magnate William Randolph Hearst, reporters have used anecdotal scare stories to claim drugs cause insanity.[88] Few drugs have endured this slander as much as LSD.

One of the most famous LSD tales is that of the man who took too much and believed that he was orange juice. He was committed to a psychiatric ward and for the rest of his life he was terrified that someone might drink him. Variations of this urban legend were circulated by the media and health professionals in the 1960s.[89]

There is no evidence that LSD causes schizophrenia or any other mental illness. LSD's effects are temporary and a user "never completely loses sight of the fact that sensual distortions are drug-induced."[90,91] There is evidence that LSD can trigger schizophrenia in people who are predisposed to it, but this effect is not limited to LSD.[92] Any highly stressful event can trigger a schizophrenic's first psychotic episode.

RESPONSIBLE TRIPPING IS SAFE:

Rates of Major Complications with LSD[93]

Per Use of LSD	%
Attempted suicides	0
Attempted suicides by those receiving mental health treatment	.1%
Psychotic reaction that lasts over 48 hours	.08%
Psychotic reaction that lasts over 48 hours in those receiving mental health treatment	.18%

LSD is not the only drug that causes temporary psychosis. Extreme usage of alcohol, marijuana, and stimulants like caffeine can also cause hallucinations. (Severe fatigue also induces artificial visions.) Even though the government has spent millions of tax dollars to prove these drugs cause permanent brain damage, the evidence is still sparse.

A recent junk science scare involved methamphetamine and led to typical understated drug headlines like this 2006 one in the *New York Times*: "This Is Your Brain on Meth: A 'Forest Fire' of Damage." Five years later reviewers analyzed the original data and found it to be bogus.[94]

E. Shiny Happy Drug Users: The Invisible Majority

Drug users are seen as unhealthy and desperate because unhealthy and desperate users are the only ones the public ever sees. The public perception of the heroin user is the "junkie." It is easy to overlook the fact that occasional heroin users ("chippers") and functioning addicts make up the vast majority of heroin users.[95]

Chippers, like the weekend user on the BBC who enjoys it when gardening, and the anonymous successful Manhattan business executive featured in the *New York Times*,[96] remain invisible to avoid criminal prosecution, job loss, and losing their narcophobic friends.[97] Words like the following from the executive almost never get media coverage: "[Heroin] is an enhancement of my life. I see it as similar to a guy coming home and having a drink of alcohol. Only alcohol has never done it for me."[98]

One of the most remarkable examples of a heroin addict leading an exemplary life is Dr. William Halsted.[99] Halsted is known as the father of modern surgery and was one of the four founders of Johns Hopkins University. This man saved his sister by doing the first emergency blood transfusion, and he did it with *his own* blood.

For the last thirty-five years of his life Halsted continued to make medical breakthroughs as a heroin addict. His skill with the surgical blade earned him a global reputation. Halsted never could quit but kept himself healthy and functioning with maintenance doses. It was only because of a book that was unsealed nearly fifty years after his death that his secret was revealed.

Halsted is not an aberration. It is openly acknowledged that modern doctors addicted to heroin (usually morphine) can perform at high levels.[100] Researchers have found well-functioning heroin addicts in all lines of work. A District of Columbia police official stated that around 1971 "more than one hundred officers were taking heroin. How did we learn about them? Not because their performance was poor . . . We took urine specimens."[101]

Even users of the relatively accepted illegal drug marijuana are covert.[102] Outside of the entertainment industry, cannabis use is reluctantly revealed. One successful user who has been outed is the billionaire Peter Lewis. As the CEO of Progressive Insurance for thirty-six years he transformed a small company with millions in revenues into a Fortune 200 company with billions in revenues. Lewis' peers regard him as a creative perfectionist, "an extraordinary businessman," and a "pothead."[103]

VI
You Will Kill Me
Drugs Make You Do Bad Things

A. The Drug Made Me Do It: Stop Lying

The popular perception is that illegal drugs cause people to do harmful and evil things. This is false. Drugs do not *make* one do anything. They can temporarily lower inhibitions, impede decision-making, and ruin coordination, however, the drug is never in control. The same occurs when you are extremely tired. Your decision-making is hampered; however, it would be inane to blame sleep deprivation for heinous acts such as murder. Yet the government and the media have been doing this to drugs for the past one hundred years.

No drug has been found to directly cause violence through its pharmacological action.[142] Drugs that have been popularly touted as violence-causing but have come up woefully short when scientists looked past colorful anecdotes and urban myths include crack, PCP,[143] and anabolic steroids.[144]

The drug most correlated with violence is the legal substance alcohol.[145] Two-thirds of people who have been attacked by current/former spouses/lovers say their assailant was drinking, and "I didn't know what I was doing when I was drunk" is the most frequently heard excuse by those who counsel violent families.[146] Yet a cross-cultural study has shown that drunken behavior is a largely learned behavior that varies widely from person to person, setting to setting, and culture to culture.[147]

At some point in Western history alcohol became a "temporary license to act like an asshole,"[148] and most people who have been intoxicated realize alcohol does not *make* one fight. The idea that drugs can make one do something horrific is due to two phenomena—scapegoating and fearmongering.

As a public defender I witnessed countless people convicted of actual crimes (crimes with victims) excuse their actions ad nauseam by implying "it was the drug that drove me to do it." It is a great excuse because the government cannot call this posturing a sham. To challenge drugs' evil power would undermine the fearmongering that drives the drug war. If a prosecutor pointed out to the sentencing judge that almost all drug users and most drug addicts never resort to non-drug crime,[149] it would raise the question, "Then why are we throwing them all in jail?"

B. Avoiding Withdrawal Hell: Avoiding the Flu

The idea that drug addicts will "do anything" to avoid withdrawal is grossly exaggerated. Perhaps the most feared addiction withdrawal is from heroin. One addiction expert called it "hell" and the "gold standard" of withdrawals.[151] Beginning with the "self-pitying vaporings of the Romantics" like Samuel Taylor Coleridge and Thomas de Quincey in the early nineteenth century, literary and screen presentations of opiate withdrawal have been even less restrained.[152]

Although heroin withdrawal is uncomfortable it is never fatal. At its worst, it is comparable to having the flu.[153] (Opiate withdrawal symptoms have been found to be frequently psychosomatic or faked.)[154] For many heroin addicts withdrawal merely means taking off some sick days.[155] In fact, some addicts intentionally go through withdrawal to lower their tolerance and the cost of their habit.[156]

Alcohol withdrawal, on the other hand, can cause psychotic experiences (delirium tremens) and can be fatal. Despite this, Hollywood presents heroin withdrawal—not alcohol withdrawal—as the demonic possession in which an addict will do literally anything to get a hit.

One woman, who used to be a heroin addict but now only uses intermittently, has led a successful professional life as a secretary and now as a social worker. The only crime she has ever committed was shoplifting a raincoat for a job interview.

> I never robbed. I never did anything like that. I never hurt a human being. I could never do that. I went sick a lot as a consequence. When other junkies would commit crimes, get money, and tighten up, I would be sick. Everyone . . . used to say: "You're terrible at being a junkie." I'm not going to hit anybody over the head. I'm sorry.[157]

C. Bananas Cause Crime: The Banana Effect

The idea that drugs make people do bad things is due to the samples of drug users who are exposed. The people who abuse drugs irresponsibly and commit crimes are the ones that get caught by the authorities and can be paraded through our courts and the media as examples for the community. The citizens who use illegal drugs responsibly and are otherwise law-abiding are much more likely to escape apprehension.

This is magnified because the media usually consult law enforcement, physicians, and drug treatment personnel for drug articles. This is the equivalent of talking to someone about ladders who has never used a ladder but is called every time someone falls off of one. For example, in 2007 I heard a therapist on a Christian

HEROIN SHOTS

Although heroin's reputation is much worse than morphine's, they are essentially the same. In the body heroin quickly turns into morphine. Heroin is simply three times stronger. That is, one part of heroin would have exactly the same affect as three parts of morphine. There are many opiates that replicate morphine's effect. Two of these are hydromorphone (six times as strong), which is still available by prescription, and etorphine (ten thousand times as strong), which is used to stun elephants.

Morphine is in opium, opium is in poppies, and poppies are in American gardens. Opium is easily taken from poppies by slicing the walls of the seed pod. The expelled gum is opium. Prior to opium's criminalization, drinking opium concoctions was a common American activity, and opium smoking is still prevalent in parts of the world. Morphine is the predominant psychoactive chemical in opium, and is easily extracted by mixing opium with boiling water and lime (CaO). The morphine rises to the top as a white suspension.

The heroin high is subtle. Ideally it "fills the user with a sense of contentment," but most people express dislike or indifference. Heroin does not grab the user and can go unnoticed by those expecting a "smack." Writers and directors who portray it as a "body-wide orgasm" are wrong and have probably never tried it. In contrast, a marijuana high is unsubtle, and marijuana aficionados are often disappointed by heroin.

A heroin high from injecting is not "substantially different" from a smoking high, but

radio program say that in all of his years of counseling he had never encountered a marijuana smoker without problems.

This biased exposure is called the "clinician's error," and it has also skewed views of homosexuals in the past.[158] When psychiatry stopped labeling homosexuality a mental disorder in the early 1970s, therapists complained, "How can you say that homosexuality is normal? I have treated many homosexuals, and they all had psychological problems."[159] This was probably true but *all* the people they saw had psychological problems—well-adjusted homosexuals never visited them.

In addition, there is a large incentive for drug users to tell the police and treatment personnel (and the media accompanying them) exactly what they want to hear—"Drugs are horrible. Don't do drugs." Any other message results in a tougher sentence or more treatment because they have not yet learned their lesson.

smoking loses much of the drug to the air. Avoiding loss is crucial to addicts because of the extraordinary cost of their habits, and they are willing to take the health risks of mainlining. (The body can develop a huge tolerance for heroin, often fifty times what was initially needed for effect.)

Mainlining is when a drug is injected into a vein. There are other less efficient injection methods, like skin popping, where the injection is put just under the skin to form a bubble. In addition to the obvious hygienic risks, another danger is possibly hitting an artery or nerve. (An artery's blood pressure is strong enough to shoot the needle's plunger back.) Despite its challenges the injection ritual can become so enjoyable that some ex-users will occasionally inject water.

—Richard Miller, *Case for Legalizing Drugs* (1991), p. 2; Francis Moraes, *Heroin User's Handbook* (2001), pp. 2, 7, 36, 64, 66–67; and Paul Gahlinger, *Illegal Drugs* (2001), pp. 367, 377.

Even if the public saw more than just the drug-using wrecks, illicit drug users' behavior would still be a poor indicator of drugs' effects. Criminalization and media propaganda can statistically link anything with crime—even bananas.

This Banana Effect can be demonstrated with a hypothetical scenario. In an imaginary United States, bananas are made illegal and the media begins spouting the idea that eating bananas is irresponsible, dangerous, and horrible for one's health. Responsible, law-abiding, health-conscious citizens would stop eating bananas.

Surveys of banana eaters would start to show that they commit more crimes and are unhealthier than non-banana eaters. Bananas did not change. The population using them changed. This is exactly what happened when drugs were criminalized at the beginning of the twentieth century.[160]

Numerous studies have found that drug-using criminals usually were criminals before their drug use began. One study found that a heroin user's first arrest typically occurs eighteen months *before* heroin use begins.[161] The ridiculously exorbitant costs of drugs caused by criminalization undoubtedly drive some addicts to crime, however, most addict-criminals were criminals first. The drugs and crime nexus is driven more by the population using drugs than by the drugs themselves.

Despite the Banana Effect and the fact that almost all research is aimed at damning drugs, statistical evidence still seeps out challenging the drugs-delinquent connection. Some of this evidence has shown that casual drug users earn as much as non-drug users,[162] and are just as likely to be employed.[163] Drug use is more common among people earning less than $12,000 a year, but also among people earning $100,000 a year or more.[164] A 1999 study of sixty-three Silicon Valley companies found productivity was sixteen percent lower in firms with pre-employment drug testing and twenty-nine percent lower in firms with random drug testing.[165] Perhaps this is because, on average, drug users have higher IQs than their peers.[166]

Another study that tracked kids from preschool to age eighteen found that adolescents who had engaged in some drug experimentation were the best adjusted. Adolescents who, by age eighteen, had never experimented were "relatively anxious, emotionally constricted, and lacking in social skills."[167] If the government's gross generalizing of drug users is applied to non-drug users, then all non-drug users are uptight cowardly geeks.

VII
You Only Think You Are Having Fun
Illegal Drugs Serve No Purpose

This is perhaps the most galling misconception. In high school in the early 1990s a question on a health test was, "What are the reasons for drinking alcohol?" I got the question wrong as did most of the class. The "correct" answer was there are no reasons to drink.

This concept has been foisted on Americans for the past century with regard to illegal drugs. It is ridiculous. There are numerous valid reasons why people take drugs. Some of these include:

A. Meeting God: Mind Expansion/Religious Reasons

Hallucinogens have been used in religious rites for tens of thousands of years. The sacred scriptures of India contain over one thousand hymns in praise of soma, a psychedelic mushroom.[168] This drug use has not been a trivial sideshow but a hallowed mystical experience central to these religions.

HIGH ON SUCCESS
Some Drug Users Who Overachieved[104]

Amphetamine—current Air Force pilots, Winston Churchill,[a] Anthony Eden (British Prime Minister),[a] Paul Erdös (mathematician), John F. Kennedy,[a] World War II & Vietnam veterans[a,b]

Dexedrine [amphetamine] is the gold-standard for anti-fatigue . . . [It] has never been associated with a proven adverse outcome in a military operation. —U.S. Air Force, 2003[105]

[Amphetamine] was a great success. It cleared my head and gave me great confidence. —Winston Churchill[106]

Barbiturate—John Kenneth Galbraith (economist),[a] Anne Sexton (poet),[a] Mao Zedong[107] (revolutionary)

Can you be addicted in a calm way that doesn't hurt anyone?

There's a difference between taking something that will kill you and something that will kill you momentarily. —Anne Sexton[108]

Cocaine—Frédéric Bartholdi (architect of Statue of Liberty),[d] George W. Bush,[109] Thomas Edison,[b] Sigmund Freud,[a] Ulysses S. Grant,[b] Pope Leo XIII,[b] Barack Obama, Robert Louis Stevenson (writer),[d] Jules Verne (first sci-fi writer),[d] Andrew Weil (doctor/author),[c] Oprah Winfrey,[110] Malcolm X[111]

Pot had helped, and booze; maybe a little blow when you could afford it. —Barack Obama[112]

LSD—Ralph Abraham (mathematician),[c] Richard Branson (CEO, self-made billionaire),[113] Aristotle,[b] Cicero,[b] Douglas Englebart (invented computer mouse),[114] Richard Feynman (Nobel Laureate in physics),[115] Michel Foucault (sociologist),[c] Bill Gates,[116] Cary Grant, Steve Jobs (Apple co-founder/CEO),[117] Mitch Kapor (software pioneer),[c] Robert Kennedy,[b] Francis Krick (Nobel laureate in physiology),[118] Groucho Marx,[c] Kary Mulis (Nobel laureate in chemistry),[c] Anaïs Nin (writer),[c] Plato,[b] Sophocles[b] Note: The ancient Romans and Greeks used a natural form of LSD (kykeon) during a ceremony of the Eleusinian Mysteries.

People who take drugs are trying to escape from their lives. LSD is a hallucinogen, and people who take it are trying to look within their lives. That's what I did. —Cary Grant[119]

I just think [Bill Gates] and Microsoft are a bit narrow. He'd be a broader guy if he had dropped acid once or gone off to an ashram when he was younger. —Steve Jobs[120]

Opiates (opium, unless noted)—Marcus Aurelius (Roman Emperor/philosopher),[c] Jane Addams (reformer),[c] Louisa May Alcott (morphine),[c] Honoré de Balzac (writer),[a] Elizabeth Barrett Browning (poet),[c] Samuel Taylor Coleridge (poet),[d] Wilkie Collins (writer),[d] Charles Dickens,[c] Gustave Flaubert,[a] Benjamin Franklin,[a] King George IV,[c] William Gladstone (British Prime Minister),[a] Edmond Halley (astronomer),[136] William Halsted (heroin),[a] Hippocrates,[c] Thomas Jefferson,[137] Samuel Johnson (writer),[a] Rush Limbaugh (OxyContin), Jack London,[138] Florence Nightingale (nurse, morphine),[c] Paracelsus,[b] Charlie Parker (heroin),[b] Pablo Picasso,[139] Plotinus,[c] Edgar Allan Poe,[140] Marcel Proust (writer),[c] Sir Walter Scott (writer),[c] William Wilberforce (reformer),[a] Oscar Wilde[c]

Marijuana—Louis Armstrong (musician),[b] Michael Bloomberg (NYC mayor, self-made billionaire), Richard Branson,[121] George W. Bush,[122] Bill Clinton,[c] Bing Crosby,[123] Richard Feynman,[124] Galen,[b] Gustave Flaubert (novelist),[a] Bill Gates,[125] Newt Gingrich, Al Gore,[c] Stephen Jay Gould (paleontologist),[c] Victor Hugo (writer),[b] Steve Jobs,[126] John F. Kennedy,[127] Peter Lewis (CEO, self-made billionaire),[128] Jack London (author),[129] Barack Obama, Sarah Palin,[130] Edgar Allan Poe,[b] Carl Sagan (astronomer),[c] Arnold Schwarzenegger,[c] Shakespeare,[131]

The importance of drug rituals can be seen with the Eleusinian Mysteries. In ancient Greece and Rome there was a cult based at the Athens temple of Eleusis. Up to three thousand people a year were initiated in an annual week-long affair that culminated in the Mysteries, rites kept secret under the penalty of death. The cult had amazing endurance, beginning around 1500 B.C. and not ending until the Romans' enforcement of Christianity shut it down at the end of the fourth century A.D..

Cult members included such celebrated figures as Aristotle, Sophocles, Plato, and several Roman Emperors. The poet Pindar wrote of the Mysteries, "Happy is he who, having seen these rites, goes below the hollow earth; for he knows the end of life and its god-sent beginning."[169] The Roman Emperor Cicero believed them to be the greatest contribution of Athens. It is now believed that the Mysteries' rites incorporated a natural form of LSD.[170] This powerful mystical experience held the cult together for two thousand years.

A mystical experience is a profound event in which one is "left with a greater awareness of God, or a higher power, or ultimate reality."[171] The ability of hallucinogens to facilitate these revelations was demonstrated in numerous studies

Clarence Thomas (Supreme Court Justice),[c] Queen Victoria,[b] George Washington,[b] William Wordsworth (poet),[b] Jesse Ventura (Navy SEAL, governor),[c] Pancho Villa (revolutionary),[c] John Wayne, Oscar Wilde,[b] Malcolm X[132]

You bet I did, and I enjoyed it. —Michael Bloomberg[133]

That was a sign we were alive and in graduate school in that era. —Newt Gingrich[134]

There's been no top authority saying what marijuana does to you. I tried it once but it didn't do anything to me. —John Wayne[135]

Others—William James (psychologist/philosopher, nitrous oxide, mescaline),[c] Richard Nixon (Dilantin),[a] William Rehnquist (Supreme Court Chief Justice, Placidyl),[141] Pancho Villa (mescaline)[c]

Note: No modern entertainers listed due to limited space.

conducted before hallucinogens were outlawed.[172] In one 1962 study, before a Good Friday church service, fifteen theology students and professors were given psilocybin and another fifteen were given placebos. Despite not knowing who received the placebos, those who received psilocybin had experiences dramatically more mystical than those who did not. The researcher behind the study later wrote,

> "The experience helped them resolve career decisions, recog-
> nize the arbitrariness of ego boundaries, increase their depth of faith,
> increase their appreciation of eternal life, deepen their sense of the
> meaning of Christ, and heighten their sense of joy and beauty."[173]

One of the participants who received psilocybin said over thirty years later, "it enlarged my understanding of God by affording me the only powerful experience I have had of his personal nature."[174]

B. I Like You: Social Reasons

Some people enjoy stimulants like cocaine for confidence in dealing with people, while others prefer sedatives, like alcohol, to help them relax. Other social motives are more esoteric. For example, Louis Armstrong said of marijuana, "When you're with another tea smoker it makes you feel a special sense of kinship."[175]

Science has found the biological underpinnings of some of these social benefits. One example is the effect of alcohol on the male brain. Men have more difficulty expressing their feelings verbally than women. The portions of the male brain that handle these matters are less integrated than in the female brain.[176] Alcohol breaks down the discrete compartments in the male brain and allows males to "open up" emotionally.[177]

Perhaps the most social drug is Ecstasy (MDMA). MDMA is a stimulant with psychedelic qualities. It releases people emotionally and allows them to relate to others. Its possibilities were demonstrated by the couple Sue and Shane Stevens.[178] In the mid-1990s Shane learned that he had terminal cancer. The resulting stress was destroying their relationship until a friend suggested they try Ecstasy.

Under Ecstasy's influence they talked about all their emotions and fears. As Sue described, "One night . . . changed our life permanently . . . . We woke up to the same people we had fallen in love with . . . There were no barriers between us, no fears, no anger . . . ."[179] Afterwards Shane was a new person. He stopped using painkillers and led an active life with their children. A month before his death in 1999 they used Ecstasy for the last time: "We wanted one last night. We spent the next six hours recapping our lives together. We talked about everything . . . We lived our entire life together in that night, plus we lived fifty more years."[180] At one point during that evening Shane said, "You know, it's really great not to have cancer tonight."[181]

Despite its promising use by psychiatrists in therapy, when kids started using it at raves in the mid-1980s the Drug Enforcement Administration (DEA) made MDMA a Schedule I drug. Schedule I is the most severe category, supposedly reserved for drugs with high abuse potential and no acceptable medical use. MDMA has virtually no addiction potential and researchers protested its criminalization.[182]

COCANALYSIS
Freud & Cocaine

Sigmund Freud invented the psychological discipline of psychoanalysis. Psychoanalysis' validity is still fiercely debated—as is the claim that without cocaine Freud would have never come up with it. Throughout the period Freud developed his theories of psychoanalysis, he successfully used cocaine to alleviate his depression and anxiety. Cocaine arguably assisted Freud in two other crucial ways.

First, a common side effect of cocaine use is becoming a chatterbox. Cocaine made Freud a talker and opened him up emotionally. It helped transform Freud from a solitary lab rat to a person who socialized at the soirées of leading intellectuals. (He wrote that he took it before going out to "untie my tongue.") Cocaine also enabled the numerous all-night discussions with a suffering friend that were the precursor of his "talking cure."

Second, another common side effect of cocaine use is instilling great confidence in oneself and one's thoughts. Although this confidence is frequently misplaced—as in Freud's bizarre belief that surgically removing parts of one's inner nasal canal could cure all ills—psychoanalysis proved worthy in the end. Cocaine possibly "gave [Freud] both the depth of vision necessary to jettison conventional thought, and the arrogance to believe that he was right and everyone else was wrong."

Note: Freud was never addicted to cocaine. He was addicted to nicotine and could not give up cigars even after cancer required that his upper right jaw be removed. This mouth cancer eventually killed him.

—Dominic Streatfeild, *Cocaine* (2002), pp. 105–116; and Louis Breger, *Freud* (2000), pp. 55–73, 357.

C. Ow!: Pain Tolerance[183]

Since the 1920s federal drug agents have harassed the medical profession into ignoring patients with chronic pain from catastrophic injuries. In 1996, *60 Minutes* ran a segment on the ludicrous ramifications of the drug war on pain treatment. It featured the hearing of Dr. William Hurwitz in which Virginia's board of medical examiners debated whether to revoke his license to practice.

The hearing involved a procession of tragic victims from all over the country testifying that Hurwitz was the only doctor who had the courage to assist them. One man was in a car crash and by the time he was discovered his legs had completely frozen. After the gangrenous parts of his body were amputated he had lost everything below his navel. He testified that morphine prevents the sensation that his lower half is still being sawed off. Another witness was a former police officer from upstate New York who had been crushed by a school bus. He threatened the board that if it revoked Hurwitz's license and cut off his prescription he would commit suicide.

Amazingly the Virginia Board of Medicine held its line in the war on drugs and revoked Hurwitz's license. As the Virginia state police manual warned, "Physicians should be alert for 'Professional Patients' showing up in wheelchairs missing various limbs."[184] None who testified were able to bewitch the medical examiners with their sob stories. One examiner said that by revoking Hurwitz's license the board might have saved other lives. The crushed police officer followed through on his threat and killed himself four weeks later.

Law enforcement continues to send undercover agents and informants into doctors' offices to lure them into writing bad prescriptions.[185] Only 3.27 percent of users of medically prescribed opiates develop any form of addiction. This figure drops to .19 percent for patients who did not have a prior history of drug abuse.[186]

D. Third Wind: Energy

Winston Churchill used amphetamine and barbiturate to help him navigate World War II.[187] The entire American military used as well. With amphetamines being packed in ration kits, the American soldier in World War II averaged one pill per day.[188] Despite going through the equivalent of a four-year speed binge, "The Greatest Generation" managed to avoid mass addiction and went on to "build modern America."[189] Nor did drugs appear to damage the faculties of greatest generation member John F. Kennedy. Kennedy continued to use uppers into his presidency, including during his summit meeting with Nikita Khrushchev in 1961 and during the 1962 Cuban missile crisis.[190]

Amphetamine was not reserved for the performance of the fighting men. Although the habit was probably widespread in sports, European cyclists were the most candid. Italian champion Fausto Coppie told French radio in the late 1950s that all competitive cyclists used amphetamine and those who disagreed did not know what they were talking about. Jacques Anquetil, who won the Tour de France, told a

KILLER DIVORCÉES
Predictors of Violence[150]

Neither drug abuse/dependence nor severe mental illness is a statistically significant predictor of violence. Even when these co-occur they still rank behind divorce and lengthy unemployment.

Top Predictors of Future Violence

1. Age (younger people are more violent)
2. History of any violent act
3. Sex (males are more violent)
4. History of juvenile detention
5. Divorce or separation in the past year
6. History of physical abuse
7. Parental criminal history
8. Unemployment for the past year
9. Co-occurring severe mental illness and substance abuse and/or dependence

journalist in 1967 that only an idiot would believe a professional cyclist who races 235 days a year could manage without stimulants.[191]

Even regular folks used amphetamine in the middle of the century.[192] It was available without prescription until 1954 and was widely used to stay awake by truck drivers and students during final exams. A historian notes, "enormous quantities of oral amphetamines were consumed in the United States during the 1940s and 1950s with apparently little misuse." It was not until criminalization in 1965 that the methamphetamine "speed freak" became responsible for "a wave of unspeakable acts of violence."

E. Don't Worry, Be Happy: Relaxation

Just as stimulants are used for energy, depressants are used to relax. The most common depressant is alcohol. During the late 1960s and 1970s, another popular depressant was Quaaludes. Brooklyn College went through five thousand pills a day and at Ohio State University, where fraternities had jars of it available, football players routinely used Quaaludes to come down after games.[193]

Before the war on drugs, other drugs were used to relax as well. One of these was opium, the precursor of heroin. Unlike alcohol and Quaaludes, opium—taken in moderation—does not interfere with performance. William Gladstone (1809–1898), one of Britain's most esteemed prime ministers, took laudanum (an opium/alcohol mix) before giving speeches to appease his nerves and keep him controlled.[194] The noted British abolitionist William Wilberforce (1759–1833) attributed all his success as a public speaker to taking opium beforehand.[195]

F. A Whole New World: Creativity

Any new experience can foster creativity, and drugs can provide fascinating and unique experiences. The ancient Greeks and Romans were well aware of this and believed drug-induced dreams, visions, and hallucinations were an avenue to self-knowledge, discovery, and creativity.[196] The most famous example of Plato's "divine madness" could be the paintings of Vincent Van Gogh. His heavy use of yellow pigment, most notably the yellow coronas in *Starry Night*, likely came from the visual distortions of the drug digitalis.[197]

Some drugs have left their imprints on entire eras. The influence of LSD's perceptual distortions can be seen all over the art of the 1960s, from the surreal music of the Beatles and Pink Floyd to the comic artist Robert Crumb, who credits acid for molding his trademark distorted figures.[198] The writer Ken Kesey came up with the idea of a schizophrenic mute narrator for his acclaimed book *One Flew Over the Cuckoo's Nest* (1962) during an acid trip.[199] Allen Ginsburg wrote the famous poem *Howl* (1956) after a night spent walking San Francisco's streets under the influence of the natural hallucinogen peyote.[200]

Just like LSD was *the* influence on 1960s artists, marijuana was *the* influence on

French artists one hundred years earlier. Members of the Hashish Club included the great literary figures Dumas (*Count of Monte Cristo*), Nerval, Hugo (*Les Misérables, The Hunchback of Notre-Dame*), Boissard, Delacroix, Gautier, and Baudelaire.[201] Across the ocean, their American counterpart, Edgar Allan Poe, was also a marijuana "adherent."[202]

The twentieth-century literary giant Norman Mailer has said that marijuana is "divine" for providing one with new associations and "extraordinary thoughts."[203] When asked if drugs aided his creativity, Brian Wilson of the Beach Boys replied, "Very much so, yeah. Marijuana helped me write *Pet Sounds*."[204] (*Pet Sounds* was ranked by *Rolling Stone* magazine as the second greatest album of all time.)[205] The contemporary novelist Tom Robbins explained further:

> The plant genies don't manufacture imagination, nor do they market wonder and beauty—but they force us out of context so dramatically and so meditatively that we gawk in amazement at the ubiquitous everyday wonders that we are culturally disposed to overlook, and they teach us invaluable lessons about fluidity, relativity, flexibility, and paradox. Such an increase in awareness, if skillfully applied, can lift a disciplined, adventurous artist permanently out of reach of the faded jaws of mediocrity.[206]

Drug-invoked creativity has not been limited to artists. A Nobel Prize-winning chemist, Kary Mullis, has credited LSD with assistance in formulating the concepts for a paper he published in 1968.[207] Arguably the most prolific mathematician of the twentieth century, Paul Erdös, attributed his creativity to amphetamines.[208] Similar credit has been given to marijuana by the psychologist Susan Blackmore[209] and the astronomer Carl Sagan.[210] Ralph Abraham, the mathematician who invented chaos theory, said, "In the 1960s a lot of people on the frontiers of math experimented with psychedelic substances. There was a brief and extremely creative kiss between the community of hippies and top mathematicians."[211]

Perhaps the most stunning acid-induced discovery was that of DNA's structure by Francis Crick in 1953. Crick, who was active in the drug legalization movement, told associates that he was on acid when he perceived the infamous double helix, the software of life. When confronted about this by a reporter he did not deny it but did threaten to sue if the reporter made it public. (The reporter went public after Crick's death in 2004.)[212]

Hallucinogens also played a role in the personal computer revolution that has transformed society. Early visionaries such as Mitch Kapor (Lotus), Douglas Englebart (invented the computer mouse), Steve Jobs (Apple), and Bill Gates (Microsoft) all used LSD. It is not coincidence that the tech capital of the world, Silicon Valley, sprouted adjacent to the psychedelic center of the universe.[213] Kevin Herbert, a programmer who was an early employee of Cisco Systems, still solves his toughest technical problems on acid and was instrumental in Cisco banning drug testing.[214]

Pharmacological muses are not limited to hallucinogens. The modern intellectual Susan Sontag found marijuana too relaxing to use while writing and preferred speed (amphetamine).[215] Most of Philip K. Dick's science fiction stories were produced on speed and it could explain his prolific output. Dick would write sixty pages a day, and nine of his works have been made into movies, most notably *Blade Runner* (1982), *Total Recall* (1990), and *Minority Report* (2002).[216]

The famous Beat writer Jack Kerouac used the amphetamine benzedrine to write his groundbreaking novel *On the Road* (1957),[217] and said: "Benny has made me see a lot . . . The process of intensifying awareness naturally leads to an overflow of old notions, and *voilá*, new material wells up like water following its proper level, and makes itself evident at the brim of consciousness."[218]

Stimulants also served writers before amphetamines were synthesized. The natural stimulant cocaine inspired Robert Louis Stevenson and he wrote his 1886 novel *The Strange Case of Dr. Jekyll and Mr. Hyde* during a sleepless six-day binge.[219]

Opiates have not received many creative plaudits from artists, but their extensive modern use by them is notable. Samuel Taylor Coleridge (*Kubla Khan*), Elizabeth Barrett Browning, and Sir Walter Scott (*Rob Roy*) all produced timeless writings while under its influence.[220]

The exceptional jazz saxophonist Charlie Parker (1920–1955) was a heroin addict. Because other jazz musicians were awed by him, heroin became the drug of jazz.[221] As the jazz sound transferred into rock and roll so did the drug use. One of the reasons the influential band the Rolling Stones used a potpourri of drugs, which included heroin, was "to identify with the jazz musicians' credo that expanding their minds would lead to greater artistic excellence."[222] Notoriously burned-out Rolling Stone Keith Richards became the model for the "elegantly wasted" rock outlaw.[223]

In 1967 The Velvet Underground & Nico became the first rockers to make overt references to drugs with their heroin songs, "I'm Waiting for the Man" and "Heroin," with "Heroin" clearly mimicking the dreamy state of a heroin high.[224] If heroin does not assist creativity, it does not appear to hurt.[225]

The Velvet Underground's open drug references have now become ubiquitous in popular music. However, outside of marijuana, the "drugs are bad" message is usually not undermined by rockers, who want to be seen as living dangerously.[226] The youngest generation of artists have lived their entire lives under the anti-drug media blitzkrieg launched in the 1980s. While they still do illicit drugs, few publicly speak of drugs in a positive manner with so much of their income now coming from corporate endorsements.[227] One of the few brave ones is Richard Ashcroft of The Verve:

> Anything that can take you to beyond where you naturally are when you wake up in the morning can have some creative effect, can have some way of spinning the way you look on life. Your fucking skunk can do that. Cocaine can do that. I don't do heroin myself, but obviously I'm sure there's an initial period where it does that. I smoke the weed every day, and to me, that is the thing I've found is best for making music.[228]

G. F The Man: Rebel Cool

Numerous people take drugs because it allows them to be rebel cool. One of the countless unintended consequences of criminalizing recreational drugs was that they became associated with anti-authoritarian risk-takers ("rebels").[229]

This can be seen by comparing caffeine use with cocaine use. Binging on caffeine can rival the effects of powder cocaine and even lead to hallucinations,[230] but people who snort No-Doz pills or pound a six-pack of Jolt Cola are seen as morons, not rebels.

One reason for this is that the caffeine binger is taking little risk. There is no danger of arrest. The person knows exactly how much she is taking so there is little chance of overdose. In addition, the media have not been able to exaggerate caffeine's dangers because everybody is familiar with it. Not even the most paranoid mother can think the caffeine binger is playing with "death" (even though people do die from caffeine overdose in rare circumstances).

Another reason is that the popular image of someone binging on caffeine is a ten-year-old kid bored at her birthday party. Thanks to the criminalization of cocaine, the popular image of someone taking cocaine is no longer a distinguished fogey drinking Vin Mariani. The popular image is now one of hell-raisers and rock stars doing lines off of strippers.[231]

Just as important to the rebel cachet as who does it is who does not do it. Rebel status can be lost when conformists ("squares") join the action, but illegal drugs will never have this problem. Squares may drink a lot of caffeinated soda, but squares will never break the law.

Rebel cool has the most appeal to self-conscious adolescents and young adults. The advent of criminalization at the turn of the nineteenth century allowed kids to use drugs to defy authority, and drug use quickly became a rite of passage for young adults.[232]

Dutch authorities brag that through legalization they have made marijuana boring. Marijuana use by Dutch teenagers actually declined in the decade following its legalization in 1976. Although it has gone up significantly since then, Dutch teens still try marijuana at roughly half the rate of American teens.[233]

Apparently marijuana is not as cool when anybody can try it. As Richard Mack, a narcotics agent who smoked it when undercover, said, " . . . I found myself wondering what in the heck the big deal was."[234]

H. Custom: Culture

People use drugs because the people around them are using drugs. The anti-drug crowd has branded this as sinister peer pressure. However, is someone who eats turkey at Thanksgiving doing it because of peer pressure? When you recommend an enjoyable activity to a friend are you peer-pressuring them into doing it?

Just as alcohol has served as a social nexus in bars and gatherings for millennia in Western culture, other drugs have served and continue to serve the same function for other groups. For example, the chewing of coca leaves in South America, the chewing of betel in Southeast Asia, the drinking of kava in the South Pacific, the chewing of khat in East Africa, and the smoking of marijuana by Jamaican Rastafarians all serve social functions.

I. It Does the Body Good: Health Reasons

Medical use is the only acceptable use of drugs, according to the government, however, medical benefits have still not been able to remove recreational drugs from the DEA's clutches. For example, in the cases of marijuana and MDMA, the DEA refused to decriminalize their medical use against the recommendations of the DEA's *own* judges.[235] The stonewalling on marijuana is astoundingly fraudulent, with no less than eighty state and national health care organizations, including the prestigious *New England Journal of Medicine*, advocating for immediate medical access to marijuana.[236]

Although criminalization has made the public forget the more natural forms of drugs, those forms have nutritional value. The plant that cocaine is derived from, coca, has been ingested by South Americans as far back as 2500 B.C..[237] The Indians claimed it was "a gift from the gods to satisfy the hungry, fortify the weary, and make the unfortunate forget their sorrows." Coca leaf chewing and coca tea were used for sustenance. Coca was an essential source of nutrients to those living in the high-altitude Andes, and without coca the Indians might not have been able to survive in that severe environment.

Perhaps the most underestimated use of illicit drugs is for self-medicating mental health issues. For example, studies have found alcoholics and smokers had less dopamine (pleasure chemical) receptors in their brains than their peers.[238] Numerous people who use the drugs that manipulate dopamine levels—cigarettes, alcohol, cocaine, amphetamines—are arguably just trying to be as content as normal people.

As a public defender I represented an adult woman who frequently used cocaine. She was one of the most hyper and unfocused adults I had ever met and I asked her why she enjoyed cocaine, since the last thing she needed was a stimulant. She told me that cocaine had the opposite effect on her and actually slowed her down.

I later learned that she was right. Cocaine allows those with attention deficit disorders to be calm, focused and clearheaded.[239] If she had the resources she would probably be diagnosed and prescribed a legal stimulant like the amphetamine Adderall. Not surprisingly, patients with attention deficit disorders are over-represented among those undergoing treatment for cocaine abuse.[240]

J. Drugs Make Life Fun: Pleasure

Recreational drugs provide pleasure. Although the preference for specific drugs—and drugs in general—is highly subjective, most people use illicit substances because they make them feel good. A scientific survey of over 4,400 subjects found that marijuana users are happier and less depressed than non-users.[241] For many, drug experiences rank among the best moments of their lives. One of these is Apple co-founder and self-made billionaire Steve Jobs:

> [Jobs] explained that he still believed that taking LSD was one of the two or three most important things he had done in his life, and he said he felt that because people he knew well had not tried psychedelics, there were things about him they couldn't understand.[242]

After a hundred years of government propaganda and media sensationalism drug users are afraid to give pleasure as a reason. The popular perception is that drugs are so evil and destructive that to take them for an inconsequential purpose such as enjoyment is blasphemy. Therefore a never-ending line of people convicted of drug possession march before judges all across America for sentencing and give "The Script." The usual themes are tragedies drove them to drugs, drugs overtook their will, and drugs drove them to do bad things. The performance ends with, "Now that I have been arrested and prosecuted I have seen the error of my ways and will repent."

As a public defender I represented a few brave defendants who wanted to say, "I enjoy the drug and it caused no negative consequences until I was arrested, went to jail, and received this criminal record," but as their counsel I advised them that would not be prudent if they wanted a lenient punishment. I learned that the judges were so

264

jaded by The Script that when I advised these defiant clients to give abbreviated and vague versions of The Script so as not to lie under oath the judges did not even notice. (It is possible they noticed but did not care.)

The Script works well because it fits into the myth that is drilled into the population from birth, and on which the criminalization of drugs is built. The Script also comforts the judge, the arresting officer, and the prosecutor. They are not ruining lives, they are saving them. Even more importantly, all the people who have never taken drugs are reassured that they are not missing out on anything and that everything is right in the world.

GOOD TIMES
Maybe *You* Are Missing Out[243]

Person	Drug	Quote
Tori Amos	Ayahuasca (Hallucinogen)	"It's not like I've never done cocaine but . . . if I can't see dancing elephants I'm not interested . . . [Ayahuasca] can grab you by the balls and just shove you up against the wall."[19]
Helen Mirren	Cocaine	"I loved coke. I never did a lot, just a little bit at parties." [20]
Rick Root	Cocaine	"It gave a very pleasant high. It gave me the impression that I could dig deeper into my mind . . . It gave me the ability to look at things in a broader view."
Jon Marsh	Ecstasy (MDMA)	"Apart from falling in love, taking Ecstasy is the most enjoyable thing I've ever done."[21]
Charlie De León	Glue	"I've asked [Guatemalan guajeros] what it feels like to sniff glue or sniff thinner and they tell me they see whatever they want to see . . . It gives them the strength to do whatever they want to do."[22]
Lenny Bruce	Heroin	"I'll die young, but it's like kissing God."[23]

William Burroughs	Heroin	"If God made anything better, he kept it for Himself."[24]
Francis Moraes	Heroin	"...being a chipper [occasional user] can be a lot of fun ..."[25]
Michel Foucault	LSD	"Foucault was about to enjoy what he would later call the greatest experience of his life..."[26]
Morgan Freeman	Marijuana	"God's own weed."[27]
Allan Mattus	Marijuana	"Pot is just really fun—that euphoric buzz you have ... A crappy day isn't a crappy day anymore ... One of my favorite things is to go to a park. There's nothing better than toking up and going to look at some great scenery."
Bill Santini	Mescaline (Hallucinogen)	"...it was one of the unique sensations of my life—patterns on patterns. Very interesting ... sounds had colors and colors had textures, and I very much liked the experience."
Bruce Rogers	PCP	"A lot of bang for the buck."

NOTES

1. *Oxford American Dictionary* (1980), p. 265.
2. "2002 National Drug Control Strategy," 9 July 2002, ret. WhiteHouseDrugPolicy.gov, 11 Jan. 2007.
3. Paul Gahlinger, *Illegal Drugs* (2001), p. 89.
4. Ibid.
5. The rule of utility is stricter with illegal drugs because unlike legal drugs, such as medication, advertising cannot positively distort them.
6. The 1990s Seattle rocker Kurt Cobain *deliberately* set out to become a junkie and eventually committed suicide via shotgun in 1994. "Watch Out, Needle's About" *Q*, Feb. 2001, p. 60.
7. Richard Davenport-Hines, *Pursuit of Oblivion* (2002), p. 12.
8. One reporter who frequently writes about research countering anti-drug propaganda is Maia Szalavitz at Time.com.
9. Antonio Escohotado, *Brief History of Drugs* (1999), p. 91.
10. Dealers frequently dilute cocaine with much cheaper caffeine to fool customers. Gahlinger, *Illegal Drugs*, p. 251.
11. Dominic Streatfeild, *Cocaine* (2001), pp. 60–61.

12.   Estimated ninety milligrams per twelve ounces. David Barlow and Vincent Durand, *Abnormal Psychology* (2004), p. 392.

13.   Coca-Cola is still flavored with coca leaves. In 1985 a formula without coca, New Coke, was tried, but it was a disaster.

14.   James Gray, *Why Our Drug Laws Have Failed* (2001), p. 54.

15.   In Pennsylvania, delivery of .04 ounces is a mandatory two-year prison sentence without parole. 18 Pa.C.S. §7508(a)(7).

16.   Crack is a "creature of the law—an artifact of [cocaine's] prohibition." Mike Gray, *Drug Crazy* (1998), pp. 106–107.

17.   Julie Deardorff, "Emerging Health Concern," *Chicago Tribune*, 21 Nov. 2006; and Lamar Heystek, "Just Say No to No-Doze," CaliforniaAggie.com, 4 Nov. 2003, ret. 21 Apr. 2007.

18.   Joseph Brean, "Caffeine Linked to Psychiatric Disorders," *National Post*, 2 Dec. 2006, ret. Canada.com, 21 Apr. 2007.

19.   Craig Van Dyke and Robert Byck, "Cocaine," *Scientific American*, Mar. 1982, p. 128.

20.   Robert Sabbag, *Snowblind* (1990, orig. pub. 1976), p. 72.

21.   From a survey of health professionals involved in addiction treatment. Daniel Perrine, *Chemistry of Mind-Altering Drugs* (1996), p. 7.

22.   Paul Gahlinger, *Illegal Drugs* (2001), pp. 129–130.

23.   Francis Moraes, *Heroin User's Handbook* (2001), p. 75; and Richard Miller, *Case for Legalizing Drugs* (1991), p. 5.

24.   Those marked with an [a] from Joyce Lowinson, *Substance Abuse*, 2nd Ed. (1992), p. 432; with a [b] from Erowid. org, ret. 4 Apr. 2012.

25.   Bennett Weinberg and Bonnie Bealer, *World of Caffeine* (2001), p. xiii.

26.   "South Korean Dies after Game Session," BBC.co.uk, 10 Aug. 2005; and Tony Dokoupil, "Is the Web Driving Us Mad?" TheDailyBeast.com, 9 July 2012.

27.   Mihaly Csikszentmihalyi, *Flow* (1990), p. 73.

28.   Mark Kram, "Playboy Interview," *Playboy*, Nov. 1998, p. 66.

29.   Most heavy long-term users do not experience any withdrawal symptoms. Paul Gahlinger, *Illegal Drugs* (2001), pp. 333–334.

30.   Michael Roizen and Mehmet Oz, *You On a Diet* (2006), p. 161.

31.   Ibid., p. 165.

32.   Maia Szalavitz, "Can Food Really Be Addictive?" Time.com, 5 Apr. 2012.

33.   "National Survey on Drug Use and Health," Fig. 1.1A, Substance Abuse and Mental Health Services Administration (SAMHSA), 2010. "Lifetime usage" refers to those who had ever used the drug in their lives.

34.   Jacob Sullum, *Saying Yes* (2003), p. 233.

35.   For more about the brutal conditions and conditioning used in animal addiction studies see Craig Reinarman and Harry Levine, *Crack in America* (1997), pp. 147–149.

36.   Letter notations indicate source. Those marked with an:
      a: James Anthony, Lynn Warner, and Ronald Kessler, "Comparative Epidemiology of Dependence . . .," *Exp. Clin. Psychopharmacol.*, 1994, 2(3), p. 251.
      b: Fernando Wagner and James Anthony, "From First Drug Use to Drug Dependence," *Neuropsychopharmacology*, 2002, 26(4), p. 479.
      c: Monitoring the Future: A Continuing Study of American Youth (12th-Grade Survey), 2004–2008—Core Data.

37.   Martin Booth, *Opium* (1996), quoted in Sullum, *Saying Yes*, p. 223.

38.   Tom Morganthau, "Kids and Cocaine," *Newsweek*, 17 Mar. 1986, p. 58.

39.   Brian Scheid, "Symposium Shown Horrors of Meth Use," *Intelligencer*, 1 Oct. 2005, ret. phillyBurbs.com, 2 Oct. 2005.

40.   *Diagnostic and Statistical Manual of Mental Disorders*, 4th Ed, (2000), (DSM-IV-TR).

41.   Stanton Peele, *Seven Tools to Beat Addiction* (2004), p. 16.

42.   Robert MacCoun and Peter Reuter, *Drug War Heresies* (2001), pp. 226, 236–237; and Glenn Greenwald, "Drug Decriminalization in Portugal," Cato Institute, 2009.

43.   Edward Epstein, *Agency of Fear* (1990), pp. 185–187.

44. Catalina Lopez-Quintero, et al., "Probability and Predictors of Transition from First Use to Dependence . . .", *Drug. Alcohol Depend.*, 1 May 2011, p. 126.

45. Jon Grant, et al., "Introduction to Behavioral Addictions," *Am. J. Drug Alcohol Abuse*, 36, 2010.

46. Ronald Kessler, et al., "Lifetime Prevalence and Age-of-Onset Distributions of DSM-IV Disorders . . .", *Arch. Gen. Psychiatry*, 62, 2005.

47. Lopez-Quintero, "Probability and Predictors of Transition from First Use to Dependence . . .", p. 126.

48. Stanton Peele, *Diseasing of America* (1995), p. 160.

49. Lopez-Quintero, "Probability and Predictors of Transition from First Use to Dependence . . .", p. 126.

50. Lee Robins, "Vietnam Veterans' Rapid Recovery from Heroin Addiction," *Addiction*, 1993, 88, pp. 1044–1045.

51. Gene Heyman, *Addiction: A Disorder of Choice* (2009), p. 92.

52. Grant, "Introduction to Behavioral Addictions."

53. Lopez-Quintero, "Probability and Predictors of Transition from First Use to Dependence . . .", p. 126.

54. D.R. Roalf, et al., "Risk, Reward, and Economic Decision Making in Aging," *J. Gerontol.*, 6 Sep. 2011.

55. Stanton Peele, *Seven Tools to Beat Addiction* (2004), p. 13.

56. "National Survey on Drug Use and Health," Fig. 5.3B, Substance Abuse and Mental Health Services Administration (SAMHSA), 2010.

57. These have occurred in a marathon and a water binging contest. Gina Kolata, "Study Cautions Runners," *New York Times*, 14 Apr. 2005; and "Ten Fired after Radio Contest Death," Reuters, 17 Jan. 2007.

58. Robert MacCoun and Peter Reuter, *Drug War Heresies* (2001), p. 125.

59. Paul Gahlinger, *Illegal Drugs* (2001), pp. 335–336, 308, 313–316, 275–276.

60. Brenda Ingersoll, "Dealer of Killer Drug Gets 10 Years," *Wisconsin State Journal*, 14 July 2006.

61. MacCoun, *Drug War Heresies*, p. 125.

62. In a three-year heroin maintenance program with over one thousand patients no one died. Gahlinger, *Illegal Drugs*, pp. 382.

63. K.A. Sporer and A.H. Kral, "Prescription Naloxone," *Ann. Emerg. Med.*, 12 July 2006.

64. The popular image of a person found dead with the needle still in their arm, like Lenny Bruce, is misleading. Sudden deaths are frequently attributable to adulterants or mixing drugs: for example, *heroin and alcohol are a deadly combination.* Francis Moraes, *Heroin User's Handbook* (2001), pp. 90–93.

65. John Sullivan, "City Stand on Heroin Antidote Risks Lives," *Philadelphia Inquirer*, 20 Aug. 2006.

66. Ibid.

67. An autopsy study found a total of thirty-three deaths of acute cocaine intoxication in Virginia in 1988. Most were from using cocaine intravenously along with other toxic substances. R. McKelway, V. Vieweg, and P. Westerman, "Sudden Death from Acute Cocaine Intoxication," *Am. J. Psychiatry*, 1990, 147, pp. 1667–1669.

68. The safety ratio is the amount that can kill divided by a common dosage. Robert Gable, "Comparison of Acute Lethal Toxicity of Commonly Abused Psychoactive Substances," *Addiction*, June 2004, 99(6), p. 689.

69. Linda Wong and Bruce Alexander, "'Cocaine-Related' Deaths," *J. Drug Issues*, Winter 1991.

70. Martin Tramer, et al., "Quantitative Estimation of Rare Adverse Events . . .", *Pain*, 2000, 85, pp. 169–182.

71. The federal system from which these statistics are usually derived openly admits this: "It is important also to remember that not every reported substance is, by itself, necessarily a cause of the death or even a contributor to the death." "Drug Abuse Warning Network, 2003: Area Profiles of Drug-Related Mortality," Dept. of Health and Human Services, 2005, p. 33.

72. John Morgan and Lynn Zimmer, *Crack in America* (1997), p. 140.

73. Sofia Santana, "Cocaine: Deadlier Than Ever," PalmBeachPost.com, 21 May 2006, ret. 11 Sep. 2008.

74. "Deaths Related to Cocaine," *Annual Report 2005: The State of the Drugs Problem in Europe*, ret. Europa.eu, 11 Sep. 2008.

75. Chelsea Carter, "Cocaine Killed Ike Turner, Coroner Says," AP, 16 Jan. 2008.

76. *These numbers should be interpreted loosely.* The variety of sources was not an attempt to massage the results. The sources and time periods used were the ones available.

77. Letter notations indicate source. Those marked with an:
    a: Ali Mokdad, et al., "Actual Causes of Death in the United States, 2000," *JAMA*, 10 Mar. 2004, p. 1240.
    b: Donna Hoyert, et al., "Deaths: Final Data for 2003," *National Vital Statistics Reports*, 19 April 2006, p. 33.
    c: "Odds of Death Due to Injury, United States, 2003," National Safety Council, ret. NSC.org, 3 July 2006.
    d: John Stossel, *Give Me A Break* (2004), p. 77.

78. Bill Masters, ed., *New Prohibition* (2004), p. 135.
79. Paul Gahlinger, *Illegal Drugs* (2001), p. 382.
80. Ibid.
81. Although it occurs, poison-laced drugs are extremely rare. Drug dealers have a large incentive not to kill their customers. As with fast-food restaurants and other purveyors of unhealthy items a slow death is less of a concern, hence the use of adulterants.
82. After an injection of heroin cut with coffee, coffee can be tasted. Francis Moraes, *Heroin User's Handbook* (2001), p. 64.
83. Robert MacCoun and Peter Reuter, *Drug War Heresies* (2001), p. 126.
84. Gahlinger, *Illegal Drugs*, p. 59.
85. Ibid., p. 173.
86. Richard Miller, *Drug Warriors and Their Prey* (1996), p. 5.
87. Gold's 2003 value varied from roughly $10–14 a gram. Alcohol was based on $1 for a twelve-ounce beer (five percent alcohol). Street values of heroin and cocaine vary widely by city and time. Drug values from average prices in mid-2003. "Price and Purity of Illicit Drugs," ONDCP, Nov. 2004, pp. 20 and 36.
88. Davenport-Hines, *Pursuit of Oblivion*, pp. 128–129.
89. Barbara Mikkelson and David Mikkelson, "Citric Acid Trip," Snopes.com, 29 Jan. 2007, ret. 20 Apr. 2012.
90. Sullum, *Saying Yes*, p. 156.
91. An obvious exception to the latter is when someone is dosed without their knowledge. This abhorrent behavior appears to be limited to immature jerk-offs and the CIA. In 1951 the CIA dosed an entire French town. Henry Samuel, "French Bread Spiked with LSD in CIA Experiment," Telegraph.co.uk, 11 Mar. 2010.
92. "Schizophrenia—Causes," NHS.uk, 18 Nov. 2010, ret. 20 Apr. 2012.
93. Sidney Cohen, "Lysergic Acid Diethylamide," *J. Nerv. Ment. Dis.*, Jan. 1960, p. 36.
94. Maia Szalavitz, "Why the Myth of the Meth-Damaged Brain May Hinder Recovery," Time.com, 21 Nov. 2011.
95. Roughly eighty percent are chippers. Gahlinger, *Illegal Drugs*, p. 99.
96. Jacob Sullum, *Saying Yes* (2003), pp. 243–245.
97. They are not invisible to academics. Hundreds have been interviewed in multiple studies. For an overview see Hamish Warburton, Paul Turnbull, and Mike Hough, *Occasional and Controlled Heroin Use: Not a Problem?* (2005).
98. Sullum, *Saying Yes*, p. 245.
99. Halsted info from Mike Gray, *Drug Crazy* (1998), pp. 53–55.
100. Keith Berge, Marvin Seppala, and Agnes Schipper, "Chemical Dependency and the Physician," *Mayo Clin. Proc.*, July 2009, 84(7), p. 625.
101. Richard Miller, *Drug Warriors and Their Prey* (1996), pp. 2–3.
102. Sullum, *Saying Yes*, p. 131.
103. Ibid., pp. 7–8.
104. Those marked with an [a] from Davenport-Hines, *Pursuit of Oblivion*; with a [b] from Gahlinger, *Illegal Drugs*; with a [c] from Russ Kick, *Disinformation Book of Lists* (2004); with a [d] from Sadie Plant, *Writing on Drugs* (1999).
105. "Air Force Rushes to Defend Amphetamine Use," TheAge.com.au, 18 Jan. 2003.
106. Plant, *Writing on Drugs*, p. 123.
107. Li Zhi-Sui, *Private Life of Chairman Mao* (1994), p. 108.
108. Davenport-Hines, *Pursuit of Oblivion*, p. 317.
109. Kitty Kelley, *Family* (2004), pp. 303–304.
110. "Oprah Reveals On Her Show She Smoked Crack Cocaine," *Jet*, 30 Jan. 1995.
111. Alex Haley, *Autobiography of Malcolm X* (1987), pp. 112, 137.
112. Barack Obama, *Dreams from My Father* (1996), p. 93.
113. Richard Branson, *Losing My Virginity* (1998), pp. 65–66.
114. Ann Harrison, "LSD," *Wired*, 16 Jan. 2006.
115. Leonard Mlodinow, *Feynman's Rainbow* (2003), p. 96.
116. David Rensin, "Bill Gates Interview," *Playboy*, 8 Dec. 1994.
117. Stephen Randall, *Playboy Interviews: Movers and Shakers* (2007), p. 97.
118. Alun Rees, "Nobel Prize Genius Crick Was High on LSD When He Discovered the Secret of Life," *Mail on Sunday*, 8 Aug. 2004.

119. Russ Kick, *Disinformation Book of Lists* (2004), p. 18.
120. Steve Lohr, "Creating Jobs," NYTimes.com, 12 Jan. 1997.
121. Branson, *Losing*, p. 112.
122. Kelley, *Family*, pp. 303–304.
123. Gary Giddins, *Bing Crosby* (2001), p. 181.
124. Mlodinow, *Feynman's Rainbow*, p. 96.
125. Stephen Manes and Paul Andrews, *Gates* (1994), pp. 59–60.
126. Randall, *Playboy Interviews*, p. 97.
127. Nina Burleigh, *Very Private Woman* (1998), pp. 211–213.
128. Jacob Sullum, *Saying Yes* (2003), p. 8.
129. Alex Kershaw, *Jack London* (1997), pp. 166, 201.
130. Eve Conant, "Pot and the GOP," *Newsweek*, 25 Oct. 2010.
131. Pipes found at his home that date to his time have marijuana residue and his Sonnet 76 arguably refers to it with phrases like "noted weed." Craig Lambert, "Shakespeare's 'Tenth Muse,'" *Harvard Magazine*, Sep.–Oct. 2001.
132. Alex Haley, *Autobiography of Malcolm X* (1987), pp. 81, 137.
133. Christian Wiessner, "New York Mayor Featured in Pro-Marijuana Ad," Reuters, 9 Apr. 2002.
134. Sullum, *Saying Yes*, p. 19.
135. Peter McWilliams, *Ain't Nobody's Business if You Do* (1996), p. 297.
136. He wrote a paper on its beneficial and enjoyable effects. David Standish, *Hollow Earth* (2006), p. 17.
137. John Ferling, *John Adams* (1992), p. 444; and Russ Kick, ed., *You Are Being Lied To* (2001), p. 245.
138. Kershaw, *Jack London*, p. 166.
139. Patrick O'Brian, *Picasso* (1994), pp. 132–133.
140. Martin Booth, *Opium* (1996), p. 49.
141. Dan Baum, *Smoke and Mirrors* (1996), p. 233.
142. Jacob Sullum, *Saying Yes* (2003), p. 198.
143. Martin Brecher, et al., "Phencyclidine and Violence," *J. Clin. Psychopharmacol.*, Dec. 1988, p. 397.
144. Fia Klötz, et al., "Criminality among Individuals . . . ," *Arch. Gen. Psychiatry*, Nov. 2006, pp. 1274–1279.
145. Peter Hoaken and Sherry Stewart, "Drugs of Abuse and the Elicitation of Human Aggressive Behavior," *Addict. Behav.*, 2003, 28, p. 1547; and Brecher, "Phencyclidine and Violence," p. 400.
146. Sullum, *Saying Yes*, pp. 196–198.
147. Ibid., pp. 12–13.
148. Frank Zappa said this about drugs in general. Ibid., p. 13.
149. Richard Miller, *Case for Legalizing Drugs* (1991), p. 63.
150. Eric Elbogen and Sally Johnson, "Intricate Link Between Violence and Mental Disorder," *Arch. Gen. Psychiatry*, Feb. 2009; and communication with Eric Elbogen, 11 Jul. 2012.
151. Adi Jaffe, "Crystal Meth Withdrawal," PsychologyToday.com, 23 May 2010.
152. See "The Supposed Agonies of Withdrawal" in Theodore Dalrymple, *Romancing Opiates* (2006), pp. 122–139.
153. Ibid., pp. 20–32.
154. Miller, *Case for Legalizing Drugs*, pp. 29–30, 165; and ibid.
155. For example, in June 2005 Artie Lange of the radio program *The Howard Stern Show* missed four days on sick leave, later revealing (Sep. 21, 2006) he had detoxed from heroin at home.
156. Jacob Sullum, *Saying Yes* (2003), p. 224, and Richard Davenport-Hines, *Pursuit of Oblivion* (2002), p. 216.
157. Sullum, *Saying Yes*, pp. 242–244.
158. For more on the "clinician's error" see Patricia Cohen and Jacob Cohen, "Clinician's Illusion," *Arch. Gen. Psychiatry*, Dec. 1984, 41, p. 1,178.
159. Jefferson Fish, *Drugs and Society* (2006), p. 80.
160. Mike Gray, *Drug Crazy* (1998), p. 53.
161. Miller, *Case for Legalizing Drugs*, pp. 60, 189.
162. Richard Miller, *Drug Warriors and Their Prey* (1996), p. 3.
163. Sullum, *Saying Yes*, p. 115.
164. Adjusted to 2010 values. Ibid., p. 115.
165. Edward Shepard and Thomas Clifton, "Drug Testing," *Working USA*, 31 Dec. 1998.

166. J. White and G.D. Batty, "Intelligence across Childhood in Relation to Illegal Drug Use in Adulthood," *J. Epidemiol. Community Health*, 14 Nov. 2011.
167. Sullum, *Saying Yes*, p. 14.
168. Paul Gahlinger, *Illegal Drugs* (2001), p. 6.
169. Ibid., p. 43.
170. Ibid., p. 44.
171. Huston Smith, *Cleansing the Doors of Perception* (2000), p. 21.
172. Ibid., pp. 20–21.
173. Sullum, *Saying Yes*, p. 164.
174. Smith, *Cleansing the Doors*, p. 105.
175. Gahlinger, *Illegal Drugs*, p. 36.
176. Anne Moir and David Jessel, *Brain Sex* (1991), p. 48.
177. A woman complained of her partner, "It's hard to talk to a drunk, and yet it's the only time he shows me any real feelings." Ibid., p. 111.
178. Sue and Shane Stevens are pseudonyms.
179. Sullum, *Saying Yes*, p. 184.
180. Ibid, p. 185.
181. Ibid.
182. Gahlinger, *Illegal Drugs*, p. 338, and ibid., p. 171.
183. Sect. from Mike Gray, *Drug Crazy* (1998), pp. 183–185.
184. Ibid., p. 184.
185. Radley Balko, "War Over Prescription Painkillers," HuffingtonPost.com, 29 Jan. 2012.
186. David Fishbain, et al., "What Percentage of Chronic Nonmalignant Pain Patients . . . ," *Pain Med.*, 2008, 9(4).
187. Gahlinger, *Illegal Drugs*, p. 206.
188. Ibid.
189. From flap of Tom Brokaw's *The Greatest Generation* (2004).
190. Nassir Ghaemi, *A First-Rate Madness* (2011), pp. 171–172.
191. Richard Davenport-Hines, *Pursuit of Oblivion* (2002), p. 308.
192. Paragraph from Jacob Sullum, *Saying Yes* (2003), pp. 208–209
193. Gahlinger, *Illegal Drugs*, p. 353.
194. Davenport-Hines, *Pursuit of Oblivion*, p. 82.
195. Ibid., pp. 55-56.
196. David Hillman, *Chemical Muse* (2008), pp. 136–137.
197. People who use large amounts of digitalis see the world in a yellow-green tint and often see yellow spots surrounded by coronas. In one of Van Gogh's paintings his doctor is holding the plant from which digitalis is extracted. Van Gogh's doctor likely gave him digitalis to treat his epilepsy. Paul Wolf, "Creativity and Chronic Disease," *West. J. Med.*, Nov. 2001, p. 348.
198. Robert Crumb and Peter Poplaski, *R. Crumb Handbook* (2005), p. 132.
199. Davenport-Hines, *Pursuit of Oblivion*, p. 331.
200. Gahlinger, *Illegal Drugs*, p. 401.
201. Hashish is marijuana resin.
202. Gahlinger, *Illegal Drugs*, p. 35.
203. Russ Kick, *Disinformation Book of Lists* (2004), p. 28.
204. Jian Ghomeshi, "Brian Wilson Talks about Drug Use on QTV," *Q with Jian Ghomeshi*, 20 May 2011.
205. Pat Blashill, et al., "500 Greatest Albums of All Time," RollingStone.com, 2003.
206. Jacob Sullum, *Saying Yes* (2003), p. 157.
207. Ibid.
208. He went off amphetamines for a month to win a bet and said, "You've showed me I'm not an addict. But I didn't get any work done. I'd get up in the morning and stare at a blank piece of paper. I'd have no ideas, just like an ordinary person. You've set mathematics back a month." Bruce Schechter, *My Brain Is Open* (2008), p. 196.
209. "I can honestly say that without cannabis, most of my scientific research would never have been done and most of my books on psychology and evolution would not have been written." "I Take Illegal Drugs for Inspiration," ret. susanblackmore.co.uk, 15 May 2007.

210. Keay Davidson, *Carl Sagan* (1999), pp. 217–218.
211. Kick, *Disinformation*, p. 14.
212. Alun Rees, "Nobel Prize Genius Crick Was High on LSD When He Discovered the Secret of Life," *Mail on Sunday*, 8 Aug. 2004.
213. See John Markoff's *What the Dormouse Said: How the 60s Counterculture Shaped the Personal Computer* (2005).
214. Ann Harrison, "LSD," *Wired*, 16 Jan. 2006.
215. Kick, *Disinformation*, p. 22.
216. Sadie Plant, *Writing on Drugs* (1999), p. 121.
217. Ibid., pp. 120–121.
218. Richard Davenport-Hines, *Pursuit of Oblivion* (2002), p. 306.
219. Paul Gahlinger, *Illegal Drugs* (2001), p. 353.
220. Kick, *Disinformation*, pp. 15, 22.
221. Gahlinger, *Illegal Drugs*, p. 36.
222. The other two reasons were to rebel and to feel good. "Kings of Drugs," *Q*, Feb. 2001, p. 88.
223. "Watch Out Needle's About," *Q*, Feb. 2001, p. 58.
224. Ibid., p. 60.
225. Tony Wilson, who founded Factory Records, said, "It's quite clear that smack [heroin] is not a problem drug for a musician. One of history's most successful record executives, who obviously I can't name, said, 'Some of my biggest acts are junkies and they've been giving me platinum albums for twenty years.' Now heroin is not a nice drug, but it doesn't take away creativity. Only cocaine does that. So I told Alan McGee to fuck off. I mean, how long did Coleridge keep writing poetry for?" Ibid., p. 58.
226. For example, Guns N' Roses' "Mr. Brownstone" and "Nighttrain" (1987) and Eminem's "Drugs Ballad" (2000) celebrate drug use but also imply horrible repercussions.
227. Rap star Ludacris was fired as a sponsor by Pepsi in 2002 when a conservative television pundit called a Pepsi boycott for hiring someone who "encourages substance abuse." Timothy Noah, "Whopper of the Week: Bill O'Reilly," Slate.com, 14 Feb. 2003.
228. "Captain Beaky and his Bands," *Q*, Feb. 2001, p. 53.
229. Researchers call this the "forbidden fruit" effect. Robert MacCoun and Peter Reuter, *Drug War Heresies* (2001), pp. 89–90.
230. Julie Deardorff, "Emerging Health Concern," *Chicago Tribune*, 21 Nov. 2006
231. One historian believes that drug use did not become an integral part of the rock star mystique until some London police officers in the late 1960s went on a crusade to get their face on the front page with a busted rock star. "Junk Science," *Q*, Feb. 2001, p. 57.
232. Richard Davenport-Hines, *Pursuit of Oblivion* (2002), pp. 193–197.
233. Jacob Sullum, *Saying Yes* (2003), p. 276.
234. Bill Masters, ed., *New Prohibition* (2004), p. 16.
235. Mike Gray, *Drug Crazy* (1998), pp. 175–176; and ibid., p. 171.
236. Bill Masters, ed., *New Prohibition* (2004), p. 164.
237. Paragraph from Paul Gahlinger, *Illegal Drugs* (2001), pp. 37–39.
238. Terry Burnham and Jay Phelan, *Mean Genes* (2000), pp. 74–75.
239. Edward Hallowell and John Ratey, *Driven to Distraction* (1994), p. 173.
240. R. Milin, et al, "Psychopathology Among Substance Abusing Juvenile Offenders," *J. Am. Acad. Child Adolesc. Psychiatry*, July 1991, pp. 569–574.
241. T.F. Denson and M. Earleywine, "Decreased Depression in Marijuana Users," *Addict. Behav.*, Apr. 2006, pp. 738–742.
242. John Markoff, *What the Dormouse Said* (2005), p. xix.
243. Bruce Rogers is a pseudonym. Unless noted, quotes from Sullum, *Saying Yes*, pp. 133, 156, 207, 217, 218.

DRUGS II

THE TABOO
YOU JUST DON'T KNOW,
YOU ASSHOLE!

A taboo is a topic that a culture prevents its people from discussing freely. The American government and media have done this effectively to drugs through almost a century of dishonest propaganda driven by a lust for votes and quotes. The two characteristics of a taboo, its unsettling nature and ignorance, are now prominent with regard to drugs.[1]

I
THE UNSETTLING NATURE
NO, YOU DON'T KNOW, YOU GOVERNMENT TOOL!

I was not certain whether drugs qualified as a taboo until I started talking to other people about heroin in social situations. The reactions were startling. People not involved in the conversation would overhear part of what I said and would come over to preach to me. The emotional reactions sometimes verged on violence, as when an enraged off-duty police officer protested that I had not seen the tragic domestic situations he had seen caused by junkies.[2]

As someone who has interviewed hundreds of heroin addicts (many of whom were detoxing as we spoke) upon their admittance to prison, represented numerous "junkies" in court whose lives had been destroyed, and has read extensively on the subject, very little of what I said could return me from pariah status in these social situations. Most of what I said would be dismissed out of hand, or narcophobes would offer silly arguments lapped up by all those around.

A surprising example of pat dismissals came when I blamed heroin overdoses on its criminalization while talking to a student pursuing his doctorate in psychology. He refused to believe me despite being well-educated in the realm of drugs, open-minded, *and* having tried heroin himself. I had to go to one of *his* textbooks to finally prove to him that there was an antidote for heroin overdoses.

An example of silliness was when I explained to one testy eavesdropper that if legalized heroin would be about as deadly as alcohol. He got emotional and angrily whipped out the fact that he knew someone who had died of alcohol intoxication. At no point did he make the connection that he was arguing that alcohol should be criminalized.

> Are you fucking kidding? Most users of heroin never become addicts?!?!?!?!?!?!?!?!?
>
> FUCK YOU FOR SPREADING BAD-INFORMTION. [sic] THIS IS LIFE AND DEATH SHIT YOU ASSHOLE.[3]

II

THE IGNORANCE
NO, HONESTLY, YOU DON'T KNOW

A. They Just Wouldn't Do Such a Thing: The Historians

In 2004 Dr. David Hillman was to defend his doctoral thesis at the University of Wisconsin. A classics scholar with a biology background (M.S. in bacteriology), he was uniquely qualified to present his dissertation on classical pharmacology. He was grilled for hours about only one chapter of his 250-page thesis on medicinal drugs in ancient Rome. This chapter showed that "just about everyone in antiquity" enjoyed recreational drugs and that they would have thought it ridiculous to outlaw them.[4]

Hillman was given the choice to either remove that chapter or fail. The department head refuted Hillman's chapter by saying, "[The Romans] just wouldn't do such a thing."[5] After a decade of study to attain his Ph.D., Hillman capitulated.

Hillman's excised chapter would later become his 2008 book *The Chemical Muse: Drug Use and the Roots of Western Civilization*. In it Hillman shows how modern translators have manipulated individual words, like opium, and entire concepts, like sorcery. Opium is translated to poppy seeds even where this makes no sense, and sorcery's true power is obscured.

Sorcerers, magicians, and witches abound in classical literature. Translators rarely reveal that their power stemmed from their great expertise in drugs. Sorcerers were classical drug dealers and the effects of drugs were seen as magical in those times. Drugs and magic were one.

For example, Medea, the wife of Jason the Argonaut, is frequently portrayed as a witch. She aided Jason by putting fire-breathing bulls asleep and giving him amazing courage. Hillman shows how translators mistranslate *polypharmakon* and *pharmaka* to present her as being skilled in the "magical arts" and a possessor of "charms." Medea was actually "drug-savvy" and possessed "drugs." She gave the bulls and Jason drugs, not spells.

Sorcerers were honored and respected members of society. They and the more run-of-the-mill drug sellers, "root cutters," had to know how to extract desired chemicals from plants and animals. This was an exact science, for the wrong amount or the wrong extraction could kill.

History scholars have also skewed the concept of libations. The Greeks' and Romans' favored method of drug administration was to mix it with wine. (The wine of most early peoples contained psychotropic drugs.)[6] This has allowed history teachers to present ancient drinkers like Plato and Jesus Christ as merely drinkers—not "illegal drug" users.

Hillman wrote about his doctoral experience:

> Unfortunately, the moral bent that so characterizes contemp-
> orary Classicists forces them to write histories that best promote
> the cultural agendas of our times, rather than the actual facts of
> the past . . . Blacklisting is not a cruelty of the distant, uninformed

past; it's a very real phenomenon that flourishes within academic circles today, whether in the humanities or the sciences.[7]

B. Give Me More Tax Money: The Government

The amount of misinformation that the government and the media flaunts is breathtaking in scope. Dr. Paul Gahlinger commented about conducting research for his 2001 guide to illegal drugs:

> I was appalled at how much of [the information] proved to be wrong. Many authors simply repeat errors, adding links to a chain of misinformation that eventually becomes accepted as fact and contributes to the widespread misunderstanding about drugs.[8]

The government is the master manipulator in numerous ways. First, it controls the manufacture of information. It collects the statistics and it finances the research. In America drug research is largely run by the National Institute on Drug Abuse (NIDA). With its billion-dollar budget, NIDA decides what studies and what institutions are allowed at the funding trough. Researchers who do not focus on the "negative consequences" of drug use do not get funding.[9]

Second, the government controls the dissemination of this information. It spends billions on snazzy anti-drug ads,[10] and spoon-feeds its spin to the popular media, which promptly gives it headlines. The Office of National Drug Control Policy's presentation of drug statistics has been so contrived over the years that the exposure of its chicanery fills an entire 2007 book—Lies, Damned Lies, and Drug War Statistics.[11]

An example of this dog-and-pony show is the recent propaganda over marijuana. Marijuana is more potent than years ago and the government has sprung on this (result of criminalization) to make absurd claims and outright lies. For example, a DEA chief was quoted in an AP article as saying, "This ain't your grandfather's or your father's marijuana. This will hurt you. This will addict you. This will kill you."[12,13]

The fact that marijuana is more potent does not make it more harmful. If anything, it makes it healthier, because users have to inhale less of the carcinogenic smoke to get the desired effect. However, the increased potency also allows the government to trot out all their fallacious claims anew.

Two of the more craptastic claims are the high numbers of marijuana users in treatment centers and emergency rooms.[14] Marijuana users do fill treatment centers, but that is because almost all of them were caught with marijuana and forced to get treatment for their "addiction" by the criminal justice system. As for "marijuana-related" emergency room visits, patients are asked to mention any recent drug use *regardless* of whether it has anything to do with their visit. A marijuana smoker bitten by a cat qualifies as a "marijuana-related" visit.

The relatively few who are there because of marijuana itself are frequently there for paranoia.[15] There isn't anything actually wrong with them. An example is the Michigan police officer in 2007 who baked himself pot brownies with confiscated marijuana and called 911 because he thought he was dying. Initial anxiety plays a large part in panicked drug reactions.[16] Where are novice marijuana users getting this initial anxiety? The same place the officer got the silly idea that marijuana could kill him.

C. Brain Shrinkage: The Scientists

The journalist John Stossel has called it "junk science and junk reporting."[17] Scientists have an incentive to find something dramatic against drugs because it is easier to get published and funded. Reporters are clueless about science and are looking for a good story.

Some of the recent asinine headline-grabbers are the claims that marijuana use causes schizophrenia and marijuana use shrinks your brain.[18] To understand how they can get away with saying this, one must first understand the difference between correlation and causation.

For example, I would assert that a thirteen-year-old kid who comes from a troubled background is more likely to have difficulty in school, have mental health problems, have a bad diet, curse, trespass, make prank phone calls, have B.O., and smoke marijuana. All of these things are correlated. Common sense and studies indicate it is the troubled background that causes all of these things.[19,20] Assuming marijuana causes the kid's mental health problems based on the correlation is as faulty as saying marijuana causes prank phone calls, or cursing causes B.O. This erroneous reasoning inundates illegal drug research.

A cabal of scientists received a lot of press coverage in 2005 for claiming that marijuana causes schizophrenia. Other scientists have pointed out the numerous flaws in their research,[21] however, the criticism rarely gets coverage.[22] Nor do reporters point out the most obvious counterargument—one that is obvious to those who actually smoke it, not just study it—where are all the marijuana psychotics? Where are all these shrunken-brained marijuana smokers? Despite steep rises in marijuana usage in past decades there has not been a change in the incidence of schizophrenia.[23]

With the spigot of research funding wide open the negative marijuana studies are never-ending. Junk science can trash almost any substance, food, or activity. The caffeine business is well aware of this fact. (High caffeine intake correlates with psychosis as well.)[24] In the 1970s caffeine came under attack from reformers when junk science linked it to pancreatic cancer. In response, Coca-Cola and other companies created the International Life Sciences Institute (ILSI) to protect their "interests from those meddlers, newborn in every generation, who would use the law to control what ostensibly free adult citizens are allowed to eat or drink."[25]

ILSI funds researchers who see caffeine as beneficial and publicizes their findings. Its efforts have had an impressive effect. Caffeine articles emphasize the "legal high," and the benefits of moderate use, not the crash and the fallout of extreme intake.[26] A study exonerated mild caffeine use but found that high daily intake (over 687 milligrams) increased the risk of cardiac arrest.[27] The ensuing headline was not "Caffeine Kills" but "Caffeine Cleared of Cardiac Arrest Charges."[28] A study of Starbucks coffee found a Venti-sized cup (twenty ounces) of Breakfast Blend can sometimes break 700 mg of caffeine.[29]

D. "Flowers of Destruction": The Objective Media[30]

Magazines, newspapers, and television lap up whatever bogus stats are thrown their way, and fearmonger even in those rare instances when government officials do not. Articles and television spots from otherwise objective news sources are almost always unabashedly misleading.

Here are some common characteristics of a drug article:

Crazy Quotes—The focus is on attention-grabbing quotes. These are put in big bold text boxes or make the headlines themselves. For example, a 2002 *Newsweek* PCP article's headline reads, "I Felt Like I Wanted to Hurt People." The text box quotes Jim Parker of the Do It Now Foundation: "PCP users 'become like a grenade with the pin missing. Any increase [in its use] is cause for alarm.'"[31]

Newsweek does not mention that a review of over 350 journal articles documenting PCP use found that "assumptions about PCP and violence are unwarranted."[32] Apparently, peer-reviewed medical journal articles are irrelevant when one has a quote from an employee of a drug-rehabilitation company.

Whack Jobs and Gorefests—After the grenade quote, the PCP article discusses Antron Singleton, who was found by Los Angeles police one afternoon walking naked down the street coated in blood. Earlier that day he had murdered his 21-year-old roommate in a gruesome manner. She had facial bite marks, a slashed cheek, and a chewed lung. Singleton had smoked PCP the night before. *Newsweek* tells us of another PCP user who bit off and swallowed his two-year-old son's thumb in a "wigged-out" attempt to combine their DNA, and another who murdered a family of four.

In the past journalists cited similar horrors by marijuana users to blame marijuana for causing insanity and violence. This type of presentation is erroneous and misleading for multiple reasons. First, these incidents are *extremely* rare among users. Second, the media never bothers to do even a cursory investigation into whether the drug caused the actions. If they did, they would find that these "drug-possessed" actors frequently have a history of mental illness or violent tendencies.

This was the case with Singleton. Before this heinous act he had been hospitalized for psychosis three times. As for possible violent tendencies, he was also a professional rapper named Big Lurch. Here are some lyrics from his song "I Did It to You:"

> Jeffrey Dahmer, Charles Manson . . . 'cuz murder's a hobby. . . .
> 'cuz I'm like a hungry lion I moves in for the slaughter. . . I'm like a
> vampire, nigga, fresh meat, I can't pass it . . . Late in the afternoon

279

the mailman was delivering, So I threw him in my house, Slit his throat and left him shivering, Just because my social security check came too late … I'll stick your hands in a freezer until them mothafuckas is frosted … Murder, kill kill kill kill, murder murder murder murder, kill kill kill.[33]

Third, one could easily portray alcohol the same way. Singleton rapped about one of America's most famous cannibals, Jeffrey Dahmer. Dahmer killed seventeen people. He ate his victims for sexual satisfaction and to make them a "permanent part" of him.[34] Dahmer was an alcoholic and was so drunk during one of his initial murders that he could not remember what happened after awaking next to the corpse.

In 2009, two Russian twenty-year-old goths drowned sixteen-year-old Karina Barduchian in a St. Petersburg bathtub. They carved up her body, ate some of her, and served her meat with potatoes to an unaware woman the next day. In interrogation they said they did it because they were hungry and drunk.

In 2009 Conner Schierman stabbed a mother, her sister, and her two children to death in her home. His defense attorney argued that Schierman could not remember committing the crime because he was blackout drunk. Singleton's attorney argued Singleton could not remember anything either because PCP had taken Singleton back to a "primal state" where he could do "acts of a beast."[35]

Geraldo Rivera of FOX News called Singleton on the phone in prison so that Singleton could tell people not to do PCP.[36] Rivera did not call Schierman, nor did he call Woody Will Smith, who strangled his wife to death in 2009 because of caffeine psychosis. Rivera did not call them because most people have tried alcohol and caffeine and know how dishonest it is to blame these drugs for murder.

For those who have tried PCP, blaming PCP for cannibalism is just as idiotic. Bruce Rogers, who used PCP about thirty times in high school, said that stories about "chopping your grandmother up with an axe [were] laughable because I never even saw anyone experience a psychotic episode and never even treaded near one at all dosage levels … It seemed more likely to calm somebody down."[37]

Pictures of Woe—Although most drug users are healthy non-addicted occasional users, drug articles almost always feature suffering addicts. The aforementioned *Newsweek* PCP article does not have a picture of the young man, "shy" Mike, who wanted to "hurt people." Shy Mike, a sixteen-year-old from suburban Hartford, Connecticut, is featured in the article, and a casual reader would assume it is he in the photograph. However, shy Mike probably looked too mainstream.

Instead, the article features a picture of a random PCP "addict" covering his face with grief in a messy dilapidated room. The man's exposed arm and half his hand are covered in tattoos and his ear sports a gauge. The caption reads, "A Terrible Toll: A 28-year-old PCP addict in recovery reflects on the time he lost to the drug." *Newsweek* does not mention that PCP is less addictive than caffeine and that users "have not shown a distinct withdrawal syndrome, even after long-term use."[38]

Feature the Victims—Journalists will only talk to someone who was addicted or was close to someone who overdosed. Despite the fact that the vast majority of users have not suffered negative consequences, none of them will be quoted or consulted. In my hometown newspaper in 2002, the front page of its "Sun Style" section featured an AP article on Ecstasy (MDMA). It featured a 3¼" by 2¼" head shot of an attractive bleached-blonde twenty-one-year-old and an immense 9" by 5½" picture of her grieving parents in their living room seated by her framed pictures. She died after ingesting Ecstasy. The headline read, "A Father's Tears: Parents Take Grief Public in Campaign against Ecstasy."[39]

The woman's death was tragic, but the entire article was subterfuge. Ecstasy deaths are extremely rare. Even taking the highest estimation of its deadliness makes it less deadly than extended aspirin use, as shown in the table below.

THE KILLER IN THE CABINET:
Ecstasy vs. Aspirin

Substance	Deadliness	Annual Deaths
Ecstasy (MDMA)	.002%–.05% [28]	3–9 [29]
Aspirin (taken for at least two months)	.08% [30]	16,500 [31]

Feature Idiots—The previously mentioned PCP article features shy Mike. Shy Mike bought marijuana in the bathroom of his high school. He did not know what marijuana was supposed to smell like. The marijuana he bought had such a "strong chemical stench" that he had to hide it in the insulation of his home's attic. Apparently, nothing tipped Mike off to something being amiss with his weed, even when he had trouble walking *the next day*. Mike's parents eventually discovered some of his marijuana in his "reeking bedroom." It turned out Mike's marijuana was laced with PCP and embalming fluid. After smoking it Mike had felt like he "wanted to hurt people" and that "everybody was after him."

Is Mike an idiot? What sixteen-year-old does not know that a dried plant is not supposed to have a "chemical stench" that can stink up a room? What sixteen-year-old does not realize something might be suspicious about marijuana when he has trouble walking *the next day*? The government was running advertisements warning kids that if they smoked marijuana they might not bother to walk the dog.[40] Did he not think the government would have it on every billboard in America if it caused paralysis?

I suspect that Mike is not an idiot. The following assertions are guesses, but it is my opinion that Mike knew exactly what he was doing. "Shy" kids who have never smoked marijuana before do not go and buy a sizable stash to start using at home. Mike had smoked marijuana before and Mike knew what it smelled like. Mike knowingly bought laced marijuana and knowingly continued to smoke it because he liked it. Mike's parents caught him, so Mike lied his ass off. Mike told his parents that it was the first time he bought marijuana.

When his father, police officer, or anybody with a nose told his mother that it was spiked, she flipped her lid that her little boy could have been hurt. Mike saw the reaction and played it up. He said that he couldn't walk, he wanted to hurt people, and that he thought people were after him. His mom probably cried. He was the victim of PCP and evil drug dealers (who were probably Mike's friends). The story worked.

Mike's parents bought it and told this horrible story to other parents and then *Newsweek* bought it too. *Newsweek* probably thought Mike did not want his picture in the magazine because he was concerned about his professional future. Mike did not want his picture in the magazine because other kids would realize he is a lying asshole. It is also my belief that if his parents were so naive as to believe his story, he probably is not even shy, but plays that part for the folks because they are so ignorant to his world that they annoy him greatly.

What is more galling than people like Mike are idiots who behave recklessly and hurt themselves and other people when using drugs with near-suicidal abandon. These people make even more wonderfully lurid press for anti-drug zealots. Of course they usually blame their behavior on drugs because they are facing serious prison time, unlike shy Mike, who was probably facing being grounded and losing his allowance.

Play the Numbers—The PCP article points to a forty-eight percent increase in PCP-related emergency room visits. To its credit, the article gives a nod to honesty by stating that PCP is "a small part of the nation's drug problem," right before comparing users to hand grenades without pins.[41]

Perhaps instead of the bomb analogy it would have been useful to point out that the forty-eight percent increase brought the number up to nearly six thousand in 2001. For some perspective, it could have been mentioned that Tylenol (acetaminophen) overdoses account for 56,000 emergency room visits a year.[42]

Flat-Out Lie—PCP does not increase strength.[43] It is less addictive than caffeine. It does not promote violence. A junkie is, by definition, someone who is hopelessly addicted to a substance. The PCP article reads:

> Known as angel dust in the 1970s, PCP, or phencyclidine, gave users superhuman strength and a numbing calm. But the addictive, psychedelic drug also made many paranoid, violent and completely out of touch with reality; they leapt off roofs and broke out of handcuffs with their bare hands. Police cracked down, and eventually the drug got such a bad reputation that even junkies wouldn't touch it.

Never Point Out Actual Source of Harm—In the above-mentioned Ecstasy story the father was quoted in a big text box saying:

> I would have given anything for some warning signs. I would

have moved. I would have locked her up, I don't care, if there were warning signs. I would have done whatever it took.

This understandable grief is demonstrated frequently by parents and loved ones of those who unexpectedly overdose, and is given wide coverage by the media. The grieving parents, like many in their position, joined the campaign against the drug with the familiar refrain that, " . . . if I save one kid, if it saves one kid . . . "[44]

Parents often latch onto the tempting drug pusher myth to exculpate the deceased,[45] and then some use their media coverage to crusade for tougher justice. The mother of a twenty-three-year-old, Kelley Baker, who "overdosed on Ecstasy," managed to blame others for even broader behavior: " . . . a dealer had taken advantage of her vulnerability and gotten her involved in selling the drug to others."[46] In a sad irony, this mother worked to have Illinois pass "Kelley's Law" to further toughen penalties for the sale and possession of Ecstasy. Now young Illinois women who use Ecstasy—like her daughter did—can go to prison for even longer time periods.

When David Nutt, one of the United Kingdom's chief scientific advisers on drugs, called for lowering criminal punishments for Ecstasy because of its relative safety, a news article quoted a father: "I'd like that professor to stand beside Siobhan's grave and say he wants to downgrade the drug. Or to stand by the graves of any of the other hundreds of kids who have died."[47]

The articles never explain that tougher laws would not have saved these lives, but that legalization probably would have. If Ecstasy was legal it would have come in a package, with exact dosage described, and it would have been accompanied by *honest* medical warnings from pharmaceutical companies wary of being sued. If parents and loved ones of overdose victims really would do anything to save one kid's life as they say, then they should press for legalization.

Preach and Teach—The article on shy Mike concludes with the reader learning he is now in treatment. It is stunning that his parents or the judge actually believe he is addicted and in need of treatment after smoking such a small amount of PCP/ marijuana— both of which are less addictive than caffeine. But it does not matter as the game must be played. The article ends, "'I never want to do PCP again,' Mike says. A lesson learned the hard way: it's just not worth the risk."

E. They Must Suffer: The Subjective Media

Until Helen Gurley Brown's *Sex and the Single Girl* in 1962, all fictional female characters who had premarital sex had to suffer. This reflects the current state of fictional characters who use illegal drugs.[48] Outside of marijuana, few writers have had the knowledge, courage, or license to present drug use accurately.

It was not always this way. The famous detective Sherlock Holmes regularly used cocaine and morphine intravenously. He was never shown to suffer because of it. In fact, the drugs stimulated his mind when a challenging case was lacking, and allowed Holmes to escape a commonplace existence and "a dreary, dismal, unprofitable world."[49]

Sherlock Holmes mysteries were written primarily in the late nineteenth century, before the drug war began. It was only when the anti-drug propaganda started gaining traction that Holmes' creator, Sir Arthur Conan Doyle, ended Holmes' habits in a 1904 tale.

Since then drug users have been presented as addicts who will do *anything* to score a hit and who will soon suffer or die. "Anything" has only been limited by the writers' imaginations, and although fatal heroin overdoses are a real danger, to have them appear in almost every movie with heroin use is mathematically absurd.[50]

Compared to their flouting of the sex taboo, modern artists have been notably silent in telling the truth about drugs. Although many of them have used recreational drugs and continue to use them, few modern artists have honestly portrayed them in their work. Instead numerous artists have exaggerated their dangers.

An egregious example of this was the star-filled cast of *Requiem for a Dream* (2000). [Spoiler warning.] Ellen Burstyn was nominated for an Academy Award for Best Actress for playing a mother who goes insane from taking diet pills (likely amphetamine) prescribed by a doctor. By film's end she is incredulously reduced to a vegetable in a mental ward.

The other three characters—Sara, Harry, and Tyrone—take heroin. As a matter of course, the pretty white female must become a prostitute to feed her habit and have the requisite sex with a black gangster.[51] Harry and Tyrone drive to Florida because they think heroin will be more available in that state than in New York City. (If heroin was actually this addictive, all heroin addicts would move to Mexico.) They

---

PARDON ME, BUT THAT'S BULLSHIT
Some Honest Voices

A sign that the taboo may be waning is that more journalists are beginning to expose the dishonesty of their kin. For decades Jacob Sullum and his libertarian cohorts at *Reason* magazine were the lone watchdogs, but in 2005 *Newsweek* ran a cover story, "The Meth Epidemic: Inside America's New Drug Crisis." The online magazine *Slate* promptly ran an article by Jack Shafer on *Newsweek*'s bogus presentation. Shafer exposed how they spun numbers to make meth a crisis. He even courageously pointed out that this old drug (amphetamine) only seems new because the drug war has forced addicts to smoke it, inject it, and mix combustible chemicals at home to make it.

This gumption may be spreading. In 2006 *The Washington Post* was quickly busted by Ryan Grim of the *Washington City Paper* for comically twisting facts to create a local "emerging meth epidemic." In 2012 Radley Balko revealed how the government manipulated "drug-related" deaths to incite a media panic over prescription painkillers, and Maia Szalavitz of *Time* repeatedly covers scientific research debunking drug war spin.

—Radley Balko, "New Panic Over Prescription Painkillers," HuffingtonPost.com, 8 Feb. 2012; Ryan Grim, "The Next Crack Cocaine? No, Not Really," *Washington City Paper*, 31 Mar. 2006, p. 14; David Jefferson, *Newsweek*, 8 Aug. 2005; and Jack Shafer, "Meth Madness at *Newsweek*," Slate.com, 31 Jan. 2007.

---

both end up in a Southern prison, but this is not enough punishment for these two drug users. Harry's infected arm is amputated and Tyrone (a black man) is left doing hard labor under racist prison guards. The manic and dazzling cinematography make *Requiem* a modern *Reefer Madness*.[52] [Spoiler end.]

Perhaps because of Hollywood's relative street credibility, *Requiem* received reactions like this one from a college student: "Forget about the anti-drug programs schools have, this is the real deal."[53]

There are reasons why artists consistently portray drugs so ominously. One, artists who use hard drugs are afraid to draw attention for fear of legal repercussions down the road. Second, most artists with anything but an anti-drugs message are afraid to portray their experiences honestly because they could lose commercial endorsements, lose opportunities (such as being sold at Wal-Mart), and be boycotted.

Because of this, the people who are willing to cover the topic are usually recovered addicts who can tell the sob story America wants to hear. Just like alcoholics, who are more likely to have stronger feelings about alcohol than casual drinkers, former drug addicts have strong feelings about their problem drug. The artistic rendition of drugs is arguably similar to the one that would be given of alcohol if only former alcoholics covered it.[54]

There is another phenomenon that influences artists who were users of hard drugs. Perhaps due to all of the exaggeration, drug addiction has gained an "I've danced with the devil" cachet. Former drug users often appear to embellish the "hell" of their addiction. By doing this they can portray themselves as a "bad ass" for their peers while simultaneously appearing as a victim for their family or their judge. In the case of artists, dramatization also entertains the audience.

Although these ornamentations usually pass unchallenged, the author James Frey was caught grossly exaggerating his "torturous drug-addled" life in his best-seller *A Million Little Pieces*. Frey wrote that he spent three months in jail because of an alcohol/crack binge that ended when he struck a police officer with his car and brawled with the boys in blue. The truth was that Frey hit a curb and was arrested for drunk driving. He was "polite and cooperative" and was released on bond.[55]

The book's sales were not hurt by this revelation. This is unsurprising as *Pieces* gave the message America likes, true or not. Drugs are bad, the war on drugs is good, and law-abiding Americans aren't missing out on any fun. This attitude is reflected in the initial response of a prominent talk-show host:

> What is relevant is that he was a drug addict who spent years in turmoil … and to take that message to save other people … To me, it seems to be much ado about nothing.[56]

NOTES

1. One historian calls our era's bizarre demonization of drugs a "cultural trance." Jennifer Hecht, *Happiness Myth* (2007), p. 71.
2. I calmed the officer down by buying him a drug—beer.
3. This was an e-mail received by Francis Moraes, a former heroin addict and the author of *The Heroin User's Handbook* (2001). Ret. HeroinHelper.com, 5 Feb. 2007.

4. David Hillman, *Chemical Muse* (2008), pp. 1–3.
5. Ibid., p. 2.
6. Ibid., pp. 176–177.
7. Ibid., p. 222.
8. Paul Gahlinger, *Illegal Drugs* (2001), p. v.
9. Gardiner Harris, "Researchers Find Study of Medical Marijuana Discouraged," NYTimes.com, 18 Jan. 2010; and Jacob Sullum, *Saying Yes* (2003), pp. 15–16.
10. In 1990 The Partnership for a Drug Free America's ad campaign trailed only AT&T and McDonald's in size. Dan Baum, *Smoke and Mirrors* (1996), pp. 296–297.
11. Matthew Robinson and Renee Scherlen, (2007).
12. "Locals Ask State Help to Battle Pot Houses," SPTimes.com, 22 June 2007.
13. FOX News also reported that "This stuff will kill you." Orlando Salinas, "High Living," 13 July 2007.
14. Paragraph from Bill Masters, ed., *New Prohibition* (2004), pp. 153–170.
15. When CNN's Elizabeth Cohen was questioned about teen ER marijuana cases she admitted that the kids were "basically freaking out . . . It's all in their head." "Pot More Potent Than Ever," CNN.com, 18 June 2008.
16. Andrew Weil, *Natural Mind* (1998), pp. 51–54.
17. Paragraph from John Stossel, *Give Me a Break* (2004), pp. 97–107.
18. Human brains are neuroplastic. They simultaneously shrink and grow different parts to suit how they are being used. Any new usage of the mind can have this effect. Internet addiction has been found to grow parts of the brain while shrinking others, as has learning taxi cab routes. Jeffrey Schwartz and Sharon Begley, *Mind and the Brain* (2002), pp. 250–254; and Tony Dokoupil, "Is the Web Driving Us Mad?" TheDailyBeast.com, 9 July 2012.
19. A study found adolescent problem drug use could be traced to early childhood and the quality of parenting. It was a symptom—not a cause of—maladjustment. Sullum, *Saying Yes*, p. 15.
20. Schizophrenia and childhood poverty do correlate. G. Harrison, et al., "Association between Schizophrenia and Social Inequality at Birth," *Br. J. Psychiatry*, Oct. 2001.
21. Graham Lawton, "Too Much, Too Young," *New Scientist*, 26 Mar. 2005; and Advisory Council on the Misuse of Drugs (UK), "Further Consideration of the Classification of Cannabis" Dec. 2005.
22. Maia Szalavitz, "Reefer Inanity: Never Trust the Media on Pot," HuffingtonPost.com, 30 July 2007.
23. Lawton, "Too Much."
24. Joseph Brean, "Caffeine Linked to Psychiatric Disorders," *National Post*, 2 Dec. 2006, ret. Canada.com, 21 Apr. 2007.
25. Bennett Weinberg and Bonnie Bealer, *World of Caffeine* (2001), pp. 189–190.
26. Anna Kuchment, "Make That a Double," *Newsweek*, 30 July 2007, p. 48.
27. S. Weinmann, "Caffeine Intake in Relation to the Risk of Primary Cardiac Arrest," *Epidemiology*, Sep. 1997, 8(5).
28. *Environmental Nutrition*, Oct. 1997.
29. Caffeine levels vary widely depending on daily brewing. Over six days of testing the lowest was half the above. Rachel McCusker, Bruce Goldberger, and Edward Cone, "Caffeine Content of Specialty Coffees," *J. Anal. Toxicol.*, Oct. 2003.
30. Title of 2003 *Newsweek* article on opium, Ron Moreau and Sami Yousafzai, "Flowers of Destruction," 14 July 2003, p. 33.
31. Suzanne Smalley and Debra Rosenberg, "I Felt Like I Wanted to Hurt People," *Newsweek*, 22 July 2006, p. 32.
32. Martin Brecher, et al., "Phencyclidine and Violence," *J. Clin. Psychopharmacol.*, Dec. 1988, p. 397.
33. "I Did It to You," *It's All Bad*, Black Market Records, 16 Mar. 2004.
34. *Dateline NBC* (TV), NBC, 29 Nov. 1994.
35. Akilah Johnson, "Man Said Insane in Mutilation Killing," LATimes.com, 17 June 2003.
36. "The Pulse," FOX, 8 Aug. 2002.
37. Bruce Rogers is a pseudonym. Sullum, *Saying Yes*, p. 207.
38. Paul Gahlinger, *Illegal Drugs* (2001), pp. 97, 390.
39. Ken Guggenheim, *Evening Sun*, 5 Mar. 2002.
40. "Walk Yourself," ret. AboveTheInfluence.com, 9 Feb. 2007.
41. Smalley, "I Felt Like I Wanted to Hurt People," p. 33.
42. Lauran Neergaard, "Misusing Acetaminophen Can Be Deadly" MSNBC.MSN.com, 22 Jan. 2004.

43. Gahlinger, *Illegal Drugs*, p. 388.

44. Guggenheim, "A Father's Tears."

45. Less than one percent of illicit drug users were introduced to drugs by a professional dealer. "One in Five Drug Abusers Needing Treatment Did Drugs with Parents," PRNewswire, 24 Aug. 2000.

46. Kate Patton, "Kelley McEnery Baker 1976–1999," ret. drugfree.org, 26 Mar. 2007.

47. Colin Fernandez, "Outcry from Families as Ministers Consider Downgrading Ecstasy and LSD," DailyMail.co.uk, 22 Nov. 2006.

48. There is more latitude in other countries. For example, in the British sitcom *Absolutely Fabulous* (1992–2004), Patsy frequently used cocaine. Although she was a dysfunctional character, she was not shown to suffer from her cocaine use.

49. Joseph McLaughlin, *Writing the Urban Jungle* (2000), p. 56.

50. One study found the annual risk of fatal overdose for a heroin addict to be one percent. M. Hickman, et al., "Drug-Related Mortality and Fatal Overdose Risk," *J. Urban Health*, June 2003.

51. An addicted pretty white girl having sex with a black gangster is also featured in the movie *Traffic* (2000).

52. *Reefer Madness* (1936) was a propaganda film that portrayed marijuana use leading to manslaughter, attempted rape, suicide, and insanity. It was so ludicrous that it became a cult classic.

53. From an August 2, 2006 review at RottenTomatoes.com by crushin russian, a Miami University student. Ret. 11 Jan. 2006.

54. This is not meant to belittle the experience of addicts, however, to only present their version is severely distorted.

55. "Winfrey Stands Behind 'Pieces' Author," CNN.com, 12 Jan. 2006.

56. Ibid.

12

DRUGS III

ITS ORIGIN
RACISM, LIES
& CRUEL SELFISH BUREAUCRATS

I

FROM THE BEGINNING
GETTING HIGH IN THE CAVE

The enjoyment of intoxication is universal. Cats hallucinate on catnip, koala bears have lifelong addictions to eucalyptus, cows and horses get destroyed on locoweed, birds get silly on marijuana seeds, and bighorn sheep risk mountain dangers to get a hit of lichen.[1] Wild elephants and chimpanzees have even raided stills for alcohol,[2] and in Pleasant Hill, California, thousands of robins annually celebrate their migratory arrival by getting high on holly berries. They stagger about and fly into walls.[3]

Getting high is so common in nature that humans probably first learned from watching animals.[4,5] With these feral enablers it is not surprising that our genetic forebears, the Neanderthals, got high some 50,000 years ago.[6] It's also not surprising that references to poppies, through a word that also meant "enjoy," are found in some of the earliest human writings dating from the third millennium B.C..[7]

Recreational drugs have not been demonized until recently. Societies have always been aware of their habit-forming nature. However, even in the case of heroin's precursor, opium, addiction was viewed as "an uncomfortable, but not especially dangerous, personal characteristic, like addiction to tobacco."[8]

In ancient Athens, the birthplace of democracy and the scientific method, liberty was valued above all else. Denying the freedom to pursue happiness via drugs would have been unthinkable.[9] In contrast, in Sparta patriotism was the grand ideal. Personal freedom, free speech, and individuality were seen as dangerous and any intoxication— even by alcohol—was a serious crime. Sparta was a brutal totalitarian military state.

Both the ancient Greeks and the ancient Romans enjoyed using drugs to "induce states of mental euphoria, create hallucinations, and alter their own consciousness."[10] Recreational drugs had no moral stigma and were used by all types of people from commoners to emperors. Any attempts to outlaw these naturally occurring substances would have been viewed as absurd. This benign attitude was also taken by biblical patriarchs, kings, and likely even Jesus.[11]

Greco-Romans knew how to get "high" via countless plants, such as ivy, daffodils, mandrake, and mushrooms, and their records of these preparations fill volumes. Their favorite drug was arguably opium, literally called "the juice." (The great philosopher/emperor Marcus Aurelius was addicted.) Their favorite method of enjoying psychotropics was mixing them with their wine. They would imbibe while debating philosophy in their symposiums or while bards regaled them with tales.[12] Drug-induced dreams, visions, and hallucinations were seen as an avenue to self-knowledge, discovery, and creativity. In fact, altered states of consciousness were considered divinely-provided madness.

Although less is known about Europe's drug usage in the Dark Ages, marijuana-smoking braziers have been found from throughout this time period, and arguably the most famous pot-smoker of the Renaissance was the giant Pantagruel, who appeared in Rabelais' sixteenth-century novels.[13]

Like the Athenians, the founders of the United States would have been disgusted by a government-led war on drugs. They fought the Revolutionary War to free themselves from government meddling. In 1776 independence was declared for the individual's right to "liberty and the pursuit of happiness."[14] Their first president, George Washington, used marijuana to soothe his toothaches and inflamed gums.[15]

Another Founding Father, Benjamin Franklin, used opium regularly in his final years for pain relief.[16]

James Madison was the country's fourth president and the "Father of the Constitution." He and his wife both enjoyed snuff and he defended tobacco as one of the "innocent gratifications" that makes life pleasurable.[17] The Madisons were not unique. As Ryan Grim wrote in *This is Your Country on Drugs*:

> Colonists also smoked an enormous amount of tobacco, often a variety that contained around fifteen percent nicotine—enough to cause hallucinations and a high far superior to the buzz that now comes from Marlboro.[18,19]

Early Americans liked to see their candidates get intoxicated at appropriate times and believed it demonstrated independence and character.[20] The third president and author of the Declaration of Independence, Thomas Jefferson, invented the presidential cocktail party and regularly drank three times as much as his guests, even though critics called him a habitual drunk.

Alcohol was the drug of choice for everyone in colonial times. It was a staple—a basic and necessary part of their diets.[21] Hard spirits were *the* beverage for adults and children. Beer did not keep, coffee and tea were expensive, and water was unsanitary. Puritans considered alcohol to be a "goodly creature of God."

II

Lying About the Bible Again
The War on John Barleycorn

Alcohol began to lose its stature in the nineteenth century as plumbing improved water quality. In addition, workers increasingly left their country farms for the city factories, where managers demanded efficient and sober workers. The Protestant religious fervor that swept the nation in the early nineteenth century sought to vanquish every sin, and in the case of alcohol, created a new one.

The total abstinence demanded by many Protestants during this period went directly against their Judeo-Christian heritage. Moses instructed the Jews to revel in alcohol,[22] Jesus approved of alcohol,[23] and the Protestant founders enjoyed drink. Even the sourpuss John Calvin warned against using the dangers of excessive drinking as "a pretext for a new cult based upon abstinence."[24]

Despite not having religious authority behind them, the zealots launched a moral crusade against John Barleycorn.[25] A moral crusade does not need to be rational. It merely needs alarmism and a scapegoat. The flaws of delinquent alcoholics, such as wife-beating and not supporting their families, were applied to every drinker. This was not effective, as people recognized these stumblebums were not representative of most drinkers.

Much more effective villains would emerge. The missing ingredient had been racism, and the arrival of Irish and German immigrants bolstered the temperance movement.[26] The cities, packed with these strange folk, made the rural Nativists nervous.[27] Irish and Germans loved their saloons and did not even bother to show token solidarity to the prohibitionists [drys]. Between 1852 and 1855, thirteen states prohibited the sale of alcohol, despite "furious opposition" from the urban populations.[28] These prohibitions were accompanied by widespread disobedience, lax enforcement, and violence. Most of the laws were soon revoked as people became more concerned with the bloody Civil War (1861–1865) than the fact that others drank alcohol.

Fifty years later World War I reinvigorated the temperance movement. Prohibitionists portrayed America as fighting three enemies—Germany, Austria, and alcohol. While German troops battled Americans in Europe, German-American companies like Pabst, Busch, Schlitz, Blatz, and Miller were internally sabotaging America with beer. During the war Americans had to be sober and chaste, and no grain could be diverted to brewers. President Woodrow Wilson and others perceived the war as a moral battle with "civilization itself seeming to be in the balance."[29]

Germans were not the only race who needed assistance maintaining sobriety. Politicians from the South were distrustful of the federal government telling them what they could imbibe, so the drys played up their greatest fear—out-of-control blacks. Liquor was blamed for transforming black men into rapists and "the grogshop" was pinpointed as "the Negro's center of power."[30] Southern opposition dissolved.

The day before the Eighteenth Amendment's prohibition of alcohol went into effect, the evangelical preacher Billy Sunday exhorted thousands over the radio:

> The reign of tears is over. The slums will soon be a memory. We will turn our prisons into factories and our jails into storehouses and corncribs. Men will walk upright now; women will smile and the children will laugh. Hell will be forever rent.[31]

This optimism was not limited to the pulpit. A journalist wrote, "There had been a liquor problem. But a Law has been passed."[32]

III

The First Drug War
Prohibition

It appears that Prohibition (1920–1933) decreased drinking significantly (a third to a half),[33,34] however, as with future drug wars, the costs of this lowered intake were horrifying and prohibition is "almost universally seen as a great social disaster."[35] Some of these costs were:

Increase in the Use of Other Drugs—The reduction in drinking is deceptive because it does not mean increased sobriety. People simply turned to cheaper alternatives. One of the biggest benefactors was marijuana.[36] Prohibition led to the opening of marijuana-smoking establishments called tea-pads. By the end of prohibition New York City had five hundred of them.

Increase in Organized Crime—Prohibition immediately made crime extremely profitable. Small-time mafia bosses who ran local gambling and prostitution outfits suddenly became obscenely rich and powerful national players. One charismatic bootlegger, George Remus, employed three thousand men and at one house party gave every woman in attendance (roughly fifty) a new Pontiac car.[37,38] A historian wrote,

295

"National prohibition transferred two billion dollars a year from the hands of brewers, distillers, and shareholders to the hands of murderers, crooks, and illiterates."[39]

Surge of Violence[40]—The exorbitant profits meant mafia bosses were willing to use exorbitant violence to protect their operations. In Prohibition's first year, the major cities' crime rates jumped twenty-four percent. The federal caseload tripled and the federal prison system operated at 170 percent capacity. The murder rate rose sharply in the decade of prohibition and promptly dropped at its end.[41]

Perhaps more spectacular than the quantity of carnage was the brazen ruthlessness. The St. Valentine's Day massacre occurred in 1929 when Chicago bootlegger extraordinaire Al Capone had seven members of a rival gang machine-gunned execution-style in a garage by operatives posing as police. Other Chicago machine-gun battles occurred in the open streets during the day.

Prohibition violence was not limited to gang warfare. Henry Joy, a founder of the Packer Motor Car Company, was committed to Prohibition until he saw its results first-hand. His lakeside estate on Lake St. Clair, north of Detroit, was on the front line of smuggling from Canada, and he regularly witnessed federal agents firing away at smugglers.

At one point, authorities ransacked Joy's boathouse unannounced and roughed up his old watchman who had eleven bottles of beer. The next week when a duck hunter on the lake did not hear agents ordering him to stop over the sound of his boat motor, he was blown away. In 1930, the *New York Times* reported that sixty-one federal agents had died and 151 civilians had been killed by agents.[42]

Erosion of Civil Rights[43]—The massive volume of alcohol cases swamping the courts cemented plea-bargaining as an intrinsic part of America's criminal justice system. In plea-bargaining, the government will make concessions, often in severity of sentence, in exchange for a guilty plea.

This works well for people who are guilty and do not wish to dispute their charges. However, it is a catch-22 for those who want to fight their charges, many of whom are innocent. The constitutional right to a jury trial is now qualified. If a citizen takes advantage of that right, she is facing a dramatically more severe punishment.[44] In effect, defendants are not being punished for the underlying crime but for contesting the charges.

This right was not the only one to suffer. It was under prohibition that wiretapping became an acceptable intrusion on the home, entrapment became common, grounds for warrantless searches were expanded, and double jeopardy was first allowed—meaning that someone could now be prosecuted under both local and federal law.[45]

Widespread Corruption[46]—The first federal agent was caught taking bribes only two weeks into Prohibition.[47] By 1929, one out of four federal agents had been dismissed for charges ranging from bribery to drinking the evidence. In Detroit, public officials received over $20 million in graft a week, while in New York City underground bars, called speakeasies, had to pay over $4,000 in bribes a week to stay open.[48] It is difficult to blame the officers who could *triple* their annual salary in one day by overlooking a ubiquitous and victimless crime.

The Cool/Forbidden Fruit Factor—Prohibition made drinking fashionable. Now only bumpkins did not have a hip flask. Previously women drank at home if at all. Drinking was unbecoming of a female and the only ones at saloons were prostitutes and dancers. Now the trendy young women, named flappers, would pack the speakeasies, leading one observer to complain that the outlawed saloons may have been depraved but at least you didn't have to fight your way through crowds of schoolgirls to reach the bar.[49] The bootleggers became romantic heroes portrayed dashingly in movies.[50] Infamous Al Capone was a hero to many who despised Prohibition and was cheered in the streets.

Alcohol Became Potent and Deadly—While beer consumption plunged, the sale of the more potent, and more easily hidden, hard liquor doubled.[51] Much of the alcohol during Prohibition was manufactured from industrial alcohol. To prevent this, the government required that industrial alcohol be poisoned. When the bootleggers did not properly remove the poison in their makeshift labs, drinkers could suffer blindness,[52] paralysis, or death. Almost 30,000 people died in this manner, while roughly 100,000 suffered permanent damage.[53] At the time, one senator called this "legalized murder."[54] During Prohibition, there were also documented cases of people injecting alcohol.[55]

This overview is crucial because the reason Prohibition was overturned in 1933 was because people could remember what life was like before it.[56] The drys could not argue that life would be horrible with legalized alcohol because people knew that life. Society under Prohibition is illustrative as the narrative turns to the criminalization of other drugs.

IV

Wright was Wrong
A Drunk Doctor Plays the USA and the World[57]

The criminalization of drugs aside from alcohol was comparatively easy. Such a tiny percentage of the population used other drugs that they did not have the political strength to defend themselves. Two wowsers[58] used the age-old formula of race-baiting and fearmongering to criminalize these people and create bureaucratic careers for themselves.

The first of these men was Hamilton Wright. Wright was a forty-one-year-old physician who became famous when he "discovered" the tropical disease beriberi was a bacterial infection. He was wrong, but it did not matter, for he quickly parlayed his stardom by marrying the daughter of a powerful senator. Through his new connection he was placed on the Opium Commission in 1908.

President Theodore Roosevelt was hoping the newly-formed commission would lend support to China in its dispute with Great Britain over opium importation into China. Opium usage was being misrepresented and demonized for political purposes in China, just like alcohol usage was in the United States.[59] The United States did not profit from the opium trade and therefore it was a costless way to seek Chinese favor.

Wright became a man on a mission. In evaluating the opium issue in America, he determined that there was a devastating problem. He either lied or lacked intelligence. The highest credible estimates at the turn of the century were that there were three opium addicts for every thousand people. These addicts were mostly harmless hardworking middle-aged Southern white women who had become unintentionally addicted via quack patent medicines containing opium.[60] For example, at the time a popular cough syrup containing heroin claimed, "It will suit the palate of the most exacting adult or the most capricious child."[61]

The number of opium addicts was actually dropping because the federal government had recently forced medicines to list their ingredients. People were now aware of addictive substances in their medicine and could be cautious.

Wright was a handsome man who looked like a "well-preserved Yale quarterback." His immense ego, propensity to lie and exaggerate, and his "bulldozer style" well suited him to solve this opium "problem."[62] The first Shanghai Opium Commission in 1909 went well for Wright, although the British, French, and Dutch did not share Wright's alarm. A British study showed opium to be no worse than alcohol and perhaps better. One official stated, "There is more violence in a gallon of alcohol than a ton of opium."[63] Despite this, the attending governments agreed to restrict opium and its derivatives in their own borders.

Wright's ambition was set afire and for the next two years he lobbied to turn the "United States into a shining beacon of drug morality."[64] In this manner, he would embarrass the world into going along with global narcotics criminalization. Wright ran into two problems. One, national drug laws would require a national police force and the Tenth Amendment of the Constitution prevented this. Wright complained to his superior that "it has been a difficult business... The Constitution is constantly getting in the way."[65]

Wright bypassed the Founding Fathers' restriction through a recently-passed Supreme Court decision that ruled the federal government could regulate anything that it taxed. Wright drew up a bill that required anyone dealing with drugs to register, pay a license fee, and keep records. This underhanded maneuver gave federal Treasury Department agents complete control over narcotics.

Wright's second problem was convincing skeptics that the federal government needed more power. Here Wright used race-baiting. Opium smoking was favored by Chinese immigrants who were imported to build the Western railways, so Wright warned skeptical Westerners that opium smoking drove white women into the arms of Chinese men. For the skeptical Southerners, Wright used a hackneyed danger, claiming cocaine turned black men into rapists. This fit nicely into the myth already circulating that cocaine made blacks unruly and gave them superhuman strength.

WHITE POWDER:
RACISM BEHIND DRUG LAWS

DRUG	IRRESPONSIBLE GROUPS	QUOTES
Alcohol (mid-1800s)	German and Irish immigrants	"Those cocaine niggers sure are hard to kill…"[32] "If I could show you what a small marijuana cigarette can do to one of our degenerate Spanish-speaking residents…"[33]
Alcohol (national prohibition, 1920–1933)	Germans and Southern blacks	
Cocaine	Southern blacks	
Opium (Heroin)	Asian immigrants	
Marijuana	Mexican immigrants	
Peyote	American Indians	
Crack	Inner-city blacks	
LSD	Hippies	

Through these lies Wright badgered foreign dignitaries and his superiors at the State Department into having another International Conference on Opium in 1911. The British were so angered by Wright's heavy-handed manipulation and exaggeration that the State Department asked Wright to find another line of work. He refused, as he was "a man with a cause."[66] At this conference he obligated the United States to pass a federal anti-narcotics law—*despite not having authority to do so.*

The unscrupulous Wright then returned to America and told Congress that this treaty gave them no choice in the matter and that they had to enact a law. The Harrison Narcotics Act would pass in 1914 because Wright hoodwinked his country. Ironically, Wright would be fired by the Secretary of State before the bill's passage because he was an alcoholic who came to work drunk.

Besides the fact that the country believed they were bound by international agreement, Wright's bill passed with little debate because it appeared to be merely gathering information about drug dispensation. However, the Treasury Department promptly used Wright's crafty wording to jail doctors who they believed were giving drugs to "addicts."[67] Thousands of drug-addicted Americans were now criminals. Six weeks after the bill's passage the *New York Medical Journal* read:

> . . . the immediate effects of the Harrison antinarcotic law were seen in the flocking of drug habitués to hospitals and sanitariums. Sporadic crimes of violence were reported too, due usually to desperate efforts by addicts to obtain drugs . . . The really serious results of this legislation, however, will only appear gradually and will not always be recognized as such. These will be the failure of promising careers, the disrupting of happy families, the commission of crimes which will never be traced to their real cause, and the influx into hospitals for the mentally disordered of many who would otherwise live socially competent lives.[68]

V

The Hoover of Drugs
A Bald Snake Disregards The Constitution for Thirty Years[69]

The next wowser was a bitter veteran of Prohibition's futile war on alcohol. Harry Anslinger believed Prohibition failed because it was not fought hard enough. As the head of the Prohibition Unit's foreign control division, Anslinger had pushed for harsher penalties for bootleggers and drinkers. Before Prohibition ended in 1933 Anslinger was temporarily put in charge of the Federal Bureau of Narcotics (FBN).

Similar to J. Edgar Hoover's lifelong seizure of the Federal Bureau of Investigation, Anslinger made the FBN his fiefdom for over three decades. Whereas Hoover was able to use his agents to blackmail and intimidate political opponents, Anslinger's ace card was his absolute control over the medical market for painkillers. He determined who had access to this lucre and, as of 1936, he only allowed eight companies. Not coincidentally, these companies have become today's billion-dollar pharmaceutical behemoths and include names such as Merck, Parke-Davis, and Eli Lilly. Just as Anslinger protected them from competition, they protected him with intense lobbying.

Pharmaceutical money and influential anti-drug zealots would make Anslinger indestructible. This was most apparent in 1932. An Anslinger memo instructing FBN agents to look for an informant described as "a ginger-colored nigger" enraged the White House and moved the senator from Anslinger's home state to call for his resignation. Anslinger did not resign and stayed on for another thirty years.

A. *Criminalizing Stuff Is Fun: Marijuana*

The Harrison Narcotics Act only outlawed opium, its derivatives (morphine, heroin, etc.), and cocaine. Anslinger was initially against criminalizing marijuana. He cogently observed that marijuana was a weed that grows "like dandelions."[70] However, a movement was building in the Western states against it and Anslinger could not resist using marijuana to get his agency more money.

Marijuana was still smoked primarily by Mexicans, although its use had spread to industrial cities as an alternative to alcohol during Prohibition.[71] Just as ill will toward Chinese immigrants was the motive behind criminalizing opium smoking, the Mexican immigrants were about to get the same recreational management.

This 1929 Montana report is representative of the deliberations behind anti-marijuana legislation:

> There was fun in House Health Committee during the week when the Marihuana bill came up for consideration. Marihuana is Mexican opium, a plant used by Mexicans and cultivated for sale by Indians. "When some beet field peon takes a few rares of this stuff," explained Dr. Fred Ulsher of Mineral County, "he thinks he has just been elected president of Mexico so he starts to execute all his political enemies. I understand that over in Butte where the Mexicans often go for the winter they stage imaginary bullfights . . . after a couple of whiffs of Marihuana . . ." Everyone laughed and the bill was recommended for passage.[72]

At the federal level passage would not be as easy, so Anslinger and his agents went on a publicity tour. Although not as funny as Dr. Ulsher, Anslinger was just as dishonest. He claimed that marijuana was more addictive than cocaine and opium, and that it caused insanity.[73] In a 1936 pamphlet, the FBN asserted that:

> Prolonged use of Marihuana frequently develops a delirious rage which sometimes leads to high crimes, such as assault and murder. Hence Marihuana has been called the "killer drug" . . . Marihuana sometimes gives man the lust to kill, unreasonably and without motive. Many cases of assault, rape, robbery, and murder are traced to the use of Marihuana.[74]

Anslinger loved to dazzle audiences with grisly crimes "caused" by marijuana.[75] One of his favorites was that of Victor Licata. Licata was a twenty-one-year-old Floridian who slaughtered his entire family with an axe. Anslinger would not mention that Licata had long been considered mentally unstable, and instead attributed his acts to the fact that Licata was "addicted to smoking marihuana cigarettes." Whenever possible, Anslinger would produce pictures of the carnage.

In the 1937 Congressional hearings on the bill before the House Ways and Means Committee, Anslinger's testimony consisted almost entirely of hearsay—newspaper clippings and anecdotes from his notes. One Anslinger note read, "Colored students at the Univ. of Minn. partying with female students (white) smoking and getting their sympathy with stories of racial persecution. Result pregnancy."[76]

The American Medical Association (AMA) opposed regulation of marijuana, which doctors had used as a medicine for over one hundred years, and had an actual doctor testify.[77] Dr. William Woodward pointed out that many of the facts and figures that Anslinger quoted from newspaper articles actually originated with Anslinger, so Anslinger was merely quoting himself. Woodward pointed out that there was no evidence of marijuana causing crime, no evidence of a marijuana crisis among children, and also pointedly asked why no one from the Public Health Service was present to testify. (The reason no one from the Public Health Service was there was that the assistant surgeon general had told Anslinger that marijuana did not produce dependence.)

This testimony incensed the congressmen. Obviously someone was jerking their chain and they responded by tearing Woodward apart.[78] He was accused of being obstructive and evasive. The chairman scolded the doctor: "If you want to advise us on legislation you ought to come here with some constructive proposals rather than criticism, rather than trying to throw obstacles in the way of something that the Federal Government is trying to do."[79]

When the bill went before the entire House of Representatives for the final vote, its discussion lasted less than two minutes. When a congressman asked if the AMA approved of the bill, the House Ways and Means Committee member Fred Vinson promptly responded, "Their Doctor Wentworth came down here. They support this bill a hundred percent."[80] The future chief justice of the Supreme Court blatantly lied and did not even bother to get the poor doctor's name right.

In the next five years Anslinger's FBN destroyed 60,000 tons of marijuana and arrested about a thousand people annually for violating the marijuana law.[81] Anslinger did not forget the AMA's act of treason either. From mid-1937 through 1939, the FBN prosecuted more than three thousand doctors. In 1939 the AMA bowed to Anslinger and came out against marijuana. From 1939–1949 only three doctors were prosecuted by the FBN for drug activity.[82]

B. Anslinger Has No Clothes but He Is Still Emperor

After adding marijuana to the war Anslinger marched forward spewing lies and propaganda for another quarter-century.[83] The figures he pulled out of his head reflected the goals he had when he opened his mouth.

While Anslinger was seeking to criminalize marijuana, the country was in a "marijuana crisis" and marijuana drove a young man to axe his entire family. After the battle was won, alarmist non-governmental organizations were told to clam it. One, the FBN now wanted to look like it had fixed the "problem."[84] Two, Anslinger's propaganda had worked too well. People actually believed marijuana dictated criminals' actions. Prosecutors were running into the defense that marijuana made defendants commit crimes. By the 1950s, Anslinger was testifying before Congress that marijuana was not "the controlling factor in the commission of crimes."[85]

NO BUD FOR ROSEBUD
The Marihuana Conspiracy

Two business behemoths stood to lose a fortune because of hemp (marijuana) in the 1930s. They were the newspaper tycoon William Randolph Hearst and the DuPont Corporation. It had just become more economical to process hemp fiber from the plant. This meant that hemp paper and textiles would be highly competitive. Hearst had a huge stake in forests and machinery to produce paper from wood pulp. DuPont had recently patented a process to make paper from wood pulp and had also begun marketing its artificial fiber, nylon.

Hearst newspapers attacked marijuana with sensational stories of Mexican mayhem, addicted children, and unspeakable violence. It was Hearst's newspapers that changed the common spelling from marihuana to the Spanish, marijuana, to give it a more foreign feel. The connections between DuPont, the anti-marijuana politicians, and Harry Anslinger are well documented.

—Peter McWilliams, *Ain't Nobody's Business If You Do* (1996), pp. 281–286.

Anslinger needed to find new villains. As the twentieth century approached its midpoint *overt* racism became more and more distasteful.[86] In addition, with World War II the politicians had no need for exaggerated fears to energize voters, as the Axis powers provided a real one. Anslinger still tried. He warned that legions of addicted GIs returning to America would need the FBN's attention. This failed to materialize, and Anslinger was disgruntled by the FBN's lack of funding.[87]

Luckily for him, a new enemy was rising. Like his fellow bureaucratic dictator, J. Edgar Hoover, Anslinger used the threat of communism to get congressional funds flowing. The Communists were trying to destroy the West not with soldiers, but with opium.[88] In 1948, Anslinger made a remarkable 180-degree turn. He testified to congress that marijuana, the drug he used to call the "killer drug," made one so tranquil and peaceful that Communists were supplying huge amounts to the American military, government employees, and key citizens to weaken their fighting spirit.[89] The FBN's budget was doubled.

Anslinger also found another drug culprit—liberal judges. Once again, he had no evidence, but he only needed a couple unscrupulous congressmen looking for a crusade to help their approval ratings. The congressmen would hold the hearings to get the press' attention and Anslinger would trot out his newspaper clippings and lies. In this manner, Anslinger had the federal government institute harsh minimum mandatory sentences and institute the death penalty for narcotics violations.

Anslinger bullied anyone who challenged him. New York City Mayor Fiorello La Guardia authorized an expert panel to study the marijuana problem. Anslinger's reacted by attacking the mayor and the panel personally and launched a flurry of accusations three years before the investigation was completed. By the time the panel announced marijuana was relatively harmless, the press had tired of the fuss, leading to almost no coverage.[90] Anslinger then banned all marijuana research in the United States so his newspaper clippings could never be challenged again.

When Anslinger had Congress institute mandatory minimum sentencing in 1951, he aroused the attention of lawyers at the American Bar Association (ABA), who thought that mandatory sentencing unconstitutionally violated the independence of the judiciary. One of its chairmen, Rufus King, began researching the legal history of the Harrison Narcotics Act and was flabbergasted.

In 1924, a respected doctor in the state of Washington had been set up by an addict on the payroll of the Treasury Department. She told the doctor she was an addict, in terrible pain, and needed medication. He wrote her a prescription for three tablets of cocaine and a tablet of morphine. The next day Treasury agents arrested him and put him in jail. He was convicted but appealed his case all the way to the Supreme Court. The Supreme Court threw out his conviction as unconstitutional, thus invalidating the Treasury Department's entire scheme of enforcement.

None of this was remarkable. What was remarkable was that Anslinger and the Treasury Department ignored the ruling. The thousands of doctor arrests made over the next decade were illegal, including the ones that had bullied the AMA into submission. When King asked his European counterparts about their countries' drug problems, they responded, "What drug problem?" The whole thing was a hoax.

King set up a joint committee between the ABA and the AMA to straighten out the situation and naively asked Anslinger to participate. Anslinger refused, but asked to be kept informed of its progress. When the committee first published their findings for a limited distribution, Anslinger immediately published an identical-looking report that personally attacked the committee members.

The FBN sent this report to media outlets all over the country at the taxpayers' expense. Anslinger portrayed the ABA and AMA as Communist tools. Treasury Department agents went to the private foundation that was funding the report and told them they were supporting a "controversial" study. The Treasury Department had control over the foundation's tax-exempt status so it withdrew its support.

Although Anslinger destroyed the report, he did not destroy King. King challenged Anslinger publicly for the next three years and Anslinger unwisely took him on in print and radio. Perhaps Anslinger had been getting by on lies, bluster, and newspaper clippings for so long he forgot what passed as legitimate evidence. One of Anslinger's rants in these debates was brought to the attention of President John F. Kennedy, and he decided Anslinger should go. Anslinger resigned several months later. The year was 1962.

Anslinger would later admit to supplying morphine to his friend and fellow fearmonger Senator Joseph McCarthy. He did this for years and his justification was that McCarthy was a fine American.[91] At the end of his life Anslinger became a morphine addict himself.[92] Neither he nor McCarthy were ever arrested, nor did they ever have to serve mandatory prison sentences.

VI

Lock Up The Disrespectful Brats
Nixon Was A Tough Guy

Despite Anslinger's resignation, the drug battle did not abate. Drug laws and decades of disinformation were in place. Most importantly, so was Anslinger's agency, the Federal Bureau of Narcotics. As President Ronald Reagan would later note, government agencies self-perpetuate.[93] A boon also arose. The anti-drug rhetoric could no longer blame racial minorities for drug problems as open racism was no longer acceptable. The 1960s would provide a stigmatized minority to take their place—the hippie.

Every generation rebels against its parents and in the 1960s the youngest generation was massive, with 76 million "baby-boomers" reaching adolescence.[94] By 1965, half of the American population was under 30. At the same time, the Vietnam

War created disillusionment among the young adults being sent to fight. This led the boomers to question their parents' values in other areas, such as race, sex, and drugs. Instead of sticking to their parents' drug—alcohol—the adventurous youth, called "hippies," turned to hallucinogens like marijuana and LSD.

Controversial anti-establishment celebrities such as Harvard psychologist Timothy Leary, Beat poet Allen Ginsberg, novelist Ken Kesey, and countless musicians such as the Beatles and the Grateful Dead openly advertised LSD as a tool to create a better world. Leary's exhortations for youth to "tune in, turn on, drop out"[95] branded hallucinogens as hostile to the American work ethic. LSD and marijuana became inextricably tied to radical politics and hippies. Forty years later, the hallucinogen/hippie link is still strong.[96]

Hallucinogens allowed elders to explain their children's bizarre and disrespectful behavior. This was assisted by the media, who served the scapegoat on a plate filled with sensational lies.[97] President Lyndon Johnson blamed hallucinogens for the 1960s social turmoil, and although he outlawed LSD, he did not ramp up the tough-guy rhetoric like his successor, Richard Nixon.[98] Nixon was elected on a law-and-order campaign, and would put the naughty baby-boomers in their proper place—jail.

Unfortunately, the Constitution prevented the federal government from usurping state control of law enforcement. This hurdle flummoxed the Nixon White House until a staff member hit on the idea of drugs.[99] The constitutional barriers to federal drug enforcement had already been trampled by Anslinger. Drugs also allowed Nixon to indirectly target the black population that he saw as the "whole problem."[100] Nixon soon began trumpeting a new national emergency.

When Nixon asserted that drugs were "decimating a generation of Americans," drugs were such a tiny health problem that they were statistically insignificant. Many more Americans were dying from choking to death on food or from falling down stairs.[101] Even Nixon's figures put the number of heroin addicts at merely three in a thousand (the same as in Wright's day), but he dishonestly presented that number as eight times higher than two years earlier, creating a junkie explosion.[102] As a White House assistant later explained, "If we hyped the drug problem into a national crisis, we knew that Congress would give us anything we asked for."[103]

Nixon used this "crisis" to create the Drug Enforcement Administration (DEA) that replaced the Federal Bureau of Narcotics. Never armed with more than a few hundred agents before, the federal drug police force now had over 4,000 agents. The DEA had "awesome powers,"[104] and its domestic and global jurisdiction was broader than that of the Central Intelligence Agency or the Federal Bureau of Investigation.

While president, Nixon would get drunk and pop Dilantin and sleeping pills from his private stash. He did not get his Dilantin from a doctor but from his financier friend Jack Dreyfuss. Nixon never had himself arrested.[105]

VII
Carter Tries[106]

Nixon's corruption pushed the country to elect a less iron-fisted leader, Jimmy Carter. Carter put a doctor, Peter Bourne, in charge of his drug policy. As someone who had exposure to drugs outside of the world of law enforcement, Bourne pushed Carter to eliminate criminal penalties for marijuana possession. This fell apart when Bourne wrote a sedative prescription for a young woman on his staff. Because she was a White House employee he made it out to a false name to protect her identity. She gave it to a friend who had it filled at a pharmacy being audited. When the friend could not produce an ID the police were called.

After decades of propaganda infiltrating American schools and media, anyone who even suggested legalization risked being tarred as a radical drug-pushing dope-smoking nut.[107] Bourne was already in the crosshairs, and this allowed him to be blown away. The press went bananas digging through Bourne's past. It came out that Bourne had attended a party where marijuana and cocaine were used openly. Despite not using any himself, Bourne and decriminalization were kicked out of Washington.

VIII
Reagan and Crack Incite Panic

The next president, Ronald Reagan, picked up right where Nixon left off. In 1982, Reagan said from the Rose Garden, "We're taking down the surrender flag that has flown over so many drug efforts. We're running up the battle flag."[108] The war was on.

A. You Look Suspicious, Give Me All Your Money: Forfeiture

The civil right that Reagan tore from the Constitution in the name of the drug war was protection from unconstitutional seizures. The Omnibus Crime Bill of 1984 threw due process out the window. Previously the government had to prove a person guilty before they could take her property. Now police could take money or property they believed to be tainted by drugs in a process called forfeiture. The property owner had to go through expensive legal proceedings to prove that it was not tainted if they wanted the property back.

In addition, Reagan gave law enforcement agents a huge incentive to abuse this extraordinary power. Seized assets would go to the law enforcement agencies that made the seizure. After twenty years of this legal innovation, law enforcement agencies and police departments across the country are now dependent on this "income." Not surprisingly, the necessity of forfeiture for the war on drugs morphed into a necessity for the war on crime. There are now two hundred federal forfeiture statutes that allow forfeiture for such heinous crimes as collecting the feathers of migratory birds.[109] The effect of forfeiture laws has been a massive shakedown of Americans who cannot afford legal representation.

B. Prohibition Creates Crack: The Media Creates a Monster

Powder cocaine became popular with high rollers and celebrities in the 1970s. Its exorbitant expense made it a status symbol, the champagne of drugs. Stories of drug-addled rock stars publicized cocaine and other drugs. The following are a taste of this genre:

Beach Boy **Brian Wilson** was so gripped by cocaine paranoia in the late 1960s that he refused to shower for fear of what would come out of the showerhead.

Avid heroin user **Nick Cave** would write lyrics in his notebooks with a bloody needle.

Sex Pistol **Sid Vicious** was shooting up in a bathroom stall with one of the

Ramones when he dipped the syringe into the toilet bowl and injected a mixture of water, urine, puke and feces.

In 1984, one of Aerosmith's Toxic Twins, **Steven Tyler**, suggested to the band that they cover a great song, "You See Me Crying," not realizing they had written and recorded the song nine years earlier. The other Toxic Twin, Joe Perry, once introduced his wife to the band even though they had all known her for years.

When **Janis Joplin**'s guitarist turned blue after shooting up heroin backstage in 1969, he was revived by Zappa groupie Suzy Creamcheese, not by the usual slapping and yelling, but by oral sex.

During one LSD fiesta, British rocker **Julian Cope** ran around a dinner table for an hour and a half evading the "paw" of his drummer who was a mountain lion. Cope's feet began to burn so he ordered milk be thrown on the carpet. This was too slippery so he added a bowl of Rice Krispies to the mix. Later that night at a picnic in his attic, another bandmate perturbed Cope, so Cope pissed in his baked beans.

At a 1973 West Berlin Rolling Stones aftershow party, two strippers were simulating sex on a fur coat when a member of the entourage lit them on fire. **Mick Jagger** and **Keith Richards** sat watching high on heroin and exhibited no reaction whatsoever. "They just sat there, radiating this numb, burned-out cool."[110]

While cocaine was "evil" enough to provide fodder for Reagan's drug war, rich white celebrities getting silly did not scare most Americans. This changed in 1985. Just as criminalization led to a 190-proof synthesized hooch called white lightning that could blind or kill, criminalization led to an easily-smoked version of cocaine called crack. Not many blue-collar people could afford cocaine, but they could afford crack. Crack brought cocaine to the masses.

The inner cities were the natural location for this market to pop. White people, the primary crack users, had easy access to the inner cities, and since its inhabitants were poor they were more willing to take the risks involved in selling it. The booming crack market set off a firestorm of inner-city violence as gangs fought for their piece of the crack pie. Predictably, the violence was erroneously attributed to its pharmacology, not its prohibition.[111]

The big media companies centered in the cities only had to go down the street to get great coverage of the ferocious bloodletting. In 1986, more than a thousand

THE REALITY OF CRACK
Like the Use of Alcohol

Harold Dow (Reporter): This is it. The drug so powerful it will empty the money from your pockets, make you sell the watch off your wrist, the clothes off your back ...
Robert Stutman (DEA Agent): Or kill your mother.

—CBS News, May 27, 1986

The sociologist Sudhir Venkatesh closely observed life in the notorious Robert Taylor housing projects on Chicago's South Side throughout the 1990s. Although few residents admitted to using crack because of its stigma, he wrote:

> After a while it became clear to me that crack use in the projects was much like the use of alcohol in the suburbs where I grew up: there was a small group of hard-core addicts and a much larger group of functional users who smoked a little crack a few days a week. Many of the crack users in Robert Taylor took care of their families and went about their business, but when they saved up ten or twenty dollars, they'd go ahead and get high.

crack stories ran in the press, with *Time* and *Newsweek* having five crack covers apiece. NBC alone showed more than four hundred reports, while CBS ran a special "two hours of hands-on horror" in the crack "war zone."[112] Whereas wasted rockers and socialites were amusing, young black men running amok with guns was too much for mainstream America.

This urban mayhem still did not sate the fervor for headlines. The fearmongers' pantheon of mythic figures would receive its newest member in 1985—the crack baby. Images of shaking emaciated preemies supported by tubes and fancy machines filled the airwaves. Journalists wrote fearfully about a crack baby epidemic brought on by cruel crack moms who despised their offspring. The country would have to financially support this generation of mentally incapacitated children.

From the beginning, there were medical experts who questioned the crack baby phenomenon. An Atlanta specialist from Emory University Medical School,

> Dominic Streatfeild, an English journalist, spent a day in a South Bronx crack house in the 1990s. He noted that the only shocking thing about watching someone smoke crack was that it was not shocking at all, and compared it to watching someone smoke a joint. From reading he expected the effects of crack to be "pretty serious," but they were not. Immediately after smoking most would become incoherent and rant a bit, but many were incoherent even before getting high. While high, users would yell out random opinions even though none of them bothered to listen to each other.
>
> The tragic life stories of the crack house patrons depressed Streatfeild. Afterwards he went to an Upper East Side bar to have a beer and contemplate whether a middle-class white guy like himself could possibly understand the desperate conditions of crack den habitués in a lower-class black neighborhood. Behind him at the bar "two well-heeled yuppies in chinos and polo shirts whinged about their lives." While the yuppies "droned on" about the "misery" of their respectable salaries and golf games, Streatfeild got thoroughly sotted (drunk) and stumbled home to puke.
>
> —Jimmie Reeves & Richard Campbell, *Cracked Coverage* (1994), pp. 130–131; Dominic Streatfeild, *Cocaine* (2001), pp. 316–323; and Sudhir Venkatesh, *Gang Leader for a Day* (2008), p. 55.

Claire Coles, told reporters that jittery preemies born to abused women who smoke and drink could not be blamed on cocaine. When she placed the blame on poverty and took away the sensational crack baby icon, reporters stopped interviewing her.[113] The crack baby epidemic was traced back to a misquoted doctor and ensuing exaggeration. It was later found that infants born exposed to cocaine fit the normal intelligence curve.

First Lady Nancy Reagan's famous solution to the drug woes was "Just say no." According to Nancy Reagan those who said yes were accomplices to murder.[114] With that rhetoric from the top and images of inner-city blacks going gangbusters and birthing crack babies, it is not surprising that drugs took center stage. In 1980 fifty-three percent of the population had supported the legalization of small amounts of drugs. By 1986 this number had dropped to twenty-seven percent.[115] In 1985 under one percent of Americans identified drugs as the "number one problem facing the nation today." By 1989 that number had rocketed to fifty-four percent.[116]

313

IX
Reagan and Bush Get Their War On and Lose

A. Declaring a War on the Coca Plant

In the mid-1980s Reagan decided to cut off the supply of cocaine at its source. DEA agents were first sent into Peru to lead teams armed with weed-whackers. This proved moronic, as the rugged coca plant grows naturally in the Andes and just one valley in Peru covers an area three times the size of Massachusetts. It also became dangerous when rebel guerrillas started attacking them. The Reagan administration hoped to do aerial spraying; however, dumping dangerous chemicals over the vast Andes' countryside was understandably rejected by Peru. The United States also tried destroying the labs that processed the coca. This too became a hopeless chase as labs were simply rebuilt or moved deeper into the jungles.

After the Reagan fiasco in Peru, America focused on Bolivia. Bolivia was a poorer country and more willing to dance for foreign aid. The United States convinced Bolivian peasants to pull up their coca fields for $800 an acre and plant alternative crops that American experts showed them how to grow. This cut cocaine production in Bolivia temporarily, however, this project failed as well. For example, one group of farmers was persuaded to plant ginger and soon "found themselves up to their asses in ginger."[117] No one knew what to do with forty tons of ginger. Other touted crops such as bananas, grapefruit, and pineapples failed to be profitable as well. Despite spending two billion dollars on the problem, total cocaine output in the Andes increased fifteen percent during President George H.W. Bush's administration.[118]

B. Daily 9/11s: Colombia[119]

Reagan and H.W. Bush would also try to take down the number one cocaine kingpin in the 1980s, the Colombian Pablo Escobar. Unlike the coca plant, Escobar fought back. Although the parallels between alcohol prohibition and cocaine prohibition were lost on the average American, they were not lost on Escobar.

Escobar idolized Al Capone, and like Capone, he became king by dealing with traitors and opponents ruthlessly. While Capone fought for millions in profit, Escobar fought for billions. Escobar fought harder.

The country of Colombia is strategically located in the geography of cocaine. At the northern end of South America, it sits at the top of the Andes' cocaine country. With access to both the Caribbean and Pacific oceans it is well situated for smuggling. The Colombian drug traffic had been handled by individual operators and wealthy traffickers who already dealt with the criminal justice system by *plato o plomo* (silver or lead). This meant: if you do what I want I will pay you, if not, I will kill you. But in 1981 an event inspired Escobar to take this further.

A daughter of a major trafficker, Marta Nieves Ochoa, was kidnapped by Marxist revolutionaries. Kidnapping the rich is a common way for Latin American rebel groups to raise funds, but this time instead of paying, the Ochoas called a council of war. Over two hundred criminal organizations were present and they each agreed to donate ten men to a new organization, Death to Kidnappers. They publicly announced the new organization and then proceeded to kill anyone suspected of involvement with the kidnapping. This included "union organizers, old ladies, young children, horses, pigs, and chickens." Marta Nieves Ochoa was released unharmed without the ransom being paid. This impressive and effective use of force inspired Escobar to form an organization, Medellín & Compañía, with two other powerful narco-traffickers who would consolidate Colombia's drug trade.

Escobar became one of the planet's wealthiest people. He became a Robin Hood character in his hometown of Medellín, spending more on public housing there than the government did and planting more than 50,000 trees in the city's slums. He had sixteen homes in Medellín alone, and his 7,000-acre country manor contained the country's finest zoo, with a kangaroo that could play soccer.

Escobar also became one of the planet's most powerful people and that power would soon be felt. The United States leaned heavily on Colombia to extradite Escobar, as it knew that *plato o plamo* would get Escobar out of any fix in Colombia. The decision to extradite Escobar would be handled by Colombia's supreme court. In November of 1985 the Palace of Justice in Bogotá, Colombia, was occupied by heavily armed guerrillas. In the chaos, eleven of the twenty-two judges on the Supreme Court were killed. All eleven of the dead judges had voted for extradition of Escobar.

When the judges reconvened they found something amiss with one of the signatures on the extradition treaty and declared it unconstitutional.

The White House was enraged, but no one in the Colombian government was willing to die to have Escobar extradited. In Colombia's presidential election of 1990 there was one extremely courageous candidate named Carlos Galán. He was the only candidate who openly supported extradition of drug lords to the United States and was far ahead in the polls. Galán was constantly under heavy protection and was wearing a bulletproof vest in August of 1989 when seven hit men drilled him.

This murder enraged the populace and emboldened the sitting president to establish extradition by decree. Although Escobar and his associates were abroad, the Colombian army impounded their mansions, ranches, and private islands and arrested 10,000 people suspected of working under the Medellín Cartel. The cartel issued a press release that read "Now the fight is with blood," and was signed "The Extraditables."[120]

The savagery that was about to befall Colombia has been compared to a World Trade Center bombing occurring every couple days for several weeks. In one day, nine banks were dynamited. In September, traffickers started picking off the wives of police and army officers when they were grocery shopping. The Bush administration sent down $65 million in military aid, including five hundred bulletproof vests. However, while they cheered from afar, they pulled all Americans out of the country except for in the heavily guarded American embassy. Bush addressed the United States on September 5, 1989. He promised to stand with the Colombian government and pledged $2 billion in aid to the Andean countries.

Of course, no anti-drug speech is complete without a little dishonesty so he proceeded to hold up a small plastic bag and said, "This is crack cocaine seized a few days ago by Drug Enforcement Agents in a park just across the street from the White House."[121] His point was to show that drugs were everywhere, however he did not reveal that DEA agents had actually lured a teenage dealer there and as the one special agent said, "it wasn't easy."[122]

In Colombia, bombs kept going off. In America the Secret Service extended protection to Bush's five grown children. Mónica de Greiff, Colombia's minister of justice, was in Washington at the time asking for aid. Her courage was inspiring considering her two predecessors had been murdered in daylight. She was a media star but then she received a phone call in which a voice gave a minute-by-minute description of her son's movements from the day before. She promptly resigned her post and requested asylum in the United States.

DeGreiff's resignation was a signal of Colombia's wilting resolve. A surviving presidential candidate who still had three bullets in his body from an earlier assassination attempt began openly calling for dialogue with the traffickers. The question hovered, "Why was Colombia paying such a horrible price because of America's lust for cocaine?" On the morning of December 6, a truck filled with a half-ton of dynamite went off in Colombia's capital, Bogotá. It blew the entire front wall from the secret police headquarters and destroyed two square miles of the city. Seven miles away the United States embassy's windows were shattered. Sixty people were killed and almost a thousand wounded. Bombs were going off in supermarkets, hotels, movie theaters, and even schools.

The cartel's stance softened slightly when one of Escobar's partners was shot down in a gun battle and the United States sent troops into Panama and seized its dictator, Manuel Noriega, for drug trafficking. In secret, the Extraditables began talks with the Colombian government. Colombian politicians who opposed the talks ceased to exist. The press was already scared into silence, except for Bogotá's *El Espectador*, and they had paid heavily, losing a publisher, several executives, and half a dozen reporters.

In September of 1990 the Colombian president offered the traffickers a deal. If they turned themselves in they would be tried in Colombia, not the United States. Although Washington was shocked and dismayed, Colombians danced in the streets.

Although his partners, the Ochoa brothers, took the deal promptly, Escobar held out for a better one. The concessions were apparent when the press saw his specially made "prison." His cell was a three-room suite. The compound had a soccer field, a disco, and a bar where at weekly parties the guards served drinks to hit men and prostitutes. America was enraged and the government was further embarrassed when it became apparent Escobar was still running the drug trade out of his prison.

The Colombian government's tolerance broke when Escobar brought some former employees to his prison to be tortured and murdered. The Colombian army moved to relocate Escobar but he was tipped off and fled. He stayed on the lam for another year and a half before he was finally gunned down on a rooftop during a shootout with police on December 3, 1993. The people of Colombia who were not on Escobar's payroll celebrated and Bush was euphoric. The head of the DEA proclaimed, "No matter how powerful they are . . . they are not immune."[123]

Although Escobar's videotaped death made a great television clip, like most drug war "victories" it was ridiculously and painfully futile. After thousands of deaths and billions of dollars were spent to break the Medellín Cartel, cocaine was cheaper and more available in America than before.[124] In addition, it is questionable how much of Escobar's downfall was due to the Colombian government and the DEA. Escobar's trail of terror had left him with scores of enemies, such as the powerful Cali Cartel that quickly replaced him.

Like his idol, Al Capone, Escobar became a global celebrity with his brazen and bloody exploits. However, just like Capone, he was not a clever drug dealer. Clever drug dealers avoid headlines, they do not make them. The best ones are never heard of at all. If Escobar did not embarrass the Colombian government with his ostentatious "prison," he might be free now, like the Ochoa brothers who only served five years.

C. A Boxed Head and a Cardinal Dead: Mexico[125]

After the decade-long battle with the Medellín Cartel, Colombians no longer had the desire to continue to fight despite the verbal and financial exhortations from the United States. And cartels are not reserved to Colombia. When Bush shut down massive importation into Florida by the Colombians, the cocaine flow switched to the Mexican border and gave rise to Mexican cartels. Like Cali, the Mexican traffickers under the leadership of the "Godfather" Miguel Ángel Félix Gallardo knew to lay low; however the top popped on May 24, 1993.

That day a cardinal arrived as an ambassador of the Pope to soothe relations with President Carlos Salinas. After His Eminence entered a car at the airport, a young man blew him away with fourteen bullets. Other gunmen lit up the area, killing the cardinal's driver and five other bystanders, including an elderly woman and her nephew.

The gunmen proceeded into the terminal flashing police badges and boarded an airplane headed for Tijuana that was supposed to have left twenty minutes earlier. Not only did the plane patiently wait for the gunmen but upon arrival in

Tijuana, Mexican police gave them an escort to the American border, where they disappeared.

This stunning hit focused the world's attention on Mexico and was likely a colossal error. The cardinal was supposed to arrive at the airport at the same time as a head of the Sinaloa Cartel. It appears the rival Tijuana Cartel mistakenly hit the cardinal, who was riding in a Mercury Grand Marquis, a popular car with drug lords.[126]

The Mexican government was negotiating the North American Free Trade Agreement and to repair its reputation it desperately tried to arrest the Arellano Félix brothers of the Tijuana cartel. Just like Escobar, the Arellano Félix brothers refused to hide and would be seen out dining and shopping. This embarrassment led Mexico City to send an elite federal squad led by the incorruptible commander Alejandro Castañeda.

In March of 1994 the commander ordered a suspicious Chevy Suburban to the side of a busy road in Tijuana. The windows of the Suburban exploded as gunmen inside blasted away at the commander's entourage. Amazingly, Castañeda escaped harm and after his men won the gun battle, he found that they had apprehended Javier Arellano Félix. Another carload of law enforcement soon arrived. They were local state police, but instead of assisting Castañeda's men they shot Castañeda in the back with an AK-47, drove off his federal troops and took Arellano Félix back into hiding.

Several weeks later a presidential candidate, Luis Donald Colosio, was assassinated at a political rally. His death was followed by the deaths of a slew of top lawmen and prosecutors put on the case. One newly installed leader of the federal police found that most of his force did not even pick up their paychecks. Their official income was so negligible compared to the bribes they collected that it was not worth the effort. For these sorts of revelations the new leader was soon poisoned in his sleep. The poison did not kill him but left him totally paralyzed.

By the mid-1990s, Mexico was Colombia North. The violence between the Tijuana and Sinaloa cartels was evidence that the "Godfather," Félix Gallardo, had lost his control of the Mexican drug traffic. (Tijuana was run by his nephews, while Sinaloa was run by his former lieutenants.) Another cartel—the Gulf Cartel—would also grow powerful under the protection of President Carlos Salinas' brother, Raul. After leaving office in 1994 Carlos Salinas fled to Ireland to avoid questioning about how that cartel had gone relatively untouched.

Succeeding Mexican presidents fought the drug war tepidly. As Mexico's foreign minister from 2000–2003 admitted in a more candid moment, "It is said that each administration in Mexico . . . will pick and choose which cartel to go after, to sort of offer them up as a sacrificial lamb to the Americans and, in a way, at least tolerate the other cartels that they don't go after."[127]

This middle course is understandable as it allowed Mexico to continue to receive American aid while avoiding turning the country into the bloody battleground seen during Colombia's all-out drug war in the 1980s. However, President Felipe Calderón scorned this path when he was elected in 2006. Just ten days after taking office in December he sent over 4,000 army soldiers into the state of Michoacán to combat La Familia cartel.

La Familia had made international news in September when it seized five men from a mechanic's shop and killed them by hacking off their heads with bowie knives. Beheadings are common in Mexican drug violence, but these perpetrators proceeded to a crowded nightclub where they got everyone's attention by waving machine guns and then tossed the five bloody heads onto the middle of the dance floor.[128]

La Familia had been aligned with the Gulf Cartel. Since the 2003 arrest of the Gulf Cartel's leader, Osiel Cárdenas Guillén, La Familia had been trying to establish itself independently. This would be prophetic for Calderón's blitzkrieg. He would successfully capture cartel leaders but these victories would create power vacuums smaller groups would violently fight to fill. The result has been an explosion in drug-related deaths. Under six years of President Vicente Fox (2000–2006) there were roughly 23,000 drug-related homicides. Under Calderón (2006–2012) there were almost 50,000 in his first five years.[129]

Although receiving financial support and backing from the United States, Mexicans may be tiring of the carnage of the all-out drug war, just like the Colombians did in 1990. A 2010 poll found only twenty-one percent of Mexicans felt Calderón's crusade had made the country safer and half felt it had heightened danger.[130] Calderón may be tiring as well. In August of 2009 Calderón's administration decriminalized the possession of small amounts of drugs in Mexico and he called for an international debate on the merits of complete legalization.

X
The Land of the Free Pisses on Other Countries

The world's illegal cocaine market has matured, just as the domestic crack market has. Territories have been divvied and underground operations have been refined. The market is still brutally violent, but the carnage of the 1980s has subsided. Although the "war" rhetoric continues from American politicians and bureaucrats sitting safely on high, wise law enforcement in America's inner-city trenches and governments abroad, whose entire countries are potential battlegrounds, know that a real war is not worth the casualties.[131]

The result is a political folly that allows America's drug bureaucracies to receive their money,[132] and allows worried mothers across America to be told the evil of drugs is being fought to the hilt. In Colombia the result is Plan Colombia. Started by President Bill Clinton, Plan Colombia is a billion-dollar program with three prongs. The first is that America gives money, weapons, and training to the Colombian army to fight narco-trafficking. However, the army is primarily used against the country's leftist rebels and is complicit in horrific human rights violations. The army aids right-wing paramilitaries that slaughter, rape, and mutilate villagers accused of leftist sympathies.[133] As of 2003 the country's main paramilitary, which frequently fought alongside the army, controlled about forty percent of Colombia's drug trafficking.[134] Since 2003 figures are difficult to come by, as paramilitaries have been officially disbanded; however, they continue to operate.[135]

Another prong of Plan Colombia is that millions of tax dollars go into spraying rural peasants' coca fields. This spraying, like the use of Agent Orange in Vietnam, is indiscriminate. Although the planes target coca, the air-dropped chemicals kill all plant life. Despite what the U.S. State Department has asserted,[136] this spraying has not been effective in lowering coca production.[137] Like marijuana, coca is a hardy plant. It is a perennial shrub that can grow on steep slopes and infertile acidic soils that cannot support other crops.

Spraying also infuriates the peasants. It kills their sustenance crops and may cause long-term damage to their health and environment. This spraying has been a recruiting boon to the country's leftist rebels who control areas of Colombia as large as Switzerland and continue Colombia's civil war. In fact, it is likely the rebels would have been rendered impotent years ago without Plan Colombia hectoring the rural population.[138]

The third prong of Plan Colombia has American money subsidizing peasants who grow alternatives to coca. This is exorbitantly expensive and still comically insufficient as coca growing can be four to ten times as profitable as other crops.[139] Like their government, which takes America's money and uses it to fight rebels, peasants take America's money and continue to grow coca.

America's international meddling goes beyond fighting narco-trafficking. Drug criminalization is a fragile proposition that does not hold up to informed criticism. It is therefore necessary to silence critics completely and that is what federal bureaucrats have done.

Since the First Amendment does not apply to foreigners, American bureaucrats can freely bully foreigners for merely thinking differently. United States ambassadors in Latin America have repeatedly demanded the dismissal of officials who oppose the war on drugs. Their ability to get foreign officers and politicians dismissed is openly acknowledged by foreign presidents.[140]

America's power in this area stems from its immense wealth. It can deny financial aid to impoverished countries, and for more economically sound countries there is the threat of economic sanctions, such as prohibitive tariffs on exports to the United States. (Tariffs hurt American consumers and honest businesses abroad.) Since the mid-1980s each drug-producing country is reviewed annually for certification based on its participation in the war on drugs. If it is not compliant, the above sanctions are taken. When a special commission in Jamaica considered decriminalizing marijuana in 2001, a spokesman from the United States' Jamaican embassy threatened to take any decriminalization into consideration when deciding whether Jamaica received certification.[141]

This micro-management was audacious considering some American states have decriminalized marijuana. Would our federal government have the gall to impose economic sanctions on California for its legalization of medical marijuana? Is it the United States' business to be threatening economic sanctions because Jamaicans want to smoke marijuana *in their own country*?

Much of the coercion is done secretly to give the appearance that the world wholeheartedly supports America's war on drugs. For example, at the end of April

2006 the Mexican legislature passed a bill decriminalizing possession of small amounts of any drug. Mexican president Vicente Fox had submitted it to allow Mexico's overwhelmed police to focus on drug traffickers. Fox was set to sign the bill when American drug authorities became involved. One of the few American papers to give coverage was the *New York Times*, which briefly reported: "Officials from the State Department and the White House's drug control office met with the Mexican ambassador in Washington Monday and expressed grave reservations about the law, saying it would draw tourists to Mexico who want to take drugs and would lead to more consumption..."[142]

It is unknown what threats or concessions were made but two days later Fox made the legislature change *his* bill so that it was "absolutely clear" that drug possession and consumption continue to be crimes in Mexico.[143] (Mexico successfully decriminalized drug possession in 2009.)

Since September 11, 2001, a popular question asked by Americans is "Why do they hate us?" United States' politicians claim foreigners hate America because they are jealous of our freedom, but perhaps they hate America because it denies them their freedom.[144]

XI
The War Continues
Stay The Stupid Course

The war has continued on all fronts. Plan Colombia is still in effect. In the United States over 850,000 people were arrested for marijuana offenses in 2010.[145] Fourteen thousand people a year die from overdosing on illegal drugs.[146] America leads the world in the percentage of its population it locks up,[147] largely due to its ardent drug prosecution.

The popular artists who are often in the vanguard of eroding taboos still portray drugs, outside of marijuana, as evil. Just as almost all movies and books used to portray people having premarital sex as bad people doomed to destruction, the same is still true of "hard" drugs. Even the few movies that show hard drug users in a nonjudgmental manner still have them die.

RADICAL NUTBALLS?

Supporters of Drug Decriminalization

Note: Decriminalization is not necessarily legalization. It includes measures such as making personal possession a minor crime, for example punishable by a fine, and authorizing medical use.

Countries—Argentina,* Belgium,[150] Brazil,[151]* Canada,[152] Colombia,* Ecuador,* Italy,* Luxembourg, Mexico,* Netherlands, Peru,* Portugal,* Spain,* Switzerland,[153] Uruguay* (*Have decriminalized the possession of small amounts of *any* drug for personal use.)

Economists—In 2005 the economist Jeffrey Miron sent an open letter to the President and Congress advocating marijuana legalization. It was signed by over five hundred economists. One of the three Nobel Laureates who signed was Milton Friedman, arguably the most influential economist of the twentieth century.[154]

Journalists—Abigail van Buren (Dear Abby),[155] Walter Cronkite,[156] Christopher Hitchens,[157] John Stossel, Jacob Sullum

Law Enforcement—Raymond Kendall (former head of Interpol), Joseph McNamara (former chief of police in Kansas City, Missouri, and San Jose, California), Law Enforcement Against Prohibition (LEAP has over 5,000 law enforcement members),[158] Norm Stamper (former chief of police in Seattle, Washington)

Political Commentators—Glenn Beck,[159] Neal Boortz, William F. Buckley, Eleanor Clift, Larry Elder, Glenn Greenwald, Arianna Huffington, Bill Maher, Clarence Page, Pat Robertson, Andrew Sullivan

Politicians—Mayor Kurt Schmoke (Baltimore, 1987–1999), Governor Gary Johnson (New Mexico, 1995–2003), Governor Jesse Ventura (Minnesota, 1999–2003), President Jimmy Carter, President Bill Clinton[160]

Publications—*The Economist* (arguably the most prestigious news magazine in the world),[161] *Mother Jones*,[162] *National Review*,[163] *The Observer* (world's oldest Sunday newspaper),[164] *Reason* magazine

States[165] (D–decriminalized small amounts of marijuana, M–allows medical marijuana)— Alaska[D,M], California[D,M], Colorado[D,M], Connecticut[D,M], District of Columbia[M], Hawaii[M], Maine[D,M], Maryland[M], Massachusetts[D], Michigan[M], Minnesota[D], Mississippi[D], Nebraska[D], Nevada[D,M], New Jersey[M], Montana[M], New Mexico[M], New York[D], North Carolina[D], Ohio[D], Oregon[D,M], Rhode Island[M], Vermont[M], Washington[M]

Perhaps because the popular media have been such lackeys regarding hard drugs, the government has decided to focus its billion-dollar propaganda on marijuana.[148] In recent years the following messages have been dramatically displayed in government television advertisements. According to this propaganda, marijuana will cause you to:

> drive over little girls riding bikes
>
> shoot your friend in the face with a handgun
>
> let little girls drown in pools
>
> forget to pick up your little brother from daycare
>
> spend your entire life sitting on a couch
>
> not bother to walk your dog
>
> lose your girlfriend/boyfriend to a space alien

These advertisements are so idiotic that it is debatable whether their real target is kids, who can easily see through this crap, or the clueless parents who want their money to go toward the bureaucratic clowns that make these ads.

The deceitful government anti-drugs campaign has a target penetration that Fortune 500 companies dream about. In 2003 the campaign's broadcast, print, and Internet ads reached about ninety percent of all teens at least four times per week.[149] This campaign does not even begin to address the ubiquitous propaganda that is now self-propagating after almost a century of government-sponsored disinformation.

This "drugs are bad" mantra is spewed in school curricula and also pitched in "public service" announcements made by companies, community service groups, and celebrities seeking goodwill. A piquant example of this infiltration was when I used a urinal at a district court house in Pennsylvania in 2005 and looked down to discover the rubber splash-guard I was peeing on read "don't do drugs."

Despite all of this blather, the drug taboo appears to be weakening. The Internet is allowing more people access to the truth. And just as people's real-life experiences with alcohol before prohibition made it difficult to sustain the myth of its peril, the same is now occurring with marijuana. Enough of the population has smoked marijuana themselves, or knows people who smoke marijuana, to realize how comical its demonization is. Despite the federal government's attempts to force the states into submission, marijuana legalization referendums are inching their way toward success in multiple states.

This trend should continue as the pre-baby-boomers are replaced by generations that have used marijuana. Current senior citizens came of age before its widespread use in the 1960s and therefore have little firsthand knowledge. They were also subject to the most blatantly alarmist propaganda and therefore only know of the drug as something used by Commie-loving hippies.

Unfortunately, the growing perspective on marijuana has not been reflected in so-called "hard" drugs. However, even with the taboo's current chokehold on hard drugs, the truth is starting to trickle through. Respected economists and other commentators that would never advocate trying an illegal drug are supporting decriminalization and taking a public health approach.

Unlike the assault on the sexual taboo, which was led by artists and the young, it appears that the assault on this taboo may be led by fiscal conservatives and libertarians. If money stops flowing into the government's anti-drug machine, which out-advertises every argument with poppycock and locks up every drug user that dares show her face, perhaps journalists and other media will start portraying every drug in an honest manner.

> The prestige of government has undoubtedly been lowered considerably by the Prohibition laws. For nothing is more destructive of respect for the government and the law of the land than passing laws which cannot be enforced. It is an open secret that the dangerous increase of crime in this country is closely connected with this.
>
> —Albert Einstein[166]

NOTES

1. Ronald Siegel, *Intoxication* (2005), pp. 10, 42–44, 50–51, 61–64, 152, 154.
2. Ibid., p. 104, and Wairagala Wakabi, "'Drunk and Disorderly' Chimps Attacking Ugandan Children," *East African*, 9 Feb. 2004.
3. Despite four to five holly berries making a full meal, a single robin will eat as many as thirty. Siegel, *Intoxication*, pp. 56–59.
4. Wild boars dig up and eat iboga roots, which causes them to jump wildly and go into fits. This is thought to have led people to this African drug. Paul Gahlinger, *Illegal Drugs* (2001), p. 301.
5. Siegel, *Intoxication*, pp. 38, 168.
6. Gahlinger, *Illegal Drugs*, p. 6.
7. Antonio Escohotado, *Brief History of Drugs* (1999), p. 6.
8. Gahlinger, *Illegal Drugs*, p. 20.
9. Section on Greeks and Romans from David Hillman's *The Chemical Muse: Drug Use and the Roots of Western Civilization* (2008).
10. Ibid., p. 87.
11. Ibid., p. 221.
12. Other less popular modes of ingestion were suppositories (anal and vaginal), snorting, and smoking. Although they did not have cigarettes or pipes they would smoke by fumigation, for example, the ancient Scythians would throw marijuana onto hot rocks to enjoy its effects.
13. Jennifer Hecht, *Happiness Myth* (2007), pp. 80–81.
14. *Declaration of Independence* (1776).
15. Gahlinger, *Illegal Drugs*, p. 33.
16. Richard Davenport-Hines, *Pursuit of Oblivion* (2002), p. 52.
17. Siegel, *Intoxication*, p. 255.
18. Ryan Grim, *This is Your Country on Drugs* (2009), p. 19
19. Commercial cigarettes now contain .5–2 percent nicotine. Gahlinger, *Illegal Drugs*, p. 192.
20. Paragraph from Siegel, *Intoxication*, pp. 254–255.
21. Paragraph from James Morone, *Hellfire Nation* (2003), pp. 283–284.
22. "When you and your family arrive, spend the money on food for a big celebration. Buy cattle, sheep, goats, wine, beer, and if there are any other kinds of food that you want, buy those too." Deuteronomy 14:26 (CEV).
23. Jesus turned water into wine for a wedding celebration, advised his disciples to drink wine in remembrance of him, was criticized as a "winebibber," and one disciple explicitly described him drinking wine. John 2:7–10, Mark 14:22–24, Matthew 11:19, and John 19:28–30.
24. Jim West, "A Sober Assessment of Reformational Drinking," *Modern Reformation Magazine*, Mar./Apr. 2000, vol. 9.2.
25. John Barleycorn was slang for beer and whisky.
26. Morone, *Hellfire Nation*, p. 285.
27. Nativists wish to protect their culture from immigrants.
28. Morone, *Hellfire Nation*, p. 285.
29. Ibid., p. 312.
30. Ibid., p. 299.
31. Ibid., p. 325.
32. Ibid.
33. Robert MacCoun and Peter Reuter, *Drug War Heresies* (2001), pp. 160–161.
34. The drinking decrease due to prohibition is debated. Some experts claim its effects were negligible. Ibid., p. 161.
35. Ibid., p. 157.
36. Richard Davenport-Hines, *Pursuit of Oblivion* (2002), p. 239.
37. Morone, *Hellfire Nation*, p. 327.
38. Remus was purportedly the basis of F. Scott Fitzgerald's character, Jay Gatsby, in *The Great Gatsby* (1925).

39. Mike Gray, *Drug Crazy* (1998), p. 18.
40. Sect. from ibid., pp. 20, 64–67.
41. MacCoun, *Drug War Heresies*, p. 160.
42. Morone, *Hellfire Nation*, p. 326.
43. Sect. largely from ibid., pp. 328–331.
44. In 2005, one of my clients pleaded not guilty to drug distribution, had a jury trial, lost, and was sentenced to state prison for at least two years. The assistant district attorney who prosecuted the case admitted that if he had pleaded guilty, he would have likely received probation.
45. MacCoun, *Drug War Heresies*, p. 160.
46. Sect. from Gray, *Drug Crazy*, pp. 67–68.
47. Morone, *Hellfire Nation*, p. 326.
48. Adjusted to 2005 values.
49. Gray, *Drug Crazy*, p. 69.
50. Ibid., p. 70, and Morone, *Hellfire Nation*, pp. 327–328.
51. Gray, *Drug Crazy*, p. 68.
52. This is likely the origin of the phrase "to drink yourself blind," and explains the many blind blues singers. Nick Davies, "Make Heroin Legal," Guardian.co.uk, 14 June 2001.
53. Antonio Escohotado, *Brief History of Drugs* (1999), p. 82.
54. These deaths are ignored by those who claim Prohibition was a success because it lowered cirrhosis rates. Jacob Sullum, *Saying Yes* (2003), p. 83.
55. Davies, "Make Heroin Legal."
56. MacCoun, *Drug War Heresies*, p. 166.
57. Sect. largely from Gray, *Drug Crazy*, pp. 40–52.
58. In the 1920s, "wowsers" referred to meddling reformers.
59. Frank Dikötter, Lars Laaman, and Zhou Xun, *Narcotic Culture* (2004), pp. 107–117.
60. An opiate authority at the time was Dr. Charles Terry. Unlike Wright, he actually conducted a study. He wrote, "…a very large proportion of the users of opiate drugs were respectable hardworking individuals in all walks of life, and…only about eighteen percent could in any way be considered as belonging to the underworld." Gray, *Drug Crazy*, p. 53.
61. Ibid., p. 43.
62. Ibid., pp. 43–44.
63. Ibid., p. 44.
64. Ibid., p. 45.
65. Ibid.
66. Gray, *Drug Crazy*, p. 43.
67. In its defense, it believed opium addiction was easily cured. However, it based this on the "research" of an uneducated insurance salesman whose "cure" was merely a strong laxative.
68. Gray, *Drug Crazy*, p. 52.
69. Anslinger info largely from ibid., pp. 72–91.
70. Ibid., p. 75.
71. Richard Davenport-Hines, *Pursuit of Oblivion* (2002), pp. 239, 346.
72. Ibid., p. 240.
73. Jacob Sullum, *Saying Yes* (2003), p. 140.
74. Ibid., p. 202.
75. This paragraph from ibid.
76. Gray, *Drug Crazy*, p. 79.
77. The AMA was only told about the bill and its hearing two days prior, despite the bill being prepared for two years. Peter McWilliams, *Ain't Nobody's Business If You Do* (1996), p. 286.
78. Although these representatives could have been asinine, they were perhaps merely bitter. The committee was filled with New Deal Democrats who despised the AMA for fighting them over Social Security and health care issues. In addition, the committee chairperson was a key DuPont Corporation supporter and DuPont stood to profit immensely from the criminalization of marijuana. Gray, *Drug Crazy*, p. 80, and ibid.
79. Gray, *Drug Crazy*, p. 80.

80. Ibid., p. 81.
81. Davenport-Hines, *Pursuit of Oblivion*, p. 348.
82. McWilliams, *Ain't Nobody's Business*, pp. 286–287.
83. Gray, *Drug Crazy*, pp. 81–82.
84. Ibid., p. 81.
85. Sullum, *Saying Yes*, p. 204.
86. James Morone, *Hellfire Nation* (2003), pp. 359–361.
87. Gray, *Drug Crazy*, p. 81.
88. Ibid., p. 84.
89. McWilliams, *Ain't Nobody's Business*, p. 287.
90. Gray, *Drug Crazy*, pp. 83–84.
91. McWilliams, *Ain't Nobody's Business*, p. 287.
92. Paul Gahlinger, *Illegal Drugs* (2001), p. 61.
93. "No government ever voluntarily reduces itself in size. Government programs once launched, never disappear. Actually, a government bureau is the nearest thing to eternal life we'll ever see on this earth!" McWilliams, *Ain't Nobody's Business*, p. 151.
94. Paragraph from Gahlinger, *Illegal Drugs*, pp. 50, 51, 63.
95. Richard Davenport-Hines, *Pursuit of Oblivion* (2002), p. 333.
96. In a 2005 drug trial of mine, the district attorney struck a woman from the jury pool who supported marijuana legalization. Afterwards a police officer poked fun of her by mimicking the stoned hippie voice popularized by Cheech and Chong in the 1970s, "Yeeeah, dude. Let's legalize pot, man."
97. A syndicated series of newspaper articles in 1967 falsely linked LSD to cancer and birth defects. Another popular myth was that LSD caused kids to stare at the sun until they went blind. Davenport-Hines, *Pursuit of Oblivion*, pp. 333–334.
98. Gahlinger, *Illegal Drugs*, p. 63.
99. Gray, *Drug Crazy*, p. 94.
100. According to his Chief of Staff, Nixon said in 1969, "You have to face the fact that the whole problem is really the blacks. The key is to devise a system that recognizes this all while not appearing to." Dan Baum, *Smoke and Mirrors* (1996), p. 13.
101. Ibid., p. 21.
102. Nixon later had the numbers cut so he could say he was fixing the "crisis" in his campaign. *Agency of Fear* (1977), pp. 174–177.
103. Ibid., p. 140.
104. Gray, *Drug Crazy*, p. 96.
105. Nixon's close friend, the evangelist Billy Graham, blamed "all those sleeping pills" for his downfall. Davenport-Hines, *Pursuit of Oblivion*, pp. 420–421.
106. Sect. from Gray, *Drug Crazy*, pp. 98–100.
107. After anthropologist Margaret Mead testified before Congress for marijuana legalization in 1969 she was mocked in national cartoons and a mother wrote that she was a "dirty louse" and a "crazy . . . dope fiend" who deserved punishment. "Margaret Mead as a Cultural Commentator," 15 Feb. 2006, ret. loc.gov, 28 May 2007.
108. Baum, *Smoke and Mirrors*, p. 166.
109. Leon Felkins, "Position Paper of Forfeiture Endangers American Rights Foundation," 27 Mar. 2002, ret. FEAR.org, 11 Nov. 2006.
110. Stories from London's *Q* magazine, Feb. 2001, pp. 53–56, 60.
111. A study of New York City homicides in 1988 found that eighty-five percent of crack-related murders stemmed from black-market disputes, another seven percent came from crimes committed to support a crack habit. Only one homicide out of 118 involved a perpetrator who was high on crack. Jacob Sullum, *Saying Yes* (2003), p. 195.
112. James Morone, *Hellfire Nation* (2003), p. 467.
113. Gray, *Drug Crazy*, pp. 100–110.
114. Gahlinger, *Illegal Drugs*, p. 66.
115. Ibid., p. 66.
116. Morone, *Hellfire Nation*, p. 467.

117. Gray, *Drug Crazy*, p. 116.
118. Ibid., pp. 116–117.
119. Sect. largely from ibid., pp. 119–131.
120. Ibid., p. 123.
121. Gray, *Drug Crazy*, p. 124.
122. When the undercover agent first made the request for that location the suspect said, "Where the [expletive] is the White House?" Michael Isikoff, "Drug Buy Set Up for Bush Speech," *Washington Post*, 22 Sep. 1989.
123. Gray, *Drug Crazy*, p. 124.
124. In 1980, thirty percent of high school seniors said cocaine was available. In 1995, forty-six percent did. In 1995 cocaine cost less than a third of what it had 1981. Robert MacCoun and Peter Reuter, *Drug War Heresies* (2001), pp. 31–32.
125. Sect. largely from Gray, *Drug Crazy*, pp. 133–143.
126. The fight between the two cartels began when a Tijuana mole installed within the Sinaloa Cartel ran off to San Francisco with the wife and two children of Sinaloa's leader. There the mole had her withdraw $7 million from the bank before removing her head and mailing it back to her husband. The mole then took the kids to Venezuela and threw them off a bridge. The Tijuana Cartel knew revenge was imminent so it launched a preemptive strike.
127. Ted Carpenter, *Bad Neighbor Policy* (2003), pp. 189–190.
128. James McKinley, "With Beheadings and Attacks, Drug Gangs Terrorize Mexico," *New York Times*, 26 Oct. 2006.
129. "Drug Violence in Mexico," Trans-Border Institute, U. of San Diego, Mar. 2012.
130. "Turning to the Gringos for Help," *Economist*, 27 Mar. 2010.
131. For the attitude in Chicago see Gray, *Drug Crazy*, pp. 11–13.
132. Before September 11, 2001, the drug war was viewed by the U.S. security bureaucracy as the cash cow that could replace the cold war. Ted Carpenter, *Bad Neighbor Policy* (2003), pp. 42–49.
133. One example was the 1997 Mapiripán massacre, in which over fifty villagers were tortured for days, hacked to pieces with machetes, and then tossed in a river. Some were decapitated with chainsaws. Roxanna Altholz, "Human Rights Atrocities Still Go Unpunished in Colombia," AlterNet.org, 28 Jan. 2008; and Jo-Marie Burt, "Massacre at Mapiripán," ColombiaJournal.org, 3 Apr. 2000.
134. Scott Wilson, "Colombian Fighters' Drug Trade is Detailed," *Washington Post*, 26 June 2003.
135. "Paramilitaries' Heirs," Human Rights Watch, 3 Feb 2010, ret. HRW.org, 1 Oct. 2010.
136. From the mid-1980s to the mid-1990s coca acreage in Peru rose steadily according to the UN, the Peruvian Ministry of Agriculture, and a respected American consulting firm. The State Department claims acreage is flat or declining. Carpenter, *Bad Neighbor Policy*, p. 97.
137. Perhaps most telling, U.S. street prices for cocaine have been unaffected. Ibid., pp. 76–78.
138. Ibid., pp. 61, 70.
139. Ibid., p. 107.
140. Ibid., pp. 142–143.
141. Ibid., p. 150.
142. James McKinley, Jr., "Under U.S. Pressure, Mexico President Seeks Review of Drug Law," *New York Times*, 4 May 2006.
143. Ibid.
144. "They hate our freedoms . . ." George W. Bush, "Address to a Joint Session of Congress," 20 Sep. 2001, ret. whitehouse.gov, 31 Mar. 2007.
145. "Marijuana Prosecutions for 2010 Near Record High," NORML.org, 19 Sep. 2011, ret. 20 Apr. 2012.
146. Robert MacCoun and Peter Reuter, *Drug War Heresies* (2001), p. 125.
147. Roy Walmsley, "World Prison Population List," (8th Ed.), International Centre for Prison Studies (UK), 2009.
148. From 1998–2006 the government appropriated nearly $1.5 billion to the Drug-Free Media Campaign. Mark Eddy, "War on Drugs," Congressional Research Service, 3 July 2006, p. 3.
149. Ibid., p. 1.
150. Belgium, Luxembourg, and the Netherlands have decriminalized marijuana. Eric Schlosser, "Up In Smoke," *New York Times*, 1 June 2003.
151. Andrew Downie, "Brazil's Drug Users Will Get Help, Instead of Jail," *Christian Science Monitor*, 4 Jan. 2002.
152. Canadian cafés where the open smoking of marijuana is tolerated by the authorities include the Hot Box

Café in Toronto and the Blunt Brothers/New Amsterdam Café in Vancouver.

153. Ian Sparks, "Swiss Cannabis Smokers . . . .", DailyMail.co.uk, 16 Nov. 2011.

154. "Milton Friedman, 500+ Economists Call for Marijuana Regulation Debate," ProhibitionCosts.org, ret. 10 July 2012.

155. Larry Elder, *Ten Things You Can't Say in America (2000)*, p. 260.

156. Cronkite was a spokesperson for the Drug Policy Alliance.

157. Christopher Hitchens, "Legalize It," *Foreign Policy*, May/June 2007.

158. "International Organization of Law Enforcement Denies UN Claims of Drug War Success," LEAP, 8 Aug. 2006, ret. LEAP.cc, 20 Feb. 2012.

159. Eve Conant, "Pot and the GOP, " *Newsweek*, 25 Oct. 2010.

160. Jann Wenner and Herb Ritts, "Bill Clinton," *Rolling Stone*, 28 Dec. 2000.

161. "Case for Legalisation," *Economist*, 28 July 2001, p. 11.

162. Monika Bauerlein and Clara Jeffery, "This is Your War on Drugs," MotherJones.com, July/Aug. 2009.

163. *McLaughlin Group* (TV), Oliver Productions, 26 June 2009.

164. "Time for Obama to Join the Debate Over the Failed War on Drugs," Guardian.co.uk, 7 Apr. 2012.

165. Largely from NORML.org, ret. 6 July 2012.

166. Albert Einstein, *World As I See It* (2006), p. 49.

DRUGS IV

REPERCUSSIONS
MAYBE WHEN IT'S
YOUR DAUGHTER
YOU'LL GIVE A SHIT

The most severe repercussions of the drug taboo are the by-products of its criminalization. It will be difficult to change the laws as long as the taboo prevents rational debate from receiving public exposure.

I
DO THE CRIME, DO THE TIME … BITCH!
THE LAND OF LIBERTY?

The United States of America prides itself on being *the* land of freedom. However, this is a questionable assertion considering that it incarcerates a higher percentage of its population than any other country in the world.

The land of the free houses over twenty percent of the world's prisoners despite having less than five percent of the world's population. It incarcerates a percentage of its citizens three times higher than the theocracy Iran, and four times higher than the Communist state China.[1] This is attributable to America's zealous drug war, with there being seven times more drug prisoners in 2000 than there were in 1980.[2] We are incarcerating more and more American drug users to "help them."

Politicians have gone to the "get tough on drugs" well so many times that the injustice now reaches absurdity. One example is Doug Gray. Gray had a wife, a son, and his own roofing business. He was a Vietnam veteran who lost his leg in the war and was a casual marijuana user. Gray was offered a pound of marijuana at a bargain price. Gray figured he could smoke it and sell the rest to his friends. The seller was paid by drug agents to make the offer and, due to mandatory sentencing, Gray is now serving a life sentence. The Alabama taxpayers will pay roughly $25,000 annually to house, feed, and medically treat Gray until his death.[3]

The situation is so unjust that numerous judges and even prosecutors have openly criticized mandatory minimum sentences.[4] In 1993, fifty senior federal judges refused to hear any more drug cases.[5] In addition, because of mandatory minimum sentences, violent offenders, such as murderers and rapists, are routinely released early to make room for people like Doug Gray.[6]

The drug war has so perverted the concept of freedom that it is questionable some even remember what it means. In response to a 2008 international study that found American drug use far ahead of countries that had decriminalized drugs, an Office of National Drug Control Policy official rationalized that Americans use more drugs because they live in a "highly free" society.[7]

FREEDOM ISN'T FREE
DRUG WAR AND U.S. PRISON POPULATION

YEAR	FEDERAL COST (BILLIONS)[34]	NUMBER INCARCERATED (MID-YEAR)[35]	PERCENTAGE OF U.S. POPULATION[36]	PERCENTAGE GROWTH OF PERCENTAGE OF U.S. POPULATION
1980	$1.5 (1981)	503,586	.22	
1985		744,208	.31	41

1990	$9.8	1,148,702	.46	48
1995	$13.3	1,585,586	.59	28
2000	$18.5	1,937,482	.69	17
2005	⊤ 37	2,186,230	.74	7

CALLING A SPADE A SPADE:
WHO IS RESPONSIBLE?

Drug Legalization Problems

1. A small minority of users become addicted. (Most of whom would have found a substance for escape under prohibition.)
2. A small minority of users act irresponsibly. (Most of whom would have found a substance to facilitate idiotic behavior under prohibition.)
3. Hundreds of annual overdose fatalities.

Drug Prohibition Problems

1. Law-abiding responsible people cannot enjoy drugs.
2. Casual drug users and functioning addicts (the vast majority of drug users) have their careers ruined by criminal records.
3. The lives of non-functioning addicts and their dependents are destroyed when they become full-time criminals to afford drugs worth more than gold.
4. The children of incarcerated drug dealers grow up without a parent.
5. Ten thousand foreign drug war fatalities annually in Mexico and other nations.
6. Thousands of annual overdose fatalities.
7. Property crimes of addicts.
8. Erosion of civil liberties.
9. Billions of dollars go to domestic gangs and international terrorist organizations instead of to tax-paying, job-creating, private-sector corporations.
10. Billions of tax dollars are spent on enforcement and incarceration bureaucracies.
11. No sales tax revenue from a massive industry.
12. Violence and weapons are a way of life for dealers of all ages.
13. Militarization of police.
14. Corruption of public officials.

II

WHAT CONSTITUTION?
CIVIL RIGHTS

Our criminal justice system had been developed over the centuries to balance the rights of the accused with the rights of the wronged. The system worked well when there were wronged parties to start the investigation process. This changed with the drug war.

Selling and using drugs are consensual activities. Just as with heresy before the Inquisition, there is not a wronged party to involve law enforcement. Under the prevailing rules prosecuting drug users was difficult.

The police, who before were restrained from participation in crime, provocation of crime, and snooping where nothing was amiss, had to be unshackled and unshackled they have become. As Judge James Gray, a Republican and former federal prosecutor, wrote in 2001, "Nothing in the history of the United States of America has eroded the protections of our Bill of Rights nearly as much as our government's War on Drugs."[8]

This has predominantly occurred in three areas—constitutional interpretation by the courts, the use of informants, and street justice.

A. Chip, Chip, Gone: Judicial Interpretation

The chipping away of our Bill of Rights is a slow but steady process. A few milestones were:

1971—Previously a search warrant could not be based solely on an anonymous tip. Anonymous tips allow anybody (including the police themselves) to easily set up anybody's property, such as a car or home, for a search. Since 1971 the courts have ruled an anonymous tip is sufficient.

1986—Previously police could not go onto private land to seek evidence without a warrant. In 1986 this was limited to land immediately surrounding a home.

1996—Previously police could not pull a car over for a minor traffic violation merely to search it for drugs. The Supreme Court decided these pretext stops are constitutional. A Pennsylvania officer admitted to me at a district courthouse in 2005 that with the countless automobile regulations, he could technically stop any car he wished on a minor violation, for example, an improperly illuminated license plate.

The Supreme Court has also allowed rights to be tossed aside by politicians. One of the most egregious has been forfeiture laws enacted by Congress in 1984.[9] This breathtakingly medieval concept clearly violates not only the Bill of Rights, but basic principles of fairness. It allows law enforcement to confiscate any property or money they believe to be tainted by drugs. This can be done on mere suspicion. The burden is then on the owner to institute expensive legal proceedings to prove the property is clean. Eighty percent of the people from whom assets are seized are never even charged with a crime.[10]

Even more comically unjust is the fact that the department confiscating the property is allowed to keep the proceeds. This creates a massive incentive to grab property—not big-time drug dealers. As one customs official admitted, "If the locals [police] have a guy with a ton of marijuana and no assets versus a guy with two joints and a Lear jet, I guarantee you they'll bust the guy with the Lear jet."[11]

In *Drug Warriors & Their Prey* Richard Miller documents the extensive abuse of these Neanderthal laws. A few examples are a forfeited family home where a kid hid his drug use from his parents, a forfeited family car when a son's *passenger* had drugs, whole apartment buildings forfeited because a tenant had drugs, taking thousands of dollars from people simply because having that much cash was suspicious, and a heinous case where a man was shot dead in a marijuana raid contrived in the hopes of forfeiting his ranch.[12]

The Supreme Court has done little to rein in forfeiture despite the fact that it was this very practice, along with wanton warrants, that helped launch the American Revolution.[13]

B. Snitch Justice

When someone is arrested on a drug-related offense, the police will often offer to make things "easy" for the defendant if she will set up someone else. The police use this technique to try to move up the chain and catch "bigger fish" in the

337

drug distribution hierarchy. However, most people are not naive enough to give up bigger fish because bigger fish tend to harshly punish the little fish for ratting them out. Instead they set up relatively harmless fellow users who only sell their stash to friends. In a scenario I've heard described by numerous defendants, a non-dealer will tell me how her friend, X, called her up begging for some of her stash five days in a row.[14] In this manner casual users rot in prison under harsh minimum mandatory sentences, while the authorities can claim they nabbed a "dealer."[15]

Our culture has so demonized drug users that entrapment may not even strike Americans as disturbing. However, what if a friend who knew you once cheated on your taxes called you up repeatedly with a great scheme on how to cheat on your taxes. If you then cheated, were caught, and learned your friend had set you up to save her own hide over an audit, would you consider this justice? Would you consider this an efficient use of police resources? It is this sort of police conduct—not protecting violent criminals—that makes "stop snitching" a popular theme in America's inner-cities.[16]

At the higher level of snitchery the stakes get bigger and the deception and manipulation get sleazier. Defendants facing exorbitant mandatory sentences are more willing to say anything and set anybody up in order to cut a deal for themselves. In addition, to sweeten the pot for witnesses who are not facing charges, the government resorts to paying them. In 1993, $97 million was spent on paying informants.[17] The informants are often worse criminals than the defendants they are testifying against. A former DEA agent has stated that federal agents have allowed "about 15,000 wild, out-of-control informants" to take control of investigations.[18]

Another unjust repercussion of this snitch culture is that the low-level people who do not have the wherewithal or connections to rat people out are hit with mandatory sentences while the higher-ups walk. For example, college student Kellie Ann Mann bought some LSD to mail to an ex-boyfriend of hers. She was sentenced to ten years despite having never been arrested and having no drug connections outside of the dealer she found at a Grateful Dead concert (likely the informant). Her ex-boyfriend set some people up and received less than three.[19]

C. But the Good Guys Play by the Rules: Please

Although there always have been and always will be a *small minority* of cops who abuse their power, the impossible mission of drug enforcement encourages abuse. For example, police officers are prevented by the Constitution from searching citizens willy-nilly. However, it is extremely difficult to pinpoint a drug transaction. All that is seen is money or a tiny package exchanging hands, often from a great distance.[20]

What frequently happens instead is police will see someone they suspect of dealing and will go up and pat her down and make her empty her pockets. (And no, they are not always gentle.)[21] This does not hold up in court so police will testify that the defendant agreed to be searched or that drugs were dropped.

This is known as "testilying" or "joining the liars' club" and is acknowledged off the record in larger jurisdictions.[22] As one Chicago sergeant said, "They lie, so we lie."[23] With an unbelievable number of drugs being dropped in front of police the judges are well aware of these fictions. One Chicago defense lawyer said, "Everybody in the building knows that the cop threw the guy up against the wall and found the shit in his pocket or his shoe."[24] In Chicago, as in many jurisdictions, perjury is considered a more severe crime than drug possession.

ROLLING BACK THE CLOCK TO 1250 A.D.
LIBERTY AND FIGHTING EVIL

DRUG WAR "TOOL"	INQUISITION EQUIVALENT
"Rubber stamping" of warrants based on anonymous tips, combined with knocking no longer being necessary in home raids.	No warrant necessary, although the Inquisition almost never pursued anonymous tips.[38]
Mandatory minimum sentences.	No mitigation allowed for age, sickness, or dependents.
Non-prosecution of police who kill or injure innocent civilians.	Suspects who died from torture were "killed by the devil."

Entrapment.	Entrapment.
RICO Conspiracy Laws, No-Fault Eviction Laws, Landlord Culpability Laws.	Merely associating with heretics is criminal.
Forfeiture laws that give property of suspects to police.	Inquisitors seized property of accused.
Informants receive money or a lighter sentence.	Informants received a portion of the accused's property.

III
It's Not My Rich White Ass
Classism & Racism

Although its current proponents are *not* generally racist or elitist, the war on drugs has racist roots and profoundly classist and racist effects.

First, poor people get shoddier legal representation than wealthy people. In addition, poor people often cannot afford to bail out so they have to await their day in court in prison. This process takes so long that they have often served enough time by the trial date to make innocence a moot point. However, these deficiencies of the criminal justice system are not unique to the drug war.

Because of the consensual nature of the "drug" offenses, drug enforcement is highly discretionary. Drug offenses are caught through proactive searches, pat-downs, sting operations, and informants. People who live in poorer areas tend to have less privacy and more exposure to police. For example, those living in a trailer park or urban subsidized housing ("projects") will have more police contact simply due to the population density, and also because there is frequently more crime to investigate in poorer areas. In addition, impoverished neighborhoods have more people subjected to the criminal justice system and therefore there are more people looking to set other people up to help themselves.

Some of the hardest-hit areas are poor black urban neighborhoods.[25] Unlike poor rural white areas that tend to be in the hinterlands, black urban neighborhoods are perfectly situated to distribute drugs to the wealthy commuters who work in the city and live in the suburbs. The financial enticement to black youth in the cities to participate in drug dealing is enormous.[26]

The reason more of America is not irate over the loss of civil liberties is that the war on drugs is not focused on suburbia. Most police know it is much easier to get away with illegal searches of the persons and property of poor groups who cannot afford lawyers. Poor people are also easier to convict. For these reasons, and others, suburban users of drugs are not targeted nearly as frequently.[27]

This racial divergence is seen in the statistics and even in the laws themselves. Despite the fact that blacks represent only fifteen percent of drug users they comprise seventy-four percent of those imprisoned for drug possession. Although youth of all races use and sell drugs at similar rates, minority youth represent sixty to seventy-five percent of the drug arrests.[28] The penalties for blue-collar crack sold on city streets are exponentially harsher than those for the powder cocaine sold in penthouses.

When Congress considered mandatory minimums for methamphetamine they excluded Ecstasy. One of the few elected officials willing to discuss drug decriminalization, former Baltimore Mayor Kurt Schmoke, explained: "Obviously, we know whom Ecstasy is going to hit. If we started putting mandatory minimum sentences on Ecstasy and the prisons started loading up with suburban Jane and John Doe's children, there might be a major change in drug policy."[29]

IV

FAT WHITE SENATORS DO NOT SCARE THEM
GENERATION G (FOR GANGSTER)

Politicians love to talk tough about the drug war. They beat their breasts and brag to nanny and pappy on the campaign trail that they are expanding mandatory minimum sentencing and pouring money into the war so little Suzie will never be able to get high. The same brazen pompousness is demonstrated by the law-and-order political pundits who blame the country's problems on "liberal" judges, even though the last four presidents have pushed "liberal" judges to near-extinction.[30]

As someone who has met some of the next generation of drug dealers, I can tell you they are not scared. The drug war has made drug dealers romantic heroes to many in the ghetto, just as prohibition did for gangsters in the 1920s.[31] The music of the ghetto, rap, has taken the ethos of the inner city worldwide and mainstream. And although it is not readily apparent to the outsider this culture is heavily influenced by the drug trade.[32]

Inner-city style is built for dealing. Hoodies and hats worn low prevent identification. Baggy clothes hide drugs and weapons. The involved handshakes can disguise hand-to-hand transfers. Hanging out on the corner masks working the corner. The strict use of nicknames, such as rapper's titles, can hide identities from outsiders, including the police. As a public defender, I was involved in several cases where the police were still looking for characters only known by nicknames like "Bugsy." When I taught in the inner city, some students were upset when I used full names when taking roll. They preferred that their surname, or in their words their "government," not be known by their peers.

These kids did not fear jail. Obscene mandatory minimum sentences have made jail a rite of passage for impoverished inner-city blacks.[33] One in three black men between the ages of twenty and twenty-nine are either on probation, on parole, or in prison.[34] A stint upstate is like going to college. They gain connections, learn from veterans how to hone their game, and by doing time they gain street credibility by proving they will not snitch. When I was teaching, the kids would know exactly when the county prison was on lockdown because so many of them had cell phones and incarcerated relatives.

These kids are not stupid. They learn about the drug world firsthand, not from the media and the government's propaganda. They know that crack and heroin users are not out-of-control demons their incarcerated relatives have pushed drugs on. They know that these users are usually functioning, often well-functioning, citizens who sought their drug-dealing relatives out.[35] They know the complexion of the buyers and they know the complexion of the prison population. They know how abusive and dishonest the police can be when fighting a frustrating and impossible battle.[36] And they definitely know that none of their jailed relatives were out in "white man's land" pushing dope on little Suzie in her playground.[37] (Only one percent of illegal drug users were introduced to drugs by a dealer.)[38]

Although the lack of opportunities for inner-city youth is highly publicized, I dare to suggest that many of these kids choose this life and it is not an irrational decision. It has been estimated that *street* dealers face a twenty-two percent chance of imprisonment in the course of a year of part-time selling, and that they could expect to spend a third of their selling career behind bars. However, broken down to single drug transactions the risk of imprisonment per cocaine sale is about one in 10,000.[39] On the other hand, dealing is an extremely lucrative and easy job with the adrenaline-popping risk and rebel cachet youth crave. Although the economics are different in the open-air drug markets (the streets' version of Wal-Mart),[40] for a smart and careful indoor dealer who runs a solo venture with a number of regular customers, a *relatively* safe and profitable living can be had.[41]

Growing up in a blue-collar town with a good school system in the 1980s and early 1990s, many of my peers followed their parents into factory jobs. Although some able kids furthered their education for higher-paying careers, many able kids did not. They liked their parents' lifestyle and chose to follow them.[42] If they were inner-city youth they probably would have entered the drug business for exactly the same reasons.

V

The Drug Didn't Do This To Little Suzie
The Government Did

A. Don't Put Me in Jail Because Prohibition Killed Suzie

What is particularly galling about the drug war is that it is defended on the basis of problems that *the war has caused*. The most poignant example of this is fatalities caused by illicit drug use. I have already covered how decriminalization could wipe out heroin overdoses, and cocaine deaths could be avoided as well.[43]

Cocaine deaths are extremely rare. Fatalities are frequently linked to respiratory failure, because the drug substantially increases the heart rate. In users with healthy hearts, death can still occur because, as with peanuts and Ecstasy, a

HIGHWAY SAFETY

Taking any drug, legal or illegal, involves risk, but these rules can minimize it greatly:

(1) Do Not Rush—Test that the drug is what it is supposed to be, its potency, and your individual reaction, by taking a little, for example half a pill. You can always take more, but you cannot go back and take less.

(2) Do Not Mix—Never mix drugs unless you know how they react, for example, heroin and alcohol can be deadly.

(3) Do Not Inject—Smoking can provide a similar effect and vaporizers are making it more efficient.

minuscule percentage of people are allergic to cocaine. This was the case of college basketball great Len Bias. His death in 1986 following his drafting by the professional basketball team the Boston Celtics was used to launch a media blitz against cocaine, and take the drug war "nuclear."[44] In the month following Bias' death the network stations aired seventy-four evening news segments about crack and cocaine.[45]

It is unlikely that any media outlets pointed out that Bias did not overdose, but had an allergic reaction. In addition, Bias was having his third convulsion before his friends sought medical attention. As countless others have done, they hesitated before seeking medical attention because they did not want Bias or themselves to be arrested.[46]

In the mid-1990s nearly twenty teenagers died of heroin-related overdoses in Plano, Texas. Friends of these kids were slow to act as well. When local authorities were asked why they did not announce that anybody reporting a drug overdose would not be prosecuted; their response was that this "would send the wrong message."[47] Since the death of Len Bias, states have passed Len Bias Laws that allow providers of a drug to be charged with homicide if the user dies from its use.[48]

B. Don't Put Me in Jail Because Prohibition Ruined Suzie's Life

Almost all drug addicts beat their addictions,[49] but criminal records are forever. Jack Cole worked twelve years as an undercover narcotics officer and intimately knew the people he sent to jail. In his words, his job was to *"do whatever was necessary to become people's best friend—their closest confidant—so I could betray them and send them to jail."*[50]

Cole was engaged in over a thousand arrests during that time period and believes he "ruined" the lives of a "huge" number of kids. In Cole's words most of these young offenders were nonviolent, casual users unlucky to cross paths with him. Convicted young adults may lose eligibility for government student loans and welfare benefits. Perhaps most burdensome, for the rest of their lives they will be marked as a drug user and a criminal in every job interview.

Working as a public defender, I regularly witnessed the shock of suburban parents whose kids were being prosecuted for drug offenses. "My daughter is not a criminal! If she has a criminal record it will ruin her future!" They were amazed that the district attorney had the nerve to prosecute their child. The hypocrisy on the drug issue is stunning. Everyone wants the government to get tough on drug users until it is their loved one. Then all of a sudden they see drug use as a medical issue.

The pinnacle of this hypocrisy was probably the performance of former United States representative from San Diego, California, Randy Cunningham. In 1994, he voted to retain the death penalty for drug traffickers. In 1996 Cunningham wrote an editorial on drug policy that criticized President Bill Clinton's "soft-on-crime liberal judges," opposed any reduction in mandatory minimum sentences, and pushed for "a real war on drugs."[51]

In 1997 his son, Todd Cunningham, was charged with smuggling four hundred pounds of marijuana from San Diego to Massachusetts. The federal mandatory minimum for this charge was five years. At sentencing Cunningham requested mercy from the judge. In tears he said of his son, "He has a good heart. He works hard."[52] The sentence was half the mandatory minimum. It would have likely been lighter, but Todd had tested positive for cocaine three times while out on bail. Meanwhile, Doug Gray sits in an Alabama prison for the rest of his life for buying a pound of marijuana pushed on him by the government.

As a public defender I noticed that although the drug war's caricature of the demonic drug user quickly evaporated for parents of kids prosecuted for drug offenses, parents of kids whose drug habits led them to commit other crimes still stuck with the drug war script. Their children, who had committed thefts and burglaries to support habits, were still not bad people. It was the drugs that were evil.

Never did they make the connection that if heroin prices were not inflated to thirty times the price of gold, Suzie would not have been reduced to stealing baby formula from Wal-Mart. If heroin was legal, Suzie would not be subject to the impurities of black market heroin, and instead of being a disgusting walking corpse Suzie would still be a beautiful, healthy, well-functioning woman.[53]

VI
My Government Has Fallen And Can't Get Up

A. Bush Got High. Why Can't I?: Hypocrisy

The hypocrisy of politicians on the drug issue is rampant. One only has to look at the last three presidential administrations. In 1992 President Bill Clinton told a young crowd that he tried to smoke marijuana but he did not inhale, then added with a smile that he wished he had.[54] His vice president, Al Gore, has admitted to smoking marijuana infrequently in college, while serving in Vietnam, and as a young reporter. However, a close friend of Gore from those days says that for periods of time he smoked every day with Gore and that Gore "loved it."[55]

President George W. Bush's brother, Florida Governor Jeb Bush, has admitted that he smoked marijuana in high school.[56] His other brother, Marvin Bush, has used illegal prescriptions to get narcotics. His daughters smoked marijuana at a Hollywood house party.[57]

Numerous people from W. Bush's earlier days allege that he used marijuana and cocaine in the past. For example, W. Bush's co-workers on a 1972 senatorial campaign in Alabama have said that he "liked to sneak out back for a joint of marijuana or into the bathroom for a line of cocaine."[58] His sister-in-law has alleged that W. Bush and one of his brothers used to snort cocaine at Camp David when H.W. Bush was president. Perhaps most telling is that W. Bush has never denied using drugs, instead saying things like "When I was young and irresponsible, I was young and irresponsible," and "If you're asking me if I've done drugs in the last seven years the answer is no."[59]

President Barack Obama has admitted to using cocaine and "frequently" smoking marijuana in his youth.[60] In his high school yearbook he thanked the "Choom Gang" for all the good times. (Chooming is Hawaiian slang for smoking marijuana.)[61]

The hypocrisy displayed by these politicians on the issue of marijuana is repulsive considering the DEA's continual prosecution of not only the Choom Gangs, but also of medical marijuana distributors obeying their state laws. As a senatorial candidate in 2004, Obama supported marijuana decriminalization, and as a presidential candidate insisted medical marijuana was best handled as a state and local issue.[62] Yet since becoming president he has overseen so many federal medical marijuana busts that he is on course to surpass W. Bush's record.[63]

During his March 2009 "virtual town meeting" Obama was forced to address the marijuana issue. Obama said with a smirk, "I don't know what this says about the online audience, but . . . this was a fairly popular question." The live audience laughed.[64] It is unknown how many of the 850,000 people arrested for marijuana infractions that year found it entertaining.[65]

B. Why They Hate Us: The DEA Pisses On the Whole World

The DEA and other federal drug toughs do not just run roughshod over the states. They run roughshod over the entire world. This is sorely evident in Latin America.

The United States has used the threat of withdrawn aid and financial sanctions to get Latin American government officials critical of the drug war canned.[66] It absurdly accused these officials of being in cahoots with the drug cartels.[67] (Legalization would put cartels out of business.) The DEA also runs raids in these countries with little respect for their respective governments,[68] and works with these countries' criminals.

In 1990 the DEA was impatient with the Mexican government's extradition of a

Mexican doctor suspected in the torture and murder of a DEA agent. The DEA paid a bounty to have the doctor kidnapped and brought to America. This egregious disregard of Mexican law ended with the doctor being acquitted by a federal judge because the case against him was so weak.[69]

The audacity of these actions is demonstrated when the roles are reversed. If the European Union used its political influence to defeat American politicians supporting the death penalty, would it not be considered meddling? If Saudi Arabia financed the fumigation of American farms that it believed were supplying barley and hops for beer being smuggled into its country, would that not be deemed ridiculous? If Iran offered a bounty for the kidnapping of an American suspected of murdering an Iranian, would Americans not be aghast?

The growing economic strength of Colombia, Mexico, and Brazil has weakened the United States' ability to intimidate Latin America into silence. The former presidents of these three countries are now leading the global push toward drug decriminalization, and they have been joined by the current presidents of Colombia and Guatemala, Juan Manuel Santos and Otto Perez Molina.[70]

C. Tax Addiction is a Moral Issue: Bloated Bureaucracy

A United States Representative described the federal drug war as "essentially a jobs program."[71] As a judge observed, if drugs were legalized the two hardest-hit groups, which would suffer almost equally, would be organized crime and law enforcement.[72]

However, law enforcement workers are not the only government employees to benefit from the drug war. *Every single* federal agency gets substantial extra funding to carry out the drug war.[73] This includes agencies such as the Department of Land Management and the Bureau of Indian Affairs. Congressmen have said off the record that all of our federal agencies are addicted to the War on Drugs funding and do not want to give up that money.[74] It is not surprising that in 2003 the federal government revamped the way it accounted for money spent on drug control to effectively hide over a third of drug spending that year and an unknown amount henceforth.[75]

In 1972, the director of President Richard Nixon's drug abuse commission observed that four years earlier, $66 million had been spent in the drug abuse area, that the budget was now approaching the one billion dollar mark, and when that point was reached, "we become, for want of a better term, a drug abuse industrial complex."[76] (In 2003 the federal drug budget was almost $20 billion.)

The strength of the industrial complex was evident in California's 1988 election. The correctional workers' association was the number-one donor to legislative races and provided the fiscal muscle for the passage of California's medieval three-strikes sentencing policy.[77]

D. Corruption Is a Third-World Thing: Wrong

Narco-dollars have so overwhelmed and infested the Latin American governments and their relatively minuscule budgets that it is questionable who is actually in charge. Drug corruption does not appear to have reached into the upper levels of the United States' government. However, one reason for this could be that the higher-ups in the federal hierarchy are unnecessary.

Between 1993 and 2000 the number of American law enforcement officers sentenced to federal prison increased 600 percent.[78] The corrupt have included notables such as DEA supervisor Rene de la Cova, who was famous for bringing Panamanian dictator Manuel Noriega into custody, and they have included large groups. In New Orleans, an FBI sting investigation led to roughly 200 police officers being fired for violence and theft of cocaine from drug dealers.[79]

In 1999, a LAPD officer confessed that he and fellow officers had been stealing drugs and money from drug dealers, using prostitutes to sell the drugs for them, planting evidence, and committing perjury repeatedly in court. Further testimony revealed that he and a fellow officer had shot and killed a suspected drug dealer for merely leaning into their undercover police car. At another time they shot an unarmed black man already in handcuffs who they suspected of drug dealing. To cover this up, they planted a sawed-off .22 rifle on him and testified the man had assaulted them. That man is wheelchair-bound for the rest of his life, and had already served three years of a twenty-three-year sentence when this testimony released him.[80] This type of police behavior should make the Los Angeles jury's decision to acquit O.J. Simpson of murder less puzzling to those living outside of the inner city.

The corrupt Americans who have been caught include officials of every sort—

judges, police commissioners, mayors, former Justice Department lawyers, FBI agents, border guards, military personnel, immigration inspectors, and criminal prosecutors.[81] This should not be surprising. The war on drugs has made the drug business arguably the most profitable venture in the world. A United States customs inspector can easily double his annual income of $45,000 by merely choosing to search truck A as opposed to truck B in the never-ending flow of trucks coming across the Mexican border. Two El Paso inspectors charged with assisting traffickers in 1995 had reportedly pocketed $1 million.[82]

In 1995 the DEA testified before Congress that Mexican drug cartels were corrupting American police agencies "on a systematic basis" with bribes of about a million dollars per week.[83] Tucson FBI Chief Steve McCraw said that the border corruption was so "pervasive . . . it's a national disgrace."[84]

Although corruption has not been discovered at senior levels that does not mean that it is not present. One hint is provided by the experience of Mike Horner, a United States Customs inspector.[85] He flagged a Mexican truck driver in the computer system as being suspected of drug trafficking. This driver was later stopped at the border and searched due to a fluke—and over a supervisor's objections—and was found with four tons of cocaine. When Horner checked the system he discovered that a number of his warnings had been erased.

When Horner later passed along a tip on a group of major traffickers out of Tijuana, the top man in his region asked for his informants. This was an odd and unnecessary request and Horner objected at first. Four days after Horner capitulated, one of his informants was found with a tire iron in one ear and out the other. The other informant was stabbed sixteen times. When Horner requested an internal investigation from the Treasury Department, the top man took an early retirement and the investigation was dropped.

Another hint is provided by CIA activities. After some brazen investigative journalism, government officials finally acknowledged there has been CIA involvement with rebel organizations active in drug trafficking.[86] This should not be surprising either, as drug profits have made drug kingpins some of the most powerful people in the third world.

Where the lines are drawn in this involvement may never be known. In the murky and off-the-record world of international power-brokering the words "national security" can stop any investigation cold. Decorated former DEA undercover agent Michael Levine has alleged the drug war is an illusion in *The Big White Lie: The CIA and the Cocaine/Crack Epidemic*. In the book he writes that major drug traffickers targeted by the DEA were repeatedly regarded by the CIA as "assets," terminating the DEA's investigations.[87]

VII
Slandering the Real Lands of the Free

A major prong in the American government's drug policy is to scare the crap out of its population. A tenet of this approach is that any letdown in the drug war will result in the nation's children being inundated with drugs, or to use the words of a United Nations drug director, a "heroin tsunami."[88]

It is practically unknown in America that numerous countries have decriminalized the adult possession of small amounts of drugs for personal use. This is not surprising, as the American media largely ignores it. When Portugal decriminalized personal possession in 2001 no major media outlets gave it coverage.[89]

The few media outlets that do acknowledge other countries' approaches give them extremely biased coverage. For example, the *Christian Science Monitor* in 1995 ran the story "Legalization Increases Drug Use by Colombians." The article itself revealed that there had been no studies on usage rates and that a Colombian counselor admitted she had not seen a rise in applicants to her rehabilitation center.[90]

Colombia is a great example of decriminalization because the United States of America spends billions attempting to keep out Colombian cocaine. Cocaine is plentiful in Colombia and cheap. Cocaine in America costs roughly twenty-five times more.[91] Not only that, but Colombia has decriminalized possession of small amounts of drugs for personal use since 1994. By drug war logic, Colombians should be drowning in addiction, and yet an international 2008 study showed that four percent of Colombians have tried cocaine, compared to sixteen percent of Americans.[92]

PEOPLE CAN'T HANDLE FREEDOM?
Lifetime Usage Rates[93]

Note: Three of the following four foreign countries have decriminalized possession of small amounts of *any* drug. Netherlands has not decriminalized but unofficially overlooks.

Country	Year of Decrim.	Usage Rate: Marijuana	Usage Rate: Cocaine
Colombia	1994	10.8%	4.0%
Italy	1975	6.6%	1.0%
Netherlands		19.8%	1.9%
Spain	1983	15.9%	4.1%
USA		42.4%	16.2%

Two scholars who have studied decriminalization policies found that enforcement has "surprisingly little measurable consequence,"[94] and no study has ever shown that decriminalization affects consumption.[95] Americans no longer remember that when drugs were legal in this country there was no drug "problem." Cocaine and heroin addicts accounted for a small percentage of the population, as they do now, but they were usually treated by their doctors and did not commit crimes.[96]

This is arguably why the federal government has so fiercely imposed its will regarding marijuana on the states and on other countries.[97] When marijuana is legalized and Suzie does not become a heroin junkie and pot smoke doesn't fill the streets, their sham drug logic will be revealed to people firsthand, and no amount of silly marijuana ads will put it back together again.

One country that has had the financial strength and political courage to tell America's drug warriors to fig off has been the Netherlands. In Holland, drug laws are still on the books (in part to obey the international treaties pushed through by America), but possession of small amounts of marijuana, heroin, and cocaine are disregarded. Dutch police support this system.[98] It leaves their prisons available for violent criminals and drug traffickers, and their drug clinics available for people who actually want to use them.

For this policy, which began in 1976, Dutch officials have had to weather decades of slander from American suits.[99] This barrage is filled with ridiculous lies that drug warriors assume, usually correctly, their audiences will not catch. One slanderous lie of former drug czar Barry McCaffrey's was that the Dutch policy of giving free heroin to addicts caused its murder rate to become twice America's. (The Dutch murder rate is half ours and heroin maintenance has been shown to *reduce* crime.)[100] Another drug czar, Lee Brown, was once bad-mouthing the Dutch at a Los Angeles town hall meeting. To Brown's chagrin a Dutch ambassador happened to be present, and he politely refuted everything Brown had said.[101]

In 2008 the top American cable news program for eight years running, *The O'Reilly Factor*, had a commentator state:

> In the Netherlands their experimentation with social tolerance, free love, free drugs, clearly has backfired. Amsterdam is a cesspool of corruption, crime. Everything is out of control. It's anarchy.[102]

In 2009, when shown an Amsterdam clip refuting these statements by demonstrating that their marijuana usage rate is almost half America's and their murder and drug overdose rates are mere fractions of America's, host Bill O'Reilly responded dismissively, "The way they do the statistics in the Netherlands is different plus it is a much smaller country, much smaller place to do the stats on."[103]

One of the issues that has arisen with decriminalizing "soft" drugs in small areas is the influx of drug tourism. Young adult foreigners can flood these zones, bringing the same issues young adults bring when they overrun spots that only allow alcohol, such as spring break destinations.

The same can happen with drug addicts when small areas are decriminalized for "hard" drugs, for example Needle Park. Needle Park was an isolated 1980s Swiss attempt to allow all drug users in one park.[104] It was a disaster because of overcrowding and poor planning, for instance using a park rather than a public health clinic. If Europe outlawed dance clubs everywhere but in tiny zones in the Netherlands, similar problems would ensue.

Overall the Dutch approach has been a success. In Holland, between 1979 and 1994 the percentage of people under twenty-two years of age who used hard drugs dropped from fifteen percent to two-and-a-half percent. In the 1980s when cocaine hysteria enthralled America, Reagan launched a domestic and international war. At the same time the Dutch explicitly mandated that their police *not* arrest people for possession of hard drugs. The results? In 1987 only 1.7 percent of adults in Amsterdam said they took cocaine in the previous year, while six percent of adults in New York City said that they had used cocaine in the previous six months. In the 1990s drug usage across the board was two to ten times lower in all relevant categories in the Netherlands than in the United States.[105]

The Dutch are not uniquely capable of handling freedom and other countries are following their lead. In 2001 Portugal decriminalized personal possession of all drugs. A 2009 study found that there was no serious push to reverse policy as by virtually every metric it had been a "resounding success." Since 2001 drug usage rates in many categories had decreased. Most notable was the large decrease in the thirteen- to nineteen-year-old age group. From 2001–2005 Portuguese marijuana usage rates were the lowest in the European Union.[106]

Decriminalization has not been the only success. Maintenance programs in which addicts are *provided* with drugs have been successful as well. Swedish heroin maintenance programs (where heroin addicts are provided heroin by prescription) have been effective in reducing crime and homelessness. They have also greatly improved the rates of addicts' employment, self-sufficiency, and success in ending addiction.[107]

In Widnes, England, Dr. John Marks was having success providing heroin, cocaine, and amphetamine addicts with maintenance doses. In the program's first five years Widnes enjoyed a ninety-six percent reduction in thefts and break-ins. Even more startling was that new addiction rates dropped by ninety-two percent.[108] It appeared that since addicts were no longer in the streets, dealers left the area.

Then Marks made a mistake. In 1992 he allowed the American news show *60 Minutes* to feature his success. It focused on Julia Scott, a heroin addict of ten years, who was a prostitute and a single mom. During three years with Marks, she held down a job as a waitress, paid her taxes, and took good care of her three-year-old daughter.

Soon after the show aired, the British embassy in Washington, DC was "getting heat over the broadcast," and a "high-level meeting" was arranged in which Americans asked the English to "harmonize" their drug policy with the United States.[109] In 1995 the funding for Dr. Marks' clinic was pulled and given to a new organization featuring the American method of forced withdrawal. Many of Dr. Marks' 450 patients ended up on the street committing crimes and abandoning their families to support their habits . . . and of course, dying like Scott soon did. However, no longer could *60 Minutes* send the wrong message to America's children.

VIII
Organized Crime's Lifeline

The more money poured into fighting the drug war the more profitable it will become. Marijuana is the largest cash crop grown in America. At the turn of the millennium, the international illicit drug business was generating roughly $400 billion in trade annually—eight percent of all international trade. This is roughly the same percentage as tourism and the oil industry.[110] All of the profits are unregulated, untaxed, and going to criminals.

In the United States this money makes ethnic gangs powerful organizations. Even worse is that it funds rebel and terrorist organizations worldwide.[111] The power of domestic gangs is only visible in the open-air drug markets where entire city blocks have been abandoned by police, but in other countries—such as Afghanistan and Colombia—these organizations are more powerful than their governments and entire regions have fallen into anarchy.

After the September 11, 2001, terrorist attacks, the White House had the arrogance to spend $3.4 million to run two advertisements during the 2002 Super Bowl accusing America's recreational drug users of supporting terrorism.[112] This is the same government that in the year prior to 9/11 oversaw the arrest of 750,000 people for marijuana possession and the arrest of only one terrorist.[113]

This is the same government that was warned by an FBI field agent a year prior to 9/11 that Osama bin Laden's followers could be training in American flight schools. The agent proposed that information be compiled on the visa applications of foreign students seeking flight school admission. This was never done because FBI headquarters regarded it as a "sizable undertaking."[114]

Meanwhile, the 2002 Super Bowl ads launched a $1.5 billion anti-drugs advertising campaign. When later evaluated by the Government Accountability Office it was discovered that this "sizable undertaking" had not reduced drug use, but instead convinced kids that illegal drug-taking is normal.[115]

THE MONEY TRAIN
ORGANIZATIONS FINANCED PRIMARILY BY DRUG PROHIBITION

GANG	ETHNICITY	PRIMARY DOMAIN
Aryan Brotherhood	White	U.S. Prisons
Bloods *	Black	Los Angeles
Crips *	Black	Los Angeles
Gangster Disciples	Black	Chicago
Hell's Angels	White	Canada
Italian Mafia (Five Families, Cosa Nostra)	Italian	New York City
Mara Salvatrucha (MS-13)	Salvadoran	Los Angeles, El Salvador
Mexican Mafia (La Eme)	Chicano	Southern California
Nuestra Familia	Latino	Northern California

* Umbrella organization with many affiliated gangs (sets).

TERRORIST GROUP	ORIENTATION	COUNTRY
Taliban (Al Qaeda's Protectors)	Islamic	Afghanistan
FARC	Marxist	Colombia
AUC's heirs	Para-Military	Colombia
Shining Path	Maoist	Peru

IX

MISSION IMPOSSIBLE
FINE, DON'T CUT AND RUN, YOU IDIOT

A. If They Say They Are Winning,
They Are Talking Out of Their Asses

The insanity of the war on drugs is most evident when it is recognized how abysmally it has failed. All twenty-three blue-ribbon commissions that have studied the issue in the past century have condemned the drug war. A 2006 survey of over 22,000 chiefs of police and sheriffs found that eighty-two percent of them disagreed with the statement that the drug war had "been successful in reducing the use of illegal drugs."[116]

The government likes to point to temporary dips in the usage of particular drugs as signs of success, but these dips are often accompanied by blips for other drugs—blips that go unmentioned. The popularity of individual drugs, and drugs as a whole, wax and wane just as with other consumer goods, regardless of government intervention.[117]

One of the few objective measures of prohibition's success is the price of drugs. If the government was successful in stifling the flow of drugs, prices should go up. However, prices for cocaine and heroin fell steadily during the heated drug warring of the 1980s and 1990s. This price drop did not appear to be attributable to less consumption or less availability; for example, in 1989 cocaine was almost twice as easy to get by high school seniors as it was in 1980.[118]

The price of marijuana has been more erratic, but its availability and its popularity are the same as they were in the mid-1970s.[119] It is also worth noting that marijuana is now the number-one cash crop in the United States, bigger than corn and wheat combined.[120]

B. Economics 101

The war on drugs will never succeed because of iron-clad economic laws. The stated goal of drug enforcement is to drive up illegal drugs' retail price.[121] This fails because recreational drugs have proven to be a necessity to the human species.[122] Some scientists have even argued that it is instinctual to desire altered states of consciousness, for instance, little children spinning to create dizziness.[123] Since getting high is impossible to stop,[124] the war on drugs is self-defeating for two reasons.

One, since drugs have proven to be a necessity,[125] when the government manages to raise a drug's price it also raises the profit (incentive) for people to supply them.

Two, criminal enforcement of drug laws actually strengthens the drug market. It is well known to those who witness the drug war firsthand that "we only catch the stupid ones."[126] Law enforcement largely locks up low-level or middle-level offenders. The drug kingpins that politicians blame for little Suzie's choices are seldom caught.[127] Law enforcement "weeds out the less effective, less ingenious participants and encourages the more ruthless and the more cunning."[128]

The rising efficiency of drug traffickers and dealers can be seen in more than just the price drop in the finished product; it can also be seen in its quality. Street heroin rose in purity from five percent in 1982 to twenty-seven percent in 1999. Street cocaine rose from thirty-six percent in 1982 to sixty-four percent in 1999.[129]

IT'S SNOWING MONEY:
Cocaine Economics[130]

The Product	Point in Chain	The Value
100 lbs. of coca leaves	Rural South America	$50

9/11:
The Drug War Hits Home

America's drug war abroad has caused decades of slaughter in countries like Colombia and Mexico. This collateral damage has not dampened America's enthusiasm to rid the world of chemical pleasure.

Perhaps a better understanding of its own tragedy might. The masterminds of 9/11, al Qaeda, were sheltered and abetted by the Taliban that controlled Afghanistan from 1996–2001. The Taliban was largely financed by opium and, in 1999, Afghanistan produced three times more opium than the rest of the world combined.

In Spring 2001 the United States gave the Taliban $43 million as a reward for "cracking down" on opium production (despite knowing it protected Bin Laden). It later was learned that the Taliban merely cut back because the country was producing so much opium that heroin prices were tanking.

—Jeffrey Bartholet & Steve Levine, "Holy Men of Heroin," *Newsweek*, 6 Dec. 1999; Bill Masters, ed., *New Prohibition* (2004), p. 33; and "Retired General Says Drug Money Fueling Taliban, al Qaeda" *Washington Times*, 1 Oct. 2005.

1 lb. of cocaine	South America	$500
1 lb. of cocaine	United States	$5,000
16 1-ounce packets	Wholesaler	$15,000
1 lb. of crack rocks	Retailer	$50,000 undiluted or $100,000 diluted

C. Common Sense

The futility of keeping drugs off of the streets is demonstrated by other facts. For example, America cannot even keep drugs out of its prisons. In 1997, nine percent of those in American prisons tested positive for drugs.[131] This is the case even in high-security "supermax" prisons, where people such as Charles Manson have tested positive.[132] The government could lock up the entire population to keep it from doing drugs and it would still fail.

359

GETTING HIGH LEGALLY
In Grandma's Garden

It is argued that if drugs were legal their use would soar. The following is a partial list of drugs found naturally in America that are legal to possess. Despite not being drug-war targets their usage is rare. Perhaps what is needed is a government campaign against them to get the word out. Warning: Legal status varies by jurisdiction and is subject to change. Users' experiences with these drugs can be found on the Internet at sites such as Erowid.org.

Amanita muscaria—This mushroom was the Soma of ancient India and grows wild in North America. Consuming one to five dried mushrooms causes sensory distortions and occasional hallucinations. Nausea and vomiting often result as well.

Broom (Cytisus scoparius)—When smoked, this yellow-flowered shrub produces intoxication and euphoria.

Calamus (Acorus calamus)—Eating two inches of the root is invigorating. Ten inches creates an LSD effect.

Catnip (Nepeta cataria)—Smoking catnip or drinking it via a tea creates a marijuana effect. An LSD effect is reported at high doses.

Coleus (Coleus blumei and Coleus pumilus)—Chewing and eating fifty to seventy-five leaves causes colorful hallucinations.

Hops (Humulus lupulus)—Used in alcoholic beverages, hops can also be smoked as a marijuana alternative. Because of this the government has asked growers not to sell them to the general public.

Morning Glory (Rivea corymbosa)—Consuming twenty to fifty powdered seeds causes restlessness and increased awareness. A hundred to 150 seeds will cause visual distortions and hallucinations. Two hundred to five hundred seeds will cause intense hallucinations, nausea, vomiting, and abdominal pain. Used by the Aztecs.

Scorpion—In Afghanistan the main part of scorpion tails are dried, crushed into powder, and smoked. They reportedly cause long-lasting intoxication and hallucinations. Effects likely vary widely between species.

—Paul Gahlinger, "Psychoactive Drugs that Are Not Illegal," *Illegal Drugs* (2001), pp. 177–194; and David MacDonald, *Drugs in Afghanistan* (2007), pp. 244–249.

Another clue is America's entry points. Media attention is given to the drug war's battles at the border. This is usually focused on smuggling through international airline flights and motor vehicle traffic running from Mexico into the United States. The fact that smugglers are even bothering to use these routes at all shows how ineffectively they are policed because there are easier alternatives. The most obvious one is walking them across deserted border areas like illegal immigrants—without drugs—do every day.

A second route is through the mammoth forty-foot-long steel containers of international commerce that are flipped from ships to railroad carts and trucks. Checking just one of these containers is a huge task and Los Angeles' port alone can bring in 130,000 of them in a month. In Los Angeles, customs inspectors struggle to check even two percent of these. The entire annual cocaine supply for the United States could fit in thirteen of the boxes. The entire annual heroin supply could fit in just one.[133] Heroin importation on the East coast practically came to a halt in the summer of 1972, but it had nothing to do with law enforcement. There was a shipping strike.[134]

Even if drug importation miraculously ceased, Americans could simply grow their own. Coca and poppies can both be grown on American soil. *Papaver somniferus*—the poppies that provide heroin—grow through sidewalk cracks in Seattle, along interstate highways, and are planted by gardeners like Martha Stewart.[135] To get opium from these plants one merely has to slit the pod with a knife. It is probably not a coincidence that poppies are frequently the top-selling dried flower.

Lastly, people can always switch to other drugs. The thorough prosecution of particular drugs in the past has simply turned people to alternatives. The prohibition on opium and cocaine drove people to use heroin. Alcohol's prohibition was the "mainspring of the marijuana boom." The raising of the minimum legal age for alcohol consumption to twenty-one in the late 1970s and 1980s also stoked marijuana demand.[136]

Little Suzies who want to get high will always be able. One readily available backup, which remains popular with Latin America's poor, is huffing inhalants (gasoline, glue, and paint thinners).[137] Unlike other recreational drugs (such as heroin and marijuana) chronic use of inhalants causes permanent brain damage.[138] The practice of huffing does not get as much government attention or media coverage despite the fact that eight percent of middle school students and fifteen percent of high school seniors participate.[139]

D. What If We Stop Being Pussies?

The response of the zealots to the decrepit state of the war on drugs is to step it up. However, the limits of punishments are being reached. When marijuana users are serving life sentences, the only thing left to do is kill them, and this has been tried before to no avail.

Saudi Arabia publicly decapitated drug smugglers to stem the flow of drugs in its country. The flow did not stop. Instead, such a backlog on beheadings was created that in 1995 weekly chopping days had to be expanded from two days to four.[140]

Harsh sentences are also not effective deterrents. Studies have shown that people who break the law are more likely to consider potential gains and probability of success than potential punishment.[141] Because the potential gains of drug dealing are so monstrous, the only possibility is to bring down the probability of success.

Because drug distribution is a consensual crime any advances in interception rates will have to include the further erosion of civil liberties. This has been happening and continues to happen. However, there is a limit and that limit will likely be reached when police start hitting little Suzie and her wealthy parents in the suburbs.

This is already in motion, with the Supreme Court removing the last remaining sanction against no-knock military-style police raids based on anonymous tips in 2006.[142] With the increasing militarization of police and SWAT (Special Weapons and Tactics) Units now responding to domestic disputes, suicidal threats, and even angry dogs, it is not surprising the affluent suburban civilian death count is now rising.[143,144]

Even if civil liberties were completely thrown out the window and the nation's entire budget was devoted to tackling drugs, it is questionable whether drug use could be stopped. When President Richard Nixon first launched the drug war he set up a program that tested the effectiveness of locking up *every* drug dealer in a particular city. With a huge amount of federal funding, the feds arrested all seventy-six drug dealers in Phoenix simultaneously. For a week drugs were unavailable in Phoenix and local drug treatment programs were overwhelmed. However, on the eighth day new dealers emerged, and within a month the drug scene had returned to its previous state. The same experiment was executed in San Diego and again by the eighth day San Diego had new drug dealers.[145]

X

Drugs Are Fun
Why Must Everyone Be Square?

The egregious costs and horrible consequences of the war on drugs have garnered opponents from a broad political spectrum that includes politicians, judges, and law enforcement personnel. But even among the decriminalization crowd the taboo stands firm in that no one concedes that recreational drugs are actually beneficial to people.[146]

It is a great irony that the country that launched its revolution explicitly on the inalienable right of the pursuit of happiness has led the global war on using drugs to be happy.[147] From the beginning of humanity drugs have been used to lighten the human condition and expand consciousness. Heroin, cocaine, PCP, LSD, mushrooms, marijuana, Ecstasy, and many others have all provided great pleasure for the vast majority of their users. However, because a small percentage of people use them irresponsibly, our society has spent the last century using propaganda to envelop them in a taboo.

Arguably the broadest cost of this taboo is that millions of responsible citizens—the very ones who would most likely use them appropriately—never experience the unique and enjoyable sensations drugs have to offer.

NOTES

1. Roy Walmsley, "World Prison Population List," (8th Ed.), International Centre for Prison Studies (UK), 2009.
2. James Gray, *Why Our Drug Laws Have Failed* (2001), p. 29.
3. William Greider and Erika Fortgang, "Mandatory Minimums: A National Disgrace," *Rolling Stone*, 16 Apr. 1998.
4. Gray, *Drug Laws*, pp. 2–4, 43.
5. Melinda Beck and Peter Katel, "Kicking the Prison Habit," *Newsweek*, 14 June 1993.

6. Ibid. and Gray, *Drug Laws*, p. 36.
7. Aliza Marcus, "US Leads 17 Countries in Cocaine, Marijuana Use," Bloomberg.com, 1 July 2008, ret. 1 Oct. 2008.
8. Gray, *Drug Laws*, p. 95.
9. The Supreme Court upheld the forfeiture of a rented yacht where one marijuana cigarette had been discovered. Richard Miller, *Drug Warriors and Their Prey* (1996), p. 110.
10. Gray, *Drug Laws*, p. 104.
11. Miller, *Drug Warriors*, p. 122.
12. Ibid., pp. 105–106, 111–113, 117–118.
13. Mike Gray, *Drug Crazy* (1998), p. 102.
14. The assertion that they were not really dealers is supported by the fact they were being represented by me, a public defender. Most dealers can easily afford private counsel.
15. For support from a former undercover officer that arrested dealers are often mere users see Bill Masters, ed., *New Prohibition* (2004), pp. 27, 28.
16. This is demonstrated by the inner-city popularity of "Stop Snitching" T-shirts. Kelefa Sanneh, "Snowman Shirts' Hidden Drug Message Raises Alarm," *San Diego Union-Tribune*, 13 Nov. 2005.
17. Gray, *Drug Laws*, p. 108.
18. Ibid.
19. William Greider and Erika Fortgang, "Mandatory Minimums: A National Disgrace," *Rolling Stone*, 16 Apr. 1998.
20. In one of my 2005 trials an officer testified to seeing a thin glassine package smaller than a dime pass hands from fifty yards away through binoculars.
21. For example see Gray, *Drug Crazy*, pp. 34–35.
22. Ibid., pp. 36–37; and Masters, *New Prohibition*, p. 21.
23. Gray, *Drug Crazy*, p. 37
24. Ibid.
25. Anti-drug policies are "unquestionably concentrated in inner-city communities." Robert MacCoun and Peter Reuter, *Drug War Heresies* (2001), p. 112.
26. As a substitute teacher in the inner city from 2003–2004 making $110 a day I would have kids counting their drug money in class. One kid once had over $500 laid out on his desk. I was tempted to deal drugs.
27. William Greider and Erika Fortgang, "Mandatory Minimums: A National Disgrace," *Rolling Stone*, 16 Apr. 1998.
28. Bill Masters, ed., *New Prohibition* (2004), p. 101.
29. Ibid., p. 65.
30. President Bill Clinton generally appointed centrist judges and he certainly did not support judges "liberal" on the drug issue. Esther Kaplan, *With God on Their Side* (2005), p. 267; and James Gray, *Why Our Drug Laws Have Failed* (2001) pp. 116–117.
31. However, the majority of black inner-city residents do not accept the trade or usage of illegal drugs. Larry Elder, *Ten Things You Can't Say in America* (2000), p. 265.
32. Recent examples of drug dealers turned rap superstars are 50 Cent of Queens, New York, and T.I. of Atlanta, Georgia.
33. Gray, *Drug Laws*, p. 45.
34. Masters, *New Prohibition*, p. 101.
35. In their words, their relatives were just there to "serve you." "Serve you" was slang for selling someone drugs. Students would often offer in jest to serve me because my jittery hands and sometimes runny nose led them to believe I was a cocaine user.
36. MacCoun, *Drug War Heresies*, p. 120.
37. "White man's land" is how my inner-city students referred to the area outside of the city.
38. "One in Five Drug Abusers Needing Treatment Did Drugs with Parents," PRNewswire, 24 Aug. 2000.
39. MacCoun, *Drug War Heresies*, pp. 26–27.
40. See "Why Do Drug Dealers Still Live With Their Moms" in Steven Levitt and Stephen Dubner, *Freakonomics* (2005), p. 89.
41. I have derived this from discussions with dozens of clients charged with drug dealing, and also from dealers who have never been caught. Two sources of downfall for drug dealers appear to be greed and sloppiness. For example, expanding your clientele beyond a trusted core and making open-air sales.
42. Advantages of blue-collar jobs can be less stress and a forty-hour work week.

43. In Holland, where cocaine possession is treated leniently, there are no cocaine-related deaths. James Gray, *Why Our Drug Laws Have Failed* (2001), pp. 218–220.

44. Mike Gray, *Drug Crazy* (1998), pp. 107–108.

45. Ibid.

46. Gray, *Drug Laws*, pp. 128–129.

47. Ibid., p. 128.

48. Lisa Curtis, "Bias Law Presents Challenges for DAs," *News Graphic*, 5 Jan. 2006, ret. gmtoday.com, 24 Apr. 2007.

49. "National Survey on Drug Use and Health," Fig. 5.3B, Substance Abuse and Mental Health Services Administration (SAMHSA), 2010.

50. Cole information from Masters, *New Prohibition*, p. 31.

51. Randy "Duke" Cunningham, "A Call to Arms Against Youth Drug Abuse," *San Diego Union-Tribune*, 24 Sep. 1996.

52. Bill Murphy, "Son of Lawmaker Sentenced to Prison," *San Diego Union-Tribune*, 18 Nov. 1998.

53. Besides chronic impotence and constipation, opiate addiction is "minimally injurious." Gahlinger, *Illegal Drugs*, p. 382.

54. Lance Morrow, "Kids and Pot," *Time*, 9 Dec. 1996.

55. Jacob Sullum, *Saying Yes* (2003), pp. 18–19.

56. Following two paragraphs from Kitty Kelley, *Family* (2004), pp. 266, 301, 302, 575.

57. Gavin Edwards, "Ashton Kutcher," *Rolling Stone*, 29 May 2003.

58. Kelley, *Family*, pp. 303–304.

59. Ibid., pp. 578–579.

60. Jacob Sullum, "Bummer," *Reason*, Oct. 2011, and Barack Obama, *Dreams from My Father* (1996), p. 93.

61. Gene Healy, "President Obama's War on His Own 'Youthful Irresponsibility,'" *Washington Examiner*, 25 May 2010.

62. Sullum, "Bummer."

63. Tim Dickinson, "Obama's War on Pot," *Rolling Stone*, 1 Mar. 2012.

64. Sullum, "Bummer."

65. Paul Armentano, "Incarceration Nation," AlterNet.org, 15 Sep. 2010, ret. 7 Apr. 2012.

66. Ted Carpenter, *Bad Neighbor Policy* (2003), pp. 142–144.

67. James Gray, *Why Our Drug Laws Have Failed* (2001), p. 88.

68. Carpenter, *Bad Neighbor Policy*, p. 140.

69. Ibid., p. 147.

70. Fernando Henrique Cardoso (Brazil), Cesar Gaviria (Colombia), and Ernesto Zedillo (Mexico), "Drugs: The Debate Goes Mainstream," HuffingtonPost.com, 9 Apr. 2012.

71. Bill Masters, ed., *New Prohibition* (2004), p. 56.

72. Ibid., p. 47.

73. Gray, *Drug Laws*, p. 42.

74. Ibid.

75. See Note 13.

76. Gray, *Drug Laws*, p. 42.

77. Ibid., pp. 38–39

78. Ibid., p. 76.

79. Ibid., p. 74.

80. Ibid., p. 75.

81. Ibid., p. 76.

82. Gray, *Drug Crazy*, p. 148.

83. Gray, *Drug Laws*, p. 77.

84. Ibid.

85. Horner info from Gray, *Drug Crazy*, pp. 146–148.

86. Gray, *Drug Laws*, pp. 139–142.

87. Ibid., p. 141.

88. Sebastian Abbot and Nasser Karimi, "West Links Drug War Aid to Iranian Nuclear Impasse," AP, 24 June 2008.

89. "Drug Possession No Longer a Crime in Portugal," *Drug War Chronicle*, 7 June 2001, ret. stopthedrugwar.org,

30 Sep. 2008.

90. Andrew Downie, "Brazil's Drug Users Will Get Help, Instead of Jail," *Christian Science Monitor*, 4 Jan. 2002.

91. "Colombia Rethinks Legalized Drugs," CBS/AP, 5 Apr. 2004.

92. Louisa Degenhardt, et al., "Toward A Global View of Alcohol, Cannabis, and Cocaine Use," *PLoS Med.*, 1 July 2008.

93. Ibid.

94. Robert MacCoun and Peter Reuter, *Drug War Heresies* (2001), pp. 236–237.

95. Danna Harman, "Debate Far from Over for Mexico's Drug Bill," *Christian Science Monitor*, 10 May 2006.

96. MacCoun, *Drug War Heresies*, pp. 194–199.

97. Richard Davenport-Hines, *Pursuit of Oblivion* (2002), p. 15.

98. Gray, *Drug Crazy*, p. 165.

99. Ibid., p. 168.

100. Larry Elder, *Ten Things You Can't Say in America* (2000), p. 260.

101. Gray, *Drug Crazy*, p. 169.

102. O'Reilly Factor, FOX News, 8 Dec. 2008; and Elian Wils and Robbert Nieuwenhuijs, "The Truth About Amsterdam," 27 July 2009.

103. O'Reilly Factor, FOX News, 4 Aug. 2009.

104. Gray, *Drug Crazy*, pp. 163–164.

105. James Gray, *Why Our Drug Laws Have Failed* (2001), p. 220.

106. Glenn Greenwald, "Drug Decriminalization in Portugal," Cato Institute, 2009.

107. Gray, *Drug Crazy*, pp. 163–164.

108. Stuart Walton, *Out Of It* (2002), p. 248.

109. Gray, *Drug Crazy*, p. 154.

110. Richard Davenport-Hines, *Pursuit of Oblivion* (2002), p. 11.

111. Bill Masters, ed., *New Prohibition* (2004), p. 33.

112. "Super Bust!" NORML.Org, 31 Jan. 2002, ret. 25 Jan. 2007.

113. Masters, *New Prohibition*, p. 7.

114. David Johnston, "Pre-Attack Memo Cited Bin Laden," *New York Times*, 15 May 2002.

115. Donna Leinwand, "Anti-Drug Advertising Campaign a Failure," USAToday.com, 29 Aug. 2006, ret. 24 Jan. 2007.

116. Arthur Benavie, *Drugs: America's Holy War* (2009), p. 5.

117. Drug trends have not correlated with anti-drug spending. The 1980s saw significant decreases in lifetime drug usage by high school seniors, but the 1990s saw significant increases despite massive budgetary increases. Robert MacCoun and Peter Reuter, *Drug War Heresies* (2001), p. 16.

118. Ibid., pp. 30–32.

119. In 1975, eighty-eight percent of high school seniors said marijuana was "fairly easy" to obtain and forty-seven percent had used it. In 2011, the numbers were eighty-two percent and forty-six percent, respectively. "Monitoring the Future," U. of Michigan, ret. MonitoringtheFuture.org, 20 Apr. 2012.

120. David Alexander, "Marijuana Top U.S. Cash Crop," Reuters, 19 Dec. 2006, ret. news.yahoo.com 19 Dec. 2006.

121. Masters, *New Prohibition*, p. 71.

122. Paul Gahlinger, *Illegal Drugs* (2001), p. 5.

123. Jacob Sullum, *Saying Yes* (2003), p. 269.

124. Gahlinger, *Illegal Drugs*, p. iv.

125. In economic terms drugs' price elasticity of demand is low, that is, its price has little effect on demand.

126. Ronald Rose said, "Believe me, after twenty years as a prosecutor and judge, I can assure you that we only catch the stupid ones." James Gray, *Why Our Drug Laws Have Failed* (2001), p. 211.

127. Masters, *New Prohibition*, p. 45.

128. Ibid., p. 72.

129. Ibid.

130. Gahlinger, *Illegal Drugs*, p. 251.

131. Gray, *Drug Laws*, p. 49.

132. Ibid.

133. Paragraph statistics from Gray, *Drug Crazy*, pp. 151–152.

134. Edward Epstein, *Agency of Fear* (1990), pp. 185–187.

135. Paragraph from Russ Kick, ed., *You Are Being Lied To* (2001), p. 249–250.

136. Paragraph from Richard Davenport-Hines, *Pursuit of Oblivion* (2002), pp. 216–217, 239, 426.

137. Huffing is hyperventilating from a plastic bag containing solvent, or breathing from a solvent-soaked cloth.

138. Gahlinger, *Illegal Drugs*, p. 186.

139. Ibid., p. 185.

140. Stuart Walton, *Out Of It* (2002), p. 192.

141. Robert MacCoun and Peter Reuter, *Drug War Heresies* (2001), pp. 79–85.

142. *Hudson v. Michigan*, 547 US 586 (2006). Radley Balko, *Overkill* (2006), p. 34.

143. Ibid., p. 13.

144. One example was Salvatore Culosi, Jr., a thirty-seven-year-old optometrist. He was unarmed and cooperative but was still killed in a heavily armed SWAT team's visit to his suburban home in Fair Oaks, Virginia. His crime was that an undercover agent had placed football game bets with Culosi. To learn more about the ongoing problem see the articles by Radley Balko on The Huffington Post. Tom Jackman, "SWAT Tactics at Issue After Fairfax Shooting," *Washington Post*, 27 Jan. 2006, and ibid., pp. 12–13.

145. Gray, *Why Our Drug Laws Have Failed*, p. 49.

146. MacCoun, *Drug War Heresies*, p. 70.

147. Richard Davenport-Hines, *Pursuit of Oblivion* (2002), p. 167.

14

THE END
DEATH

You will die. Death is inevitable. Despite weakening considerably since its peak in the 1950s and 1960s, death is still taboo in America.[1] Death must still be discussed sensitively in many contexts and people with life-threatening illnesses are still stigmatized.[2] It is a taboo that permeates and empowers other taboos. How people consider death affects how they live their lives.

I
DEATH IN AMERICA
SANITIZED AND DISTORTED

In nature, death is omnipresent. Starvation, unmitigated disease, and being eaten alive are some of the unsavory ends common in the wild. The guillotine is tender in comparison to the innate cruelty of pathogens and predators. In sharp contrast to their kin in the natural world, many Americans have never witnessed the death of a large animal, much less another human being.

The eating of meat is now so far removed from the slaughter that most McDonald's patrons could not fathom what it is like to kill and butcher a docile cow. People approaching their deaths are frequently sequestered in hospitals, where the only witness may be a cold machine eking out the body's life signs as long as possible.[3]

Prior to the last century, death was not concealed. It was an accepted part of life. Cemeteries were in the centers of towns. Rural populations raised and then killed the animals they ate. Almost all people died in their homes under the watch of their loved ones. Today many would consider it appalling to be the mortician of a loved one, but historically it was the family that prepared the cadaver for burial and conducted the services. Children were not separated from these proceedings and would sometimes even sleep in the same room as the corpse.[4]

While firsthand exposure to death has been almost completely removed from the non-medical population, deaths are now ubiquitous in the media. These media deaths are sanitized: they are either fictional or reduced to mere words and numbers by American news sources, which rarely show graphic images of death.[5]

The most extreme example of this expurgation is the fact that the United States managed to wage war in Iraq for five years with over four thousand American combat deaths, and most of its population never saw an image of a dead American soldier.[6] In cultural contrast, the Arabic news network Al Jazeera showed a "tidal wave of very graphic pictures." Its spokesman said of its Iraq War coverage, "Our audience actually expects us to show them blood, because they realize that war kills. If we were not to show it, we would be accused by our viewers … of perhaps hiding the truth or trying to sanitize the war."[7]

Media deaths distort peoples' perceptions of how death occurs. Fictional shows, like the pervasive crime drama, fixate on murder. The news industry also focuses disproportionately on sensational deaths. Studies have found that people who watch the local news overestimate crime rates and have greater fear for their safety. Crime rates in the United States have been dropping for the past twenty years. However, for almost every one of those years a supermajority of Americans believed that there was more crime now than the year before.[8]

Not only do these skewed media portrayals distort Americans' conceptions of what causes death, but they also promote the belief that death is something that happens to us instead of something that we all do.[10] This belief is abetted by the medicalization of death. The countless medical breakthroughs of the past century have made death a medical condition to be battled unceasingly, not a natural life process to be accepted.

This overly combative view is demonstrated by the billions of dollars wasted by Medicare annually to treat near-death patients with scant hopes of recovery. It is estimated that twenty to thirty percent of the medical expenditures in patients' last two months have no meaningful impact, for example, surgically implanting a defibrillator for heart problems in a ninety-three-year-old man with terminal cancer or keeping an unconscious person barely alive for months in an intensive care unit at the cost of $10,000 per day.[11] Even when terminally ill patients *want* a physician to help them die it is often prohibited. Physician-assisted suicides for deathbed patients are still illegal in forty-seven states.

SPINNING DEATH
MEDIA COVERAGE OF MORTALITY[9]

CAUSE OF DEATH	MORTALITY RISK	PERCENTAGE OF MORTALITY COPY IN PRINT NEWS	DISPROPORTION RATIO
Diet and Activity Patterns	14%	15.9%	1.1
Suicide	1.1%	1.4%	1.3
Homicide	1.2%	8.8%	7.3
Illicit Drug Use	1%	15.7%	15.7

Vast curative advances have also given the tacit impression that all diseases can and will be conquered eventually.[12] When a person dies from disease it is now often someone's fault. Either the person did not have a healthy lifestyle, or scientists have not yet figured out how to cure the affliction. Death is no longer an inherent part of life, but an evil to be beaten by health, safety, and medical research.

II
YOU WILL DIE
THINK ABOUT IT

Science has not been able to tell us what death is like. For most Americans, this is unnecessary, because almost ninety percent believe in heaven.[13] The Christian concept of heaven was a remarkable form of social control in the Middle Ages. Medieval rulers did not have to worry about the happiness of the peasants' lives because Earth was merely to be suffered through for the joys of the afterlife. For the dutiful Christian, living life according to an interpretation of the Bible is still the most important accomplishment before death.

For those who value reason more than faith, the speculative nature of an afterlife puts the emphasis on joy on earth. The recognition of death is one of the keys to terrestrial joy. According to the historian Jennifer Michael Hecht, there are four doctrines of happiness found in all philosophy, psychology, wisdom literature, and self-help. One of these is to be mindful of death.[14]

Survivors of near-fatal experiences are happier people. The vivid reminder of death forces them to appreciate how precious each moment is and how important it is to live fully. Recognizing that life is limited gives it value. The power of regularly pondering death has been extolled by wise men as varied as the Buddha, Plato, and Christian saints. Medieval monks often kept real human skulls in their cells. These *memento mori* would help remind them of death.[15] Under the modern taboo, keeping human skulls would mark one as weird or even mentally disturbed.

Although obsessing about death can be depressing, periodic meditations can help give people greater perspective on the often trivial troubles that cause distress. Being mindful of the ultimate deadline reminds one to seize the day. The full line of the famous Roman poem by Horace is "*Carpe diem quam minimum credulo postero,*" or "Seize the day, never trust the next." The reason you cannot trust tomorrow is because you might be dead. Seizing the day is another of the four universal doctrines of happiness.

III

The sole means now for the saving of the beings of the planet Earth would be to implant again into their presences a new organ . . . of such properties that every one of these unfortunates during the process of existence should constantly sense and be cognizant of the inevitability of his own death as well as the death of everyone upon whom his eyes or attention rests. Only such a sensation and such a cognizance can now destroy the egoism completely crystallized in them.[16]

In America seizing the day often means fully engaging in the competition for money, power, or fame. Materialism is drummed into the population's heads with ubiquitous commercials whose underlying message is that you are not as happy as you could be. However, the wise have never advocated seeking any of these superficial goals.[17] Even the father of capitalism, Adam Smith, knew pursuing wealth was a trivial and unsatisfying pursuit.[18]

Happiness cannot come via these superficial means because of four instinctual characteristics that evolved to aid the propagation of our species.[19] First, humans quickly acclimate to any situation. Riding in a limousine, living in a penthouse, receiving critical acclaim, or having screaming adoring fans is an awesome rush for the uninitiated, but when they become the norm even these delights quickly lose their uniqueness. A study of major lottery winners found that after the passage of mere months, their happiness levels were not higher than their peers.[20]

Second, happiness is dependent on expectations. The adage is "Satisfaction equals performance minus expectations." A Soviet labor camp prisoner can be happier after receiving an unexpected piece of bread than a rock star whose album only reaches number five on the sales charts.

Third, happiness is dependent on your reference group. Americans experience innovations beyond anything queens, kings, and emperors of past eras could imagine. Food and music from every land is easily accessible. Driving, flying, and movies are marvels available to almost everyone. Yet we are not ecstatic. The average American is earning almost three times as much in real income as fifty years ago, but the average American is not any happier. Since innovations and income have risen for everyone, no one is happier.[21]

Fourth, we will always want more. Subconscious greed is encoded in our chromosomes. International studies have found that for every dollar rise in experienced income, people's estimation of how much income they *need* to support their family rises by at least forty cents.[22] A palliative care worker found that one of the most common regrets of her dying patients, and one expressed by every single male, was that they wished they had not worked so hard.[23]

Wealth is not irrelevant, as anyone who has been unemployed is aware. However, studies have shown that wealth's influence on happiness decreases markedly after the point of providing for basic needs. Additional income does not influence a country's happiness level for countries with more than a $20,000 annual income per person.[24] Contrary to many Americans' conceptions, being able to pay for your children to go to college and having a plush retirement are not basic needs.

To combat these irrational instinctual traits regarding wealth one should follow another of Hecht's universal happiness doctrines—control your desires. "To want what you have," is simple to understand, but difficult to practice due to our DNA. According to Eastern philosophy, not just avarice, but all suffering stems from the desires of the self—the ego. To find bliss one must discard the ego.

Western psychologists are also beginning to battle the ego. The "talking cure" of psychoanalysis, which indulges the ego, is being supplanted by cognitive therapy. Cognitive therapy teaches people to battle depression by challenging the ego's irrational negative thoughts. It also teaches that self-worth should not be based on externalities like love or accomplishments. If one must retain the concept of self-worth, it should be that everyone has an equal and unchanging unit of worth. However, it is best to throw the concept out completely.[25]

The psychologist Mihaly Csikszentmihalyi has also found that people are happiest when the ego is erased in "flow."[26] Flow can occur whenever someone is using skills to achieve a challenging and clear goal. Flow experiences are marked by high concentration, forgetting about your worries, losing track of time, and the loss of self-consciousness. When in flow the action is being undertaken for the sake of the action itself. Ulterior motives like money, recognition, or winning are forgotten. Remarkably, people experience flow at work more often than at leisure.

In Hindu philosophy, to completely destroy the ego and all of its wants is to reach nirvana.[27] There are multiple routes to this end. The shortest and steepest is the path of knowledge that involves realizing that complete consciousness is buried underneath your ego. An ego-bound adult compared to an enlightened person is like a child who cries over trifling matters because she lacks perspective. You must understand how "I" and "me" are merely cultural concepts, and that even your personality is a mask.

The process is aided by visualizing yourself in the third person. In this context, personal failures and setbacks are seen as trivial, as if one is playing a loser in a play. Antagonists and enemies are characters that make life challenging and interesting. Negative emotions and thoughts are not suppressed but simply allowed to pass through. You are a bemused observer of life, the last form of the ego.

Beneath this final layer is the full awareness that links you to all people, all life, and the cosmos. Your separateness from the universe is a deceit of the ego, a deceit that ends when the ego is vanquished by either death or enlightenment. Like a drop of spray returning to the ocean, when the ego dissolves completely nirvana is reached. Alan Watts wrote:

> When this new sensation of self arises, it is at once exhilarating and a little disconcerting . . . there is indeed a certain passivity to the sensation, as if you were a leaf blown along by the wind, until you realize that you are both the leaf and the wind.[28]

In Hinduism there are numerous routes and combinations of routes to nirvana. The path of knowledge is for cerebral people. Other paths include the path of love for emotional people, and that of work for active people. Christianity is an example of the path of love. A personification of the eternal, Jesus is loved above all else and for no ulterior motives. The attachment to the ego is thus replaced by an attachment to Jesus. The path of work is to throw oneself fully into one's job. One works not for the superficial rewards of wealth or prestige, but as an exercise in focusing on something other than one's ego. This path is similar to the Western concept of flow.

Those who reach nirvana do not float away to heaven or even a temple in the mountains. A successful business executive may be more enlightened than a monk. Those who attain full awareness are serene, joyful, radiant, and their love flows to all.

While nirvana and complete ego annihilation may appear to be an unrealistic and supernatural aspiration, it is still useful to see life as *lila*, or play. Play inherently requires ego detachment and lightheartedness. The universe has arranged itself in the form of you for a tiny moment in time. To let the ego—that genetic code programmed solely for voluminous breeding—interfere with your happiness is folly.

Hecht advises to play life like a game but to keep in mind that the game is "somewhat stupid." As examples of its stupidity, she points out that in business, government, politics, and even the arts, the "winners" are often the heartless, the greedy, or the well-connected. Play the game. Enjoy the game and the rewards that you attain, but do not take it seriously.[29] In time everyone—even presidents—will be dead and forgotten. From the perspective of a lifetime, most setbacks, enemies, mistakes, and grievances are mere bagatelles.

IV

Seize the Day
Authenticity

For existentialists such as Martin Heidegger, embracing death is the key to life.[30] Recognizing your finitude creates existential angst. Life is absurd. No meaning is provided for you. It is marvelously bizarre, random, and comedic.[31] You are brought here to wander and coexist for a brief moment, and then you are gone just as inexplicably and suddenly as you arrived.[32] Many people never ponder death and merely accept the beliefs of those around them. They get pulled into the temporal concerns of the ego and the routine of robotic conformity.

Existential angst jars people out of this passive mimicry. This is supported by those forced to confront death. The most common regret of the dying patients of the aforementioned palliative care worker was that they hadn't had "the courage to live a life true to myself, not the life others expected of me."[33]

To existentialists, seizing the day means to live authentically. This means you make a rational examination of what goals, values, and recreations are true to you. You alone can determine what meaning to give your brief existence.[34] This process involves the fourth and last universal happiness doctrine of knowing yourself. Knowing yourself takes work. It requires exposing yourself as broadly as you can to different knowledge, ways of thinking, and experiences. It is in this manner that you can find meaning that is genuine to you.

Living authentically is difficult. Conforming to social norms is easy and you will have the reassurance of the people around you that you are doing the right thing. Family and friends may resent you if you turn from their lifestyle. If your path leads you into taboo territory you can be branded as weird or even criminal for acts that harm no one.

Liberty protects those people whose authentic life strays from the mainstream. The philosopher John Stuart Mill believed that liberty required that the government not punish offenses where the alleged harm is to the perpetrator. Mill argued that individuals knew what made them happy more than politicians did and that politicians used these laws to force conformity with the majority's cultural norms.

Mill believed that authentic people with the courage to step away from the herd give more value not only to their lives but also to society. Without original individuals to try out new "experiments in living" a culture becomes a "stagnant pool" mired in custom. Mill believed that the amount of eccentricity in a society correlates with its mental vigor, moral courage, and genius.[35]

V
Ecstasy Denied

With our current era's fixation on longevity and productivity, happiness advice often focuses on a "happy life." This type of guidance deals with discipline and long-term planning. Ecstasy is ignored. Ecstasy is intense and unforgettable happiness.[36] It is rare almost by definition. The frequent pursuit of ecstasy can lead to acclimation and interfere with the responsibilities necessary for a "happy life"; however, to have none at all is just as tragic because ecstasy is one of life's sweetest offerings.

Historically, there have only been four common types of ecstasy—sex, drug, religion, and festival.[37] Frequently all four would overlap into majestic orgies of joy in honor of a god. Some of these included the ancient Greeks' festival of Dionysus, the ancient Romans' Liberalia, and the medieval Catholics' celebration of carnival. These public celebrations involved everyone and included dancing, costumes, music, drug use, nudity, and sex. The annual occasion of unrestrained glee enriched peoples' lives.

Two of the four classic types of ecstasy are now trammeled by taboo and criminal laws. Due to this, these festivals now seem dangerous and irresponsible. The drug Ecstasy, which is used in modern festivals by young adults, was criminalized for everyone due to a handful of deaths out of tens of thousands of users. Despite it being less dangerous than horse riding,[38] the public debate centered on the fatalities. The merriment and pleasure it provided were ignored. Americans fought the Revolutionary War to establish a country based on the principles of "life, liberty, and the pursuit of happiness." It is now run on the principles of "health, safety, and the avoidance of death."

According to existentialists like Søren Kierkegaard and Friedrich Nietzsche, living authentically means cultivating risk and danger. Kierkegaard called those who do not take risks cowards. Nietzsche called them slaves. How would the participants in those ancient festivals view us? How do the citizens of Amsterdam view us? We have become an anal country—trying desperately to protect ourselves from the accidents of life and the danger of death.[39]

NOTES

1. Michael Bartalos, ed., *Speaking of Death* (2008), pp. 6–8.
2. Lynne DeSpelder and Albert Strickland, *Last Dance* (2005), pp. 185–186.
3. The sequestration of the dying has been greatly ameliorated in recent decades by the hospice movement.
4. DeSpelder, *Last Dance*, p. 6.
5. The morbid imagery of the 2010 Haitian earthquake was an exception and it caused controversy for being offensive. Arielle Emmett, "Too Graphic?" AJR.org, Mar. 2010.
6. After five years of the Iraq War there were fewer than six graphic photographs of dead U.S. soldiers found in media searches. Michael Kamber and Tim Arango, "A Sanitized View of the Iraq War?" NYTimes.com, 26 July 2008.

7.   Jacqueline Sharkey, "Al Jazeera Under the Gun," AJR.org, Oct./Nov. 2004.
8.   Adam Saeler, "Unreality TV," *Civic Column* (Mercyhurst College Civic Institute), June 2011.
9.   Karen Frost, Erica Frank, and Edward Maibach, "Relative Risk in the News Media," *Am. J. Public Health*, 1997, 87, p. 842.
10. DeSpelder, *Last Dance*, p. 23.
11. "Cost of Dying," CBSNews.com, 3 Dec. 2010.
12. Par. from Daniel Callahan, "Death and the Research Imperative," *New Engl. J. Med.*, 2 Mar. 2000, p. 654.
13. Dalie Sussman, "Poll: Elbow Room No Problem in Heaven," ABCNews.go.com, 20 Dec. 2005.
14. Jennifer Hecht, *Happiness Myth: Why What We Think is Right is Wrong* (2007), p. 17.
15. *Memento mori* is Latin for "remember you will die." It can refer to any object reminding one of death, and is also a genre of artwork with that theme.
16. George Gurdjieff, quoted in Alan Watts, *Book* (1989), p. 39.
17. Hecht, *Happiness Myth*, p. 46.
18. Darrin McMahon, *Happiness* (2006), p. 330.
19. Terry Burnham and Jay Phelan, *Mean Genes* (2000), pp. 122–124.
20. Philip Brickman, Dan Coates, and Ronnie Janoff-Bulman, "Lottery Winners and Accident Victims," *J. Pers. Soc. Psychol.*, Aug. 1978, 36(8), p. 917.
21. Richard Layard, *Happiness* (2005), p. 30.
22. Ibid., p. 43.
23. Bronnie Ware, "Top Five Regrets of the Dying," HuffingtonPost.com, 21 Jan. 2012.
24. Layard, *Happiness*, pp. 32–33.
25. David Burns, *Feeling Good* (1980), pp. 341–345.
26. Mihaly Csikszentmihalyi, *Flow: The Psychology of Optimal Experience* (1990).
27. Hinduism parts taken largely from Huston Smith, *World's Religions* (1991), and Alan Watts, *Book* (1989).
28. Watts, *Book*, pp. 124–125.
29. Hecht, *Happiness Myth*, p. 53.
30. Christopher Panza and Gregory Gale, *Existentialism for Dummies* (1998), p. 180.
31. Anyone who cannot understand this has never hung out with an ostrich, much less taken a good close look at one.
32. Jostein Gaarder, *Sophie's World* (1996), p. 196.
33. Ware, "Top Five Regrets of the Dying."
34. Living authentically is similar in concept to Simon Gibson's life theme, Abraham Maslow's self-actualization, and Friedrich Nietzsche's noble individual.
35. John Stuart Mill, *On Liberty and Other Essays* (1998), pp. 71, 74, 89.
36. Jennifer Hecht, *Happiness Myth* (2007), p. 10.
37. Ibid., p. 257.
38. David Nutt, "Equasy," *J. Psychopharmacol.*, 2009, 23(1), pp. 3–5.
39. Ernest Becker, *Denial of Death* (1973), p. 32.

APPENDIX ONE
GREAT PHILANDERERS
TWENTIETH-CENTURY WORLD LEADERS

Albert Einstein (physicist)—Einstein developed the Theory of Relativity and his name is now synonymous with genius. Einstein's devotion to physics appears to have had priority over his marriages. He once wrote, "I treat my wife as an employee whom I cannot fire."[1]

Einstein had an illegitimate daughter, Lieserl, with his first wife, Mileva Maric. Einstein never went to see the child and she appears to have been raised by others before soon dying of scarlet fever. Einstein later married Maric but it was an unhappy union. Despite being a pacifist, Einstein's first marriage was marred by violence, with Maric once appearing with a bruised and swollen face.[2]

During a separation from Maric and their legitimate children due to World War I, Einstein visited them infrequently and instead moved in with his lover and cousin, Elsa Löwenthal. Within months of the eventual divorce, Einstein married Löwenthal (after being rejected by her twenty-year-old daughter, Ilse). He once said, "It is a sad fact that man does not live for pleasure alone."[3]

Henry Ford (business leader)—Ford was the founder of Ford Motor Company. Despite being a "straitlaced guardian of sexual morals" and a traditional family man, it appears he kept a less-traditional family next door. A zesty teenage office worker at a Ford plant, Côté Wallace, attracted him. Thirty years his junior, Ford arranged that she marry one of his executives and built them a home adjacent to his with a secret stairway leading to her bedroom. Thirty years after Ford's death, her son, John, wrote a book that exposed that Ford, not his mother's husband, was his father.[4]

Mahatma Gandhi (nonviolent revolutionary)—Gandhi brought India independence from Great Britain through civil disobedience. He was married at the age of thirteen and, at the time, saw it as merely the acquisition of a "strange girl to play with."[5] He adopted celibacy in his mid-30s. He kept a long line of devoted secretary/nurses who would massage him, bathe him, and give him enemas. Gandhi also had naked teenage girls sleep with him (supposedly platonically) to keep warm.

Rudolph Giuliani (mayor)—Giuliani was the celebrated mayor of New York City during its September 11, 2001 terrorist attack. He was first married to his second cousin for fourteen years. He had that marriage annulled and married his second wife, Donna Hanover, while mayor. This did not prevent him from having a public relationship with a "very good friend," Judith Nathan.[6] In 2000 Mayor Giuliani sent the press into a fervor by marching with Nathan in the city's St. Patrick's Day parade, and later told the press that he was leaving Hanover—before telling Hanover. At the divorce proceedings, Hanover said Giuliani had cheated on her prior to Nathan. Giuliani is now married to Nathan.

Martin Luther King, Jr. (civil rights leader)—King was the Baptist minister who led the black civil rights movement. Due to the FBI's unconstitutional bugging, explicit details of King's adulterous ways are known. Some of the phrases he supposedly said during sexual forays were "I'm fucking for God," and once at ejaculation, "I'm not a Negro tonight."[7] King frequently enjoyed adultery. Although he only slept with black women,[8] the lighter their skin color the better.[9] King had used the motel where he was assassinated for a tryst the night before.[10]

Mao Tse-Tung (revolutionary)[11]—Mao led a peasant army to create the modern Chinese state. Despite the fact that Mao refused to brush his teeth his entire life, he did well romantically after his first marriage. The first marriage was arranged by his father. Mao went through the traditional wedding ceremonies, but then to spite dad, refused to live with her, or even touch her.

His second wife was a fellow revolutionary, Yang K'ai-hui. When enemy forces captured her, she refused to renounce Mao and was therefore publicly beheaded. Mao was already living with another woman half his age at the time of Yang's death. She became his third wife. The Long March, a 6,000-mile retreat that reduced his army from 100,000 to 5,000, was what arguably drove her insane.

His fourth and final wife was a scandalous actress who slept her way into multiple roles. Her later political activity indicates she probably saw Mao as another career move. In his later years, Mao enjoyed weekly ballroom dances with a rotating bevy of attractive young women, some of whom he selected for private sexual activities.[12]

Pancho Villa (revolutionary)—A gifted guerrilla fighter, Villa helped lead the successful Mexican Revolution. He had a Robin Hood-like side but was also astonishingly ruthless. The United States sent six thousand troops and its first-ever airplane combat mission to capture him, but was unsuccessful.

Villa generously called himself a "son of a bitch with the ladies."[13] He and his soldiers sometimes attacked towns to rape the women. Once Villa tied a father up and raped his young daughter in front of him. Another time, a Juárez pawn shop owner was bound and forced to watch Villa and his men gang rape his wife. They then shot the man multiple times and made the raped wife clean up the resulting gore.

Numerous women were still smitten by him and he married compulsively, perhaps seventy-five times. After he quickly bored of a wife he would simply gallop off on his horse. Ironically, he believed unfaithful women should be shot. When he was assassinated his last words were "Don't let it end like this. Tell them I said something."[14]

NOTES

1. Quote and most of Einstein sect. from Dennis Overbye, *Einstein in Love* (2001), pp. 92, 95, 260, 342–344, 349.
2. "Einstein's Wife: The Life of Mileva Maric Einstein," PBS.org, ret. 19 June 2006.
3. Irving Wallace, et al., *Intimate Sex Lives of Famous People* (1982), p. 521.
4. Quote and Ford sect. from Ibid., pp. 454–455.
5. Quote and Gandhi sect. from Ibid., pp. 406–410.
6. "Giuliani's Legal Dish Drenches Front Pages," *Chicago Tribune*, 23 June 2002.
7. All King quotes from Michael Dyson, *I May Not Get There with You* (2001), pp. 162–164, 346–347.
8. Ralph Abernathy, *And the Walls Came Tumbling Down* (1991), p. 472.
9. Dyson, *I May Not Get There*, pp. 193–194.
10. Abernathy, *And the Walls*, pp. 433–441, 470.
11. Sect. largely from Wallace, *Intimate Sex Lives*, pp. 421–424.
12. Li Zhi-Sui, *Private Life of Chairman Mao* (1996), pp. 93–94.
13. Quote and Villa sect. largely from Wallace, *Intimate Sex Lives*, pp. 445–447.
14. Ray Robinson, *Famous Last Words . . .* (2003), p. 177.

Appendix Two

Great Philanderers
American Presidents

This list is not meant to be comprehensive. Also, because of their private and consensual nature, extramarital sexual activities are difficult to discover and prove. If one requires irrefutable evidence in these matters, almost none of the following is valid. On the other hand, it is likely that numerous presidential activities have successfully been hidden from historians and journalists, particularly those from the United States' first century.

George Washington—There are no illegitimate children to prove that our first president committed adultery, however, that is not surprising since Washington was likely sterile. It is apparent that his true love was not the wealthy widow he married, Martha Dandridge Custis, but his friend's wife, Sally Fairfax, with whom he exchanged passionate letters that only allude to adulterous consummation.[1]

Thomas Jefferson—After much scholarly jousting over the issue of whether Jefferson fathered the children of his slave, Sally Hemmings, it now appears that he did not. It is more likely his brother, Randolph, did instead.[2] Jefferson promised his wife on her deathbed, when he was thirty-nine, that he would never remarry and he kept his promise. However, he made no promise to stay chaste and it appears that he did not. One of his relationships was in Paris, France, with the Italian artist Maria Hadway Cosway, who likely had an open marriage with her bisexual husband.[3]

His best friend's wife, Betsey Walker, accused him of pursuing her sexually for eleven years. This led John Walker to challenge Jefferson to a duel that never occurred. The eleven-year term is likely a gross exaggeration. However, in regards to the matter Jefferson did concede "that when young and single I offered love to a handsome lady. I acknolege [sic] its incorrectness."[4]

Grover Cleveland—When Cleveland was a sheriff in Buffalo, New York, and known as "Big Steve," he had an illegitimate son by a widow, Maria Crofts Halpin. Cleveland put the boy in an orphanage until foster parents could be found. When Halpin protested, she was committed to an asylum for five days. She later gave up on fighting for custody when Cleveland gave her a generous payment. When political opponents later tried to derail him with the story, his open honesty about the affair deflated the issue.

Later in life his law partner, Oscar Folsom, died and Cleveland became a father figure to Folsom's eleven-year-old daughter, Frances. When "Frank" turned twenty-one, the forty-nine-year-old president married her in the White House.

Andrew Jackson—Jackson met Rachel Donelson Robards while she was living with her widowed mother. They fell in love. Unfortunately, Rachel was still married to a Lewis Robards, from whom she was separated. Robards retrieved Rachel from her mother's home in Tennessee. Jackson—a man who would eventually survive over one hundred duels—was not cowed, and he abducted Rachel from Robards' home in Kentucky and took her back to Tennessee. Robards was going to conduct another raid, but Jackson and Rachel fled to Mississippi to avoid it. Robards then filed for divorce, and Jackson and Rachel were married. Unfortunately, the court denied Robards' divorce, petition making Rachel a bigamist. Years later the divorce and wedding were finally repeated successfully.

James Buchanan—Many believe that Buchanan was a homosexual.[5] As a young man, his fiancée broke off their engagement and then died shortly thereafter. Buchanan never married and lived with a man, William Rufus King, for twenty-three years. King was a bachelor as well, and served as vice president under Franklin Pierce. King was considered effeminate by his associates and referred to in the derogatory homosexual terms of the day.

Woodrow Wilson—While married, Wilson had an affair with a Mary Allen Peck, whom he met while vacationing in Bermuda. His presidential opponent in 1912, Theodore Roosevelt, refused to use the affair against Wilson in his campaign saying, "It won't work! You can't cast a man as a Romeo who looks and acts so much like an apothecary's clerk."[6]

Warren Harding—Harding was aggressively wooed by a wealthy "unattractive divorcée" named Florence Kling DeWolfe, and married her.[7] Not being physically attracted to his wife, Harding turned to brothels and affairs for release. Florence would have him followed and would scold him with the evidence but he did not care.

Harding had a fifteen-year affair with his good friend's wife, Carrie Phillips, and would write her love letters (some were over forty pages) describing her physical features and his overwhelming lust: "Carrie, take me panting to your heaving breast."[8] When he ran for president in 1920 she used these letters to get hush money from the Republican National Committee.

As a fifty-two-year-old senator he took the virginity of a voluptuous twenty-one-year-old daughter of a family friend, Nan Britton. As president he continued their affair rather indiscreetly at the White House, most notoriously once having intercourse in a White House closet. Britton had a daughter by Harding, whom he supported financially.

Franklin Roosevelt[9]—Roosevelt had an affair with Lucy Mercer, the secretary of his wife, Eleanor. Five years into it, Eleanor found love letters and confronted Roosevelt. It is believed that he and Eleanor discontinued sexual relations around that time. It is probable that he later had sexual relations with his young secretary, Missy LeHand. Other partners are more speculative. (His paralysis did not hamper his sexual capability.)

It is also possible that Eleanor had her own affairs including one with a woman, reporter Lorena Hickock. Hickock lived at the White House for four years and some of their voluminous correspondence discusses passionate embraces. While there is uncertainty about Eleanor's sexuality, Hickock was likely a lesbian.

Dwight Eisenhower—Eisenhower had a relationship with his World War II driver, Kay Summersby. President Harry Truman confirmed that Eisenhower requested military leave after the war from General George Marshall so that he could divorce his wife, Mamie, and marry Summersby. Marshall refused the request and threatened to make Eisenhower's life hell if he divorced.

Summersby claimed in her memoirs that their passion did not go beyond heavy kissing because Eisenhower had impotency issues that he blamed on Mamie. Summersby quoted Eisenhower as saying his marriage "killed something in me. Not all at once, but little by little. For years I never thought of making love, and when I did . . . I failed."[10] The ghostwriter of her memoirs, Sigrid Hedin, later said that Summersby confided in her that Eisenhower was not completely impotent, but that she did have to teach him lovemaking.

John F. Kennedy—Kennedy lost his virginity in a Harlem brothel at the age of seventeen. As a young man he named his penis "JJ,"[11] and had an affair with a married ex-Miss Denmark who had smitten Adolf Hitler and was allegedly a Nazi spy. After learning the FBI was wiretapping their trysts, Kennedy broke up with her.[12]

As a single congressman he was always with women, however, he developed a reputation for being a quick sexual performer who preferred to stay on his back. (In his defense, he suffered from back problems his entire life.)

A senator with whom he shared an apartment for affairs said Kennedy had the most active libido of any man he had ever known, and that Kennedy enjoyed having sex with two women at once. Kennedy was nonchalant about his promiscuity and once told reporters, "I'm never through with a girl until I've had her three ways."[13]

After marriage his breezy attitude did not waiver. He entered one of his inauguration parties with the words, "Where's the broads?" before picking a sex partner out of a lineup of six starlets.[14] When his staff panicked over a picture of him lying next to a naked buxom brunette he merely said, "Yes, I remember her. She was great!"

He liked to swim naked in the White House pool and of his numerous secretarial partners there were two prominent ones in the White House, known to Secret Service agents as Fiddle and Faddle. Fiddle and Faddle would sometimes join Kennedy in the pool sans clothes.

Kennedy was not averse to paying for sex either, reportedly using call girls as warm-ups before his famous televised presidential debates. Some of his more prominent trysts were with the stripper Blaze Starr, with whom he reportedly had intercourse in a closet while her governor fiancé hosted a party in the next room, and, of course, Marilyn Monroe.

Lyndon Johnson—Johnson's most prominent affair was with the socialite mistress of his mentor and benefactor Charles Marsh. Her name was Alice Glass and Johnson's wife, Lady Bird, said of her, "She was very tall, and elegant, really beautiful . . . I remember Alice in a series of long and elegant dresses and me in—well, much less elegant."[15] Glass' sister and best friend say she overlooked his big ears and nose, and fell for his expressive eyes, loving hands, and his aspiration to help people.[16] Although he would have future affairs, Glass appears to have been his true love and he probably would have divorced Lady Bird and married her if it would not have been political suicide.

Johnson was extremely blunt and open about sexual matters, for example in college he would frequently tout his naked penis, called "Jumbo," in front of his roommates, saying things like, "Jumbo had a real workout tonight."[17] Proud of its size, even in Congress he would ask fellows at the urinals if they had ever seen anything so big. He would openly pee in the House of Representatives parking lot in front of women, and once dropped his pants to show his staff, male and female, a hernia injury.

A frequent crotch-and-rear-scratcher/adjuster, he complained his tailor never gave him enough "ball room."[18] He once fixed a staffer's tie knot because it looked like a "limp prick,"[19] and in the White House instructed a staffer to assuage a female reporter critical of Johnson by taking her out on a date: "Give her a good dinner and a good fuck."[20] His repeated instructions regarding this strategy indicated Johnson was not joking.

As a congressman he had an open affair with fellow congresswoman/actress Helen Gahagan Douglas. Despite the fact they were both married, they would drive to Congress together in the mornings and walk in holding hands.[21] His poor treatment of the excessively shy Lady Bird extended beyond adultery to public disrespect: "You look so muley, Bird. Why can't you look more like Nellie?"[22] (Nellie was a friend of Lady Bird's.) In college Johnson was open about wanting to marry a woman only for her money and it appears that he did.[23]

Ronald Reagan[24]—Reagan's first wife, the Academy Award-winning actress Jane Wyman, left him for being a boring stiff and an endless talker. When he was once rambling at a Screen Actor's Guild (SAG) meeting, of which he was president, she shouted at him, "Oh, for God's sake, Ronnie, shut up and go shit in your hat."[25] Wyman also claimed his sexual skills were as good as his acting. (He was only a B-level actor.) This evaluation was echoed by others.

Reagan was devoted to Wyman. He even publicly gave his blessing to an affair she had prior to their divorce. When his attempts at reconciliation failed he went on a two-year tear of trysts that began before his divorce was official. He slept with so many women that he found himself in bed one morning with a woman whose name he had forgotten, telling himself, "Hey, I gotta get a grip here."[26] During this time Reagan loved to drink heavily and when he was not having sex, he liked talking about it. Reagan went out clubbing with so many celebrity women that he was called a "wolf" by one movie magazine.[27]

Unfortunately, the non-celebrities who passed through his bed did not get the same treatment. One model, Betty Underwood, recalls that he would not even pay for her to take a cab ride from his apartment late at night and she had to take a bus. During the months of their affair he never took her out and when she called him one day to tell him she was pregnant, he pointed out they had never been seen in public together and hung up on her. Scared she would lose her SAG card if she pursued the matter, she got an abortion.

Selene Waters, a nineteen-year-old starlet, was hit on by Reagan when she was with a date at Slapsie Maxie's. Waters was excited about the possibility of being seen in public on the SAG president's arm. After getting her address and phone number and verifying she lived alone he showed up unannounced at three that morning. He pushed his way in and forced sex on her. As she said in 1989:

> They call it date rape today—I hate that word rape—but then I was so shocked and angry because he had spoiled everything. I told him, too, but he said, "Oh, I just couldn't help myself. Don't worry about a thing. I'm going to call you and we're going to go out and then we'll talk some more about your career."[28]

This was a tumultuous time period for forty-two-year-old Reagan. His previous marriage proposal to twenty-one-year-old actress of the Baha'i faith, Christine Larson, had been rejected. Roughly a week after the Waters event, Reagan reluctantly proposed to a thirty-year-old B-level actress, Nancy Davis, who was pregnant with his child. Two weeks later an abbreviated marriage was held, to which Reagan did not invite his family.

Davis had slept her way into Hollywood,[29] and had adored Reagan for years. She even joined the SAG board to get closer to him. It was known even before the pregnancy became public that Reagan and Davis' sexual relationship had already begun because Reagan never closed his bedroom curtains.

When the baby, Patricia Reagan, was born to Davis, Reagan was not present. He was with Larson, crying to her that his life was ruined. He angrily broke off his affair with Larson shortly after the birth of Patricia, when he arrived at Larson's one day to be met at the door by a French actor wearing only a bath towel. Reagan appears to have stayed committed after that, except for a brief dalliance in 1968, definitely nothing as sensational as Davis' affair with Frank Sinatra in the early 1970s.

George H.W. Bush[30]—H.W. Bush's first reported affair occurred with an Italian woman with whom he shared an apartment in New York City. She sought legal counsel in 1964 when H.W. Bush did not follow through on his promise to divorce his wife, Barbara, and marry her. In the early 1970s a North Dakota woman divorced her husband and moved to Washington, DC, to be near him. In 1980 he had an affair with a young blonde photographer covering the presidential campaign.

In 1981 Bush was in a minor traffic accident with a "girlfriend" and he used his political clout to keep it out of the police logs so as not to attract attention. Another time in the 1980s, H.W. Bush was visiting a woman late at night when a fire in the building brought the Fire Department. His Secret Service detail would not let the firemen in the building until he was whisked out a back door.

The longest-lasting relationship H.W. Bush has had was with a divorcée eight years his junior, Jennifer Fitzgerald. He appears to have begun his romantic involvement with Fitzgerald in the early 1970s. He made her his secretary in 1974 when he became Chief of the United States Liaison Office in Peking, China, under President Gerald Ford. He kept her as a personal assistant when he was later put in charge of the CIA, and would continue to keep her employed in positions close to him.

This would change when H.W. Bush ran for president in 1988. In 1987, presidential candidate Senator Gary Hart confronted allegations of an affair by denying it and challenging reporters to follow him. They did and soon pictures emerged of a model sitting on his lap in a boat named *Monkey Business*. Originally the Democratic frontrunner, Hart's campaign was wrecked. This incident ended the

YOU WILL DIE — Appendix Two

press' gentleman's code that had protected politicians' extramarital affairs.

In this new environment, Fitzgerald was moved to the State Department to keep her out of the White House during H.W. Bush's presidency. When H.W. Bush ran for re-election against Democratic nominee Bill Clinton the candidates did not attack each other on the fidelity issue. As one Clinton aide said:

> Our guy was more susceptible on that issue. After I went to Arkansas and saw what we were dealing with—lists longer than the phone book—I started doing a little research on the other side and found that Bush also had other women in his life . . . I took my list of Bush women, including one whom he had made an Ambassador, to his campaign operatives. I said I knew we were vulnerable on women, but I wanted to make damn sure they knew they were vulnerable too.[31]

In 1992 the Fitzgerald affair received press coverage from a book and a *New York Post* article. In the first press conference following the article, Bush made sure his entire family was standing by his side, including his children's spouses, grandchildren, his 91-year-old mother in a wheelchair, and their pets. Despite this domestic protection the query still came and he furiously responded:

> I'm not going to take any sleazy questions like that from CNN. I am very disappointed you would ask such a question of me. I will not respond to it. I haven't responded in the past. I am outraged, but nevertheless in this kind of screwy climate we're in I expect it. But I don't like it and I'm not going to respond other than to say it is a lie.[32]

One of his granddaughters then burst into tears. Fitzgerald has never responded to the allegations publicly.

Bill Clinton—When Clinton was a sixteen-year-old Boys Nation senator he shook President John Kennedy's hand at the White House. Young Clinton aspired to Kennedy's political greatness, and whether or not he knew it, his relations with the opposite sex would follow Kennedy's as well. Upon returning to high school life in Arkansas, the young man who was always "on the hunt" had a new pick-up line.[33] "Shake the hand that shook the hand of John F. Kennedy."[34]

Clinton was president in the post-Gary Hart era, and with the help of his political opponents the press had no difficulty finding Clinton's *Monkey Business*. In terms of quantity, Clinton undoubtedly has been a womanizer on par with Kennedy. However, the financial rewards and political climate that brought his paramours out in droves makes numerous stories suspect.

Nevertheless, Clinton appears to have lost his virginity to his childhood sweetheart, Dolly Kyle, sometime in high school. Although Clinton and Kyle moved on to other relationships in college, Kyle reappeared to become Clinton's first act of adultery his senior year in college. Kyle was eight months pregnant by her husband when she met back up with Clinton on a trip to a national Catholic women's conference. (Kyle would return the favor and sleep with Clinton when he was married.)

His proclivity for volume came when he broke up with his college girlfriend his senior year. Despite his girth, Clinton had no problem having dates almost every night and he soon developed a reputation for insisting on lights, but no condoms, during sex. It does not appear that Clinton ever slowed down. The summer after college he was "a very, very, very busy boy."[35] One of the women who kept him busy that summer was the reigning Miss Arkansas. (Clinton would eventually be romantically linked to three other Miss Arkansas title-holders as well.)

As a Rhodes Scholar at Oxford for two years, one friend believed Clinton had sexual relations with "a minimum of thirty women—and I stress the word 'minimum.'"[36] A common Oxford technique Clinton used was strip poker in his room with groups of women. He also took advantage of possibly being drafted for the Vietnam War by coaxing several women to sleep with him because his life might soon be over.

After Oxford, Clinton attended Yale and met his future wife, Hillary Rodham. Their courtship and engagement did not slow Clinton's spiraling tally. One co-worker of Clinton's in the early 1970s said that despite Hillary's frequent presence he remembered Clinton "sleeping with at least three women in a one-week period."[37] During Clinton's first run for Congress in 1974, Clinton's biggest campaign contributors were former lovers, who by his own estimate were "maybe fifty."[38] Some of his campaign staffers estimated that he had thirty lovers on the campaign trail, "one for each of the twenty-one counties plus some spares."[39]

It was during the 1980s, when Clinton was Arkansas' governor, that Gennifer Flowers alleges most of their twelve-year affair occurred. Flowers was a well-endowed news reporter in Arkansas' capital when their relationship began in the late 1970s. Flowers revealed their relationship in great detail in two books. She claimed that Clinton was insatiable, however, his penis, "Willard," was "not particularly well-endowed."[40] Flowers also alleged that early on in their relationship Clinton impregnated her and that he paid for the abortion. Over the years Clinton explored mild kinky sex with Flowers, using condiments, spanking, phone sex, having her tie him up, and requesting the vibrator be used on him. Flowers, however, drew the line at hot wax and a suggested threesome.

Clinton's most famous marital affair would occur as president with his intern Monica Lewinsky. Her fellatio of him during his phone conversation with a congressman, his ejaculate on her blue dress, and his use of a cigar on her has been officially recorded by Congress' investigation into the matter. Oddly, considering his past, his affair with Lewinsky was remarkably reserved. During their numerous dalliances he refused to penetrate her and often refused to orgasm. Clinton appears to have become sexually conservative with age.

George W. Bush[41]—Despite Bush's notorious partying as a youth, which led to at least three arrests and eventual alcoholism, there are no credible reports of dalliances. Part of this may be because, as one of his fraternity brothers recollected, "[W. Bush] certainly was not an ass man, he could barely get a date in college."[42]

Another possibility is that he was so intoxicated as a young adult that neither he, nor his female partners, remember what exactly happened or with whom it happened. A high school friend recalled hearing stories of W. Bush when they were both in college, saying, "Poor Georgie. He couldn't even relate to women unless he was loaded . . . There were just too many stories of him turning up dead drunk on dates."[43] This was a man who became president of his fraternity, "the drinking jock house," as only a junior and once rolled his drunk self home from a college party in the middle of the street.[44]

394

Another possibility is that W. Bush's political handlers were able to successfully cover up the stories. Many have speculated that some of his father's old friends at the CIA have played a part in the suspicious absence of *any* extramarital sex stories from W. Bush's raucous past. Fuel for this speculation appeared during his run for Texas governor. A former call girl from W. Bush's hometown of Midland, Texas, showed up in Austin claiming she had a past relationship with him and was willing to sell her story. According to a local political consultant, "she got a visit from some men who made her realize it was better to turn tricks in Midland than to stop breathing." She described the men as "intelligence types" and quickly left Austin.[45]

In 2000, wealthy pornography publisher Larry Flynt was irate about W. Bush's hypocrisy regarding abstinence-only education. He hired investigators, who found a woman W. Bush impregnated in the early 1970s and for whom W. Bush arranged an abortion. This occurred before the Supreme Court struck down laws preventing first-trimester abortions in *Roe v. Wade* and therefore it was illegal. Flynt knew the doctor's identity and had four affidavits from the woman's friends supporting the allegation. However, the mainstream press never publicized it (nor would they even ask W. Bush if it was true), because the woman, now married to an FBI agent, refused to come forward publicly.[46]

Even if the above allegations have validity, it appears that, unlike his presidential predecessor and father, W. Bush has stayed faithful to the wife he married at the age of thirty-one. However, it is highly unlikely that prior to marriage W. Bush partook so liberally in the immoral pleasures of alcohol and drugs,[47] but remained sexually chaste. When his brother, Jeb Bush, made the statement that the only woman he ever slept with was his wife, and it was relayed to W. Bush, he was shocked. "Jeb said that? Oh, boy. No comment. I mean Jeb is setting a tough standard for the rest of us in that generation."[48] This is also a man who once responded to a reporter's question of what W. Bush and his father spoke about with one word—"Pussy."[49,50]

NOTES

1. Joseph Ellis, *His Excellency: George Washington,* large print ed. (2004), pp. 61–63, 71–72; and Wesley Hagood, *Presidential Sex* (1995), pp. 6–9.
2. Robert Turner, "Truth About Jefferson," *Wall Street Journal,* 3 July 2001.
3. Hagood, *Presidential Sex,* pp. 22–25.
4. Ibid., pp. 11–15.
5. Ibid., pp. 41–42.
6. Ibid., p. 74.
7. This quote and most of Harding sect. from Irving Wallace, et al., *Intimate Sex Lives of Famous People* (1982), pp. 394–396.
8. Hagood, *Presidential Sex,* p. 89.
9. Sect. largely from Wallace, *Intimate Sex Lives,* pp. 390–394.
10. Quote and sect. from Wallace, *Intimate Sex Lives,* pp. 394–396.
11. Hagood, *Presidential Sex,* p. 140.
12. FBI director J. Edgar Hoover kept a file on Kennedy's sex life. It is believed this is why Kennedy did not fire him, even though Kennedy thought he was a "queer son of a bitch." Ibid., p. 145.
13. Wallace, *Intimate Sex Lives,* p. 398.
14. Hagood, *Presidential Sex,* p. 138.
15. Robert Caro, *Means of Ascent* (1991), p. 58.
16. Robert Caro, *Path to Power* (1990), p. 484.
17. Robert Caro, *Master of the Senate* (2002), pp. 121–123
18. Ibid., pp. 121–123
19. Ibid., p. 147.
20. Ibid.
21. Ibid., p. 141.
22. Ibid., pp. 224–225.
23. Caro, *Path to Power,* pp. 161, 198, 294.
24. Sect. largely from Kitty Kelley, *Nancy Reagan* (1991).
25. Ibid., p. 74.
26. Ibid., p. 78.
27. Ibid.
28. Ibid., p. 82.
29. Davis' actress mother was friends with the actor Spencer Tracy. Tracy fixed Davis up with Clark Gable in the late 1940s and Gable took her out several times when he was in New York City. Gable must have enjoyed the dates because a number of his friends would date her when they were in New York. "Nancy was one of those girls whose phone number got handed around a lot." This led to an affair with MGM executive Benny Thau. MGM signed her. Kelley, *Nancy Reagan,* pp. 56–63.
30. Sect. from Kitty Kelley, *Family* (2004).
31. Ibid., p. 522.
32. Ibid., p. 524.
33. Christopher Andersen, *Bill and Hillary* (1999), p. 63.
34. Ibid.
35. Andersen, *Bill and Hillary,* p. 76.
36. Ibid., p. 83.
37. Ibid., p. 119.
38. Ibid., p. 128.
39. Ibid., p. 131.
40. Wesley Hagood, *Presidential Sex* (1995), pp. 207, 208–209.

41. Sect. from Kitty Kelley, *Family* (2004).
42. Ibid., p. 264.
43. Ibid., p. 265.
44. Ibid., p. 261.
45. Ibid., pp. 550–551.
46. Ibid., pp. 599–600.
47. Numerous people allege that W. Bush has used marijuana and cocaine in the past, and he was frequently in drug-using environments. Perhaps most telling is that he has never denied it. Ibid., pp. 578–579.
48. Ibid., p. 550.
49. Ibid., p. 584.
50. Clinton's close friend Vernon Jordan was once asked what he and Clinton were always talking about; Jordan had the same response. Christopher Andersen, *Bill and Hillary* (1999), p. 305.

feralhouse.com